46.83

of

   *Oracle Press*™

Oracle8 Design Using UML Object Modeling

Dr. Paul Dorsey
Joseph R. Hudicka

Osborne/**McGraw-Hill**

Berkeley New York St. Louis San Francisco
Auckland Bogotá Hamburg London Madrid
Mexico City Milan Montreal New Delhi Panama City
Paris São Paulo Singapore Sydney
Tokyo Toronto

Osborne/**McGraw-Hill**
2600 Tenth Street
Berkeley, California 94710
U.S.A.

For information on translations or book distributors outside the U.S.A., or to arrange bulk purchase discounts for sales promotions, premiums, or fund-raisers, please contact Osborne/**McGraw-Hill** at the above address.

Oracle8 Design Using UML Object Modeling

1234567890 AGM AGM 90198765432109

ISBN 0-07-882474-5

Publisher	**Proofreader**
Brandon A. Nordin	Pat Mannion
Editor in Chief	**Indexer**
Scott Rogers	Caryl Lee Fisher
Acquisitions Editor	**Computer Designers**
Jeremy Judson	Jani Beckwith, Michelle Galicia
Project Editor	**Illustrators**
Mark Karmendy	Brian Wells, Lance Ravella
Editorial Assistant	**Cover Designer**
Monika Faltiss	Lisa Schulz
Technical Editors	**Cover Photograph**
Martin Fowler, Sandeepan Bannerjee	Comstock
Copy Editors	
Jan Jue, Dennis Weaver	

About the Authors

 Dr. Paul Dorsey is the founder and President of Dulcian, Inc. (www.dulcian.com). He specializes in project management, system design, and application development. He is coauthor with Peter Koletzke of *Oracle Designer Handbook* (now in its second edition) from Oracle Press. He is also coauthor with Peter Koletzke of an upcoming book from O'Reilly Press, *Very Rapid Application Development (VRAD) in Oracle Developer.* Paul is an Associate Editor of *SELECT* Magazine. He is the Vice President of the New York Oracle Users' Group. Paul is very active in the Oracle user community and an award-winning speaker.

 Joseph R. Hudicka is the CEO of Dulcian, Inc. He is a member of the Oracle8 Customer Advisory Council providing insight regarding future enhancements to the Oracle8 Server technologies. He is a systems design specialist for Decision Support (OLAP) and Online Transactional Processing (OLTP) systems with specific business knowledge in finance, health care, pharmaceutical, and manufacturing areas. Mr. Hudicka is the chief architect of DataMIG (patent pending), a complete data migration management tool suite. He delivers presentations regularly at major Oracle conferences and local Oracle user groups.

About Dulcian

Dulcian, Inc. provides a wide variety of consulting services, customized training and products for the Oracle development environment. They provide products and services to large government and private sector companies worldwide. Services include new project development, auditing existing efforts, and rescuing failed projects. Training is available on all Oracle products, relational or object/relational data modeling, and DBA mentoring. Dulcian's vision is to deliver top quality systems in record time. To this end, they have automated or streamlined every possible portion of the development lifecycle to create a flexible strategy that is adapted for each project.

Files containing code from examples in this book are available from the Dulcian web site, www.dulcian.com.

Contents At A Glance

PART III
Basic Modeling

PART IV
Time Related Modeling: Tracking History

Contents

PART I
Foundations

PART II
Database Building Blocks

PART III
Basic Modeling

PART IV
Time Related Modeling: Tracking History

Acknowledgments

I never seem to be content with writing a book on a single topic. In this book, we tried to combine both Database Design and Object Theory. As a result, I needed to draw on many different sources to complete this project.

First, my coauthor, Joe Hudicka, worked tirelessly with the people at Oracle to make the code syntax come out correctly. All of his efforts to help implement the data models are greatly appreciated.

Noted object-oriented theorist and author, Martin Fowler, tried to keep me honest with respect to the object-oriented community. He graciously accepted my evening and weekend calls, providing valuable advice and answers to many questions.

Thanks to David Hay, whose insight helped me to focus some of my opinions (mainly because we disagree about everything!).

Eyal Aronoff was kind enough to read some chapters and provided valuable feedback.

Thanks to Dai Clegg, who gave us some important input concerning ODD directions.

We appreciate all of the efforts of Sandeepan Banerjee and his team at Oracle who gave us feedback on our implementation strategies and insight into Oracle8i new features.

Special thanks to Tom Baum of the Lancaster County Tax Collection Bureau and David Heinaman of Heinaman Consulting for graciously allowing us to use their project for the Business Rules chapter.

Appreciation and thanks to Caryl Lee Fisher for all of her work in putting this whole project together and for not complaining each time I added more text and drawings for her to type up.

We greatly appreciate the efforts of Jeremy Judson, Mark Karmendy, and Ron Hull of Osborne McGraw-Hill who worked under a very aggressive schedule to get this book finished on time.

Many thanks to my coworkers at Dulcian, Inc. They are responsible for building many of the systems used as examples throughout the book. It is a privilege to work with them every day.

My love and gratitude go to my wife, Kathie Duliba. She has patiently endured my endless evening and weekend work schedule while writing this book.

Finally, to my dog Popper, thanks for always greeting me with the same enthusiasm no matter when I came home.

Paul Dorsey
Lawrenceville, NJ
September, 1998

Who would have thought I would write a book cover to cover, before I would read one from beginning to end without skipping around? The fact that you are reading this is a testament to the way Dulcian approaches every working day. Anything is possible with a sound game plan and a team of superstars.

I would like to extend both professional and personal thanks to my coauthor Dr. Paul Dorsey, for introducing me to the worlds of writing and presenting. His assistance has lifted me to levels of industry expertise and notoriety that would have otherwise been unattainable.

A debt of gratitude to Sandeepan Banerjee and the rest of the crew in Oracle's Data Server Product Management group for their work as technical editors of our manuscript. They spent many hours enlightening us on the strategic direction of Oracle8i. I anxiously look forward to the shift to Object-Relational systems design and development. Thanks also to Louis Consalvo of Dulcian who was instrumental in testing the code included in the book.

Caryl Lee Fisher took my thoughts and ideas and helped turn them into book chapters. Thanks for all of the help and support during my first major writing project.

I cannot put into words what the support of my family and friends has meant to me during this effort. I think the cutest reference I can recall is my nephew learning the names of the United States, starting with the ones I have been working in.

All of the gratitude in the world could not replace the time that this project has taken away from those closest to me. My heartfelt appreciation goes to my parents, who have provided me with unwavering support and inspiration throughout my life. Finally, and most specially, love and gratitude to Lora, my wife, who patiently and cheerfully endured late nights at the office, endless weekends spent writing during this, our first year of marriage. She has been my partner and helpmate in every sense of the word.

Joseph R. Hudicka
Manville, NJ
September, 1998

Foreword

n the last decade, the practice of software development has been permanently marked by the arrival of object technology. It has grown from a hopeful buzzword into the underpinning of a whole new range of technologies such as component software, GUI frameworks, and language design. The movement of objects into databases has, thus far, been somewhat less sweeping. Object database companies, who expected to conquer the world ten years ago, are still used only in the margins. Most new database development is solidly relational.

I believe that this situation will change substantially over the next few years, if not in the way that object database vendors hope. I do think that object databases will gain ground, but their share of the world's data will still be very small. The big change will come from the relational databases, as they extend their databases to support more object-oriented features. This process has already begun. All relational databases boast some object features already, although they are still very early steps to a confirmed object bigot like me. I expect this pace to pick up markedly in the next few years, and object capabilities will spread rapidly.

This presents a challenge for database designers. Current database design techniques are targeted for databases without objects. Although database modelers have striven hard to build implementation independent models, the truth is that implementation capabilities do affect business models. To take advantage of these new features, database designers need to adopt many ideas from the object-modeling world. Object modeling techniques have developed well over the last decade, and indeed there is now a standard notation: the Unified Modeling Language (UML) for object models.

Yet this should not be a blind rush from data models to object models. It is true to say that most object modelers tend to ignore the kind of modeling that database developers need. Many lessons that have been learned by data modelers are ignored by object modelers. Furthermore, it is not enough to build brave new object models; we need to know how to use them with databases—databases as they are now, not as they might be in the future.

This is why this book is important. It is written by someone with long experience working with databases who has actively been using the UML over the last couple of years. As such, Paul brings his experience of database development into the object world, and the notions of object modeling into the database world. As such, he is able to convey the important ideas that data modeler should absorb in order to use this new object-relational technology. His experience in databases teaches him what data modelers should not forget, but object modelers never learned. He is also able to explain how to implement object models in databases today. This book is a bridge between object and data modeling, a key to a whole new world of database systems, and a whole new world of object systems, too.

Martin Fowler

Martin Fowler is an independent software consultant. You can find his Web page at:

http://ourworld.compuserve.com/homepages/Martin_Fowler/

Preface

his is a book about how to design and build databases. It covers both logical and high-level physical design concepts. This book does not try to explain the entire systems development lifecycle. That information is contained in *Oracle Designer Handbook, Second Edition*, by Dr. Paul Dorsey and Peter Koletzke (1999, Oracle Press). This book is only concerned with the small portion of the system design process pertaining to the building of the logical data model and the implementation of that logical design.

There are three levels to database design. The first of these is the logical model, which captures the data-related business rules of the system, but is relatively unconcerned with table design or performance considerations. The second level is the physical data model. This model specifies the way that the physical tables are laid out. It provides the description of the database from developer's perspective. The third level consists of the actual physical implementation where we define indexing, storage details, and database parameters. This book will cover the first two levels (logical and physical design), but will not cover physical implementation issues.

We will be using an object-oriented approach to data modeling. This will be something of a change for people familiar with entity relationship modeling. Even though we still end up with tables and relationships at the end of the process, the way you think about the modeling process should change as a result of this book. Following the method described in this book, your data models will have several advantages over traditional data models:

- They will require fewer entities (or "classes" in object-oriented terminology).

- They will be more robust, in that they will support not only the specific user requirements gathered during the analysis phase, but will also usually support a broader class of requirements.

- They will be more stable, in that, as new requirements arise, the models will require fewer changes than traditional models.

We will show all of our examples using traditional ERDs and with the new object-oriented standard called the Unified Modeling Language (UML). You can create object-oriented models using traditional ERD notation; however, it is somewhat easier to model using UML. We acknowledge that the transition to UML and object-relational databases may not occur in the immediate future. We wanted to make this book useful to systems developers who will be working in relational databases, using Oracle Designer's ERD data modeling tool, in addition to easing the transition to the new standard.

This is a technical modeling book. It doesn't compare very easily to any other book on the market that we have ever seen. Much of it can be compared to Richard Barker's book, *CASE*METHOD: Entity Relationship Modeling,* (Addison-Wesley Publishing Company, Wokingham, England, 1990), in as far as we will cover much of the same material that Barker covers from an object-oriented perspective. But this book is more than a description of logical modeling. We are also trying to cover a topic that few other books have, namely physical database design from start to finish. We will include the basics of what you will need to know in order to set up a database including:

- Setting domains

- Naming conventions

- How to set up the tables

■ When and how much to denormalize

■ Different ways that logical structures can be implemented physically

In summary, we will cover all of the topics necessary to actually design and build databases.

Intended Audience

This book is written for the Oracle database community. There is no explicit assumption that the reader understands relational theory; however, knowledge of basic relational theory would be helpful. We have included an easy overview of basic relational theory in Chapter 2.

The authors have tried to show comparisons between UML and traditional ERDs for each new concept. We hope this will make the book easier to read for those already familiar with entity relationship modeling techniques.

This book is aimed at logical and physical database modelers (who, from our perspective, should be the same person). However, developers can also benefit from the information contained in this book in order to be intelligent consumers of data models even if they do not design and build data models themselves.

One of the directions that object-oriented modeling has gone in is the building of libraries of object structures. Recently, there have been a few books in the relational database community that followed this same model. *The Data Model Resource Book* by Len Silverston, Kent Graziano, and William Inmon (John Wiley & Sons, 1997) and David Hay's *Data Model Patterns: Conventions of Thought* (Dorsey House, 1995) present generic problems and archetype models for each problem. Our book attempts to present some of the concepts behind how such models are built. We will demonstrate some of the different modeling techniques and structures required to support these archetypes. However, these patterns have only limited usefulness. There will probably never be a time when all systems can be built simply by bolting together various generic model components. Good modeling techniques will always be at the center of a successfully implemented system.

Merging Analysis and Design—A New Approach

Traditional database development requires that the designer build two data models. The first is the logical data model that supports the user requirements but is not concerned with physical implementation. The second is the physical data model where the logical data model is transformed into a physical data model and can be implemented. Traditionally, the logical and physical data model can be quite different.

In the traditional approach, the designer performs analysis and generates a logical data model. At the end of analysis, the model is frozen. The logical data model captured most of the data-related business rules. No attention is given to physical design considerations in the building of the logical design.

The design team then moves to physical database design. They build a data model that is a physical implementation of the logical data model. It is possible (perhaps even desirable for performance reasons) for the physical data model to be quite different from the logical data model. The physical data model is then used to generate the actual database.

This approach has much appeal. Analysis can be focused on gathering logical requirements and not muddying our thinking with performance considerations. At the end of Analysis, we can be confident that we have a model that supports the majority of the data-related business rules gathered. This model is then frozen and a database is generated. Modifications to make the system run are then made at this point in the process.

Unfortunately, such a nice theoretical approach does not entirely conform to the way the world of system design works. Even though we can say that the analysis phase is complete, it does not mean the end of discovering user requirements. New requirements inevitably crop up.

The design of the screens and reports always turn up new requirements. The process of showing users screen and report layouts helps to deepen their understanding of their processes. New fields will show up in most applications and frequently, structural changes are needed to support the new requirements.

Data migration never leaves a system design untouched. Through the process of migrating the data from the legacy system, new fields are uncovered. We may also discover that many of the existing fields in the legacy system are actually used to hold more than one attribute. Sometimes a field holds the value of one attribute in one context and a different attribute in another context. Some fields will hold multiple attribute values concatenated together, as is often the case with attributes such as part numbers or contract numbers.

During development, the developers' understanding of the system matures, leading to changes in the model. The data model designed during analysis is never exactly the way that the system ends up. Entities get combined or are split up; new reference tables and new generalizations are discovered.

Using the traditional method, we must maintain two models—logical and physical. Given the current tools available, these two models are not easily kept in synch. Furthermore, it is often unclear when creating a data model whether a performance-related business rule should be represented in the logical model or not.

This schism between logical and physical models has persisted for two reasons:

- In the past, the Oracle database engine and hardware were so slow that the physical model needed to be quite different from the logical model for performance reasons.

- Analysis and design tasks are frequently performed by different people. Requirements are gathered by an analyst and the logical data model is put together by the lead analyst. Then the physical database design is created by someone with implementation experience.

Today, we have a much more efficient database engine. Computers are faster and the cost of disk storage continues to plummet. Oracle8's partitioning ability makes it feasible to allow logical table sizes to be very large without impacting performance. The efficiency of the development tools makes it possible for a small, highly skilled team to bring up an entire system from start to finish. Finally, the modeling process itself has evolved. Using the object-oriented techniques discussed in this book, it is now possible to create a logical model and not make major changes to it during physical implementation.

We are proposing a different way of thinking about modeling. We do not want to consider the building of a logical model as a separate step from building a physical model. During analysis, we will create an analysis model, largely unconcerned with physical implementation issues. When analysis is complete and development begins, the model will evolve to represent not only a maturing understanding but will also include the modifications needed to support implementation requirements. So, rather than having a logical and a physical data model, we will instead have a data model that starts out as a purely logical data model, which evolves into a data model that fairly represents all of the data related system requirements *and* can be used to generate the physical database.

This approach produces a single data model to support both the logical and physical aspects of building a system. The advantage to this unified approach is that there is only one model to maintain. This allows for a seamless transformation from the logical to the physical data model. The data models should still be periodically versioned. But when we are ready to physically generate the database, we will have a model that accurately represents the data-related business rules and can generate a working database.

Data modelers who specialize in logical design often believe that the logical data model only serves to capture business rules and has no explicit connection to the final database. This approach is both flawed and inefficient. In a data model there are always multiple ways to represent a set of user requirements. There is no reason not to choose the one that is reasonably close to the way that we believe the model will be physically implemented. If we can build a logical model that will require less effort to turn into a good physical model, then we should make every effort to build the model that will minimize overall project cost.

In order to build a logical data model that will require a minimum of modifications to become a good physical data model, the following conditions are necessary:

- The data modeler understands how to physically build systems, having acted as project lead or in a similar role throughout an entire SDLC.

- The data modeler understands both the logical and physical sides of data modeling.

We are assuming that the data model will not require severe denormalization and that the logical and physical data models are similar. However, many small changes may take place when physical implementation occurs. If you need to perform severe denormalization, then it becomes difficult to have a unified data model for both the logical and physical sides of the system since the physical data model may obscure the logical business rules. However, such a level of denormalization is rarely necessary. Good physical data models should be quite close to good logical data models.

Just because we are advocating a unified logical and physical model does not mean that there are never instances where a separation of these two is necessary. Keep in mind, however, that if you try to maintain two data independent data models, considerable expense and energy will be required to keep the two versions of the data models synchronized.

In this book, we will discuss data models and how to physically implement those data models. We will not discuss how to keep logical and physical data models synchronized, since (when we build systems) there is only one data model.

While on the surface, this approach may be a bit unnerving to most data modelers, upon further review we can all identify at least one project where we found that the physical data model made a distinct break from the logical model and the two never synchronized again. One consolidated data model prevents this separation from occurring.

The main reason for two separate models in the relational paradigm was a result of the different goals of analysis and design. In analysis, we are trying to capture business rules. In design, we are determining the best way to meet the requirements gathered in analysis. We should not encumber the analysis process with physical data model restrictions.

Experience has shown weaknesses that arise by separating analysis and design data models. The main problem is that analysis never really ends. New requirements always crop up during the design phase. If we force ourselves to maintain both an analysis and a design model, then we are doing extra work.

Second, we have learned from hard experience that if we denormalize our logical models too much, these models become inflexible with respect to future modifications. The best physical model is one that comes close to the logical model.

Finally, we recognized that it is possible to fully capture business rules and design a physically implementable data model. Of course, there will be extra "attributes" that are added to the model purely for physical implementation reasons, but we have found that such denormalized fields (as long as they can be easily identified) do not detract from the readability of the model. Sometimes, exactly the opposite is true. Many denormalized fields store information that users think should be in the model in the first place. For example, in a Purchase Order table, we frequently add a redundant attribute that stores the total of the purchase. Of course, such information is derivable from summing up the detail records, but users often expect to see the total in the master record anyway.

UML provides far more flexibility in the definition of our data models. Oracle's Object Database Designer allows us to develop detailed data models that serve us throughout the system development life cycle, as well as the ability to generate DDL from them. This section will review the methods used to create physical data structures for a sample class.

Approach of This Book

In each chapter, we will present the UML syntax along with the types of models that can be built with this syntax and show how these models can be physically implemented with both traditional relational syntax and Oracle8 objects. We will give you our opinions about the best ways to create models and implement them. Although object modeling has been around for some time, applying it to relational databases has not been widely discussed. Most database systems have been built using relational modeling. Object modeling is a relatively new way of thinking about the problem of database design.

In this book, our goal is to build upon the past history of relational databases, include state-of-the-art modeling techniques, and add the richer language of UML in order to push the ideas of object-orientation and genericization a bit farther with the goal of ultimately creating more efficient and flexible systems without sacrificing modeling clarity or performance considerations.

PART
I

Foundations

CHAPTER
1

Introduction

n this chapter we will briefly discuss the object-relational model and outline the evolution of the database industry from the flat-file structures of the '60s and '70s to the latest trends in database theory. We will also provide a brief introduction to the Unified Modeling Language (UML) as well as an overview of the Oracle environment and introduction to some of the new features available in Oracle8i.

The Evolution of Object-Relational Databases

When information systems people first began working with databases, the databases consisted of sets of files. We largely accessed these structures using CODASYL extensions to COBOL. CODASYL gave us the ability to use commands like FIRST_RECORD, NEXT_RECORD, and LAST_RECORD when dealing with files. This was our first look at database cursors. CODASYL gave us the ability to work more efficiently with data files than by reading to text files. We used indexing to these structures, and used ISAM and VSAM files. Such structures were based on linked lists and separate index structures.

For the first time, we could say that we had a database management system (DBMS). We had some level of independence between data and programs. Unfortunately, there were still some problems. Programs were still very large, and even minor changes to the system requirements might require hundreds (if not thousands) of programmer hours. You need only look at our now infamous Year 2000 problem to recognize the limitations of such systems.

Relational systems gave us a big theoretical advantage over traditional CODASYL-based systems. Developers could treat files as simple logical flat files. All indexing and SQL query parsing was handled by the relational DBMS (RDBMS).

Unfortunately, there were still some problems. Queries ran so slowly that developers had to override the default SQL parser algorithms. In the '80s it was frequently so difficult to achieve good performance that some database designers felt the need to heavily denormalize their data models.

Relational Databases

The relational model is a very elegant, clear model. It has provided the foundation for the database industry for almost 20 years. The relatively small number of concepts in relational theory has helped make relational databases the industry standard. The relational vendors have been able to largely isolate the complexity of the physical implementation of the database from the logical design of the system, thus providing a simple interface to the application developers.

During the last two decades we have matured as an industry. Many of us have felt the need for a richer modeling environment that would better fit the recent moves toward generic modeling. In addition, we recognize that there are concepts from object-oriented theory that could be brought into the database industry to give us even greater efficiencies.

Relational databases have a relatively limited vocabulary. We implement structures through judiciously designed flat files and then place a few different types of indexes on various fields in those files. As far as access is concerned, links between tables are only logically specified, so reference pointers are implemented through foreign keys. We do not really have explicit links between tables. Referential integrity constraints are merely code snippets that prevent a few specific kinds of invalid data from being placed in the data model. We can add triggers to our tables to explicitly perform some activity when a record is inserted, updated, or deleted, and store program units in the database. Finally, we can cluster tables to improve performance. These strategies still constrain us to a fairly limited way of thinking. In a relational database, every table is virtually an independent structure.

In logical entity relationship (ER) modeling, we have entities that are subsets of other entities. For example, salaried employees are a subset of all employees. Likewise, we have entities dependent upon other entities such as PO details, which are dependent upon Purchase Orders. However, our ability to represent such structures within a relational database paradigm is limited.

Paradoxically, object-oriented databases retain some of the concepts of earlier database theory. Just as in the days of CODASYL, as we bring object orientation into the relational database world, we find ourselves meeting up with "old friends" such as linked lists and pointers.

It is important not to forget the reasons we abandoned linked lists and pointers in the first place. We need to remember what the database world was like before the advent of relational databases in the early 1980s. There are still (at least until Year 2000 problems kill them off) high-performance databases running using CODASYL, ISAM, and VSAM files largely written in COBOL. Modifications to CODASYL databases usually required months of effort. An early COBOL project we encountered had a simple requirement to change the width of a field from 10 to 12 characters. This one change required hundreds of hours of programming. Now, in a relational database environment, such a change would only require a few days, at most. If the applications were generated out of Oracle Designer (or some other integrated CASE tool), such a change could be implemented in one to two days, even in a large system.

In the prerelational database days, supporting reporting requirements was very difficult. If a particular report was not planned for in the original design specifications of the system, it could easily require several weeks to write a new report (assuming it was even possible to write the report). Modifications to the underlying data structures were cumbersome. Seemingly minor changes could require a major system redesign. We will not assert that all of these problems disappeared with the advent of entity relationship diagrams (ERDs) and relational databases, but the situation certainly improved.

Early relational databases looked much like their flat-file predecessors. Normalization was considered an academic curiosity. Eventually, at least through Third Normal Form, normalization was found to be not such a bad idea after all. With our heavy denormalizations of the 1980s, we had many of the same problems with relational structures as we did with flat files. Modifications to the data structures were still difficult and expensive, as were modifications to the applications. By 1990 most data modelers had figured out that the heavy denormalizations of the '80s were causing massive problems when those systems needed to be modified. Normalization was finally "in style."

In the mid-1990s, some early object-oriented thinking began shifting into relational databases. In the Oracle world, this involved genericizing our models by creating more abstract structures, while still working within the relational database environment. Over the last few years some portion of the relational database community has already embraced object-oriented thinking.

Now it is common to see some level of generic modeling in most systems. For example, it is the industry standard to represent organization units as a simple recursive structure, rather than using separate tables for regions, divisions, and departments (or whatever the structure for a particular organization).

Even more abstract models are becoming commonplace. At a recent conference, someone designing a questionnaire database asked how to support a table with several hundred columns. Each questionnaire had several hundred questions. Several people in the audience responded that the person should model the questionnaire by placing the answers into a separate table and store the structure of the questionnaire as data in the database. A quiet revolution is taking place. Object-oriented thinking is finding its way into data models.

Recently, two more steps in the evolution toward object-orientation have followed. First, the databases themselves have included new object-oriented features. Second, we have a new, richer modeling language in UML than was available with ERDs. As mentioned earlier, these new concepts actually include some of the old concepts of prerelational thinking with linked lists and pointers. This new integration of old and new presents a great opportunity, but must also be viewed with caution. We can now build relational structures that operate more efficiently. But if we are not careful, we may lose some of the flexibility of the structures that evolved from the relational database paradigm.

Object-Relational Databases

Object-relational databases are coming. "Object oriented" has been the hottest buzzword in the computer industry for the last decade. It is hard to pick up any magazine in the computer industry without seeing some article dealing with object orientation. Often mistakenly used as a synonym for reusable code, *object orientation* implies a precise set of theoretical computer science structures that can affect every aspect of the system, including programming languages, tools, and databases.

The main impact of this technology has been on programming. Object orientation is helping to transform how programming is done. However, we should recognize that not every program in C++ is object oriented. The most important aspect of the system that must be object oriented is the thinking of the design team. It is still common for programs to be written with no reusable components or standards. A while back, we audited a large system failure, written in C++, in which every programmer had set his or her own standards. Only one small part of the system was written by use of object-oriented programming standards.

To some extent, this object-oriented revolution has already had an impact on the database community. The move toward generic models so strongly espoused by leading database modelers is a reflection of this revolution. Likewise, the almost universal use of templates with reusable object components in application development is now the norm in leading programming shops. At this point, Oracle is now enhancing the RDBMS, Oracle Designer, and Oracle Developer to better support this object orientation.

What Does "Object Relational" Really Mean?

If you ask a half-dozen experts what "object relational" means, you will get at least a half-dozen answers. We are still trying to integrate the relational paradigm with the object paradigm. Combining the two is not going to be easy.

True object databases are a tiny portion of the market, and object-relational databases are still evolving. The problem is deciding what we really want in this new paradigm. We have 20 years of relational history during which relational technology has matured into a sophisticated environment. We finally have full referential integrity, stored procedures, and triggers, and many of us have figured out how to avoid mutating tables. Similarly, object-oriented programming started taking off at about the same time as relational databases, providing an additional 20-year history.

We should not look to object orientation as a panacea. Object-oriented programming has not solved all the problems of programmers. On the contrary, object structures require a different way of thinking about programming. Object-orientation adds an additional level of complexity to the environment. Many programming shops have had great difficulty making the transition to object-oriented programming, where others report that their programming efficiency has greatly increased.

Object-oriented databases allow for objects to exist as nonvolatile structures. Rather than connecting objects through referential integrity, they use reference pointers. Inheritance is fully supported, and access to objects is typically restricted through the use of associated methods and operations.

In object-relational systems we are trying to combine the best of both worlds. We will have both object identifiers and primary keys. Objects will be related both through object references and referential integrity. We will have both triggers and methods. Tables can be built independently, or can inherit attributes and methods from some parent structure (called a *class*).

It is, however, hard to implement all of this into the relational model. Currently, in Oracle8i, we have object identifiers and methods, but only primitive inheritance.

The biggest challenge from the developer's perspective is how to best use all of this new functionality. We have all the standard tools from relational databases plus all the new structures from object databases. Where and how should we use these new structures? What will be the performance, design, and maintenance impacts?

This book will attempt to answer these questions. Unfortunately, we are shooting at a moving target. Advice that we give in this book may already be out of date by the time you read this. We will therefore try to write not only about what is the best way to do things now, but also discuss the best way to design and model in general, so that as the tools catch up with our vision, you will be prepared to effectively exploit this new technology.

Creating Object-Relational Systems

We should not judge the effectiveness of the object-relational paradigm by its current implementation in Oracle8i. Objects in Oracle8i are still relatively new. We can assume that the level and quality of object support will significantly increase over the next few years. We will discuss what a full implementation of an object-relational database might provide for us.

What advantages does the object-relational paradigm have that simple relational databases do not?

- We will be able to build systems faster, and for less cost.

- We will be able to maintain systems more easily, and for less cost.

- Our systems will be more flexible and robust so that changes to the business or newly discovered requirements can be accommodated more easily, and for less cost.

This is the vision of the object-relational approach. With the current state of the object extensions in Oracle8i, we are not able to fully realize these benefits. But as the products mature, we do expect this vision to be realized.

What is it about using an object-relational approach that provides these advantages? Object-relational thinking is an improvement over traditional relational thinking. Using an object-relational approach, you ask not only what are the correct "things of interest" about the organization to model, but you also try to discern what are the appropriate generalizations (or groupings) of "things of interest."

Many of us are already starting to think in an object-oriented fashion. Every time a supertype/subtype is modeled, object-oriented thinking is being used. In the traditional person supertype with customer and employee subtypes, we are recognizing that person is a generalization of both person and customer. Unfortunately, there is no clean way to implement subtypes in a relational model. Either we dump all of the attributes into one table, or we split them apart into two or more tables, but there is no clean way to express "generalization of" in a relational database.

One of the major theoretical differences between relational and object thinking is that in a relational database we think of data and applications separately, whereas in object thinking we consider data and its associated operations and methods together.

In the Oracle community we have always thought about data and applications separately. In Oracle Designer we connect functions to entities through interaction matrices. In Oracle Developer, applications are hooked to data in the same way that programs have always interacted with data structures. Logically, data and code should not be considered separately. The object-oriented idea that data objects and their respective operations and methods should be considered together is a much more natural and logical approach.

The development and maintenance speed improvements that we expect come from this more natural approach to modeling. The greater the disconnect between the way we think about our systems and the tools we are using, the longer our development process will take. If we can get the RDBMS and tools to be more consistent with this object-oriented approach, we will be able to build better systems faster.

The second reason we can expect an improvement is that our data models are smaller (fewer tables), more robust, and easier to develop against. Examples at the end of this chapter will illustrate this point.

What Is UML?

With the advent of increasingly complex systems, a clear and concise way of representing them visually became increasingly important. The *Unified Modeling Language* (UML) was developed by Grady Booch, Jim Rumbaugh, and Ivar Jacobson in response to that need. In an attempt to create a single system for modeling and documenting information systems and business processes, UML was created with an underlying object-oriented analysis and design philosophy. To build successful systems, a sound model is essential. It communicates the overall system plan to the entire development team. Like any language, UML has its own elements and guidelines and will be used throughout this book to illustrate examples of various modeling patterns and actual systems we have built.

As stated in the UML Summary Document (UML Summary, version 1.1, 1 September 1997, Rational Software, et al.), the primary goals in designing UML were the following:

- "Provide the users a ready-to-use visual modeling language so they can develop and exchange meaningful models.

- Provide extensibility and specialization mechanisms to extend the core concepts.

- Be independent of particular programming languages and development processes.

- Provide a formal basis for understanding the modeling language.

- Encourage the growth of the OO tools market.

- Support higher-level development concepts such as collaboration, frameworks, patterns, and components.

- Integrate best practices."

For all of the reasons stated earlier, we believe that UML is the language of choice for designing object-relational systems.

UML is not just a replacement for entity relationship diagramming. UML encompasses several parts that together provide a complete object-oriented development environment. The part of UML that deals with data modeling is the *class diagram*. This book will cover the UML class diagram exclusively.

We will only briefly mention any of the other parts of UML. It should be noted that UML covers the entire system design environment, not just data modeling. A complete discussion of UML can be found in any of the books written on UML available in any computer book outlet.

The parts of UML are

- **Class diagram** This is the data modeling diagramming language. It is similar in scope to ER modeling.

- **Object diagram** This is a class diagram for only one set of objects. Think of it as a data model where you show example data rather than the whole data model. This is very useful for explaining complex diagrams.

- **Use case diagram** A use case is similar to the idea of a "function" in Oracle's CASE method. A use case diagram shows the interaction among actors (e.g., customers, employees) and use cases. There is no analogue to this diagram in Oracle's methodology.

- **Sequence diagram** A sequence diagram shows an interaction of objects arranged in a time sequence. This is similar to the process flow diagrammer in Oracle Designer.

- **Collaboration diagram** A collaboration diagram shows the objects and messages that are passed between those objects in order to perform some function. There is no analogue to this diagram in Oracle's methodology.

- **Statechart diagram** Statechart diagrams are standard state transition diagrams. They show what states an object can be in and what causes the object to change states. There is no analogue to this diagram in Oracle's methodology.

- **Activity diagram** An activity diagram is a type of flowchart. It represents operation and decision points. This is similar to the data flow diagram in Oracle Designer.

- **Implementation diagram** An implementation diagram shows the system components and how they interact. The implementation diagram can either show the software or hardware components of the system.

Using UML

For people familiar with ER modeling, it is important to recognize that the shift to UML class diagrams will not be traumatic. Serious modelers are well acquainted with the limitations of entity relationship diagrams (ERDs). With UML, some, but by no means all, of the limitations are eliminated. Some of the things we dislike about ERDs are still present with UML.

It is important to be clear about the terms being used with regard to relational and object modeling. Keep in mind that the notion of an "entity" in ER modeling is being replaced with the notion of a "class" in UML. The proper definition of a class in this context is broader than that of an entity. You can use objects to describe process information as well. However, for this discussion, "object" will be used in the context of data objects.

A *class* is something of interest to the organization, or a means of classifying something of interest. The crucial point is that an entity or class always represents something in the real world. This is one of the key mechanisms you can use to check the validity of your data model. Can you articulate precisely the real-world "thing" that each object in the class corresponds to? If it cannot be precisely articulated, then you do not have a valid data model.

For ER modelers, simply think of a class as being synonymous with an entity. However, there is one significant difference, namely that classes are associated with "methods." *Methods* can be thought of as PL/SQL, Java, or C/C++ functions and procedures that act on the class. If you think about classes translating into tables, methods are PL/SQL, Java (Oracle 8i), or C/C++ functions that interact with the tables. For example, for an Employee class, the associated methods might include Hire, Fire, Give Raise, Assign to Dept., and Assign to Committee. It is possible to make this list of methods exhaustive so that developers need only interact with these methods rather than directly manipulating the data in the classes. This ability to isolate the developers from the physical structure of the classes is considered a primary advantage of the object-oriented technique. However, we will need to consider carefully how we should structure our development teams. If the same developers are building the methods as developing the applications, then there might be little benefit to encapsulation.

Object-Oriented Products in Oracle

Oracle8i is not the first time that object-oriented thinking has found its way into an Oracle product. In Forms 4.5 we had our first taste of object orientation through property classes. We could set and enforce standard sets of properties for any object in our applications. PL/SQL used with libraries and object groups was a rich enough set of features to provide us with some ability to create reusable program components. A few of us even went so far as to encapsulate whole parts of our applications into reusable structures. Now the products are starting to better support this evolution to object-oriented thinking.

In the RDBMS, starting with release 8.0 (released June 1997), Oracle provided our first taste of an object-relational database. Release 8i has gone to beta as of this writing and is expected to be available late in 1998. In the object extension, primary keys were supplemented with object identifiers (OIDs), traditional referential integrity was extended with object pointers, and two non–First Normal Form constructs were added: nested tables and tables of references. Oracle Developer 2.0, first released in March 1998, provided explicit template and object library support, even though for years many of us were doing workarounds to produce this template functionality. The inheritance model was improved so that referenced objects could be modified. Finally, the ability to hook blocks to PL/SQL procedures was added, acting as a precursor to attach blocks to Oracle8i object extensions.

Oracle Designer, v. 2.1 (June 1998), presented the first object extension by including a new component called the *Object Database Designer* (ODD). This component gave us the ability to use a subset of Unified Modeling Language (UML) class diagrams to generate the Oracle8i object extensions DDL code.

With the object extensions in the RDBMS, Oracle Developer support to write applications against the object extensions, and Oracle Designer support of DDL generation, are we now ready to create object-relational systems? Not quite. So far, this combination of relational and object-oriented databases is still quite new. As of this writing, we still don't have full inheritance of attributes or methods in Oracle8i. Oracle8i provides only limited inheritance. In Oracle Designer's ODD, many of the important features of UML have not yet been implemented. This does not mean that object-relational databases are a bad idea, just that they are still evolving. In the next few years, object-relational databases will completely supplant traditional relational databases as the standard for new systems.

It is clear that object-relational databases are the wave of the future. However, we are not yet ready to build production object-relational systems. First, the Oracle8i object extensions need to go through another iteration. At a minimum we need full inheritance to be able to say we have an object-oriented system. In Oracle8i, inheritance is so far a language interface issue. The problem is that languages do not agree on what "inheritance" means; C++ supports multiple inheritance, Java does not. Each of Oracle's language interfaces (C++, Java) fully supports that language's model of inheritance. (Java inheritance in the server is available in Oracle8i.)

In Oracle Designer we need a full implementation of the UML class diagrams in the Object Database Designer, and we need to see some other parts of UML make their way into the product. We also need to be able to generate modules to work with the object structures. Oracle Designer supports static database UML modeling. It is estimated that 85 percent of UML users confine themselves to static modeling. Oracle Designer supports a subset of UML that is adequate for generating Oracle8i structures. This should satisfy most users. However, this book advocates use of all the UML class diagram syntax for designing data models. While Designer is adding more UML support, third-party tools can be used with the object-relational features of Oracle8i to get a full UML modeling solution.

New Features in Oracle8i

Oracle8i includes some new features, many of which pertain specifically to the availability of object-relational data structures. This section will provide an overview of many of the new Oracle8i object features, most of which we have expanded upon in more detailed examples throughout the book.

Object-Relational Data Structures

We will begin the discussion of new Oracle8i features with those pertaining to the object layer, because this is the area with the most significant improvements. While there are a number of enhancements in Oracle8i that are not specifically object relational, the majority of these enhancements are relevant to object-relational structures.

Column and Row Types

Types are physical structures that serve as templates or building blocks for other types and/or tables. *Column* types are types that define the organization of one or more attributes or members that will collectively describe the structure of one or more column objects. Code Example 1-1 defines a column type, NAME_T, which describes the structure of columns that store Name information, such as first and last names of people.

```
CREATE OR REPLACE TYPE NAME_T AS OBJECT
(COL            VARCHAR2 (50))
/
```

Code Example 1-1

    Row types are types that define the entire structure of an object table. Code Example 1-2 defines a type PERSON_T. The PERSON_T type contains four attributes, PERSON_ID (i.e., sequence-generated unique identifier (UID)), LNAME_TX (i.e., last name), FNAME_TX (i.e., first name), and BIRTH_DATE (i.e., date of birth).

```
--example_01_01 is prereq
CREATE OR REPLACE TYPE PERSON_T
AS OBJECT(
PERSON_ID       NUMBER (10),
LNAME_TX        NAME_T,
FNAME_TX         NAME_T,
BIRTH_DATE       DATE)
/
```

Code Example 1-2a

    Notice that since datatype specifications for the LNAME_TX and FNAME_TX columns are not explicitly defined as VARCHAR2(50), the typical relational syntax for DML statements would not work. Instead, the datatype references NAME_T, the new column type defined in Code Example 1-1. Similarly, any DML statement must also identify the column type.

Column types are analogous to domains in Oracle Designer in that they genericize the structure of columns. If we ever need to modify the datatype or length of every name field in the system, we can simply modify the NAME_T column type, because its structure is shared by every name field.

Similarly, row types genericize the structure of object tables. The PERSON_T row type in Code Example 1-2a describes the structure of tables that store information about people. Code Example 1-2b defines a table EMP based on the PERSON_T row type.

```
CREATE TABLE EMP OF PERSON_T (
PERSON_ID      NOT NULL,
LNAME_TX       NOT NULL,
FNAME_TX       NOT NULL,
BIRTH_DATE     NOT NULL,
PRIMARY KEY (PERSON_ID))
/
```

Code Example 1-2b

The only drawback of tables based on row types is that these tables are strictly bound to the structure of their associated row type. In other words, object tables cannot deviate in structure from their associated type. Any modifications to their structure must be performed to their type and will then be inherited by the table(s).

Note that the columns of the EMP table have been restated in the CREATE TABLE statement. While columns are inherited by the EMP table from the members of the PERSON_T row type, there are additional features of physical implementation of these members that are defined at the table level.

Example 1-2b has declared that all four members (i.e., PERSON_ID, LNAME_TX, FNAME_TX, and BIRTH_DATE) cannot be null. Integrity constraints and DEFAULT values must also be specified within the CREATE TABLE statement.

Items such as default values and optionality would be useful parameters at the type level and may be implemented as such in a future release of Oracle8i. Column types are not limited to single attribute implementations, either. For instance, you will probably want to create an ADDRESS column type as follows in Code Example 1-3.

```
CREATE OR REPLACE TYPE ADDRESS_T AS OBJECT
 (ADDR1                  VARCHAR2 (50),
  ADDR2                  VARCHAR2 (50),
  CITY_TX                VARCHAR2 (50),
  ST_CD                  VARCHAR2 (2),
  CTRY_CD                VARCHAR2 (3),
  ZIP_CD                 VARCHAR2 (9))
  /
```

Code Example 1-3

You would most likely reference the ADDRESS_T object type within the creation of any object type that will contain address information. For example, a CONTACT table might contain a primary address to be used for communicating with a given contact. We could define a CONTACT_T object type, and base it upon both the PERSON_T and ADDRESS_T datatypes, as shown in Code Example 1-4.

```
--EXAMPLE_01_03 IS PREREQ
--members of multi-member types not supported as key components
CREATE OR REPLACE TYPE CONTACT_T AS OBJECT
 (PERSON            PERSON_T,
  ADDRESS           ADDRESS_T)
  /

CREATE TABLE CONTACT OF CONTACT_T (
PERSON.PERSON_ID NOT NULL)
 /
```

Code Example 1-4

Object tables are tables whose structure is based on object types. If we were to create a table called EMP to store employee information, based upon an object type, the two structures might look like the following Code Example 1-5.

```
--example_01_01 is prereq
CREATE OR REPLACE TYPE PERSON_T
AS OBJECT(
LNAME_TX          NAME_T,
FNAME_TX          NAME_T,
BIRTH_DATE        DATE)
```

```
/

CREATE OR REPLACE TYPE EMP_T AS OBJECT
(EMP_ID          NUMBER (10),
PERSON          PERSON_T,
HIRE_DATE       DATE)
/

CREATE TABLE EMP OF EMP_T
(EMP_ID          NOT NULL PRIMARY KEY)
/
```

Code Example 1-5

Relational Versus Object-Relational Tables

The arrival of object-relational data structures in Oracle8i has left many of us wondering about the stability of existing systems built using prior releases of Oracle. Rest assured that relational data structures are not a thing of the past either for Oracle or anyone else.

Oracle8i provides the ability to create both relational and object-relational tables. A future release of Oracle Server will support an ALTER TABLE command to transform a relational table into an object table. So the logical question is, will we still want to create relational tables? We have found that, in some circumstances, there are certain features of relational tables that still make them a better choice than object-relational tables.

Relational tables are quite flexible in that the user can add columns at will. As of Oracle8i, we can also delete columns from existing tables. This is an invaluable feature. There have been countless situations where we have been forced to rename a table and then issue a CREATE TABLE... AS SELECT FROM... statement, followed by a DROP TABLE statement for the original table. At this point, you find that the integrity constraints and indexes all have to be re-created with the appropriate names and locations. All of this tedious work has now been eliminated.

In Oracle8i, object tables are tightly bound to the object type that they are instantiated upon. You cannot add columns to object tables directly. Rather, you must add them to the object type that the object table is based upon.

Relational tables can contain columns that are based upon user-defined column types, such as the NAME_T column type in Code Example 1-1. Therefore, the key difference between relational and object tables is whether they are based on a single type. SQL statements can reference both relational and object-relational tables in a single query.

For example, let's say you were to create an object table called PERSON to store information about people. The PERSON table will require a unique identifier and fields for last name, first name, and birth date. The appropriate object-relational strategy would be to create the following object type and object table as shown in Code Example 1-6.

```
CREATE OR REPLACE TYPE PERSON_T AS OBJECT
PERSON_ID            NUMBER,
 LAST_NAME            VARCHAR2 (50),
 FIRST_NAME           VARCHAR2 (50),
 BIRTH_DATE           DATE)
/

CREATE TABLE PERSON OF PERSON_T (
PERSON_ID  NOT NULL PRIMARY KEY,
LAST_NAME   NOT NULL,
FIRST_NAME NOT NULL,
BIRTH_DATE NOT NULL)
/
```

Code Example 1-6

If we needed to add an additional column to the PERSON table to store a gender indicator (i.e., GENDER_MF), we would have to add it to the PERSON_T object type. Currently, we must drop all tables that are instantiated upon an object type in order to modify an object type. However, a subsequent release of Oracle8i will provide the capability to modify object types that have been referenced by other objects.

Currently, the following syntax must be issued to add the GENDER_MF column to the PERSON table as shown in Code Example 1-7.

```
--EXAMPLE_01_01 IS PREREQ
DROP TABLE PERSON
/

CREATE OR REPLACE TYPE PERSON_T AS OBJECT
(PERSON_ID            NUMBER,
 LAST_NAME            NAME_T,
 FIRST_NAME           NAME_T,
 BIRTH_DATE           DATE,
```

```
GENDER_MF            CHAR (1))
/

CREATE TABLE PERSON OF PERSON_T (
PERSON_ID    NOT NULL PRIMARY KEY,
LAST_NAME    NOT NULL,
FIRST_NAME   NOT NULL,
BIRTH_DATE   NOT NULL,
GENDER_MF    DEFAULT 'F' NOT NULL)
/
```

Code Example 1-7

In Oracle8i, you will have to stage the data previously stored in the
PERSON table, and reload it into the new PERSON table. A common
practice would be to RENAME the original PERSON table to something else.
After creating the new PERSON table, you would issue an INSERT
INTO...SELECT FROM... statement to transfer the data from the old
PERSON table to the new PERSON table. The appropriate SQL statements
appear in Code Example 1-8.

```
RENAME PERSON TO ORIG_PERSON;
CREATE TABLE PERSON OF PERSON_T;
INSERT INTO PERSON (PERSON_ID, LAST_NAME, FIRST_NAME, BIRTH_DATE)
SELECT PERSON_ID,LAST_NAME,FIRST_NAME,BIRTH_DATE FROM ORIG_PERSON;
```

Code Example 1-8

Let's now consider a situation where we may create multiple tables that
store information about people. INSERT INTO...SELECT...FROM handles
this situation quite nicely. Unfortunately, there is a substantive flaw when
using the CREATE TABLE...SELECT...FROM syntax. The CREATE
TABLE...SELECT FROM statement does not automatically create integrity
constraints that mirror those of the table being selected from. Therefore,
you must be sure to manually declare each referential integrity
constraint that you expect to have on the target table as part of the
CREATE TABLE statement.

Object references will also be lost during this process, because they are
system-generated values that uniquely identify each row. While the contents
of the rows in the PERSON and ORIG_PERSON tables are equivalent, their
unique identifiers will not be, provided that they have been system

generated. This is because each row of the ORIG_PERSON table has been copied and inserted into the PERSON table, with the result that they are now copies of the original individual rows. Any object references that were dependent upon the OIDs of the ORIG_PERSON table will end up in a dangling state. In other words, tables that reference the ORIG_PERSON table will contain invalid references to the new PERSON table.

Oracle8i has introduced a new integrity constraint that enforces integrity across object references. Another approach would be to declare object references based upon user-defined columns such as PERSON_ID in Code Example 1-8. The latter would cause object references to replicate the functionality of traditional primary key/foreign key validation.

We could create any number of object tables based upon the PERSON_T object type. However, this violates our naming standard for primary key columns (i.e., System Generated PK column name is TABLE_NAME||'_ID') described in Chapter 5 because this would result in multiple tables having a PK consisting of a column named PERSON_PK.

Instead, we could create relational tables. Relational tables can then reference the PERSON_T type as a column datatype, rather than a row object type. We would first remove the PERSON_ID member from the PERSON_T object type definition, because it is not characteristic of all tables that will contain references to the PERSON_T type. The following Code Example 1-9 uses the PERSON_T type as a datatype.

```
CREATE OR REPLACE TYPE PERSON_T AS OBJECT
(LAST_NAME            VARCHAR2 (50),
 FIRST_NAME           VARCHAR2 (50),
 BIRTH_DATE           DATE,
 GENDER_MF            CHAR (1))
/

CREATE TABLE EMP (
EMP_ID          NUMBER (10) NOT NULL PRIMARY KEY,
EMP             PERSON_T)
/
CREATE TABLE CONTACT (
CONTACT_ID      NUMBER (10) NOT NULL PRIMARY KEY,
CONTACT         PERSON_T)
/
```

Code Example 1-9

The two preceding examples demonstrated how to use a type as both a column object type and a row type. Notice that in using a multiattribute type as a column type, the syntax implies that you are adding a single column (i.e., the EMP column in the EMP table, because it references the PERSON_T column type). If you DESCRIBE the EMP table from SQL*Plus, it would look like the following:

```
SQL> desc EMP
  Name                                Null?     Type
  ----------------------------------- --------  ----
  EMP_ID                              NOT NULL NUMBER(10)
  EMP                                          PERSON_T
```

To insert an object into the EMP table for the members of the PERSON_T datatype, you must use the type constructor within the INSERT statement, as follows in Code Example 1-10:

```
SQL> INSERT INTO EMP VALUES
(1,PERSON_T('SMITH','JOE','06-JUN-98','M'));
```

Code Example 1-10

Failure to reference the PERSON_T constructor within the earlier INSERT statement would generate an error.

The database treats column object types as embedded objects and therefore requires that they be referenced explicitly in all DML statements. SELECT statements can still use wildcards such as SELECT* to return all columns for all rows.

NOTE
Object tables do not support replication as of Oracle8i.

Object Identifiers (OIDs)

OIDs have been included in Oracle8i to bridge the gap between relational databases and C++/Java development environments. For the purpose of native Oracle database development, SQL, PL/SQL, Forms, and Reports, ROWIDS are the fastest path to locating specific rows in the database.

However, ROWIDs have no meaning outside the context of the database itself. OIDs are essentially logical pointers used in programming outside the scope of the database itself. Once data has been extracted from the database and loaded into memory for a given C++/Java application, the language needs some way of navigating between object rows. OIDs provide this level of unique identification. OIDs might sound very similar to primary and/or unique keys. They can be system generated or based upon one or more user-defined columns. System-generated OIDs are encoded values, the contents of which are of absolutely no use by themselves. However, keep in mind that while their values are guaranteed to be unique when they are system generated, the database cannot guarantee the uniqueness of values from user-defined columns. Oracle8i includes a new integrity constraint that prevents redundancy in OIDs.

OIDs can be primary key components. Essentially, the evolution we are experiencing is simply an extension of referential integrity that can be utilized effectively as pointers in applications written in languages outside the scope of the Oracle Server.

The two categories of data objects that can be created from types are *column* and *row objects.* Column objects were shown in Code Example 1-2b from the previous section that created a column in the EMP table called EMP, which was a reference to the PERSON_T type. Column objects are not independent. They are embedded within other tables and therefore do not receive an OID. Row objects are created for object tables, based upon object types. It is important to note that, to access data through OIDs in external applications, you have to either store your data in object tables, or create object views atop the relational tables, because OIDs can only be generated by object tables and views. The primary benefit of OIDs within the database world is the way they have greatly simplified the specification of WHERE clauses. If you are using an OID to relate two tables, SQL will interpret this relationship and automatically specify the appropriate JOIN clause.

Object References

An *object reference* is merely a pointer that can simultaneously support referential integrity and external programming languages. The REF keyword is used to specify an object reference. If an object reference has been defined using the SCOPE parameter, SQL will execute this statement as a JOIN. The reason for this is that you have specified for the engine the precise object table where the object pointed to by the object reference value resides. If the SCOPE parameter is not used and there have been multiple tables instantiated upon the given object type, then the optimizer will chase the object reference values, as opposed to performing a JOIN.

The following Code Example 1-11 creates a table with an object reference to the PERSON_T type, specifically targeting the rows in the EMP table, created from the PERSON_T type.

```
CREATE OR REPLACE TYPE PERSON_T AS OBJECT
(PERSON_ID              NUMBER,
 LAST_NAME              VARCHAR2 (50),
 FIRST_NAME             VARCHAR2 (50),
 BIRTH_DATE             DATE,
 GENDER_MF              CHAR (1))
/


CREATE TABLE EMP OF PERSON_T
/


CREATE TABLE TASK (
 TASK_ID                NUMBER (10),
 PERSON                 REF PERSON_T   SCOPE IS EMP)
/
```

Code Example 1-11

Code Example 1-11 defines the type PERSON_T, which serves as the template of the EMP table. The TASK table contains a REF to the PERSON_T type.

Without the SCOPE being limited to the EMP table, the optimizer would automatically navigate the object reference values in pursuit of the requested data. Oracle manages a comprehensive list of OIDs in memory for the sake of expediting data retrieval. Navigational access would result in the database searching through this set of OIDs and determining the location(s) of the row(s) to satisfy the requested query. However, since we have limited the scope, we have instructed the engine to perform a JOIN, which can then be optimized with indexes. When the user supplies a string predicate, such as EMP_ID = '23495', navigational access will be performed. Otherwise, expect the engine to perform a JOIN.

At some point in the foreseeable future, it is likely that the performance of object references may exceed that of JOINs; however, any such benefit is still some time away. For now, JOINs are the optimal access path to data within the Oracle Server.

DEFERRED/NOVALIDATE Constraint Options

The DEFERRED and NOVALIDATE options are a pair of similar features that are geared to manipulating the validation performed by integrity constraints. The DEFERRED option is a parameter of the SET CONSTRAINTS command, issued from within a SQL*Plus or comparable active session. The two values this parameter accepts are IMMEDIATE and DEFERRED.

By default, this command is set to IMMEDIATE, which means that the RDBMS will validate the constraint immediately. DEFERRED provides the ability to pass validation of constraints until a COMMIT is issued. The DEFERRED option is generally useful in situations such as PO and PO_DTL, where you may wish to perform DML operations on multiple, related tables simultaneously, with no assurance as to the order these transactions will be validated.

The NOVALIDATE constraint clause allows contraint checking to be performed only on new or modified records. This is specifically targeted to databases having new constraints being added, or databases where large data migrations are taking place.

The single most expensive component of data migrations is the cleansing/transformation of legacy data that simply does not conform to the integrity constraints of the new environment. For example, let's assume you are migrating a list of contacts, and their home state is included in the data set.

CONTACT_ID	LAST_NAME	FIRST_NAME	STATE
1	SMITH	JOHN	NJ
2	JONES	PAUL	X
3	WHITNEY	JED	
4	KRAUS	LIZZIE	PA

Assuming that the new CONTACT table would require all four of these fields to be mandatory, and that the STATE_CD field would be validated against the REF_STATE table, then contacts 2 and 3 would violate both the NOT NULL constraint on the STATE_CD column, and the foreign key constraint on the STATE_CD column. The code is shown in Code Example 1-12.

```
DROP TABLE CONTACT;
DROP TABLE REF_STATE;

CREATE TABLE REF_STATE (
STATE_CD        VARCHAR2(2) NOT NULL PRIMARY KEY,
DESCR_TX        VARCHAR2 (50) NOT NULL)
/

CREATE TABLE CONTACT (
CONTACT_ID      NUMBER (10) NOT NULL PRIMARY KEY,
LAST_NAME       VARCHAR2 (40) NOT NULL,
FIRST_NAME      VARCHAR2 (40) NOT NULL,
STATE_CD        VARCHAR2 (2) CONSTRAINT STATE_CD_NN NOT NULL DISABLE,
CONSTRAINT CONTACT__STATE_FK FOREIGN KEY (STATE_CD)
  REFERENCES REF_STATE(STATE_CD) DISABLE)
/

INSERT INTO REF_STATE (STATE_CD, DESCR_TX) VALUES ('NJ','NEW JERSEY');
INSERT INTO REF_STATE (STATE_CD, DESCR_TX) VALUES
('PA','PENNSYLVANIA');

INSERT INTO CONTACT (CONTACT_ID,LAST_NAME,FIRST_NAME,STATE_CD)
VALUES (1,'SMITH','JOHN','NJ');
INSERT INTO CONTACT (CONTACT_ID,LAST_NAME,FIRST_NAME,STATE_CD)
VALUES (2,'JONES','PAUL','X');
INSERT INTO CONTACT (CONTACT_ID,LAST_NAME,FIRST_NAME,STATE_CD)
VALUES (3,'WHITNEY','JED',NULL);
INSERT INTO CONTACT (CONTACT_ID,LAST_NAME,FIRST_NAME,STATE_CD)
VALUES (4,'KRAUS','LIZZIE','PA');

ALTER TABLE CONTACT ENABLE NOVALIDATE CONSTRAINT STATE_CD_NN;
ALTER TABLE CONTACT ENABLE NOVALIDATE CONSTRAINT CONTACT__STATE_FK;

SQL> SELECT * FROM CONTACT;

CONTACT_ID LAST_NAME FIRST_NAME ST
---------- --------- ---------- --
1          SMITH     JOHN       NJ
2          JONES     PAUL       X
3          WHITNEY   JED
4          KRAUS     LIZZIE     PA
```

Code Example 1-12

As you can see, the constraints are now enabled with invalid values remaining in the table, as previously populated. In short, you no longer have to perform data cleansing on data you do not intend to work with in the future.

If, however, you insert a new record, or update a column of an existing record that violates a given constraint, the value you enter will be forced through the appropriate validation. Note that you can update other columns of a table that are not part of the violated constraint.

Object Views

An *object view* is very similar to a relational view. Object views are based upon a single SELECT statement that could reference one or more relational and/or object-relational tables. The most common use of views is still primarily for providing a secure level of access to the contents of the actual data structures. A key benefit of using object views is that they serve as a migration path between relational design and object-relational design. You can create object views that are based upon object types, and access data stored in relational tables. This allows utilization of object references and methods in conjunction with your relational data, without changing any data structures.

Essentially, you can maintain existing relational applications, and add an object layer on top of them at your convenience, providing an excellent opportunity to compare and contrast the two techniques in your own environment. Object views enable you to effectively use Oracle8i objects without having to migrate your existing relational data.

Object views are typed strongly, as are object tables. In other words, both object views and object tables must be instantiated as a single object type, and their structure can never deviate from that object type. Although the text implies that the relational tables should already exist, we have added the CREATE TABLE statements for the relational DEPARTMENTS and EMPLOYEES tables to Code Example 1-13 for demonstrative purposes. Any structural modifications required must be performed upon the object type and then inherited by the object table. Therefore, the first step in creating an object view is to define an object type. Let's assume we have a relational table called EMPLOYEES, which contains information about employees, and we would like to add an object layer atop it. The EMPLOYEES table contains a foreign key to the DEPARTMENTS table as shown in Code Example 1-13.

```
CREATE TABLE DEPARTMENTS (
DEPT_ID        NUMBER (10) NOT NULL PRIMARY KEY,
NAME           VARCHAR2 (50) NOT NULL)
/

CREATE OR REPLACE TYPE DEPT_T AS OBJECT (
DEPT_ID        NUMBER (10),
NAME           VARCHAR2 (50))
/

CREATE VIEW DEPT_OV OF DEPT_T WITH OBJECT OID (DEPT_ID)
 AS SELECT DEPT_ID, NAME
 FROM DEPARTMENTS
/

CREATE TABLE EMPLOYEES (
EMP_ID         NUMBER (10) not null primary key,
LAST_NAME      VARCHAR2 (50) not null,
FIRST_NAME     VARCHAR2 (50) not null,
HIRE_DATE      DATE not null,
DEPT_ID        NUMBER (10) REFERENCES DEPARTMENTS (DEPT_ID))
/

CREATE OR REPLACE TYPE EMP_T AS OBJECT (
EMP_ID         NUMBER (10),
LAST_NAME      VARCHAR2 (50),
FIRST_NAME     VARCHAR2 (50),
HIRE_DATE      DATE,
DEPT_ID        REF DEPT_OV)
/

CREATE VIEW EMP_OV OF EMP_T WITH OBJECT OID (EMP_ID)
 AS
SELECT EMP_ID, LAST_NAME, FIRST_NAME, HIRE_DATE,
MAKE_REF(DEPT_OV,DEPT_ID)
FROM EMPLOYEES
/
```

Code Example 1-13

Notice that the OID has been defined based upon the EMP_ID column values from the relational EMPLOYEES table. OID values can be system generated or user defined. The MAKE_REF command simulates an object reference by allowing the reference to point to the primary key of a relational table.

CAST-MULTISET is a SQL expression that is used to create a strongly typed collection from the resulting set of a subquery. Using the EMP/DEPT example, we can create the EMP_BY_DEPT_OV object view with the CAST-MULTISET expression as shown in Code Example 1-14.

```
--example_01_12 is prereq
CREATE TYPE EMPS_T AS object (
EMP_ID            NUMBER(10),
LAST_NAME         VARCHAR2(50),
FIRST_NAME        VARCHAR2(50),
HIRE_DATE         DATE)
/

CREATE TYPE EMPSET_T AS TABLE OF EMPS_T
/

CREATE OR REPLACE TYPE EMP_BY_DEPT_T AS OBJECT (
DEPT_ID           NUMBER(10),
NAME              VARCHAR2(50),
EMP               EMPSET_T)
/


CREATE VIEW EMP_BY_DEPT_OV OF EMP_BY_DEPT_T
WITH OBJECT OID (DEPT_ID)
AS SELECT DEPT_ID, NAME,
CAST (MULTISET(
SELECT E.EMP_ID, E.LAST_NAME, E.FIRST_NAME, E.HIRE_DATE
FROM EMPLOYEES E
WHERE E.DEPT_ID = D.DEPT_ID)
AS EMPSET_T)
FROM DEPARTMENTS D
/
```

Code Example 1-14

The CAST-MULTISET command basically clusters associated detail records with master records. Code Example 1-14 returns all employee records from the EMPLOYEES table that are associated with a given department record from the DEPARTMENTS table. CAST-MULTISET is essentially a new syntax to embed a subquery, which enables the user to group related rows together for retrieval purposes.

Querying data from the EMP_BY_DEPT_OV object view will return employees correlated by their Departments. The query within the CAST-MULTISET clause is called the *collection query*. Note that the subquery must also be assigned an object type. In this case, we reused the EMP_T object type created in Code Example 1-13.

As part of each object view's definition, you can now include methods for generic access to data. As Chapter 13 discusses, a future release of Oracle8i will provide the ability to encapsulate methods and columns. As of this writing, we can imitate such functionality by building additional object views. In fact, object views even support inheritance, to a degree, by the casting of object types.

Of course, there is no pressing need to select either relational or object-relational structures. The choice is up to each organization. Each type has its own unique features. Future systems will likely result in some hybrid of relational and object-relational systems design.

INSTEAD OF Triggers

Views are often made up of complex expressions that are typically aliased. In the past, Oracle has been unable to provide DML support for complex views. INSTEAD OF triggers have been supplied to support DML operations through views. These new triggers actually fire instead of the actual DML statement, and can be created for views, but cannot be created for tables. The code you write inside the INSTEAD OF trigger is the DML that will be executed. Applications can now be based upon views and issue DML operations to the view. Then the INSTEAD OF trigger intercepts these DML operations and instead executes the code embedded within the INSTEAD OF trigger. INSTEAD OF triggers have access to the NEW and OLD global variable references, as do the other row-level triggers, as shown in Code Example 1-15.

```
--example_01_13 is prereq
CREATE OR REPLACE TRIGGER IOI_EMP
INSTEAD OF INSERT ON EMP_OV FOR EACH ROW
DECLARE
INVALID_DEPT_ID    EXCEPTION;
```

```
BEGIN
IF :NEW.HIRE_DATE > SYSDATE - 30 THEN
INSERT INTO EMPLOYEES VALUES(:NEW.EMP_ID,
                             :NEW.LAST_NAME,
                             :NEW.FIRST_NAME,
                             :NEW.HIRE_DATE,
                              NEW.DEPT_ID);
END IF;
EXCEPTION
WHEN INVALID_HIRE_DATE THEN
RAISE_APPLICATION_ERROR(-20001, 'HIRE DATE '||
'MUST BE WITHIN LAST THIRTY DAYS OR IN FUTURE.');
END;
/
```

Code Example 1-15

Remember, however, that views are intended primarily for retrieval of data and not for manipulation. Therefore, views do not automatically support referential integrity when DML is performed via INSTEAD OF triggers. If you create an object view with an INSTEAD OF trigger that is based upon a relational table with referential integrity defined, then you will not have to perform the Foreign key validation manually. Otherwise, roll up your sleeves and start writing!

Large Objects (LOBs)

Large Objects (LOBs) are new datatypes available with the release of Oracle 8.0. LOBs provide substantially greater storage as compared with their predecessor, LONG. LOBs can store up to 4Gb of data. They can essentially be stored inline (up to 4K) within a row, or otherwise out of line. There are a number of different datatypes that correspond to LOBs, such as CLOB (character LOB), NCLOB, BLOB (binary LOB), and BFILE. BFILE stores a pointer to a physical location on disk where a file resides. Of course, BFILE offers no security over this file, because it is stored outside the database. If the security of these files is expected to be handled by the database, then these files should be stored using LOB datatype.

Data can also be stored inside a LOB, although the authors do not recommend this option. For example, you might want to store secure data such as salaries in a LOB, because LOB data is not directly accessible from SQL. It is essentially stored in an uninterpreted, binary format. The suggested approach to viewing data stored within a LOB would be through the implementation of methods. Methods are PL/SQL, and PL/SQL is required to view/manipulate data stored within LOBs.

You can also do context-sensitive querying of LOBs, such as requesting the first 500 characters of the column where LONGs required return of the entire value, or occurrences of a series of alphanumeric characters. You can have multiple LOBs in a single table, unlike LONGs, which were limited to one per table.

Server Side Code

Oracle8i offers the ability to develop and store server-side Java code within the database. These Java program units can be executed from PL/SQL triggers, procedures, and/or functions. Uncompiled Java code offers reasonably comparable performance to PL/SQL, though not quite as good, given the number of years that have gone into the optimization of PL/SQL within the server.

However, compiled Java code can execute up to ten times faster than PL/SQL. Couple this statistic with the fact that Java is extremely portable, and you can see a new trend. As is the case with relational data structures, PL/SQL will not go away. There are far too many systems already that are based upon PL/SQL, and many more are in development. PL/SQL is a robust, veteran programming language that has served us well for many years.

Keep in mind, however, that there are several organizations worldwide working to make Java as efficient as possible. The assemblage of these resources will most likely provide an end product with superior performance and usability not easily matched by any single organization. Do not be surprised if before long we can create database triggers, procedures, and functions written in Java, as opposed to simply referencing Java!

Collections

Collections are a means of storing a series of data entries that are jointly associated to a corresponding row in the database. Collections model a 1-to-many relationship between a row and a collection without necessitating integrity constraints and a separate data structure. Oracle8i provides two types of collections: VARRAYS and nested tables.

VARRAYS

VARRAYS, or varying arrays, are typically stored inline with respect to their containing row. VARRAYS are assigned an outer limit of values. A VARRAY is implemented as shown in Code Example 1-16.

```
CREATE OR REPLACE TYPE TEMP_T AS VARRAY (3) OF NUMBER (5,2)
/
```

Code Example 1-16

The TEMP_T type is used to define a VARRAY that will be used to maintain three temperature recordings. The DAILY_TEST table expands upon the TEMP_T type to record three temperature samples daily, as shown in Code Example 1-17.

```
--example_-1_15 is prereq
CREATE TABLE DAILY_TEST (
DAILY_TEST_ID        INTEGER,
DAY_ID               INTEGER,
TEMPERATURE_SAMPLE   TEMP_T)
/
INSERT INTO DAILY_TEST VALUES(1,1,TEMP_T(1))
/
```

Code Example 1-17

You can insert multiple occurrences into a VARRAY in a single INSERT statement using the following syntax shown in Code Example 1-18:

```
INSERT INTO DAILY_TEST VALUES(1,1,TEMP_T(75,85,80))
/
```

Code Example 1-18

If you need to add values to a VARRAY later, you must turn to PL/SQL syntax as of Oracle8i as shown in Code Example 1-19. A future release may provide SQL syntax to add values to a VARRAY.

```
CREATE TYPE vart AS VARRAY(3) OF INTEGER;
CREATE TABLE tab1 (c1 INTEGER, c2 vart);
INSERT INTO tab1 VALUES(0, vart(1, 2));
DECLARE
varvar vart;
```

```
BEGIN
 SELECT c2 INTO varvar FROM tab1 WHERE c1 = 0;
 varvar.EXTEND();
 varvar(varvar.COUNT) := 3;
 UPDATE tab1 SET c2 = varvar WHERE c1 = 0;
END;
```

Code Example 1-19

VARRAY values are typically stored inline with respect to the owning or master row. This results in a direct performance benefit, because the VARRAY values are always accessed simultaneously with the master record. VARRAYs are suggested when the number of elements you plan to track is small, or when you expect to bring the entire collection back within a single select call. If a column is based upon a VARRAY whose maximum size exceeds 4K, then the values are stored as "inline" LOBs, where the portion of the VARRAY value that exceeds 4K is stored out of line in the LOB segments, but the portion less than 4K is stored inline with the master row.

Nested Tables

Nested tables, the second collection type, are similar to the notion of clustered tables from Oracle7, though they are not implemented in the same manner. A nested table is essentially an additional relational table. It is not stored inline with the master table, as are clustered tables. Therefore, nested tables do not inherently offer a performance benefit. The following example represents a collection of purchase order detail (i.e., PO_DTL) rows embedded within the purchase order (i.e., PO) table as shown in Code Example 1-20.

```
CREATE OR REPLACE TYPE PO_DTL_TYPE
   AS OBJECT(
ITEM_ID  VARCHAR2 (5),
QTY      NUMBER (5))
/
CREATE OR REPLACE TYPE PO_DTL_TABLE_TYPE
   AS TABLE OF PO_DTL_TYPE
/
CREATE OR REPLACE TYPE PO_TYPE
   AS OBJECT(
PO_ID    VARCHAR2 (5),
DESCR_TX  VARCHAR2(40),
```

```
VENDOR_ID VARCHAR2 (5),
PO_DTL PO_DTL_TABLE_TYPE)
/
CREATE TABLE PO
  OF PO_TYPE(
PO_ID      NOT NULL PRIMARY KEY,
DESCR_TX  NOT NULL,
VENDOR_ID NOT NULL
  REFERENCES VENDOR (VENDOR_ID))
NESTED TABLE PO_DTL STORE AS PO_DTL
  (PRIMARY KEY (NESTED_TABLE_ID, PO_DTL_ID)
  ORGANIZATION INDEX)
  RETURN AS LOCATOR
/
```

Code Example 1-20

Nested tables cannot be limited as VARRAYs can. Querying nested tables in general will be more efficient with nested tables as opposed to VARRAYs, because you can create secondary indexes on nested tables.

You can deliver queries that aggregate rows of nested tables independent of the master table. Suppose you wanted to issue a query that would return the total quantity of items sold, per item. The SQL query shown in Code Example 1-21 would suffice.

```
SELECT D.ITEM_ID, SUM(D.QTY) QTY
FROM PO P, TABLE(P.PO_DTL) D
GROUP BY D.ITEM_ID
/
```

Code Example 1-21

As you can see, the master table, which in this case is PO, must be referenced within the FROM clause. You cannot simply issue a query based upon a nested table without also referencing the master table. The reason is, although nested tables are actually stored as independent relational tables, they do not allow the same access to their data. The TABLE(...) command instructs the SQL parser to act upon the nested table PO_DTL of table P (P is the alias assigned to the PO table) as though it were a typical table. This same example could be performed in PL/SQL.

Index Organized Tables (IOTs)

Nested tables can be defined as *index organized tables* (IOTs), which are tables that are stored within the structure of, or as, an index. The entire table and its contents are pinned in memory, eliminating the need to identify the appropriate ROWID values to satisfy a given query. Instead, the lookup is performed directly on the contents of the nested table. Object tables cannot be stored as index organized tables in Oracle8i, though this functionality may become available in a future release. Index organized tables should be used when you plan to query detail rows by the master rows. In fact, IOTs outperform clusters in this respect.

The example in the preceding "Nested Tables" section defined a primary key for the nested table—PO_DTL with two components: NESTED_TABLE_ID and PO_DTL_ID. PO_DTL_ID is a real column residing in the PO_DTL table that will be assigned system-generated identifiers, likely integer increments beginning with "1," per purchase order detail. NESTED_TABLE_ID is an alias for a system-generated value that serves as a pointer from nested table rows to the rows of the master table they reference.

The primary key of a nested table serves as the basis of defining this table as an index organized table (IOT), which is specified by the ORGANIZATION INDEX declaration. The default locator values that IOTs return in queries are the actual values stored within the table. This example specified that a locator, instead of a value, will be returned. This locator really is a pointer that supports higher performance of data retrieval.

Table Partitioning

Oracle8i provides the ability to partition subsets of data within a common table into separate physical storage locations within the database, for obvious performance benefits. The current release of Oracle8i only supports partitioning at the column level (i.e., YEAR = '1997'). However, a future release will provide the ability to partition based upon the evaluation of database functions (i.e., START_DATE = substr('01-JAN-1997',8,4)). This feature is necessary because we may choose to partition on dynamic scenarios. The current implementation requires you to store a redundant column that would contain the value of the year the transaction was committed, which is not a practice that we suggest.

Partitioning was developed to enhance data access in tables that have large data volume. The general approach is to store common rows of data together in separate partitions, based upon the typical method of retrieval.

For example, suppose a large bank issued credit cards that generated millions of transactions per month. One way that the TRANSACTIONS table might be partitioned is by month and year, especially if transaction level reporting is typically performed on monthly subsets of data.

Another approach might be to partition by the SIC codes of transactions. This partitioning method might be useful to the marketing group to get an idea of who is really using the cards, and what the most common purchase types are.

If we were to partition the TRANSACTIONS table, the code would be as shown next in Code Example 1-22:

```
CREATE TABLE TRANSACTIONS (
TRANSACTION_ID          VARCHAR2 (15) NOT NULL,
CARDHOLDER              VARCHAR2 (60) NOT NULL,
SIC                     VARCHAR2 (5)  NOT NULL,
PURCHASE_AMT            NUMBER (9,2)  NOT NULL,
TRANSACTION_DATE DATE                 NOT NULL)
/
```

Code Example 1-22

If we were to partition the preceding TRANSACTIONS table by month and year starting with transactions from the month of January, 1998, for two months, it would look as follows in Code Example 1-23.

```
CREATE TABLE TRANSACTIONS (
TRANSACTION_ID          VARCHAR2 (15)        NOT NULL,
CARDHOLDER              VARCHAR2 (60)        NOT NULL,
SIC                     VARCHAR2 (5)         NOT NULL,
PURCHASE_AMT            NUMBER (9,2)         NOT NULL,
TRANSACTION_DATE DATE ('MM-DD-YYYY')         NOT NULL)
MONTH_YEAR              VARCHAR2(6)          NOT NULL)
PARTITION BY RANGE (MONTH_YEAR)
(PARTITION TRANS1 VALUES LESS THAN ('011998')
TABLESPACE TRANS1_TS,
  (PARTITION TRANS2 VALUES LESS THAN ('021998')
TABLESPACE TRANS2_TS,
/
```

Code Example 1-23

It is important to note that you only specify the maximum value of the range for each partition. Oracle automatically determines the minimum value.

The MAXVALUE keyword could be used instead of a value in the VALUES LESS THAN clause to add a partition to store any data that did not satisfy the criteria of the other partitions, as follows in Code Example 1-24:

```
ALTER TABLE TRANSACTIONS ADD PARTITION
BY RANGE (MONTH_YEAR)
(PARTITION MAX VALUES LESS THAN (MAXVALUE))
TABLESPACE MAX_TS
/
```

Code Example 1-24

Notice that the BY RANGE parameter requires a column as the data source to partition by. This required the creation of a redundant field called MONTH_YEAR, in which we stored a six-character value, with the first two characters representing the month and the latter four characters representing the year (i.e., MONTH_YEAR = '011998'). You cannot specify a function in the BY RANGE parameter (i.e., PARTITION BY RANGE (SUBSTR (TRANSACTION_DATE,1,2)||SUBSTR (TRANSACTION_DATE,7))).

Partition Indexes

There are two ways to index partitioned tables: local and global. *Local* indexes will set up an index that is partitioned the same way as the table is defined. If we were to create a local index on the TRANSACTIONS table, it would look as follows in Code Example 1-25:

```
CREATE INDEX TRANSACTIONS_BY_MONTH_IDX
ON TRANSACTIONS (MONTH_YEAR)
LOCAL
(PARTITION TRANS1       TABLESPACE TRANS1_IDX,
 PARTITION TRANS2       TABLESPACE TRANS2_IDX,
 PARTITION MAX          TABLESPACE MAX_IDX)
/
```

Code Example 1-25

This index will create three separate indexes and one partition, hence the LOCAL keyword, since there is a separate index created per partition.

The GLOBAL keyword of the index creation command allows you to specify ranges for index values that differ from those of the table partitions. For example, if we chose to create an index that combined the transactions for the months of January and February into one partition, and create a second partition for all other transactions, the statement would look as shown in Code Example 1-26:

```
CREATE INDEX TRANSACTIONS_BY_MONTH_IDX
ON TRANSACTIONS (MONTH_YEAR)
GLOBAL PARTITION BY RANGE (MONTH_YEAR)
(PARTITION TRANS1 VALUES LESS THAN ('021998')
TABLESPACE TRANS1_IDX,
PARTITION MAX VALUES LESS THAN (MAXVALUE)
TABLESPACE MAX_IDX)
/
```

Code Example 1-26

Methods

Methods are really nothing more than stored procedures and functions that are associated with a type. The primary purpose of methods is data retrieval. For instance, a method may be created on the EMPLOYEE table to determine the duration of employment by subtracting SYSDATE – HIRE_DATE.

Today, the only method type intended for DML operations is the constructor method, which is automatically created in direct 1-to-1 correspondence with the type, itself. However, a future release of Oracle8i will provide the ability for user-defined constructor methods. These user-defined constructor methods will not perform DML directly on rows of a table. Rather, they will construct the row to be transacted, and pass that to the parser.

Encapsulation

Methods are thought of as columns, not as stored procedures and functions, and therefore fall under the SELECT portion of the Privileges/Rights model. Therefore, if you wish to grant access of a given method to a specific user, you will have to issue a GRANT SELECT… statement. This is sort of different from the way we have thought about stored code in the past, but it should not take long to get used to.

Encapsulation is not fully supported in Oracle8i, though it is planned for subsequent releases. It is possible that the ability to mark type members (columns, embedded column types, methods, collections) as private and/or restricted may eliminate the use of views somewhere in the distant future. For now, we can only state whether a user can access an object as a whole. A future implementation will enable us to grant explicit access to type members.

The current release of Oracle8i includes the notion of "invoker's rights," where a method is executed under the rights of the database account that is invoking the method. This replaces the previous implementation, which invoked a stored procedure under the definer's rights, which seemed to do nothing more than confuse matters during development.

Advantages of an Object-Oriented Approach

With Oracle8i, we are still conceptually in roughly the same environment as we were with Oracle6. With Oracle6, we could declare referential integrity constraints, but the database didn't enforce them. Similarly, we have some object-oriented structures in Oracle8i, but they are not yet fully implemented.

This does not mean that we shouldn't start creating object-oriented designs. There are some places where we might take advantage of the new Oracle8i structures. Even if we choose to implement our object-oriented designs using traditional relational constructs, our designs will be better if we shift our thinking in an object-oriented direction.

The authors started shifting logical database designs toward object-oriented structures around 1996. Since that time, we have seen our database designs improve greatly because of the object-oriented approach. Specifically, the biggest advantage we've noticed is that the number of entities (and ultimately tables) in our models has greatly decreased. The structures are much more robust and flexible so that, as the inevitable new user requirement pops up, the probability that we will have to make a significant change to the data model is greatly reduced. A few recent examples have made this advantage very clear to us.

In designing a retail system, we found many small sets of business transactions that all looked similar from a structural standpoint, namely PO Requests, POs, Invoices, Receipts of Goods, and Inter-Company Transfers. Applying object-oriented thinking allowed us to recognize that, in all of these cases, we were talking about movement of merchandise. As a result, instead of having separate structures for all these constructs, we created a single structure called "Merchandise Movement" that greatly simplified the model. The model was also more robust. Late in the design process, the users came up with a new requirement to support Purchase Returns back to vendors. Because of the object-oriented approach, we were able to easily accommodate these changes without any changes to the data model. Later in the project, the client decided to add a distribution warehouse. Again, no changes were required to support this change to the business.

In another situation at a large financial organization, we were faced with different aggregation paths for stock portfolios. The existing legacy system required two sets of structures, one for the main aggregations and a separate one for the ad hoc rollup structure. This required a great deal of manual intervention and maintenance. Because of the two separate structures, the original database had 81 entities. After redesign using object-oriented structures, the total number of entities was reduced to 27. This not only created a smaller, easier to maintain system, but also included more flexibility and capabilities than the original system.

Finally, in a large logistics system, we modeled an approval process for purchase orders. Later we modeled a similar approval process for projects. We noticed that we would eventually need seven to ten different approval processes modeled. This one aspect of the system would have eventually added approximately 50 tables to the data model. Instead we wrote a generalized approval process structure that would work for all of the different places where we needed approvals. The generalized structure required only ten tables.

In all these cases, object-oriented thinking resulted in cleaner data models, increased system flexibility, and easier maintenance. All systems were created using Oracle Designer 1.X running on Oracle7. This illustrates that object-oriented designs can be implemented without having access to fully object-oriented tools.

CHAPTER
2

Database Basics

ne of the disturbing comments that keeps cropping up with the advent of object modeling is that we no longer have to worry about relational design and normalization. This is completely false. All of the principles of good relational database design and proper use of normalization still apply in the object-relational model.

It is not the purpose of this book to provide basic database information. In this chapter, we assume that the reader is a database professional or has taken one or more database classes. Our readers should have been working in a relational database environment and want to make the shift into object-oriented models. This chapter will provide a brief review of some salient points in relational and object-oriented theory.

Quick Review of Relational Database Theory

What exactly is a relational database? Just because you have a bunch of tables stored within a relational database product such as Oracle does not guarantee that you have a relational database. A *relational database* implies that you have designed your database tables in such a way that they conform to basic relational theory and practices. These theoretical guidelines are expressed through the *rules of normalization*.

In this chapter, we will present a few examples of the way this data might be stored in flat files that do not conform to the rules of normalization. We will explain why these structures are not desirable, and show the relational equivalents and how these improve upon the design.

Example 1   Consider a standard Human Resources Employee data file laid out as shown in the following EMPLOYEE table:

EMP

EmpNo	Ename	DeptNo	DeptName
1	Al	10	Acct
2	Bel	10	Acct
3	Cil	20	Fin
4	Del	20	Fin
5	Ed	10	Acct

There are some problems with this structure:

■ If you delete all of the employees in the Finance (FIN) department, all evidence that the Finance department exists will be removed.

■ If the department name were changed from FIN to FINANCE, you would have to make that change to every employee's record in the Finance department.

According to relational theory, the solution to this problem is to represent the information in two tables (DEPT and EMP) structured as shown in Table 2-1.

Notice that with this structure, we have the department information and employee information stored in two tables. If we want to know the name of the department that Al works in, we look in the EMP table to determine that Al works in department 10. We then go to the DEPT table to determine that department 10 corresponds to the Accounting department.

DEPT

DeptNo	DeptName
10	Acct
20	Fin

EMP

EmpNo	Ename	DeptNo
1	Al	10
2	Bel	10
3	Cil	20
4	Del	20
5	Ed	10

TABLE 2-1. *Relational Representation of DEPT and EMP Tables*

It could be argued that storing the information in a single table would be much more efficient. This is true. However, the resulting database would be difficult to work with, requiring a great deal of complex code in order to overcome the limitations mentioned with respect to the single data-file example. Furthermore, the problem of joining information together in multiple tables is exactly what relational databases are designed to solve. In the physical implementation of the database, there are usually indexes placed on these linking columns (called *foreign keys*) of which DeptNo in the preceding example is an instance. This is done so that the searches to find the information requested are very efficient.

Example 2   We will use the example of a Purchase Order (PURCH_ORDER) as shown in the following table:

PURCH ORDER

PO_NBR	DATE	ITEM I	QTY I	PRICE I	ITEM2	QTY2	PRICE2
1001	1/1/1999	Ball	3	$4.00	Bat	3	$5.00
1002	2/2/1999	Bat	1	$5.00			
1003	3/3/1999	Glove	2	$2.00	Ball	2	$4.00

In this case, we have a structure where each Purchase Order is stored in its own record. This structure has the following problems:

■   To find out the total price of a Purchase Order, you need to multiply QTY times PRICE in two places (QTY1 * PRICE1 + QTY2 * PRICE2).

■   How is it possible to order three items? We would have to create a second PO for the additional item(s).

Using a relational structure as shown in the following tables, both of these problems are solved:

PURCH ORDER

PO_NBR	DATE
1001	1/1/1999
1002	2/2/1999
1003	3/3/1999

PURCH_ORDER_DTL

PO_NBR	LINE_NBR	ITEM	QTY	PRICE
1001	1	Ball	3	$4.00
1001	2	Bat	3	$5.00
1002	1	Bat	2	$5.00
1003	1	Glove	2	$2.00
1003	2	Ball	2	$4.00

Notice how a PO can have any number of lines associated with it. We link these two tables through the PO number.

Basic Terminology and Concepts

In both Examples 1 and 2, we have looked at tables and columns. In relational database design, we discuss the logical versus the physical data model. The *logical* data model represents the design of the database, whereas the *physical* data model represents the implementation of the design. Different words are used to discuss logical design as opposed to physical design. This can be confusing. The following chart helps to clarify the terminology for purposes of discussion:

Logical Relational	Logical Object	Physical
Entity	Class	Table
Attribute	Attribute	Column, Field
Instance	Object	Row

To ensure consistency, it is important to clarify the definitions relevant to the discussion:

- **Entity**   This is something of interest to the organization, such as an Employee, Department, or Sale. From a theoretical perspective, an entity may merely be a collection of attributes. However, this is not a useful way to think about entities. It is much better to consider an entity as corresponding to something in the real world. Each instance of the Department entity, for example, corresponds to a specific department in the organization—or, in the case of the Person entity, to a specific person. Entities and instances of entities in relational theory correspond directly to classes and objects, respectively, in object theory. For example, for the entity Department, we can talk about the class Department, which includes the object Accounting.

- **Attribute**   This is a piece of information that we track about an object or instance of an entity, such as department names or ages of employees. Notice that the word "attribute" is used in both relational and object theory.

- **Primary key**   This is a relational theory concept describing the attribute(s) of an entity that uniquely identifies a specific instance of the entity. For example, the Employee ID is an appropriate primary key for the Employee entity, because no two employees have the same ID. Primary keys must be unique. No components may ever be null, and once they are assigned, they should not change. This final requirement is practical rather than theoretical, because primary keys are used in lieu of pointers in relational databases. Changing the primary key would mean changing it everywhere it is used as a pointer, potentially affecting thousands or even millions of records.

- **Candidate key**   Frequently, in an entity, it is possible for more than one attribute to serve as the primary key. One of the candidate keys is designated as the primary key. Other attributes that may act as primary keys are designated as candidate keys.

Building a Simple Relational Database

We will use a simple example to illustrate the basic concepts of relational databases. More detail about these topics will be provided throughout the book. The following steps are used to create a simple relational database:

1. Define the entities (items of interest) DEPARTMENT and EMPLOYEE.

2. Determine the appropriate primary key for the entities:

Entity	Primary Key
DEPT	DeptNo
EMP	EmpNo

3. Identify relevant attributes about each entity:

Entity	Attributes
DEPT	Name, Location
EMP	Name, Age, Gender

4. Determine the relationships, if any, between these entities. Note that these relationships will eventually translate into the overlapping columns called foreign keys (FKs).

5. Identify the cardinality of each relationship. In relational theory, these can be classified as 1-to-1, 1-to-many, and many-to-many.

6. Keep all of the information organized by using a diagramming notation to pictorially represent the database design.

Types of Relationships

This section will describe the three different types of relationships between entities, provide examples of how they are diagrammed in both ERD and UML notation, and show how these diagrams are translated into physical database designs.

1-to-Many Relationship

A 1-to-many relationship between the DEPT and EMP entities would be drawn as shown in Figure 2-1.

Both syntaxes mean the same thing, namely that a Department is associated with any number of Employees including zero, and an Employee is associated with, at most, one Department. In ERD notation, both sides of the relationship are named as shown. This allows you to create a pair of relationship sentences to describe the relationship. In this case:

"Each department may be the Employer of zero or more Employees."
"Each Employee may work for, at most, one Department."

In UML, the notation typically just names the relationship once and indicates the relevant direction of the name. Usually, the most intuitive name goes from the "many" class to the "1" class. We have already seen how this is implemented in Table 2-1. We can redraw this with slightly more formal notation as shown here:

DEPT

DeptNo	DName
PK	CK
10	Acct
20	Fin

EMP

EmpNo	Ename	DeptNo
PK	NN	FK (DEPT)
1	Al	10
2	Bel	10
3	Cil	20
4	Del	20
5	Ed	10

ERD   UML

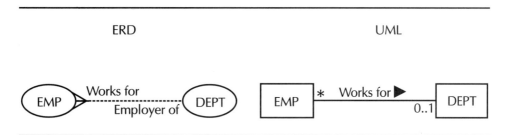

FIGURE 2-1. *1-to-many relationship*

In the DEPT table, the "PK" designation indicates that this is the primary key of the table. "CK" denotes a candidate key, implying that it is both not null and must be unique. In the EMP table, "NN" stands for not null. Each employee must have a name, but the name need not be unique. "FK" (foreign key) in the EMP table indicates that any value in the DeptNo column must also exist as a value in the DeptNo column in the DEPT table. Furthermore, if there is an attempt to delete the parent department, this deletion must be prevented or must cascade to prevent the orphaning of an Employee (pointing to a nonexistent Department). This so-called *referential integrity* must be enforced not only when child records are created or a Department is changed, but also whenever there is an attempt to delete a parent record.

We can now state the rule for implementing a 1-to-many relationship.

Take the primary key from the "1" side of the relationship, and place it as a foreign key in the table on the "many" side of the relationship.

Sometimes, we may want to say that each Employee must work for some Department at all times. In this case, the relationship with respect to the Employee is mandatory. To indicate this in an ERD, we make the line solid nearest to the Employee entity. In UML, we change the cardinality next to DEPT from "0..1" to "1," as shown in Figure 2-2.

To implement this in a relational system, we designate that the FK in the EMP table must not be null. This forces all Employees to be attached to some Department.

If we wish to say that each Department must have at least one Employee, we would draw the relationship as shown in Figure 2-3.

In this case, there is no simple thing we can do to the tables to enforce this rule. There is nothing to prevent you from making both sides of the

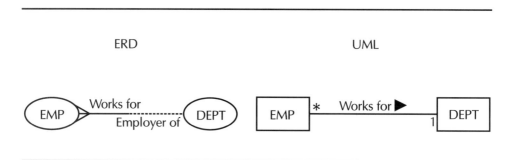

FIGURE 2-2. *1-to-many relationship—mandatory on Employee side*

relationship mandatory. However, you are only able to enforce the mandatory portion of the relationship on the "many" side.

To summarize, with a 1-to-many relationship, take the primary key of the "1" side and place it as a foreign key on the "many" side. If the "many" side is mandatory, designate the foreign key in the child table as "not null." To enforce the mandatory condition on the "1" side of the relationship, you must either write triggers to do this or enforce it through the application.

1-to-1 Relationship

One of the less common relationships between entities is the 1-to-1 relationship. Every instance of the entity is associated with at most one instance of another entity. For illustration purposes, we will use the EMP and DEPT example but use the relationship "manages" as shown in Figure 2-4.

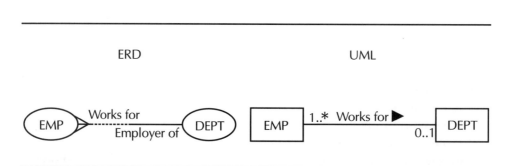

FIGURE 2-3. *1-to-many relationship—mandatory on Department side*

ERD   UML

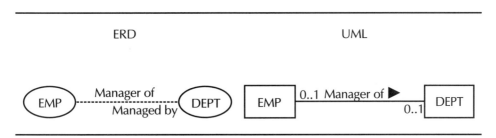

FIGURE 2-4.   *1-1 Relationship diagrams*

In this example, an Employee can manage at most one Department, and a Department can be managed by at most one Employee. The tables for this structure would be laid out as shown in Table 2-2.

EMP

EmpNo	Ename
PK	NN
1	Al
2	Bel
3	Cil
4	Del
5	Ed

DEPT

DeptNo	DName	MGR_EmpNo
PK	CK	FK (EMP), U
10	Fin	1
20	Acct	2

TABLE 2-2.   *Tables for 1-to-1 Relationship Between DEPT and EMP*

Notice that we have placed "FK" in the DEPT table to link the two tables. This is done because there are likely to be fewer departments than employees, so the FK field would have fewer null values than if stored in the EMP table. The "U" designation on FK in the MGR_EmpNo column serves to enforce that the values in this column must be unique. Without the unique indicator, this would be a one-to-many relationship. It is this uniqueness that changes the relationship from a 1-to-many to a 1-to-1.

Note that the FK is not placed in both tables. The rule is to place the FK in the smaller table. There is no reason to put it in both places, which would be redundant. One of the fundamental principles of relational databases is that all information is stored in exactly one place in the database. You can also declare that a 1-to-1 relationship is mandatory on either side, just as with a 1-to-many relationship. If you want to insist that every department must be managed by someone, a solid line would be used on the DEPT side in the ER diagram as shown in Figure 2-5.

In this case, just as with the 1-to-many example, we add the "not null" designation to the FK in the DEPT table. If you place the mandatory constraint on the employee side of the relationship, there is no way to enforce the rule through any structural change to the tables. To make both sides of a 1-to-1 relationship mandatory indicates that the two entities are representing the same thing and should probably be combined. The only time we have ever used a 1-to-1 relationship that was mandatory on both sides was to partition attributes in an entity between secure attributes (such as salary and home phone numbers) and public attributes (such as name and date hired).

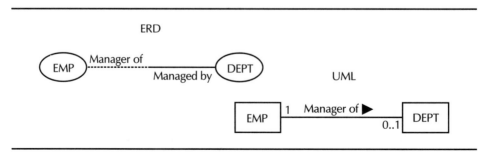

FIGURE 2-5. *1-to-1 relationship—mandatory on DEPT side*

Many-to-Many Relationship

The third basic relationship used in entity relationship modeling is *many-to-many,* as shown in Figure 2-6.

This structure cannot be implemented with only two tables. You might think that it is possible to place a "FK" in both the EMP and COMMITTEE tables. However, using a simple example of two Committees and two Employees, with both Employees serving on both Committees, you can easily verify that it cannot be done. The solution is to store the relationship in its own table that might be called "Committee Membership" with the table structure as shown in Table 2-3.

In this example, we have modeled that Al, Bel, and Cil belong to the Recreation (REC) Committee; Bel, Cil, and Del belong to the Employee Relations (ER) Committee. Ed belongs to no committee at all. Note that we have a FK as part of the primary key of the table. This is common in the case of tables arising from many-to-many relationships.

If you make either side of the many-to-many relationship mandatory, you cannot enforce this condition through any simple changes to the underlying tables. It must be enforced either through triggers or through application logic.

The entity arising from the many-to-many relationship is called an *intersection entity.* In UML, we call it an *association class.* The foreign keys in the intersection entity look like the foreign keys from standard 1-to-many relationships. Frequently, we draw our models to reflect this. UML supports a special syntax for just this type of structure, as shown in Figure 2-7.

The small horizontal lines on the ER relationship are called *UID bars,* indicating that the foreign keys will be part of the primary keys in the intersection entity. It is usually a good idea in ER modeling to remove many-

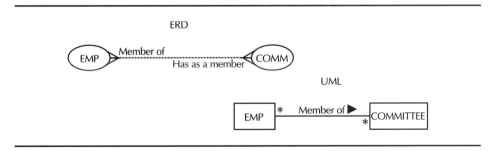

FIGURE 2-6. *Many-to-many relationship*

EMP

EmpNo	Ename
PK	*CK*
1	Al
2	Bel
3	Cil
4	Del
5	Ed

COMMITTEE

COM_CD	CName
PK	*CK*
REC	Recreation
ER	Employee Relations

COMMITTEE MEMBERSHIP

EmpNo	COM_CD
FK (EMP)	*FK (COMMITTEE)*
PK	
1	REC
2	REC
3	REC
2	ER
3	ER
4	ER

TABLE 2-3.   *Tables for Many-to-Many Relationship Between EMP and COMMITTEE*

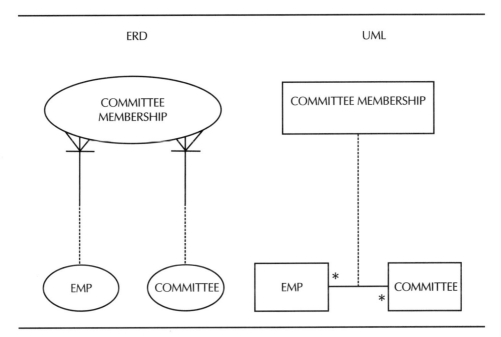

ERD   UML

FIGURE 2-7. *Many-to-many relationship between EMP and COMMITTEE*

to-many relationships and replace them with 1-to-many relationships along with intersection entities. This enables the designer to add relationships to the intersection entity and to create additional attributes for the intersection entity.

Rules of Normalization

When we say that a database has been normalized, it is not "normal" in the sense of "regular" or "ordinary." In this context, "normalized" originated from the mathematical notation of normal, meaning orthogonal. Going back to those linear algebra classes, remember that the term *normalized* was used in conjunction with orthogonal vectors in a vector space and in discussions of whether a linear combination of a set of vectors could be said to span a vector space.

The notion of normalization in a database follows a similar idea in that we are trying to develop a set of database tables that do not inappropriately overlap and allow us to store all of the information in the database in much the same way that three orthogonal unit vectors span $\Re^3$. We will not provide a formal discussion of normalization here. This can be found in books such as *A First Course in Database Systems* by Jeffrey D. Ullman, numerous works by Chris J. Date, or any other basic academic books on databases. We will present practical definitions of normalization more appropriate to the goals of this book.

Why must we build normalized databases? Normalization was derived in conjunction with the theoretical SEQUEL programming language. The fundamental theorem of relational theory is that if your database is normalized, you can extract any subset of data from it using basic SEQUEL operators. This is why normalization is so important. Without a normalized database, it may be difficult to extract information from the database without writing complex procedural code. These rules of normalization were important in relational modeling and are still important in object-relational modeling.

We are still using Oracle's SQL+ or an object extension of SQL (an implementation of SEQUEL) to manipulate information in the database. If we do not normalize, SQL may not work. People who have worked in the Oracle environment for their entire careers may not be aware of the environment before relational databases. The typical turnaround in a nonrelational system for an ad hoc report request was at least two weeks. Frequently, requests for even minor changes to data structure took months or even years of developer time. Requests for additional functionality were met with blank stares, shaking of heads, and the response that, given the current architecture, the modifications simply could not be done. If we abandon the rules of normalization in creating object-oriented databases, we run the risk of taking a giant step backward in terms of the flexibility of our systems.

First Normal Form

First Normal Form is defined as not having any multivalued attributes. We will illustrate this by showing a table structure that violates First Normal Form. For example, with a Purchase Order entity, we might want to have an attribute in the PO called "Items Ordered." Since it is possible to order multiple items, you would have the ability to store multiple items in the entity. The table shown in Example 2 illustrates this type of violation.

The problem arises if there is a third item. You can only order two items using this structure. Of course, we could always add more columns to allow for more items. We could add enough columns that we would never have to worry about ordering more items than we allow for. However, then we run into a different problem. The only way to find the number of times a particular item was ordered is to look in all of the item columns. Even finding out the total value of the invoice requires looking in multiple places.

In the relational model, we have a way to get around First Normal Form. The structure to solve First Normal Form violations is illustrated in Table 2-1.

It is possible to build good databases without adhering to First Normal Form. Relational theorists long ago worked out what extensions to relational theory would be required to support non–First Normal Form databases. The idea is to allow an array as a datatype. This can provide better performance than a standard relational database, but requires more complex queries to retrieve the data.

Within the Oracle8 object extensions, there are two ways to implement non–First Normal Form structures:

■ Array of references

■ Nested tables

Oracle allows queriability over nested tables and VARRAYS. Implementations using these structures will be discussed as appropriate throughout the book.

It is not appropriate to violate First Normal Form as discussed in the PO Example 2, but it is possible to implement your table in a non–First Normal Form fashion using Oracle8 object extensions structures.

You shouldn't feel nervous about Oracle extending the database into non-First Normal Form structures. For years, the database community has wrestled with the issue of whether First Normal Form is even desirable. You cannot simply take a standard relational database and violate First Normal Form without cost. The question remains: Are there occasions when you want to structure a table where a particular column in the table is actually an array, or either values or records? The answer is an unqualified "Yes."

There are many places where we have inherent and compelling needs for non-First Normal Form structures. Years ago, Cobb published the necessary extensions to SQL to support arrays as a datatype. There is some increase in complexity in the SQL language needed to support non-First Normal Form structures, but it is up to each designer to determine whether they want to implement these structures. The technology is currently too new for us to provide explicit guidelines for the optimal places to use these structures. We are still waiting for the tools to more easily support non-First Normal Form structures and for developers to become more experienced in dealing with them. These structures will be discussed in Chapter 9.

Second Normal Form

Second Normal Form arises when you have a multi-attribute primary key. This means that attributes are present that are dependent upon a portion of the primary key. Understanding Second and Third Normal Form requires an understanding of the concept of dependency.

Dependency

Dependency is a subtle concept. It is a data-related business rule concept. If Attribute B is dependent upon Attribute A, then, if you know the value of A, you know enough to find the value of B. This does not mean that you can derive the value of A. It means that logically there can only be one value for B. For example, in a Person entity, if we have a unique ID for a person, such as Social Security number, we could also know the person's height, employer, eye color, and so on. All of these attributes are dependent upon the unique identifier that identifies a specific person. Knowing one of these attributes, such as age, would not allow us to determine the person's height. From a relational database perspective, height is not dependent on age. Practically, this means that the primary key is the unique identifier of the instance of the entity. Therefore, when discussing dependency using the example of Person, if the person is known, then the height, weight, and so on will be known. The primary key acts as a surrogate for what the instance of the entity represents.

If we are dependent on only a portion of the primary key, we are violating Second Normal Form. For example, if we are discussing an entity such as Telephone Call, uniquely identifying a telephone call requires both the originating phone number and the time at which the call was initiated. We could use other candidate keys as a primary key, but these are adequate.

In this entity, let's assume that we have an attribute called "Phone Location." Depending upon what is being modeled, this may or may not be a violation of Second Normal Form. If the telephone is stationary on an office desk, then we have violated Second Normal Form, because the location is dependent only upon the source telephone number. However, if we are modeling a cellular phone, every call could be from a different location and no violation of Second Normal Form would exist. This example underscores the need to clearly understand the business rules in order to correctly model the organization in the database.

Another violation of Second Normal Form arises when you misspecify the primary key. For example, there is the ever-popular video store example, where we are trying to determine an entity that represents the rental of a videotape. Even in textbooks, you will sometimes find the primary key to be designated as the Customer ID, Tape ID, and date rented. You can uniquely identify the rental of a tape using the tape ID and time rented, because a single tape cannot be rented twice at the same time. Thus, any attributes associated with rentals (late charges, and so on) depend only upon Tape ID and date rented. By including Customer ID in the primary key, Second Normal Form is violated. However, in this case, the violation is not particularly serious.

Third Normal Form

A violation of Third Normal Form occurs when you have a *transitive dependency*. Operationally, it means having an attribute that is dependent upon an attribute that is neither part of the primary key nor part of a candidate key. Third Normal Form violations are always extremely serious. Any Third Normal Form violations detected must be corrected. What these violations indicate is that the database design is wrong. Our first example of a poorly designed database (previously shown in the Example 1 section) is the classic example of a violation of Third Normal Form. It is vitally important when you have an attribute in an entity or table that the attribute must be dependent on the primary key or on any one of the candidate keys, and not on any other attribute in the table. When this is the case, it is always true that either the attribute is in the wrong table, or that the data model is flawed.

Boyce-Codd Normal Form

The rules of normalization will not help you build a good data model. What they provide is a test of whether the data model you have created is correct. In theoretical computer science in college or graduate school courses, normalization is frequently taught as an algorithm to convert a flat-file structure into a normalized database. However, we have never known anyone who actually built databases using this algorithm. Instead, it is usual to develop the best data model possible and scrutinize it to determine if any of the rules of normalization have been violated. To this end, there is another rule of normalization, which effectively combines the first three rules. The concept is called *Boyce-Codd Normal Form* and can be loosely defined in the following way: "In a table, you will have one or more columns designated as the primary key. There may be additional sets of columns that are candidate keys. There are other attributes in the table as well. Ignoring the candidate keys, the only dependencies in the table are between each of the attributes and the entire primary key." Any other dependencies constitute a violation of Boyce-Codd Normal Form.

We believe that Boyce-Codd Normal Form is the easiest way to think about normalization. In creating a data model, we evaluate the dependencies in the table using Boyce-Codd Normal Form as the standard. If violations are detected, we identify the violation as First, Second, or Third Normal Form, mainly for the purpose of communicating the violations to other developers. We believe this is a much more intuitive way to think about normalization.

Basic Object Theory

Object theory is a broad topic. We assume that you are familiar with basic object theory. For those unfamiliar with the concepts, we suggest any of the numerous books available on object-oriented programming. We will present a brief review of the basic terminology that is most important to object-relational database development.

As already mentioned, objects and classes closely resemble instances of entities and entities in relational theory. As you might expect, objects in classes usually map very closely to rows in tables in the physical design. Thus, the basic concepts of objects and classes are already familiar to relational practitioners. Of course, there are important differences. For example, classes include *methods* (code that governs the behavior of the class), which will be discussed in Chapter 13, but the basic idea of a class is the same as a relational entity.

Encapsulation is a basic concept in object theory. A class is encapsulated if we define all of the interface methods to the class and restrict access to the class to only those methods. This would mean that no applications would have direct access to a table. For example, rather than inserting records directly into a table, the application would have to call an insert method that would handle the actual inserting into the table.

Inheritance is similar to relational subtyping. A subclass can inherit both attributes and methods from a parent class.

There are pure object database products on the market that support persistent objects. These products fully support both encapsulation and inheritance. Some use an extension of SQL to access the data, although few support server-side queriability of objects. The products are very interesting but we were unable to find any large implementations of object-oriented databases.

CHAPTER
3

Why Use Object Modeling?

ithin relational database design, the standard way we create logical models for databases is by using entity relationship modeling (ER modeling). The most common syntax used within Oracle is that laid out by Richard Barker in his relational modeling book CASE*METHOD: Entity Relationship Modelling (Addison-Wesley Publishing Company, Wokingham, England, 1990). Relational modeling has served us well for the last ten years. Its small number of symbols made it easy to learn. Its flexibility gave us the ability to build robust data models. But relational modeling has a somewhat limited vocabulary for representing data-related business rules.

With the advent of object-oriented technology, other modeling techniques and notations have emerged. We are not advocating that we jump on the object modeling bandwagon simply because it is the latest trend—but rather because many modelers, including the authors, feel hampered and constrained by the limitations of the ER modeling structure. ERDs do not provide a rich enough vocabulary to accommodate these new structures. It is now time to reengineer the way we think about database modeling. There are three alternatives:

- Make extensions to ERD notation to support object orientation.

- Use the existing ERD notation for logical design, and make more decisions when creating a physical data model.

- Use UML or another modeling notation.

The first alternative is viable, but ERDs would require significant rework to support object-oriented extensions. Some could argue that UML is such an extension to the ERD notation; however, this still entails a significant change in the way we think about ER modeling.

There is nothing wrong with the second alternative. If we believe that ERDs are good enough, there is no reason for Oracle and other vendors not to go in that direction. However, this is not the whole story. UML class diagrams provide some advantages over ERDs even if you are not planning to use Oracle8's object extensions. UML is a logical modeling tool just as ERDs are. There is nothing to prevent you from taking a UML diagram and implementing it with tables and constraints in the traditional way in an Oracle7 database. In fact, for a variety of reasons, you may wish to do exactly that. However, even working in an organization where, for political or technical reasons, you are unable to upgrade to Oracle8 or choose not to use Oracle objects, you can still design your databases using UML.

Oracle8 is a superset of Oracle7. Given the many new features other than the object-relational ones Oracle8 has, it is appropriate to migrate to Oracle8 even without using the object relational features.

One obvious impetus for making the transition from ERDs to UML is Oracle8's object extensions. To take advantage of the object extensions that currently exist in Oracle8 and of a full implementation of object-oriented structures that is sure to follow in future releases of Oracle8, UML (or some other modeling notation) will be needed. We believe that this third alternative of using UML or something equivalent is the best approach. There are significant changes to modeling arising from object-oriented theory. We should be taking advantage of these theoretical improvements.

Perhaps the most compelling reason to use UML is that it is emerging as a standard modeling language. The relational and object communities suffered from having multiple modeling tools. The object-oriented community took the lead in bringing together a coalition with the purpose of developing a modeling language that can support everyone. If the database community had been in complete control of UML, it probably would have looked a bit different. However, the advantages of using a cross-industry standard are too compelling to ignore.

Limitations of Entity Relationship Modeling

It is important to recognize that there is nothing inherently wrong with the current standard. ER diagrams have served the industry well for more than a decade. Many modelers will choose to stay with ER diagrams because of their simplicity and elegance. If data modelers are neither interested in pursuing the types of generic structures outlined in this book nor in using Oracle8 object extensions, then traditional ER modeling is probably adequate for their needs.

However, taking a broader perspective, some problems with ER modeling arise. The first of these problems with the ER paradigm is reflected in its name. The core idea behind ER modeling is that we can reasonably represent the data model of an organization solely through entities and their relationships with one another. Even on the surface, this seems to be a grossly oversimplified and inadequate vocabulary for describing an organization's information. A major advantage of UML is the addition of *process information* to the data model. Even without this information, ER modeling still has other serious data-related limitations.

"Association" or "intersection" entities that arise from a many-to-many relationship between two other tables are clearly a different type of entity. However, there is no way to indicate these differences in a traditional ERD. Entities that are time related (that is, time is part of the unique identifier) also cannot be distinguished, although in many cases, this distinction would enhance the effectiveness of the diagram.

In this chapter we will point out many of the limitations of ER modeling. We hope you will understand why we believe there is a compelling need to replace the current industry standard of ER modeling with the much more flexible, robust, and object-oriented UML.

The Unified Modeling Language (UML) Alternative

For better or worse, UML comes out of a tradition of object programmers and not data modelers. The Internet list traffic is loaded with comments that demonstrate a lack of experience in data modeling among many of the people interested in UML. Therefore, most of the thought and attention focused on UML has been directed at supporting structures in languages such as C++ or SmallTalk. As a result, we still don't have the perfect data-modeling tool; we have something that can be used as a data-modeling tool that was designed by people more focused on object-oriented programming than on data modeling.

Some of the opinions expressed in the Internet lists and by other authors are that UML is not a data-modeling tool at all. They assert that UML is not well suited for database design. This is clearly not the case. UML is able to model all of the relationships that ERDs do. In addition, UML is able to describe relationships that ERDs cannot. The conclusion: UML is not perfect but it is a more flexible modeling tool than ERDs. We will not pretend that Unified Modeling Language (UML) solves all of our modeling needs. We will still deal with an environment where some of the data-related business rules cannot be nicely represented by the UML data model. However, UML certainly gives us a much more flexible system that allows us to accurately represent a greater percentage of the data-related business rules.

Using UML

For people familiar with ER modeling, the shift to UML will not be very difficult. Serious modelers are well acquainted with the limitations of entity relationship diagrams. With UML, some, but not all, of these limitations are eliminated. But some of the things we dislike about ERDs are still present with UML.

Keep in mind that the notion of an "entity" in ER modeling is being replaced with the notion of a "class" (group of "objects") in UML. There is some discrepancy in the literature concerning what is meant by an "object." Here are some definitions from various sources:

1. "Something you can do things to. An object has state, behavior, and identity; the structure and behavior of similar objects are defined in their common class. The terms *instance* and *object* are interchangeable." Glossary definition from Grady Booch, *Object-Oriented Analysis and Design With Applications,* Addison-Wesley, 1994, p. 516.

2. "...Object-oriented systems represent information in units called objects which consist of data and a set of operations to manipulate them. An object can be an invoice, a filing cabinet, a type of employee, or a computerized representation of a part in a jet engine. Each includes data and logic enabling it to do certain things. For example, the engine object includes data about the characteristics of the engine and software that determine the kinds of things that the engine can do, such as rotate in a certain direction." Don Tapscott & Art Caston, *Paradigm Shift,* Osborne/McGraw-Hill, 1993, p. 172.

3. "Object: An element of a computer system that has a unique identity, state (represented by public and private data), and public and private operations (methods) that represent the behaviour of the object over time." Glossary definition from George Wilkie, *Object-Oriented Software Engineering,* Addison-Wesley Publishing Co., 1993, p. 386.

4. "An object is some distinct, identifiable thing for which the system must store data in order to perform the fundamental activities in the system." James A. Koval, *Analyzing Systems,* Prentice-Hall, 1988, p. 184.

5. "Objects are active components that exhibit behavior when stimulated by messages, or transactions." Andersen Consulting—Arthur A. Andersen & Co. S.C., *Foundations of Business Systems, 2nd Edition*, The Dryden Press, 1989, p. 233.

6. "Object: A component of a logical database description that represents a real-world entity about which information is stored." Glossary definition from James Martin, *Information Engineering: Book II—Planning & Analysis*, Prentice-Hall, 1990, p. 474.

7. "Object....(2) A structure in an object-oriented program that contains an encapsulated data structure and data methods. Such objects are arranged in a hierarchy so that objects can inherit methods from their parents. (3) In DB2, a term used to refer to databases, tables, views, indexes and other structures." Glossary definition from David M. Kroenke, *Database Processing*, Prentice-Hall, 1995, p. 583.

8. "Object...(2) In object-oriented approaches, a distinct person, place or thing with relevant knowledge or actions." Glossary definition from Thomas A. Bruce, *Designing Quality Databases with IDEF1X Information Models*, Dorset House Publishing, 1992, p. 535.

Note that with the exception of methods, which can be implemented as PL/SQL, Java, or C/C++ functions and procedures, the definition of a class (or group of objects) is the same as the definition of an entity. In particular, James Martin's definition (#6) is exactly how many of us would describe an entity. The proper definition of a class is broader than that of an entity. You can use objects to describe process information as well. However, for this discussion, "object" will be used in the context of data objects. A class is something of interest to the organization or a means of classifying something of interest. The crucial point is that an entity or class always represents something in the real world.

The working definition of a class we have formulated is somewhat narrower than the way that the object-oriented community thinks about a class. The reason for this variation is that the object-oriented community approaches this concept from a programming (frequently C++ or SmallTalk) environment perspective—in the database world, however, we are thinking about building databases. It is nice to think that when we are creating logical models, it shouldn't matter how structures are implemented. However, in reality, this implementation does influence our thinking. From the C++ programmer's perspective, classes are defined data structures, and objects are run-time instantiations of those defined data types. In the database world, classes correspond to tables, and objects correspond to rows in those tables.

Since we are approaching these concepts from different perspectives and solving different problems, it is only natural to think that our working definitions should be different. In his book *Object-Oriented Software Construction* (Prentice-Hall, 1997), Bertrand Myer defines an object by first defining an abstract data type (ADT) as "a set of mathematical elements specified by listing the functions applicable to all these elements and the formal properties of these functions" (Glossary, p. 1193). A class, then, is "a partially or totally implemented abstract data type" (Glossary, p. 1194). Although taken out of context, this definition clearly comes from an object-oriented programming perspective as opposed to database design perspective. When you're designing object-relational databases, the working definition we are proposing is more appropriate.

ER Diagramming Relationships and Their Limitations

If you use the ER modeling paradigm, there are three types of possible relationships:

- Cardinality
- Dependency (the UID bar)
- Subtype/supertype

This list does not provide nearly enough flexibility to describe the myriad possible relationships in a complex data model. The limitations of each type will be discussed separately along with the UML alternatives for expressing these relationships.

Cardinality

The full cardinality model between two entities can be described as:

"Somewhere between N_1–N_2 instances of Entity1 relates to somewhere between N_1–N_2 instances of Entity2."

This concept of full cardinality representation in modeling is not new with UML. Even some of the early ER diagramming techniques used similar notation. Barker's "crow's feet" notation is slightly more readable, but still terribly limiting. All that can be described using Barker's cardinality is that 0, 1, or N of one entity is related to 0, 1, or N of another entity. In Oracle ERDs, cardinality is extremely limited. This prevents us from representing many data-related business rules. We will compare how cardinality is handled differently between ERDs and UML.

You can easily represent 1-to-many relationships in both ERDs and UML, as shown in line 1 of Figure 3-1. In UML, this reads as 0 or 1 objects in Class A relate to any number of objects in Class B. (Note: * is shorthand for 0...N.) However, in practice, cardinalities other than *, 0..1, 1, 1..* are infrequently used. On rare occasions, the cardinality "2" may be used. Almost never are any other cardinalities used. Given that many of the business rule examples cited sound reasonable, one might expect to encounter other cardinalities. You might be inclined to use other cardinalities slightly more often early in the analysis process; but as the model matures approaching implementation, you will find that the exceptions to the rule actually occurring in real life prevent you from implementing such constraints in the database. For example, if a basketball team must have at least five players, when creating the team, how do you add the first person to the team? Unless there is some ability in the database to declare that a number of distinct insert statements belong to the same transaction, many of these more complex cardinality constraints cannot be easily implemented. Although this more flexible cardinality exists within UML, it will rarely be used in practice.

Other relationships cannot easily be represented in an ERD. Trying to represent these relationships would result in the generation of convoluted tables. For example, if our business rule is that there are exactly five people on a team, trying to represent such a business rule with an ERD is quite difficult. UML makes this much simpler, as shown in line 2 of Figure 3-1.

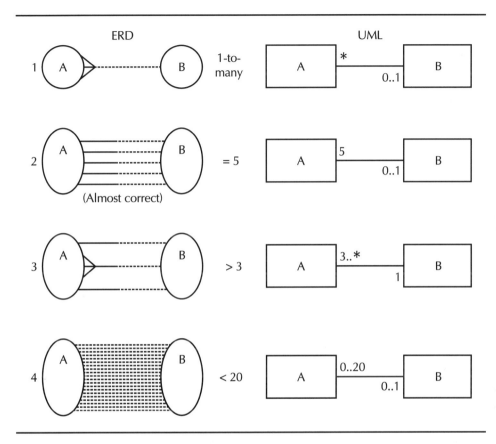

FIGURE 3-1. *Cardinality relationships*

For a business rule that says "we have at least three members on a committee," a clumsy ERD is necessary to even poorly describe this rule. But it is easily represented in UML, as shown in line 3 of Figure 3-1.

Finally, a rule that says "you cannot have more than 20 people on a committee" is virtually impossible to represent clearly on an ERD, but is simple in UML, as shown in line 4 of Figure 3-1.

Subtypes

Subtypes in ERDs are used when we can divide one entity into a number of mutually exclusive and collectively exhaustive subsets. The most common example is employees who are either paid at an hourly rate or who are salaried.

At first glance, UML syntax appears to be equivalent to ERD syntax when it comes to subtypes. If you use the example of hourly/salaried employees, there is no apparent advantage to UML syntax over ERD syntax, as shown in Figure 3-2.

However, because of the UML syntax, we can represent a particular class being subtyped simultaneously in multiple ways. An example of this is a class for Contracts, which can be classified as either fixed price, or time and materials (T&M), and also as either government or private. To represent this in UML is simple, as shown in Figure 3-3.

Representing this as an ERD requires a Cartesian product of all possible subtypes. In this example it is possible. However, if each of the subtypes were to have five or more values, then the Cartesian product would become unwieldy.

Many-to-Many Relationships

ERDs are again limited in their ability to represent many-to-many relationships. In an ERD, a many-to-many relationship is represented by an intersection table with two 1-to-many dependent relationships—with UML, however, we can use a much more natural notation that identifies the intersection entity as clearly belonging to the relationship, as shown in the UML 1 diagram of Figure 3-4.

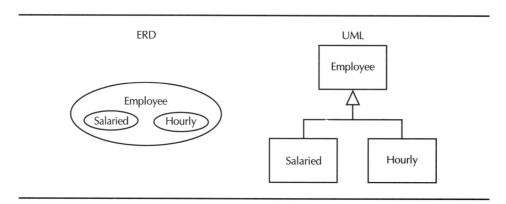

FIGURE 3-2. *Subtype Example A*

ERD   UML

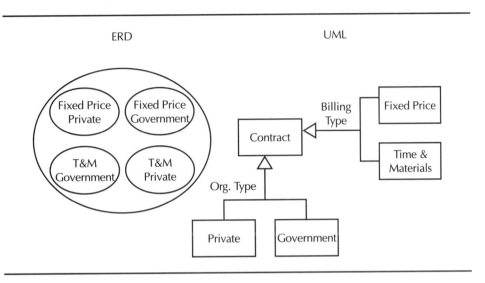

FIGURE 3-3. *Subtype Example B*

In UML, the intersection entity is called an *association class.* According to UML theory, this association class is a formal intersection whose unique identifier is exactly one object from each of the subordinate classes. In this case, it would provide an unreasonable restriction that an employee can only be associated with a particular company, at most, one time. This structure does not yet exist in Oracle's Object Database Designer. We hope that when this is implemented, Oracle will not adhere to standards requiring such a restriction.

Fortunately, UML provides a way to extend the modeling notation. Notice that in Figure 3-4, UML 1 next to the many-to-many relationship, we added «dupes allowed». This notation is called a *stereotype*. Stereotypes allow us to redefine or modify UML structures. UML's ability to support extensions is one of its greatest strengths. We could model this same concept formally in UML as shown in UML 2 or UML 3 of Figure 3-4, but both of these alternatives make for a less elegant model. For these stereotypes to generate our code correctly requires explicit support in tools such as Oracle's ODD. Otherwise, the stereotypes only provide documentation information.

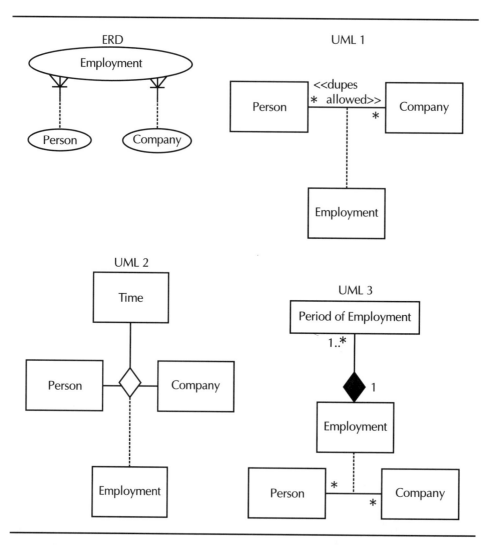

FIGURE 3-4. *Many-to-many relationships*

Multiple Classification

A particular class may exist that consists of two or more other classes. For example, a person can be both a customer and an employee. In ERDs, this phenomenon is referred to as a *nonexclusive subtype.* This standard object-oriented construct of classification is traditionally handled with either a single entity with all attributes from all types included and filled in where appropriate, or with separate entities for each structure using optional mandatory 1-to-1 relationships, as shown in Figure 3-5.

The UML notation for this is somewhat cleaner and clearly shows the classification relationship between the classes.

Disadvantages of UML Diagramming

As mentioned earlier, UML is not a panacea. It does not solve all the problems associated with ER modeling, but does make our task somewhat easier. There are some disadvantages to UML. We are still missing a way of denoting time-related entities without using stereotypes. These entities are an important type of class, just as they are an important type of entity requiring special treatment. It would be useful to be able to visually identify time-related classes. This problem in ERDs has still not been solved in UML.

UML does provide for extensions. Such extensions are allowable and supported within UML. The appropriate syntax for a time-related entity is shown here:

```
+-----------------------------+
|                             |
|          Employment         |
|                             |
|          <<time>>           |
|                             |
+-----------------------------+
```

This diagram uses the stereotype "time" as part of the unique identifier for the Employment class.

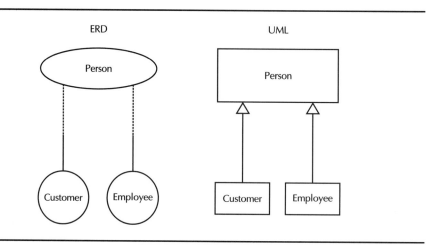

FIGURE 3-5. *Multiple classification*

Advantages of Using an Object-Oriented Approach

At the end of the Preface, we presented some examples of how object-oriented thinking improved our models. It is important to point out that, in these examples, we were not generating to Oracle8 structures or using UML, but merely thinking in an object-oriented way. These examples underline the fact that we don't have to wait for object-oriented databases to take advantage of object-oriented thinking and techniques. On these projects, UML would have helped by providing us with a better vocabulary—but we had to be trying to develop the object-oriented structure in the first place.

UML will not magically make you design object-oriented databases any more than using ERDs made you develop Third Normal Form data structures. It will be just as easy to build bad databases using UML as it has been to build bad databases using ERDs. In addition, because UML products such as Oracle's Object Database Designer (the UML portion of Oracle Designer) will generate some sophisticated object structures automatically, there may be a greater likelihood of building databases that are completely unusable than was the case with the more limited Oracle7.3 structures.

Oracle's Object Database Designer

Oracle's Object Database Designer (ODD) product uses a partial implementation of UML to help design object-relational databases. It is distributed as part of the Oracle Designer product to assist designers in building Oracle8 DDL.

Currently, this product is only a partial implementation of UML. It was designed primarily as a tool to help generate Oracle8 object structures rather than as a full UML modeling tool. A number of key structures are missing, including multiple classification, intersection classes, and dynamic classification for reference tables. Nevertheless, the product is a good first effort and could be used to design object-relational databases.

Conclusion

Though still somewhat flawed, UML represents a significant step forward in modeling notation. Not only are we able to represent more data-related business rules using UML, but this notation also encourages us to think in a more object-oriented fashion with respect to our designs. Although Oracle's Object Database Designer is not a full implementation of UML, it is nevertheless a significant improvement over ER modeling and should be used.

You will have to decide for yourself if UML class diagrams provide an improvement over ERDs. For our models, which rely heavily on generic structures, we believe that UML provides significant advantages over ERDs.

PART II

Database Building Blocks

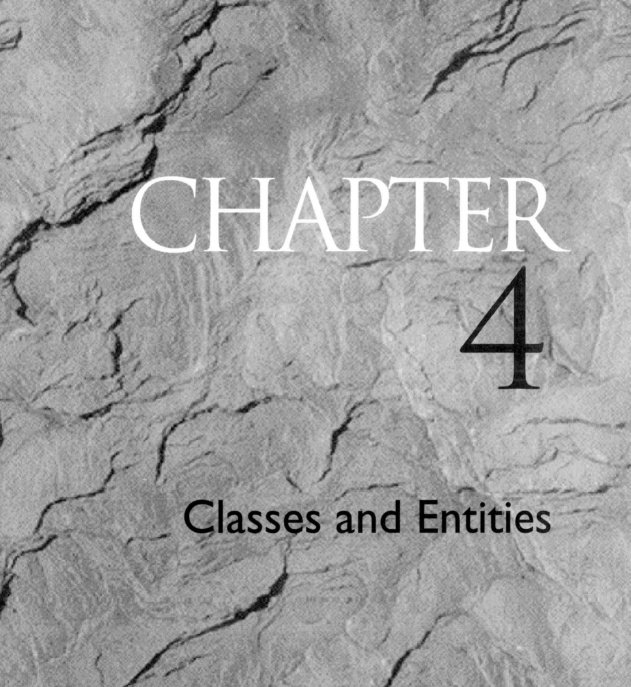

CHAPTER
4

Classes and Entities

he identification of the correct classes and the relationships between them is the essence of the data model. This chapter will discuss how classes are found, identified, and described. It is not possible to reduce modeling to a simple step-by-step process. Ultimately, modeling is an art. For a given complex situation there is no one correct data model. However, there is such a thing as a good data model, and, conversely, there are bad data models as well. One model of a business or organization can be better than another, but there are no unique solutions as to how to create a data model for a particular system.

The goal of a good model is to minimize the cost of the project over its lifetime. It is usually a mistake to focus on minimizing development cost. Good models take into account the probable changes to the system over time and are designed to more easily accommodate these changes.

Modeling is also very subjective. There are different styles of data modeling. Designers come up with different ways of handling the same type of problem. The optimal data model is not just a function of the situation being modeled. It is also dependent upon the following factors:

Skills of the team	More generic structures require more skill on the part of the designer as well as the developers.
Design environment	Most CASE products are somewhat limited with respect to the structures they can generate. The designer may need to temper the design to be CASE friendly.
Development environment	Development tools (particularly 4GLs) are limited in the kinds of structures that they can easily support. CASE-generated applications are even more limited. The designer may want to modify the design to suit the chosen development environment.

Expected lifetime of the system	Short-term projects (for example, a system to support the Olympics or an engineering project) have a lower probability of being used for the long term.
Time/cost pressures on the project	Even though flexible models decrease long-term project costs, if there is enormous pressure to keep time short and costs low in version 1 of the system, some flexibility may need to be sacrificed.

Because of the greater richness of tools and notation with UML, modeling becomes even more of an art than with ERDs. We now have new relationship types that give us more ways to model the same situation.

Although this chapter discusses class identification and a separate chapter covers relationships (Chapter 8), we do not want to give the impression that a sequential process is the correct method for designing a database. Databases cannot be designed by separately identifying first the classes and then the relationships between the classes. Both processes must occur simultaneously. Determining all of the entities first and then hooking them together with relationships was never possible with ERDs in the past, either. However, many bad data models were built using this technique.

In this chapter we will provide specific example situations, along with questions and answers to help you correctly identify classes, attributes, and primary keys.

Identifying a Class

In Chapter 3 we listed several definitions of objects. At its core, a class (group of objects) is something of interest to a particular organization that will be tracked in the database. Traditionally, in ERD-style model development, the analyst implicitly asked: "What needs to be kept track of?"

To some extent, the object modeler can start with the same question. However, the object modeler must also think about abstractions of the items of interest. For example, at the end of the Preface, we briefly mentioned a retail system for which we identified Invoices, Purchases, POs, and so on as classes relevant to the organization. We also recognized that all of these classes could be generalized into the class "Merchandise Movement." This single abstraction allowed us to decrease the size of the model by about 30 percent. Therefore, it is important to identify not only items of interest, but also relevant abstractions of those items.

We will present a series of examples with accompanying questions and answers to more fully illustrate ways of identifying classes.

Example 1   A piece of equipment needs maintenance. In this particular organization, the required maintenance generates a work order. The individual work order can be broken down into a number of tasks. Each of these tasks can be further divided into a number of actions. Finally, each action can be broken down into a number of steps. These tasks, actions, and steps can be applied to the entire piece of equipment, or to some assembly or subassembly of part of the equipment. Usually, the work order that is placed applies to an entire piece of equipment, whereas tasks, actions, and steps apply to some subassembly component of that equipment.

Question   What are the relevant classes in this example?

Answer   The obvious classes are

- Equipment
- Assembly
- Subassembly
- Work Order
- Task
- Action
- Step

Looking ahead to the full data model, we see virtually every one of the work order tasks, actions, and steps will interact with equipment, assemblies, and subassemblies. This involves a great deal of interaction between classes.

Two additional, more "abstract" classes can also be identified:

- Work: A generalization of work order, task, action, and step

- Maintenance Object: A generalization of equipment, assembly, and subassembly

Using these classes would allow us to only be concerned with the interaction between Work and Maintenance Objects, rather than the seven classes mentioned initially. The point is to carefully identify not only items of interest but also generalizations of those items.

It is important to have a precise definition of each class. A class always refers to something in the real world. Coming up with a good definition of the class is even more important than naming the class. In working with clients, we are usually willing to let clients name the class anything they want. The words in a class name may have specific meaning within the organization where the system is being developed. The description of the class determines exactly what the class represents. In modeling, we try to set the descriptions of the classes before allowing the development team to worry about the best name for a class. There is no point in trying to come up with the name of a class until it has been determined exactly what the class represents. When creating a data model, we insist on all classes being described before any arguments can take place about class names.

As obvious as this sounds, class descriptions must *accurately* describe the class. Keep in mind that a class represents something in the real world; therefore class descriptions specify something in the real world and not a table in a database. It is quite common to see descriptions begin with "This table contains information about...." Such descriptions (although not wrong per se) usually mean that what follows does not describe a real-world object. A better phrase to start descriptions with is "Every object in this class is a...." This phrase more naturally leads the designer to describe a real-world object.

Descriptions of classes should also contain the relevant information necessary for the developer to be able to understand the class. If the class is overloaded (meaning that it is storing more than one type of object), then all types of objects that can be stored in the class should be covered by the description. If particular attributes can modify the meaning of the objects in the class, then such notes can also be placed in the class description.

The name of the class should never be referenced in the description in case the name of the class changes at some future time.

Example 2   Description of the class "Sale" for a retailer: "A sale of merchandise to a customer. Note that the customer need not be specified if it is a cash sale. This class includes all kinds of sales (for example, cash, credit, and layaway) which are distinguished by sale type. Sales erroneously entered are not deleted, but their status is changed to 'ERROR.' The items that are purchased are stored in a detail table."

Note that the phrase "Every object in this class represents a..." is assumed to be part of each class description and has been omitted.

It is critical to identify real things in the environment of the organization to associate with classes, because we are trying to identify items or actions of interest to the organization. The designer should think in terms of modeling the organization, not designing a database.

A common mistake is to translate files from the legacy system directly to classes. Legacy files (even those from a relational system) are usually not equivalent to classes. Bringing forward the legacy system, without analysis, will cause the designer to replicate all of the mistakes and inefficiencies it contains. The legacy system must be carefully analyzed. It is a primary source of system requirements. However, we should not simply accept that the legacy tables can be mapped directly to classes.

A second mistake is to model documents that arise from a transaction to be the same as the transaction class itself—for example, building a class for Bills of Lading rather than one for Shipments. Usually, an organization's bills of lading, packing slips, POs, and invoices are not suitable classes (although they may correspond 1-to-1 with the appropriate associated class for the transactions). Purchases, shipments, requests for purchases, and requests for funds are all real transactions that might be of interest to be tracked and are therefore appropriate to be modeled as classes.

Of course, it is possible to have a class called "Invoice" or "Purchase Order" as long as we keep in mind that these represent the transactions associated with "requests for payments" and "requests for purchases." Recall that we are more concerned with the *description* of a class than with the name we attach to it. However, we do not recommend the practice of creating such classes. Frequently, it is important to track both the transactions and the documents. If the document name is used as a surrogate for the transaction, it is easy to forget that you haven't modeled the document at all but only the transaction.

In addition to tracking transactions, it may also be important to track the activities associated with the pieces of paper themselves. For example, in a loan company, it may be important to track every invoice, letter, and contact associated with a given client and what information those documents contained. In this case, it is appropriate to have classes to track actual documents (in addition to the underlying transactions), because it is recognized that what is being tracked are documents and transactions. To sum up, it is appropriate to track documents, but be sure that you are also modeling the relevant transactions and that the differences between the two are clearly understood.

Example 3   Assume that the client is the IRS. Tax returns are initially submitted by taxpayers. In addition, people may send amendments to their returns. They send us payments, we send out refunds. If refunds are lost by the taxpayer, we resend them.

Question   What are the relevant classes?

Answer   This is actually more complex than it appears. The trick is to notice that we are really talking about two things: the tax return and the person's tax liability. The documents, payments, and refunds all affect the tax liability. The relevant classes are

- Taxpayer
- Tax Return
- Payment
- Refund
- Request for Refund
- Annual Tax Liability

Once again, we need to think more abstractly about the classes in order to come up with the class "Annual Tax Liability."

Identifying an Attribute

Recognize that, along with classes, there are potentially two sets of attributes. The first set is what we would traditionally think of as attributes in a relational table. This kind of attribute is a property of a class that associates a particular value for that property with each object in the class. For example, if the class is Person, an attribute might be "Age," which would associate a specific number (a person's age) with each person in the class. Attributes draw their values from particular domains. The domain may be relatively general. For example, the Age domain would be "positive integers between 0 and 150." Domains may also be very specific, such as Gender: "M/F." Domains are discussed in depth in Chapter 6.

The second set of attributes is what a person (called a *client* in object terminology) who is developing applications against the table would see as attributes on the class. Because of encapsulation, it is possible to completely hide the actual attributes (since they are stored in the object table) and to display a different set of attributes to the client. For example, we might store DATE_OF_BIRTH as an attribute in an Employee class, but we might want to only manipulate age when using the Employee class. We could provide access to age through parameters on the methods but store the information as DATE_OF_BIRTH in the implemented table. In this book, we will only consider the attributes as they are stored in the implemented tables.

Each class may have many attributes associated with it. A simple class may have anywhere from two to ten attributes. A complex table could have 100 or more attributes. Frequently, classes with large numbers of attributes are poorly designed. Most typically, classes in a well-designed system have 50 or fewer attributes. Determining the appropriate attributes for a class is more challenging than it may appear. It is important to identify attributes that are definitely attributes of the class with which they are associated. If you inappropriately place an attribute, it can make your data model difficult, if not impossible, to maintain. Usually, misplacement of attributes arises from an imprecise understanding of the definition of the class.

Identifying Primary Keys

A primary key is the combination of the values of one or more attributes that collectively and uniquely identify an object in a class. Each component of a primary key must never be null. Because of physical implementation issues, primary keys must never change. In object modeling using classes, it is still appropriate to identify one or more attributes that determine the primary key. With Oracle8 object extensions, the requirement of primary keys remaining unchanged can be relaxed somewhat. If you are implementing your database using a traditional relational structure, your primary keys should remain unchangeable. OIDs, a new feature in Oracle 8, are logical pointers used by C++ or Java applications to navigate between rows of independent object classes. OIDs allow you to manipulate data stored in the database from external applications.

Example 4 An organization needs to determine appropriate primary keys for the classes within its system.

Question For the class Person within an organization, what is the primary key?

Answer There are several obvious answers, most of which are wrong:

■ Name is not a good primary key, because different people may have the same name.

■ Social Security numbers are also unsuitable as primary keys for several reasons. First, people such as employees in other countries working for a multinational organization may not have Social Security numbers. Second, it may be necessary to enter the employee into the system when the Social Security number is not known. Third, numbers may be entered incorrectly and must subsequently be changed. Fourth, there are also privacy concerns associated with Social Security numbers. Usually these numbers are hidden from most users. In a traditional relational system, primary keys are propagated to many places in the system, thus undermining the security considerations. Finally, we have been told that Social Security numbers are not always unique. Although it is very rare, there are people in the United States who have the same Social Security numbers.

The only viable candidate for a "Person" primary key is a system-generated number. In most organizations, this is an Employee ID.

Sometimes the determination of the primary key can be quite challenging, as illustrated in the following example. This is one of the most interesting examples, because the answer appears to be very easy; however, most designers select an incorrect combination of candidates the first time around.

Example 5   An organization wishes to track the cost of telephone calls and associate them with specific projects. A class called Telephone Call is created.

Question   What is the appropriate primary key for the Telephone Call class?

Answer   Several candidates may be considered:

- Person making the call
- Person receiving the call
- Phone number of the phone from which the call was made
- Number called
- Date/time of the call

The most common incorrect answer is to pick the source and destination phone number together as the primary key. This is incorrect because that would mean that a particular phone could only dial another particular phone once. The next most common error is to pick the destination phone number plus time of call. That seems correct at first glance, but it would mean that two people in an organization could not call the same number at the same time (something which is clearly possible unless "time" is tracked as a continuous variable). The appropriate primary key for a telephone call consists of the originating telephone number combined with the date and time of the call. This makes sense logically, but does not provide an intuitively attractive unique identifier (UID). The allocation of that call to one or more accounts for billing purposes requires logistical work and care in a relational system. By using object identifiers (OIDs) or system-generated Ids for the primary key, these problems disappear.

There are other benefits to using an OID. If there are structural modifications to the database that affect the UID when system-generated IDs are not being used, the changes will propagate to other tables and constraints. This could influence triggers, applications, and other work occurring after the UID is generated. If you're using a generated ID, modifications can be made that do not propagate through the system. For reference tables (value list classes), it doesn't make sense to use sequence-generated IDs. These are typically never going to change or they change infrequently. The UID for these classes should be the code attribute.

Determining appropriate primary keys is crucial to understanding the class. The process of determining primary keys acts as a secondary check of the precise definition of the classes within a system. It will be difficult to determine an appropriate primary key for a poorly defined class. Also, if primary keys are not properly specified, finding a particular object within a class may be difficult. Without a primary key, such a task may be impossible. It is not uncommon to have multiple potential primary keys to select from in a class. Such alternate keys are called *candidate keys* in relational theory.

Normalization Is Still Important

Now that we have OIDs, why do we still need to worry about normalization? The reason we still care is that normalization adds a level of precision to the design process. It acts as a test to make sure we have placed our attributes correctly and helps us to confirm that our classes have been correctly specified. One of the most important factors in creating object-oriented database designs is the correct placement of attributes. In object-oriented database design, correct attribute placement is completely dependent upon the experience and skill of the designer, without an overall underlying theory for guidance.

Some relational modelers have been working in an environment similar to the object modelers for some time. Those modelers used system-generated primary keys for all tables. When we have been brought in to audit such systems, we usually find a higher percentage of modeling mistakes than we find in other strictly relational systems. Removing logical primary keys and not worrying about normalization seems to encourage poor modeling techniques. Therefore, we strongly encourage designers to define a logical primary key for all classes, exactly as if they were traditional relational entities, even if they plan to implement the model using object technology.

Simply because we are creating object-oriented models does not mean that the rules of normalization do not apply. Database access will still be accomplished using SQL. SQL's ability to extract arbitrary subsets from the database is dependent upon the normalized structure of the classes or tables in the database. Therefore, rules of normalization must still be followed. As attributes are added to classes, take care not to violate these rules.

Violations of First Normal Form

As discussed in Chapter 2, a violation of First Normal Form arises when you add multiple attributes that are repeated measures of the same property. For example, if you have a PO and want to say that there are only a few items on a purchase order, namely Item1/Quantity1–Item5/Quantity5, this would be a violation of First Normal Form. The reason to avoid this is because it makes the aggregation of information difficult, requiring five sources of information. This problem could be solved through the clever creation of views on a table. The most serious problem occurs when there needs to be a sixth item on a PO. This is the main reason we attempt to avoid First Normal Form violations.

A continuing debate exists concerning a class storing weekly sales figures for a department that had seven attributes in it—for the sales figures for each day of the week. Is this a violation of First Normal Form? From a theoretical perspective, this is unequivocally not a First Normal Form violation. There are exactly seven days in a week, and each day is different from the other. However, building your data structure this way brings with it many of the same problems as a non-First Normal Form structure. Therefore, from an implementation perspective, storing information such as multiple days of the week as attributes is not the best way to build. The decision of whether to use this structure is purely based upon optimization of the physical implementation, but does not violate the rules of normalization.

Oracle8 Performance Features

Oracle8 offers two new techniques for use in implementing non-First Normal Form designs: *nested tables* and *VARRAYS*. Both offer the capability of storing related data close together, providing highly efficient retrieval. These structures are simply alternatives to storing 1-to-many associations in separate yet related tables.

Objects within nested tables are stored independent of the master objects they are tied to, requiring indexes to enhance retrieval performance. However, objects within a nested table have no real existence independent of the master object class from which the nested table originates. Therefore, you can only access objects within nested tables via the objects of the master object class they are tied to. As demonstrated in Chapter 1, you can 'unnest' rows stored in a nested table, but you still must specify the master table in the query. The current version of Oracle8 only supports one level of nesting. In other words, a nested table cannot, in itself, contain a nested table.

VARRAYS, or variable arrays, have been implemented as a new datatype. VARRAYS can support the earlier example of recording daily sales figures. To accommodate this, we can create an object type based upon a VARRAY with seven occurrences in this case, one for each day of the week, called DAILY_RECORDING. We would create a table called WEEKLY_TEST that has a column of this new datatype, the purpose of which would be to track the daily recordings as shown in Code Example 4-1.

```
CREATE OR REPLACE TYPE DAILY_RECORDING
AS VARRAY (7) of number (5,2)
/

CREATE TABLE WEEKLY_TEST (
WEEK_ID      NUMBER (10) NOT NULL,
DAILY_NBR    DAILY_RECORDING)
/
```

Code Example 4-1

VARRAYS, similar to NESTED tables, cannot be nested in and of themselves. The data they contain is also inaccessible outside the scope of objects within the master object class. VARRAYS cannot be indexed, though it is unlikely that you would ever want to do so because they are usually used for small to moderately sized repeating groups. Also, the current release of SQL cannot access data stored within VARRAYS, so they should be implemented when the only required access path is PL/SQL.

Violations of Second Normal Form

Second Normal Form is a different type of rule, in that you can sometimes violate it without impact. As explained in Chapter 2, Second Normal Form arises when you have a multicolumn primary key. Violations of Second Normal Form occur when you have an attribute dependent on only part of the primary key. If all of the attributes are dependent on part of the primary key, it means that the primary key has an extra column in it. Problems occur when a subset of the nonkey attributes is dependent on a part of the primary key. This indicates that either the attribute has been placed with the wrong class, or that an even more serious problem exists in that you have not created a necessary class.

Violations of Third Normal Form

Third Normal Form violations occur when an attribute is dependent upon a nonkey attribute. Third Normal Form violations are always disastrous and should be avoided whenever possible. Example 6 is an illustration of this type of violation.

Example 6   We have a table for SALE and SALE DETAIL with the following structure:

SALE
Sale Number   **PK**

Transaction date

ID of Employee who sold the goods

Name of Salesperson

SALE DETAIL

Sale Number	**PK, FK(sale)**
Sale Detail Number	PK
Item Number	
Quantity	
Item Style	
Item Model	

Question   Which of these attributes violates Third Normal Form?

Answer   There are three attributes that violate Third Normal Form. The Item Model and Item Style are dependent upon only the Item Number. The Name of Salesperson is dependent only on the employee ID. Those attributes should be moved to Inventory and Person classes, respectively.

Value List (VL) Classes

It is frequently useful to store a valid list of values for an attribute. This is particularly important if the list of valid values can change over time. Therefore, having a class to store gender does not make sense. However, valid statuses for a project could easily change merely through the whim of a manager who might redefine project workflow. Storing the valid values in a class is appropriate in that situation. To distinguish such classes from the primary classes, this type of class will be called a *Value List (VL) class.*

Commonly used VL classes include Color, Status, and Type. Each of these stores all possible values of a particular domain for an attribute. We have even seen circumstances where it was appropriate to build a domain class for Date. This would store relevant information about the year's calendar, such as End of Week, End of Month, End of Fiscal Quarter, Fiscal Year, status of computer production runs for that given date, and so on. Such VL classes can frequently be supported through database functions; however, the attributes such as production run status cannot be supported through functions; however, the other attributes did provide value.

There is a debate in the database community about whether something should be an attribute (with a list of values check constraint) or a VL class.

For reasons unknown to the authors, much time has been spent arguing about whether a particular item should be modeled as an attribute or VL class. This is a relatively simple design question. The question to ask is, "Is it relevant to keep a valid list of values in the domain?" If the answer is yes, then you should be using a VL class. If the answer is no, then no such class is necessary. VL classes are common, frequently comprising up to 50 percent of the classes in a data model. They will be discussed in depth in Chapter 7.

Physical Implementation of Entities/Classes

As explained earlier in this chapter, entities and classes are, at some level, the "things that need to be kept track of." While Oracle Designer maintains two distinct modeling methods for logical versus physical data modeling, ODD replaces Entity Relationship modeling techniques with UML for logical modeling. ODD's server model allows integration of relational and object relational structures into a single model. Additional information regarding ODD is available in Chapter 19.

Relational Implementation

In Oracle's relational architecture, entities and their attributes evolve into tables and columns, in a 1-to-1 manner—with the exception of subtypes, which tend to roll up the multiple subtypes into one generic structure.

We will use the example of U.S. states, which is data that might need to be tracked in many systems of various types. The following table displays a subset of the data we will store in the STATE table. After the data we have provided the syntax in Code Example 4-2 for defining a table STATE, which corresponds to the entity STATE.

STATE_CD	DESCR_TX
NJ	New Jersey
MD	Maryland
PA	Pennsylvania
CA	California
FL	Florida

```
    CREATE TABLE STATE(
STATE_CD   VARCHAR2(5)   NOT NULL PRIMARY KEY,
DESCR_TX   VARCHAR2(40)  NOT NULL UNIQUE)
/
```

Code Example 4-2

The state codes will be stored in the STATE_CD column, while the names will be stored in the DESCR_TX column. Note that the data length for the STATE_CD column is 5, three characters longer than the state code values. One could argue that the correct data length for the STATE_CD column would be 2. However, we have decided to classify all columns of type "code" in this system to be of type VARCHAR2 with a length of 5. Any applications that are built upon this table can limit the display characters of this column to 2, eliminating the concern of a user entering inappropriate data into this column. A more comprehensive discussion of the physical implementation of domains can be found in Chapter 6.

Note that the naming conventions declared in the STATE entity and its attributes have been used for naming the STATE table and its columns. In some cases, it is preferable to use fully spelled-out names for entities and attributes and then apply a standard set of abbreviations when creating the table and column definitions. Our team used that approach, but we found that a clear set of abbreviations (each word is abbreviated to five characters or less) can be used for both logical and physical data structures. For a complete discussion of our naming conventions, see Chapter 5.

Also note the definition of the datatypes and lengths. At the attribute level, we can apply domains to define datatypes, lengths, and precision. This is a useful technique for ensuring consistency in datatype specification throughout your data model. Domains can be defined in Oracle Designer to genericize the structure of your columns, but this is merely metadata and therefore is not available in the actual CREATE TABLE statement. Also, you cannot define whether a given column is mandatory through the use of an Oracle Designer domain, although it is clearly an additional characteristic of the attribute.

It is possible to create a physical domain in the database of type CODE, which can then be applied to every column definition with a datatype of VARCHAR2(5). User-defined domains can be developed as object types, provided that they do not require specification beyond the datatype and maximum length. Nothing can be specified outside of this realm, as of the current release. To insert rows of data into the STATE table, we would use the following RDBMS statement as shown in Code Example 4-3:

```
INSERT INTO STATE (STATE_CD, DESCR_TX
VALUES ('NJ', 'New Jersey')
/
```

Code Example 4-3

You are not required to list the columns you plan to insert into, as long as you supply values for every column in the table, although we strongly recommend that you do so. Otherwise, you must specify the subset of columns you are supplying values for. All mandatory columns must be supplied a value, unless a default has been specified in the table definition.

To retrieve the state name "New Jersey" from the STATE table, we would use the following SELECT statement in Code Example 4-4:

```
SELECT DESCR_TX
FROM STATE
WHERE STATE_CD = 'NJ'
/
```

Code Example 4-4

This example uses the basic Oracle7 syntax for the SELECT command, with the WHERE clause as the means to filter the number of records to be returned by the query.

Object-Relational Implementation

Oracle8 has improved a great deal upon the functionality available for defining data structures. The first significant difference in the physical definition of a data structure is that we can initially define a type for the object. These object types can be implemented in three ways:

- As domains for columns
- As extensions to tables that add a common set of columns
- As complete definitions of the structure of an object class

The second difference is that UML provides separate alternatives for relating two object classes to each other. The following sections will explain each of these areas in more detail, while the last section will discuss some overall disadvantages of using object types and classes.

Creating Object Types

The function of an object type is to define the basic structure of the class(es) you plan to create, specifically the format of the attributes that pertain to the class and their respective datatypes. You do not specify optionality in the object types, but rather in the definition of the objects themselves. Note that we do not need to differentiate between the logical (attribute) and physical (column) implementation of the elements describing the object. Instead, we can simply refer to them as attributes, regardless of the project phase. Object classes equate to TYPES, not tables. Instances of each type can be stored in multiple tables or columns. The following Code Example 4-5 is an example of a class type definition:

```
CREATE OR REPLACE TYPE STATE_TYPE
AS OBJECT
(STATE_CD   VARCHAR2(5),
DESCR_TX    VARCHAR2(40) )
/
```

Code Example 4-5

The STATE_TYPE class type will be the foundation upon which we define the STATE object. Our STATE definition declared that we needed two columns: a code column used to uniquely identify each occurrence of the STATE class, and a textual column that serves as a more detailed descriptor of each STATE.

Creating Classes

Classes can be created in two different ways: explicitly and implicitly. The *explicit* method would be to define the class, its columns, and its data formatting information using the relational CREATE TABLE statement, just as in Oracle7 syntax. An example of explicit class creation is as follows in Code Example 4-6:

```
CREATE TABLE STATE(
STATE_CD VARCHAR2(5)NOT NULL,
DESCR_TX VARCHAR2(40)NOT NULL )
/
```

Code Example 4-6

Explicit table creation is essentially the same technique we used in Oracle7. We name the table and its columns and define the datatypes and their optionality, all in the same statement.

The *implicit* method defines a class based upon an object type. The following Code Example 4-7 shows the creation of the STATE table, based upon the STATE_TYPE that we declared in the "Creating Object Types" section earlier.

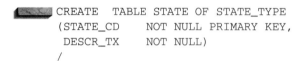

```
CREATE   TABLE STATE OF STATE_TYPE
(STATE_CD     NOT NULL PRIMARY KEY,
 DESCR_TX     NOT NULL)
/
```

Code Example 4-7

In the STATE table, we have two columns, STATE_CD and DESCR_TX, whose characteristics are inherited from the STATE_TYPE object type definition. The implicit STATE table and the explicit STATE table will look and act exactly the same. The difference is that we can create multiple classes with the same structure as the STATE class, by basing them upon the STATE_TYPE object type.

Whether explicit or implicit, tables that do not contain object references can be populated using Code Example 4-3.

We might have created a more generic class type such as Territory, or TERR_TYPE, as opposed to STATE_TYPE. The reason for defining an object type with a generic name such as TERR_TYPE is so that we can use its structure as the foundation for defining many other geographical subdivisions such as county, country, province, and so on. In this way, we can take advantage of including a single object type in the definition of many classes.

At the column level, using Oracle Designer, you have the ability to define domains. *Domains* are the collective definition of characteristics that data must have in order to be inserted into a column. Some of these characteristics might be a set of valid values such as status codes, where "O" would stand for "Open" and "C" would stand for "Closed." Value ranges can also be specified using the High and Low value attributes. There are other data characteristics in addition to these that are useful to define as components of domains, such as Optionality, Format, and Structure.

Oracle8 provides some limited ability to implement domains, although the domains cannot extend beyond the capabilities of the base datatypes. Unfortunately, you cannot add a column or change the datatype of an existing column within an object type once an object class has referenced the object type, although these capabilities and more are planned for future releases of Oracle8. This will be discussed in greater detail in Chapter 6.

CHAPTER
5

Naming Conventions

onsistently applied and appropriate naming conventions are a critical success factor for any system. Standards must be set to enforce consistency. The following general principles should be kept in mind when creating naming standards:

1. The names selected should be clear and understandable to the audience that will use them. For example, for a data warehouse, end users will be the audience, whereas for a physical database, the audience will consist of systems professionals and developers. Appropriate names for each of these groups may be very different.

2. Names should not be too long. The names selected will need to be typed over and over. Long names increase the chance of errors in addition to requiring more time to type. Even when you're dealing with generated code, long names can make the code unreadable. Sometimes products allowing you to select variable names will only display the first ten or so characters. For example, in some parts of Oracle Designer long domains names are truncated when assigning a domain to an attribute.

3. The names should communicate as much meaningful information about the object as possible. Often, it is useful to place prefix or suffix characters on system element names to categorize them.

NOTE
A balance must be achieved in applying principles 2 and 3. It is easy to go overboard in creating long names in order to communicate more information, but these names are more difficult to use over and over. On the other hand, very short names are only understandable to the person who initially designed the system and are ambiguous.

4. Names should be easy to remember. For example, we do not use any linguistic endings ("-ing," "-ed," plural), so that only one form of the word is used throughout the system. The root word is always used. This also helps keep the names shorter.

5. Any textual information found anywhere in the database requires a precise naming convention. This includes the data itself. For example, we use uppercase for all primary key codes in value list classes in the database.

6. You must create complete naming standards for everything at the same time. You cannot create database-naming standards and then later create development standards, because these standards interact. The standards must be set for the entire development environment. In this book, because we are describing database design, we will only mention decisions to be made with regard to the database. However, in a traditional development environment, naming conventions will be needed for Forms objects (pop lists, check boxes, etc.), application file names, etc.

Creating Naming Conventions

There are many elements in a database that require consistent naming conventions. We have divided these elements into two categories.

1. On the logical (data model) side, all of the elements appearing in the class diagram need to be named:

   - Schemas

   - Class diagrams

   - Classes/tables/entities

   - Attributes

   - Domains

   - Relationships

   - Operations/methods

2. On the physical implementation side, the following elements need to be named:

   - Sequences

   - Short table naming aliases

- Constraints

- Indexes

- Object types

- Table aliases

We will discuss suggested naming conventions for each of these system elements.

Logical (Data Model) Naming Conventions

Systems can be quite large, easily including several hundred tables. The largest systems may have over 1,000 tables. It is in these large systems that we often see terrible table names such as AX145_6. We need to divide the system being worked on into several manageable parts or schemas.

Naming Schemas

A *schema* is a collection of tables that can either be implemented as a database or as a separate user account. Schemas allow us to reference tables throughout the system. There should be one schema for each subject area within the data model. There should not be a large number of schemas. A schema should include approximately 30 to 50 tables. To be easily managed, a single schema should not contain more than 100 tables.

Schemas should be named with very short abbreviations. Since most systems have fewer than 10 schemas, two-letter abbreviations are adequate, such as "CO" for Core and "FI" for Finance. Whenever possible, we use the first two letters of the logical name of the schema. Because we will use the convention of SCHEMA NAME.TABLE NAME, schema names need to be kept very short.

Complications occur when there are tables arising from many-to-many associations where each table in the relationship is in a different schema. The question is where to put the intersection table. One possible algorithm is to store the association table with the most logical table. For example, if we were assigning people to projects, we would store the association with the schema containing the Project table; however, if we were assigning equipment to people, the association would be stored in the schema containing the People table.

A similar problem exists with the Employment relationship between Employee and Department. Where should the association table be stored? The answer is not clear-cut. It is equally valid to store the Employment association table with either the Employee or the Department table. Therefore, we use a different algorithm for storing association tables. Whenever there is an association table and the tables making up the relationships exist in two different schemas, the association table should be stored with the table whose name comes first in alphabetical order. In the DEPT/EMP relationship, if DEPT and EMP exist in two different schemas, we would store the employment relationship in the schema that contained the DEPT table, because DEPT precedes EMP alphabetically. This is an arbitrary rule, but there was no logical rule to consistently and unambiguously determine the schema where an association table should belong.

SQL has a command called CREATE SCHEMA, which is used to bundle multiple DDL statements together into a single statement. No single DDL statement will be committed to the database unless all components of the CREATE SCHEMA statement have been validated. In essence, the word "schema" actually refers to a set of DDL statements that exists in a single Oracle database account. You cannot create schemas that are independent of a database account. In fact, the syntax of the CREATE SCHEMA statement references the name of the database account that will own the objects. It does not receive a name of its own because it is not a separate collection in any way except in a logical sense. The following Code Example 5-1 would create the DEPT table for the database account SCOTT:

```
CREATE SCHEMA AUTHORIZATION SCOTT
CREATE TABLE DEPT (
DEPT_ID            NUMBER(2)     NOT NULL PRIMARY KEY,
NAME_TX            VARCHAR2(14)  NOT NULL,
LOC_TX             VARCHAR2(13)  NOT NULL)
/
```

Code Example 5-1

The CREATE SCHEMA statement can be executed any number of times for a specific database account. You can then issue the following CREATE

SCHEMA statement as shown in Code Example 5-2 to create the EMP table, which contains a foreign key to the DEPT table:

```
CREATE SCHEMA AUTHORIZATION SCOTT
CREATE TABLE EMP (
EMP_ID                NUMBER(4) NOT NULL PRIMARY KEY,
NAME_TX               VARCHAR2(10) NOT NULL,
JOB_TX                VARCHAR2(9),
EMP_ID_RFK            NUMBER(4),
HIRE_DT               DATE NOT NULL,
SAL_NBR               NUMBER(7,2) NOT NULL,
COMM_NBR              NUMBER(7,2),
DEPT_ID               NUMBER(2) NOT NULL REFERENCES DEPT (DEPT_ID))
/
```

Code Example 5-2

However, the CREATE schema statement generates the following error when you attempt to create multiple tables within one CREATE SCHEMA statement, as follows in Code Example 5-3:

```
CREATE SCHEMA AUTHORIZATION SCOTT
CREATE TABLE DEPT (
DEPT_ID               NUMBER(2)     NOT NULL PRIMARY KEY,
NAME_TX               VARCHAR2(14) NOT NULL,
LOC_TX                VARCHAR2(13) NOT NULL)

CREATE TABLE EMP (
EMP_ID                NUMBER(4) NOT NULL PRIMARY KEY,
NAME_TX               VARCHAR2(10) NOT NULL,
JOB_TX                VARCHAR2(9),
EMP_ID_RFK            NUMBER(4),
HIRE_DATE             DATE NOT NULL,
SAL_NBR               NUMBER(7,2) NOT NULL,
COMM_NBR              NUMBER(7,2),
DEPT_ID               NUMBER(2) NOT NULL REFERENCES DEPT (DEPT_ID))
/
```

ERROR at line 9:
ORA-00942: table or view does not exist

Code Example 5-3

The problem here is that we are attempting to create a table EMP with a foreign key to the table DEPT simultaneously. DEPT must be physically instantiated in order for another table (i.e., EMP) to be permitted to reference it with a foreign key. The CREATE SCHEMA statement does not perform integrity constraint validation during execution.

Naming Class Diagrams/ERDs

Many class diagrams may be used to depict a system. For example, one diagram may be called "Enterprise," which encompasses the whole system. Other class diagrams will include one for each schema. However, because schemas may have up to 100 classes, you may need more than one diagram per schema. If you need smaller diagrams, use the schema name plus a descriptive diagram name. We will assume that we are in a Windows-like environment and are not restricted in our selection of names. For example, if in a CORE module we were to show the tables associated with Security, the diagram name would be CO1 Security ("CO" indicating the CORE schema, "1" for schema precedence number, and "Security" to describe the tables contained in the diagram).

Diagram names should be meaningful. The same classes may appear on multiple diagrams. When creating subset diagrams, you should include all relevant classes for that subject area. Any class diagram showing an association class should always show both classes from the original many-to-many association. All value list classes (reference tables) that are referenced by any class in the diagram should be shown. For example, with a Project Class, both the Project Type and Project Status classes should be shown on the diagram.

VERSIONING   There may be many different diagram versions as you proceed through the SDLC. This information should be embedded in the diagram name. We recommend adding a suffix to the diagram name that includes what version of the system is being worked on, the life cycle phase of the project, and the diagram version. Project phase codes are "STR" for Strategy, "ANA" for Analysis, "DEV" for Development, and "PRO" for Production. Some examples of complete class diagram names are as follows:

- **ENTERPRISE V1 ANA1**   This name indicates the first version of the Enterprise data model in the Analysis phase of the first version of the system.

- **CO ACCESS CONTROL V2 DEV3**   This name indicates the third version of the CORE portion of the data model that deals with the Access Control Subsystem in the Development phase of the second version of the system.

These diagram names may seem unwieldy, but keep in mind that these names will not be typed but merely selected from a list. Since they are merely filenames, they will only appear once in the system.

Naming Classes/Tables/Entities

Good class names are important, because these names usually translate directly to table names. The goal is to have the class names match the table names. An unfortunate convention predominant in the Oracle community is that of naming entities in the singular and tables in the plural. Thus, when you're looking at an ERD, the tables have different names than the entities shown. During Analysis, one name is used, and the associated database table would have another name. Similarly, long names can be used in ERDs, but when the database is implemented, abbreviations for the long words are used. This makes a bit more sense, because the longer names are easier to show to users, but are not useful for developers. These situations where a mismatch between model and table names occurs can cause much confusion.

We recommend that classes and tables have the same names from the start. To show users more meaningful names, abbreviated words can be converted to their longer versions. Working in Oracle Designer, we created a utility to automate this process of translating abbreviations into their longer word equivalents.

The *name* of the class is not nearly as important as the *description* of the class. People selecting class names should recognize that the current corporate culture may influence the selection of names that do not make sense to the outside world. One manufacturer we worked with wanted to call equipment malfunctions "Tickets" because all malfunctioning equipment was reported via a document called a "ticket" and the name had stuck. Against our better judgment, the class was named "Ticket." While relevant to many users at the time it was selected, it may easily cause confusion for future personnel working on the systems project. In another case, an HMO had a notion of a "Medical Claim" that was a specific document representing a request for payment for medical services. There were also other types of requests for payment for services that were not claims but were bundled into the same class. The question arose of whether to name the class "Claim" or "Payment Request for Services." The class ended up being called "Claim" even though there was other information included in it. Both of these situations underscore the need for selecting class names that are clear and that leave no room for ambiguity.

The names selected should correspond to the way that the database community at large thinks about naming, rather than any organization or industry-specific standard. Classes should be named with one or more words that, as closely as possible, represent the kind of information stored by the class. The same phrase mentioned in Chapter 4 should be used to help name a class, specifically "Each object in this class is a ...." The item in the blank should be the name of the class.

ABBREVIATIONS When you name classes and other items within your system, it is important to develop a fixed list of abbreviations and words for the entire database. This same list of names and abbreviations will be used in every name, class, attribute, constraint, etc., throughout the database. We have seen organizations where different abbreviations were used in different contexts in various parts of the organization because users referred to the same objects by different names. The system designers mistakenly replicated these inconsistencies in the data model, with confusing results.

When the abbreviation list is complete, it should contain not only the words and their abbreviations, but also a brief description of the circumstances under which the word is used. This helps to ensure consistency throughout the system. A sample set of good class names, their abbreviations, and descriptions is shown in Table 5-1. Note that all class names are used in their singular form.

The strategy in determining useful abbreviations is to find a shortened version of the word that can easily be translated back into the original word. Abbreviations should be shown to several people to see if they reconstruct the same word. The number of characters selected for the abbreviation

Class Name	Abbreviation	Description
EMPLOYEE	EMP	Any person working for the organization on a full- or part-time basis
DEPARTMENT	DEPT	An internal logical grouping of Employees within the organization, such as Accounting, Purchasing, etc.
PURCHASE	PO	The act of ordering an item
TASK	TASK	A workflow event item to be completed by an Employee
PERSON	PERSON	The name of a person of interest to the organization
ADDRESS	ADDR	The address of a person or organization of interest to the organization
MODIFY	MOD	The act of changing a record within the database
MERCHANDISE	MERCH	An item for sale by the organization
MOVEMENT	MOVE	The action of transferring merchandise from one location to another
SALE	SALE	The action of receiving money in exchange for merchandise
TRAVEL	TRAVL	An employee travel event from one location to another

TABLE 5-1. *Sample Class Names, Abbreviations, and Descriptions*

should also be controlled. In most cases, we use five-letter abbreviations. We found that this was the smallest number of letters that could produce easily translated abbreviations. In cases where there are standard abbreviations, using different numbers of letters (ST for street, ADDR for Address, etc.), the commonly accepted abbreviation should be used. Although it may take new developers some time to get used to, we found that five-character abbreviations strike a reasonable balance between minimizing typing and clarity of meaning.

CLASS TYPES   There are different kinds of classes, each of which has its own appropriate naming conventions:

- **Primary Classes**   These classes include the main transactions and items of interest within the system, such as Employees, Sales, Departments, etc. Primary classes should be named with one or more meaningful words of approximately five letters, connected by underscores. If words are too long, abbreviations from the approved abbreviation list should be used. Only words on the list should be used. If you need to use a word that is not on the current list, the new word should be added using whatever control mechanisms are established for changing the list. Examples of these types of names can be found in Chapter 19.

- **Value List Classes**   These are very different from primary classes. They are merely lists of valid values for attributes. Since value list classes are conceptually different from other classes, it is useful to group them together. Value list classes are looked at much less frequently than other classes. Also, because classes are usually listed alphabetically, we recommend using a Z_ prefix followed by the name of the attribute. Thus, all value list classes will be automatically grouped at the end of an alphabetical list, making them easy to identify. For example, for the list of possible statuses for a project, the value list class name would be Z_PROJ_STS. For all of those value list classes that are "types" of items of interest, the word "type" can usually be omitted, because the Z_ prefix already identifies the class as a value list class. Using this system, Z_PROJ would mean Project Type and Z_EMP would mean Employee Type. When you're showing these classes to users, including the word "type" may be useful to improve clarity. We support this with our abbreviation utility by replacing the word "type" with the null string for Z_ tables.

■ **Redundant Classes**   Any class that is an aggregation class as a result of denormalization (i.e., redundant) should be prefixed with X_. For example, the Ledger Account History class that stores daily summaries of transactions on ledger accounts would be called X_LEDG_ACCT_HIST. A redundant class is any class that could be reconstructed if deleted.

■ **Association Classes (Intersection Entities)**   Classes that arise from many-to-many relationships pose more difficult naming problems. The first thing to recognize is that an association class usually represents a real thing that can be articulated in a straightforward manner. Some examples include the following:

   ■ The association between Course Offering and Student can be called "Enrollment."

   ■ The association between Person and Equipment can be called "Assigned Equipment."

   ■ The association between Person and Department associations can be called "Employment."

   ■ The association between Person and Role can be called "Assigned Role." "Assigned" is a useful clarifying designation when one side of the association does not obviously correspond to something in the real world.

In almost all cases, you can find a better alternative to naming an association using a concatenation of the two underlying classes.

■ **Detail Classes**   Explicit master-detail relationships frequently exist in data models. PO-PO Detail and Sale-Sale Detail are two examples of such relationships. In all cases where one class is essentially a line item detail of another class, the naming convention for the detail class will be <PARENT CLASS NAME>_DTL. Using the preceding examples, the names would be PO_DTL and SALE_DTL, respectively. Some people might prefer to use _LINE rather than _DTL. We recommend the "DTL" suffix, because it is somewhat more general. If you're describing a document such as a purchase order or sale, "line" and "detail" are synonymous. However, in other situations, the same type of relationship may exist apart from a document. For example, a task may be broken down into exactly one level of subtasks that can be called Task Details, but there may be no task document, so that TASK_LINE makes no sense.

■ **Generalization Classes**   Classes that are generalizations of other classes will be named using the same conventions used for primary classes. Keep in mind that the name of the class must stand on its own. If EMPLOYEE is a generalization of Salaried and Hourly Employees, then the appropriate name is EMP, EMP_SALARIED, EMP_HOURLY, or the appropriate abbreviations for these words. Simply having a class called SALARIED or HOURLY is not sufficient, because each item in those classes is an Employee.

Naming Attributes

Attributes are named using the same system and abbreviation scheme as classes, namely logical words to describe the attribute concatenated together. Each attribute should have a suffix that identifies the category of the domain to which it belongs, such as date, number, text, etc. In Chapter 6 we will list the many different domains we use. Using this list, we attach the appropriate domain suffix to the attribute name. The suffixes used and their descriptions are shown in Table 5-2.

In object-oriented practice Boolean fields are usually named with an "is" prefix. For example, an active flag would be named "isActive". We thought carefully about adopting this syntax. We chose not to use it. Our reasons were as follows:

■ In Oracle, mixed-case attribute names are not yet supported. "ISACTIVE" is not nearly as readable as "isActive". We could have used "IS_ACTIVE" but we decided against it.

■ We really liked the suffix notation for attribute names. We didn't want to abandon it.

■ We could have combined the two syntaxes and named the field IS_ACTIVE_YN, but we thought that was redundant.

We thought about appending an abbreviation that represents the actual domain for each attribute, but in practice, text lengths and numeric precision may change over time. We wanted the categories to be broad

Suffix	Description
_ID	Numeric primary keys
_CD	Character primary keys and any attributes that come from a restricted list of character values
_YN	Boolean
_DT	Dates stored to the nearest day
_TM	Dates stored to the nearest second
_TX	All other text formats not covered by CD, YN, including LONG variables
_CY	Numeric values representing currency amounts
_NR	All numeric fields not covered by ID or CY
_GR	Graphics, images, large binary objects

TABLE 5-2. *Attribute Suffixes*

enough so that change would be rare—but we also wanted to provide some information about the datatype in the field to assist in application development. By use of these suffixes, a utility can be built to assist in quickly assigning the appropriate domains for each attribute. If we were to suffix the attributes with the actual domains and, during the development process, we decided to change domains, all code accessing that attribute would have to be modified. We have found that it is quite common for lengths of attributes to be changed in a system, but rarely does an attribute change from one of these categories to another.

As will be mentioned in Chapter 7, the primary key for a value list class is named <NAME OF VALUE LIST CLASS>_CD. The longer value is <NAME>_TX. If we use system-generated primary keys for the value list class, then we would use the ID suffix in place of the CD suffix.

SPECIAL ATTRIBUTES   There are several specialized attributes that require slightly different naming conventions. A list of these is shown in Table 5-3.

Attribute Name	Description
ACTIV_YN	Active flag to indicate if a record has been deleted
ORDER_NR	Sort order for class used when using an order independent from other attribute classes
DESC_TX	Long text description fields for remarks, notes, etc.
_BY	Special class system user names
CREAT_TM	Date and time that a record is created
MOD_TM	Last date and time that a record has been modified
CREAT_BY	System user name of person creating a record
MOD_BY	System user name of person last modifying a record

TABLE 5-3. *Special Attributes*

Naming Domains

The main concern with domain names is that they must be short enough to fit in the small boxes within the tools used to assign them. For a standard name domain such as ID or CODE, simply use the word or its appropriate abbreviation.

Domain names should be descriptive. If the field is simply the domain of a particular length, you might even use the actual domain, i.e., VARCHAR240. A list of domains can be found in Chapter 6.

Naming Relationships

ERD relationship naming standards are discussed in Richard Barker's book, *CASE*METHOD: Entity Relationship Modeling* (Addison-Wesley Publishing Company, Wokingham, England, 1990). We will discuss the UML naming standards. Keep in mind that in ERDs, we have only two things to name in a relationship. In UML, we have three—the relationship itself and each side of the relationship. The semantics of what names are used is quite different in UML than in ERDs. ERDs use verb phrases on both sides of the relationship. In UML the verb phrase is only used once, and you must declare in which direction the phrase goes. Other discussions of relationship names and conventions can be found in Chapters 4 and 8.

UML relationships are described using a verb phrase consisting of a verb and a preposition. In addition, you can name the roles on either side of the relationship. These role names use the same naming conventions as classes and should be explicit clarifications of the roles the objects in that class play in the relationship. The archetypal example of a relationship is shown in Figure 5-1.

The direction of the relationship name should go from higher to lower cardinality, only adding roles when necessary.

Naming Operations/Methods

Methods that are *procedures* (they do not return a value other than a status) should be named with a P_prefix followed by a verb phrase. Because the method explicitly belongs to the class, the class name does not need to be a part of the method name. For example, if on the EMP class, we have a method "Hire," the appropriate name would simply be "HIRE" and not "HIRE_EMP." Methods that are functions and do return a value should be named F_<ATTRIBUTE NAME RETURNING>. Examples of procedure and function names are shown in Table 5-4.

Creating Descriptions

Describing a class accurately is even more important than selecting a name for the class. To describe a primary class, we implicitly start with the phrase "Each object in this class is a...." For more details about class descriptions, see Chapter 4.

Any notes for the developers associated with a class can be placed in the description or in a notes field. For association classes, we will frequently

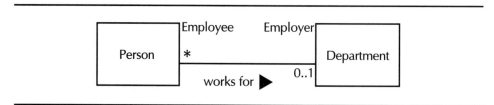

FIGURE 5-1. *UML diagram showing relationship names*

Procedure Examples

Combine budgets	P_COMBN_BUDGT
Close project	P_CLOSE_PROJ

Function Examples

Retrieve primary address	F_PRIM_ADDR_TX
Calculate total amount owed	F_TOT_AMT_OWED_NR

TABLE 5-4. *Procedure and Function Examples*

reference each of the underlying classes. For example, to describe Enrollment (association between Student and Course Offering), each object in the class is "a particular student enrolled in a particular course offering."

For value list class descriptions, begin with the implicit phrase "Each object in this class is a valid value for...." These value list descriptions must always include at least two examples.

Attribute descriptions should only be used where necessary. Many are self-explanatory and do not require descriptions. For example, the City attribute in an Address class is obvious, and creating a description is a waste of time. Attribute descriptions are needed whenever there is ambiguity about the nature of the attribute. Attributes that seem self-explanatory during Analysis may not seem so later on in the SDLC. All attributes requiring descriptions should include at least two sample values. For example, in a PERSON table, we might have an attribute called "Suffix." The description of this attribute would be "honorific or other appendage to a name used primarily for mailing labels that appears after the last name on the label such as MD, Ph.D., III, etc."

Physical (Implementation) Naming Conventions

There are other elements within a system that are not part of the logical data model and only appear during physical implementation. These elements also require consistent naming standards.

Naming Sequences

For every system-generated primary key column, we generate a unique sequence. There is never more than one sequence per table. Therefore, the name of the sequence should be <TABLE NAME>_SEQ. For example, the sequence used to generate PROJ_ID in the Project table would be PROJ_SEQ.

Short Table Name Aliases

To keep names short, it is often necessary to create short table name aliases. To generate these aliases, use the first letter of each word in the class name and concatenate them. For example, PURCH_ORDER would be shortened to PO. If this does not make the name unique, use an additional single integer (1,2,3) suffix to force uniqueness, for example, "PO" and "PO1".

Naming Constraints

If a referential integrity constraint exists between two tables, the constraint name should consist of <FIRST TABLE NAME>_ _ <SECOND TABLE NAME>_F. For example, if there were a constraint between PURCH_ORDER and PURCH_ORDER_DTL, the constraint name should be PURCH_ORDER_ _ PURCH_ORDER_DTL_F. If this is too long (the maximum number of characters for a constraint is 30), you can use the short table name aliases without the double underscores. In this case, the name would be written PO_ POD_F.

For check constraints, the naming convention should be

<TABLE NAME>_ _<COLUMN NAME>_C

If these are too long, use the short table name aliases without the double underscores. If these are still too long, create an abbreviation for the column.

For primary key constraints, the naming convention should be

<CLASS NAME>_PK

Examples of constraint names are shown in Table 5-5.

Type	Table	Column	Constraint Name
Primary key	EMP		EMP_PK
Check	MY_TABLE	MY_COL	MY_TABLE__MY_COL_C
Check	A_VERY_LONG_TABLE_NAME	MY_COL	AVLTN_MY_COL_C
Check	A_LONG_TABLE_NAME	A_LONG_COL_NAME	ALTN_ALCN_C

TABLE 5-5. *Examples of Constraint Names*

Naming Indexes

For naming indexes, use the following format:

<SHORT TABLE NAME ALIAS>_<1st COLUMN NAME IN INDEX>_
_<2nd COLUMN NAME IN INDEX>_I

Each column name should be separated by two underscores. If this is too long, abbreviate the column names using the short table name aliases abbreviation method. If you use short abbreviations, then the double underscores are not necessary. Some examples of index names are shown in Table 5-6.

Table	Index Columns	Index Name
EMP	DeptNo	EMP_DEPTNO_I
MY_TABLE	MY_FIRST_COL	MT_MFC_MSC_I
YOUR_TABLE	COL_ONE COL_TWO	YT_COL_ONE__COL_TWO_I

TABLE 5-6. *Examples of Index Naming Conventions*

Naming Object Types

For object types, use the same naming conventions as for classes with the suffix _T attached to the name.

Naming Procedures and Functions

We use P_ prefixes for procedures and F_ prefixes for functions.

Stored Programming Units

Stored programming units are programs that are stored within an Oracle database instance that perform one or more specific tasks. These stored units can be executed from user interfaces such as SQL*Plus, or referenced within applications such as those built using Oracle Developer.

The three types of stored programming units available to use are procedures, functions, and database triggers. *Procedures* are programs that perform one or more actions, and that optionally return values and/or statuses based upon the completion/termination of the program's logic.

All procedures and functions stored in the database should always be stored in packages. Packages help to organize functions and procedures into logical groups. All packages use a K_ prefix to indicate that they are packages usually followed by a single word to describe the package. Package names should be kept very short because every reference to a function or procedure inside the package must have the package name added to the beginning when called. If the package pertains to a particular table, it should be called K_<SHORT_TABLE_NAME>. If the package pertains to a group of tables, then you should choose a short package word to describe that group of tables. For example, K_ACCT could be the package for all accounting functions and K_BUDG could be used for all budget-related functions.

When naming functions or procedures inside packages, keep in mind that the context of the function or procedure is determined by the package so that names can frequently be abbreviated. For example, a procedure to post an accounting transaction could be named P_POST_ACCT_TRAN. However, since this procedure would reside within the Accounting package, it can be named POST_TRAN or simply POST because it is clear what K_ACCT.POST means.

In naming a procedure to insert objects into the DEPT table, we would concatenate the "P_" to the name of the table that the procedure is acting upon "DEPT." The result would look something like the following Code Example 5-4:

```
--****reference example_05_01 as prerequisite
CREATE OR REPLACE PROCEDURE P_DEPT IS
BEGIN
INSERT INTO DEPT (DEPT_ID, NAME_TX, LOC_TX)
        VALUES (95, 'ADVERTISING', 'HOUSTON');
END;
/
```

Code Example 5-4

The same construct is followed for stored *functions*. Stored functions are designed to perform a single specific task, and then return a status based upon the completion/termination of the function's logic. The key difference in the naming of procedures and functions is the prefix as shown in Code Example 5-5:

```
--****reference example_05-02 as prerequisite
CREATE or replace FUNCTION F_CHECK_EMP_SAL (P_EMP_ID IN NUMBER)
RETURN NUMBER
IS
CURSOR C1 IS
SELECT SAL_NBR
FROM EMP
WHERE EMP_ID = P_EMP_ID;
FLAG  NUMBER;
BEGIN
FOR C1_REC IN C1 LOOP
IF C1_REC.SAL_NBR < 5000 THEN
RETURN -1;
ELSE RETURN 1;
END IF;
END LOOP;
END;
/
```

Code Example 5-5

Another helpful bit of information you might consider adding to your naming standard for procedures and functions would be DML indicators. In other words, add a prefix that indicates "I" for Insert, "U" for Update, "D" for Delete, and/or "S" for Select. This section would declare the main utility of the stored programming unit. Also, this standard would guide your developers in writing more modularized code, which certainly helps from a documentation standpoint. This standard is exemplified using database triggers next.

Parameters in procedures are named using the same conventions as attributes with the exception of an additional prefix indicating how they are used in the procedure:

I_	Input parameter
O_	Output parameter
IO_	Input/output parameter

Naming Database Triggers

Database triggers are the last type of stored programming unit we need to review. *Database triggers* are programs that are attached to specific tables, and executed based upon the specified action criteria. Database triggers fire based upon Insert, Update, and/or Delete requests to the table in which the trigger exists.

The following conventions are used for database triggers:

■ The first character is B or A for Before or After.

■ The second, third, and fourth characters would be I (Insert), U (Update), D (Delete), or any relevant subset of these.

For example, a trigger on the EMP table that would fire before Insert and Update would be named BUI_EMP. A trigger that fired after Insert and Delete (if this combination made sense) would be named AID.

These triggers can be specified to execute BEFORE, AFTER, or INSTEAD OF the DML statement (i.e., INSERT, UPDATE, or DELETE) that executed the trigger. The naming convention makes the first section of the trigger name a single character—B for "Before," A for "After," and "I" for Instead of. The next three characters will indicate the DML actions for which this trigger will fire.

For example, should a trigger on the DEPT table fire BEFORE INSERT and UPDATE, then the trigger code would be as follows in Code Example 5-6:

```
--***reference example_05_01 as prerequisite
CREATE OR REPLACE TRIGGER BIU_DEPT
BEFORE INSERT OR UPDATE
ON DEPT
FOR EACH ROW
BEGIN
NULL;
END;
/
```

Code Example 5-6

Notice that only the relevant DML types (i.e., I and U in the BIU_DEPT trigger example) show up in the trigger name. You will not always use all three characters set aside for DML operations, but only those that are relevant in each case.

CHAPTER

6

Domains of Datatypes

omains first became popular in the Oracle community through the use of Oracle Designer. This product allowed database designers to specify predefined sets of parameters that could be applied to database columns. The parameters that could be set are shown in Table 6-1.

In Oracle Designer, parameters can be set at both the logical and physical levels. In addition, designers can set average length so that Oracle Designer can accurately estimate how much space a table will consume.

Users of Oracle Designer vary greatly in their use of domains. Some users never use domains, others make a different domain for each column. Our philosophy is to create a number of domains, then to apply one to each attribute in the data model. That way we are able to manage the amount of variability in our datatypes. This makes it easier to build our applications, because there are only a few different field lengths to accommodate.

Until Oracle8 objects, there was no way to specify domains in the database. Now we can subtype a column using the Oracle8 object extensions. The parameters that we can specify are shown in Table 6-2.

Creating Domains

When you're designing a database, it is useful to avoid having too many different domains. If you keep your datatypes to a small number, it is easier for coders to build their applications. From a GUI design standpoint, fewer datatypes make screens easier to design, because there will only be a limited number of field sizes. The way to limit the number of datatypes is by basing them upon a relatively small number of domains.

Domains are descriptions of the data parameters of the variable. However, you may also want to include triggers, validation, and other information as part of the domain definition.

One caution that we should give designers is to be careful about making their domains too restrictive. The more restrictive the domains, the more unstable the data model will be. By this we mean that there is a cost to restrictive domains. If you carefully match the domain to exactly what you perceive the business rules to be, and those rules change at all, then the database structure will have to be modified. For example, let's say we are modeling the Sale Detail table for a small retailer. No item in the store is over $100, so we restrict the maximum value on the sale amount field to be

Datatype	The standard Oracle datatypes, VARCHAR2, char, number, etc.
Length	The maximum length of the field
Precision	For numeric fields, the maximum number of digits after the decimal point
Default	The default value to be used when the data being inserted to the record has the value of NULL for this column
Low, high	For numeric and character fields, the minimum and maximum allowable value
Values	The explicit allowable values for the field

TABLE 6-1. *Initial Oracle Designer Parameters*

$100. If the store ever gets an item that sells for over $100, then the field will have to be modified.

As a second example, let's restrict the sale amount to be greater than 0. This seems like a reasonable restriction, but prevents us from using the same table to store sales returns (which would have a negative sale amount). Many restrictions on data should be placed in the applications rather than in the database. This is particularly true of contingent constraints, as discussed in Chapter 8.

In general, make your domains as restrictive as possible given your perception of what the system requirements will be in the future. It requires

Datatype	The standard Oracle datatypes, VARCHAR2, char, number, etc.
Length	The maximum length of the field
Precision	For numeric fields, the maximum number of digits after the decimal point

TABLE 6-2. *Oracle8 Parameters*

a careful balance to enforce as many data-related business rules as possible through domains without requiring extra work to relax the constraints later because the requirements changed.

There are several schools of thought on specifying domains:

1. Rarely use domains at all and only use them for a few special kinds of fields such as Boolean (Y/N).

2. Use a separate domain for every attribute in the data model. This approach is not useful, because the only thing that is accomplished is that, if a field changes its datatype, the datatype will propagate with the foreign key if the field is a primary key field or if you are maintaining separate logical and physical models.

3. Use a small number of domains that only support a few kinds of objects. With this strategy, you might have a total of 10 to 15 domains.

4. The approach we recommend is to have a relatively large, rich set of domains that supports a detailed set of data-related business rules, enforcing not simply field lengths but also some relatively meaningful validation information. By use of this last strategy, every attribute in the database is assigned a domain from a relatively rich list of domains.

You will need to determine how diverse a set of domains to create. This becomes a question of style. If you are working on a small system, fewer domains may suffice. However, keep in mind that you are rarely building only one system in isolation. Domains should be set to support the entire development environment rather than a specific system. Think in terms of future systems as well, so that both your data models and development environment can remain relatively stable. We have created systems with as few as ten domains. However, now our development environment has grown to approximately 50 domains. We will present our full domain environment in this chapter and discuss the criteria necessary for selecting domains. If using domains is new to you, we suggest beginning with a relatively limited set of domains (10 to 20), building one project, and seeing if the domains selected fit your vision of how databases should be designed. Then you can refine your domain list to best fit your style of development.

Domain Types

A domain is intended to provide characteristics about an attribute. Datatype, length, and precision for numbers (where appropriate) are supported in the database. Even for these parameters, we still want to set the allowable datatypes and lengths for a particular database. Consistency in domains across the database simplifies the database as well as the maintenance and the writing of applications.

In the database, there should be relatively few distinct types of data objects. For applications, even something as trivial as accommodating only a few different data lengths can make screen and report design much easier. However, you must be careful about being too restrictive with domains. Using our generic style of modeling, if we are storing more than one type of object in the same table, it may be necessary to relax the domain somewhat to accommodate the different types of objects. For example, for a class that stores information about the sale of a product, you should restrict Sale Amount and Quantity to positive numbers. However, if you intend to use the same class to support other transaction types, such as Sales Returns, then negative numbers for Quantity and Sale Amount may be appropriate. Similarly, a particular attribute may be mandatory for one type of object in the table and optional or not even used by another. This means that the database constraint must allow the field to be optional. Fortunately, the relaxing, removal, or disabling of constraints is well supported within Oracle and would not disrupt a production system. On the other hand, tightening a constraint on a production system is frequently an expensive and time-consuming task.

In this chapter, we will discuss each type of domain and provide examples and suggestions for appropriate uses in building systems.

Character Constraints

Most of the data in any database is nonnumeric. There are many useful restrictions we can place on character information. You can have a fixed-length character field (CHAR) or a variable-length data field (VARCHAR2) in a database. CHAR uses marginally less storage space than VARCHAR2 if the field is entirely filled. However, with the cost of disk storage resolutely following Moore's law (approximately every 18 months, the speed and storage capabilities of available computers will double), saving a byte here and there is no longer a relevant consideration. As a result, many designers have adopted the practice of only using VARCHAR2 for text fields. We believe this is a mistake. If the business rule for a database is that text fields are always of a particular fixed length, not to enforce this rule is a mistake. For example, U.S. Social Security numbers are fixed 9-character numeric fields where each field should be CHAR(9).

Numeric ID fields such as Social Security numbers, where a leading 0 is relevant, should always be stored as character fields rather than number fields. In the same way, telephone numbers, employee IDs, contract numbers, loan numbers, etc., should be stored as character fields.

TIP
The rule we use is the following: If the numbers to be stored are a count or measure of something, they should be stored numerically. If the field is being used as an identifier, the numbers should be stored as a character field.

Fixed-Length CHAR Domains

Most fixed-length character domains have only a few characters (fewer than five). However, in some cases, it may be appropriate to include CHAR domains with a greater number of characters. This is useful when information from one system needs to be fed into a second system with an existing fixed-length CHAR domain. One system we worked on included government contract numbers that had to be exactly 12 characters in order to be accepted by a downstream system. A CHAR(12) datatype enforced this business rule.

You will often need a number of CHAR domains for specific attributes that may only be used once in a particular system but may be used across systems. For example, there should be a domain for ZIP codes (5 characters), ZIP+4 (9 characters), and Social Security numbers (9 characters). There is no reason to store hyphens in either ZIP+4 numbers or Social Security numbers. We suggest making two separate domains for ZIP+4 and Social Security numbers even though both are numeric with nine characters. We could create a domain called "9-character numeric codes," but because of the frequent use of both ZIP codes and Social Security numbers, it makes more sense for each to have its own domain. Also, if either should change in format, separating out the two from a single domain would require considerable effort.

You can choose to store hyphens and parentheses in character fields such as Social Security number and telephone number, or you can display them using a display format mask. The advantage to storing them in the database is that the data is easier to read when doing simple queries in SQL*Plus. The disadvantage is that there is some wasted space in the database. We choose not to store formatting characters in the database, but it is a matter of preference as to how you want to store these fields.

All of these examples can be enforced relatively easily using minimum and maximum (000... and 999...) values, which effectively prevent any character entries. However, there are domains where such a simple approach doesn't work. Canadian postal codes that alternate letters and numbers for six characters could only be enforced with a trigger or by storing letters and numbers in separate fields.

Unfortunately, Oracle Designer does not explicitly support triggers for domains. To implement this structure in Oracle Designer, you could write the trigger code in a user extension or explicitly mark it in the description for the attribute and write an API utility to apply the trigger to each attribute based on that domain.

Boolean Fields

For Boolean attributes, we always use Y/N for Yes/No and True/False and therefore always name Boolean attributes with an underscore YN suffix. (See Chapter 5 for more details.) There are three domains for Booleans:

- Mandatory—defaults to Yes or True

- Mandatory—defaults to No or False

- Optional—no default

Include an explicit null value on indicator values because searching for a specific value is more efficient than checking to see if a column is null or not. For optional Booleans, you can use a single-character CHAR field with three possible values (Y, N, X).

It is also possible to have CHAR domains explicitly delineate all possible values for that attribute. The most common examples of this are Boolean fields. Logically, Boolean fields allow three values: T, F, and unknown. We use Boolean variables for all two-value or two-value + null attributes including Gender. Boolean is not a valid datatype in Oracle8, so it must be stored with datatype CHAR(1) with allowable values T and F for True and False, respectively.

Boolean fields are the only place that we use a named set of values for an attribute. We believe that the practice of using check constraints to support small lists of values is ill conceived, because most lists of values (no matter how apparently stable during analysis) often become more volatile during production. The cost of placing a valid list of values into a value list class as discussed in Chapter 7 is low enough from a performance perspective to justify doing it in all cases. For example, status attributes often generate arguments about using a valid list of values. Potential Status values include Initial, Pending, Completed, and Canceled. Invariably, someone will want to make a modification, such as adding "Approved." Oracle Designer does allow for storing named lists of values in one large Reference Code table. We do not recommend this approach. The reasons for this are discussed in Chapter 7.

We recommend including the CHAR domains shown in Table 6-3 and Code Example 6-1 in your system. They can be created using the following code. We will show how to implement domains in Oracle8i tables later in this chapter.

```
CREATE OR REPLACE TYPE CHAR1 AS OBJECT (
COL         CHAR (1))
/

CREATE OR REPLACE TYPE CHAR2 AS OBJECT (
COL         CHAR (2))
/

CREATE OR REPLACE TYPE CHAR3 AS OBJECT (
COL         CHAR (3))
/

CREATE OR REPLACE TYPE CHAR5 AS OBJECT (
COL         CHAR (5))
/

CREATE OR REPLACE TYPE SSN AS OBJECT (
COL         CHAR (9))
/
```

```
CREATE OR REPLACE TYPE ZIP AS OBJECT (
COL           CHAR (5))
/

CREATE OR REPLACE TYPE ZIP_4 AS OBJECT (
COL           CHAR (9))
/

CREATE OR REPLACE TYPE CODE AS OBJECT (
COL           CHAR (10))
/
```

Code Example 6-1

Single column, user-defined datatypes are referenced by their name, eliminating the need to provide an intuitive name to the member place

Name	Type	Length	Precision	Min	Max	Values	Default
Char1	Char	1					
Char2	Char	2					
Char3	Char	3					
Char5	Char	5					
ZIP	Char	5		00000	99999		
Zip+4	Char	9		000000000	999999999		
SSN	Char	9		000000000	999999999		
Bool Yes Opt.	Char	1				Y, N, X	Y
Bool No Opt.	Char	1				Y, N, X	N
Bool Opt	Char	1				Y.N, X	X
Bool Yes	Char	1				Y, N	Y
Bool No	Char	1				Y, N	N
Code	Char	10					

TABLE 6-3. *Recommended CHAR Domains*

holders within the datatypes. As you will see throughout this book, we tend to alias datatype members commonly by the string 'COL', as each of these members forms the basis of COLumns of tables that reference these datatypes. Naming the datatype member CODE within the CODE datatype would result in references to it looking redundant (i.e., CODE.CODE). By naming the type member COL, references now look like CODE.COL, which is cleaner. In the end, it's the name of the datatype that's important, not its member.

Boolean datatypes should always be mandatory with default values supplied. Oracle8i does not support default values and check constraint conditions at the Type level, though this type of support is planned for a future release.

We have taken this into consideration as we defined our Boolean datatypes. As you can see below, we have given each of our Boolean types a prefix of 'BOOL'. Each suffix indicates the allowable values to support this type. The first value supplied is the default value for columns of this type.

For example, columns instantiated upon the 'BOOL_YNX' type would require a default value = 'Y', and two additionally allowable values, 'N' and 'X'. 'Y' typically stands for Yes or True, 'N' stands for No or False. 'X' has been added for BOOLEAN flags that are optional in nature. Queries perform better when every row contains a value because these values can be indexed, and assigning an actual value instead of 'NULL' removes all ambiguity.

```
CREATE OR REPLACE TYPE BOOL_YNX AS OBJECT (
COL          CHAR (1))
/

CREATE OR REPLACE TYPE BOOL_NYX AS OBJECT (
COL          CHAR (9))
/

CREATE OR REPLACE TYPE BOOL_XYN AS OBJECT (
COL          CHAR (1))
/

CREATE OR REPLACE TYPE BOOL_YN AS OBJECT (
COL          CHAR (1))
/
```

```
CREATE OR REPLACE TYPE BOOL_NY AS OBJECT (
COL          CHAR (1))
/
```

Code Example 6-2

The Boolean domains cannot be fully implemented as data types, because they require default values as a component of their specification. Oracle Designer provides the ability to specify defaults. Types within the database do not. Default values are implemented on the physical instantiation of columns in tables. Therefore, to enforce a domain with a default value at the database level, two or more steps are required. The first step is the definition of the object type. The second is the implementation of the default value at the time that each column is instantiated upon the object type. A third might be a check constraint to define a limited value set. If you generate your DDL from Oracle Designer, all three steps can be performed for you automatically.

In creating an example for the Boolean domain that defaults to Yes, we might use the following scenario shown in Code Example 6-3:

```
CREATE OR REPLACE TYPE BOOLEAN_Y AS OBJECT (
COL          CHAR (1))
/

CREATE TABLE PERSON (
EMPNO        NUMBER (10) NOT NULL PRIMARY KEY,
NAME         VARCHAR2 (60) NOT NULL,
MALE_YN      BOOLEAN_YN DEFAULT BOOLEAN_YN ('Y'))
/
```

Code Example 6-3

From this example, you can see that the implementation required two steps. The first step was the creation of the BOOLEAN_Y object type. You could argue that because there is no ability to store default values as part of object types, we should instead create only one BOOLEAN object type that will be applied to all occurrences. However, because Oracle Designer maintains default values as part of domains and it will generate the appropriate DDL to satisfy both the data structure and default value, it makes sense to create object types that correspond to Oracle Designer domains in a 1-to-1 manner.

NOTE
Default values can be specified for columns based on column types, based on column types, but they are not supported in DML statements as of v.8.0.4.

VARCHAR2

VARCHAR2 domains consist of variable-length fields that support information of various lengths. We try to limit the number of different fields to the following list:

VARCHAR2 (10)	For short names
VARCHAR2 (20)	For displaying names on the screen because 40-character names use up a lot of space on reports and screens
VARCHAR2 (40)	For names of real-world objects
VARCHAR2 (2000)	For descriptions

We used to use smaller domains of 200, 500, and 1000 for shorter descriptions. However, in practice, we have found that this is more trouble to maintain and has no impact on screens and reports. A VARCHAR2 (2000) field storing 80 characters requires no more storage space than a VARCHAR2 (250) field storing 80 characters.

We use a separate Telephone Number domain (VARCHAR2 (40)) with a complex formatting trigger to enforce correct input. Usually, users are only interested in looking up the telephone number. If it is stored in multiple fields, users usually make enough data entry errors that the benefit of storing the number across several fields is lost. For most systems, we do not store area codes and phone numbers separately, because this is not relevant to the users' needs. Of course, if the project were for a telephone company, you would want every component of the phone number stored in separate fields.

E-mail and web addresses (250 each with no format masks) are given a domain. The large length is used to ensure that the domain can accommodate the potentially large values of web addresses.

Handling people's names is more complex than it may appear. Decisions must be made regarding the order of first and last names, middle names, honorifics and titles, professional designations, nicknames, and the possibility of a person having only one name. Using our generic approach, it is tempting to have all of the fields mentioned earlier included in the system. This would include a validated honorific (Mr., Mrs., Ms., Dr.), first name, middle name, last name, list of professional designations (Ph.D., MD, CPA, etc.), and nickname (used for conference badges or informal address). For a personnel system, all of these together would form the appropriate structure.

The problem is that this cannot be used for normal business contacts and customer lists, because the people supporting this information are usually not careful enough to gather all of this information and enter it correctly. Using this elaborate name structure for non–human resources–related systems creates the potential problem of having the same person in the database many times. Often names are reentered when they cannot be located. As a result, we tend to use a simplified structure for client and customer contact databases that uses last name, first name (including honorific), and suffix for professional designations. Usually, these are enough.

Enforcing mandatory character VARCHAR2 fields is difficult, particularly for descriptions. Users will not always enter descriptions. If descriptions are mandatory, users may enter a space. If you code a validation trigger to present a single space from being a valid value, a period may be used instead. If a period is not allowed, an "X" will be used. If you enforce that the length of the field is 10 to 15 characters, a string of letters will be used. Trying to enforce a description through mandatory constraints is a futile effort that will clutter the database with invalid data. We recommend that you do not enforce mandatory VARCHAR2 data.

Depending upon your specific system requirements, you may want a VARCHAR2 domain where the formatting is restricted to numbers. This is useful for product numbers, contract numbers, vehicle ID numbers, etc. Be warned that some "numbers" may include embedded characters such as "20Ta." Changing a datatype from number to character after a system is in production is an expensive prospect. If the data being entered is not going to be used computationally, it should be stored in a CHAR or VARCHAR2 field.

Our recommended VARCHAR2 datatypes are shown in Table 6-4 and Code Example 6-4.

```
CREATE OR REPLACE TYPE VC2_10 AS OBJECT (
COL          VARCHAR2 (10))
/

CREATE OR REPLACE TYPE VC2_20 AS OBJECT (
COL          VARCHAR2 (20))
```

```
/

CREATE OR REPLACE TYPE VC2_40 AS OBJECT (
COL           VARCHAR2 (40))
/

CREATE OR REPLACE TYPE VC2_2000 AS OBJECT (
COL           VARCHAR2 (2000))
/
```

Code Example 6-4

Sometimes we want to define datatypes that have special meanings or usages. For example, we could use the domain VC2_40 for phone numbers, but for better clarity in our data models and miscellaneous documentation, we would instead add a second datatype called PHONE_TX, as described below in Code Example 6-5.

```
CREATE OR REPLACE TYPE PHONE_TX AS OBJECT (
COL           CHAR (40))
/

CREATE OR REPLACE TYPE WEB_TX AS OBJECT (
COL           CHAR (250))
/
```

Code Example 6-5

Name	Type	Length	Precision	Min	Max	Values	Default
VC2_10	VARCHAR2	10					
VC2_20	VARCHAR2	20					
VC2_40	VARCHAR2	40					
VC2_2000	VARCHAR2	2000					
Phone	VARCHAR2	40					
Email Web	VARCHAR2	250					

TABLE 6-4. *Recommended VARCHAR2 Datatypes*

Although splitting these two datatypes apart does not add much value to implementations today, it allows us to implement systems that will accept smoothly integrated future enhancements such as check constraints and default values attached to the datatype. This is the core of differentiation between the vanilla VC2_40 datatype and the PHONE_TX datatype. We would likely write code within a check constraint that essentially applies a format mask over the phone number string as it is entered that validates the structure of the string. This check constraint would only apply to columns of type PHONE_TX, not VC2_40.

Therefore, when we have the ability to attach check constraints to datatypes, our only change will be to add the check constraint to the PHONE_TX type. Since the PHONE_TX type had already been assigned to the appropriate columns throughout the database, the new check constraint would be automatically inherited, system wide.

Dates

Dates in Oracle are stored as numeric fields, accurate to the nearest second. A day is exactly 1.000 long; minutes and seconds are fractional parts of a day. If you are storing dates and are not interested in the time that a given event occurred, you should store the TRUNC of whatever date is entered. This will ensure that the date is stored as an integer and will be stored as midnight on the transaction date.

You will have one domain for dates and a second for date and time. There is no reason to ever store date and time separately. If you need to display them separately in an application, you can display the same field twice, each time with a different format mask.

Because of this numeric storage, no special attention needs to be paid in an Oracle database to make it Year 2000 compliant. Oracle has had dates stored this way for many years. As long as dates are stored in fields of type "Date," there are no Year 2000 compliance issues to resolve.

There are some problems when you're trying to store date information that is not to the nearest second. When you see the date of January 7 at 12 midnight as a value in a field, you don't know whether you are seeing the day January 7 or the time midnight on January 7. You cannot specify a date without implicitly declaring a time. You do not have to display the time in applications, but it exists in a database. This can cause problems when your level of precision in a date may be monthly or quarterly, such as magazine publishing dates, which only list a month and year. What is stored for July 1999? If we know that precision is only quarterly, it is not a problem. For weekly magazines published on a specific day, how can this be handled? You can create a separate field to store periodicity information, or create a separate field for each different type of periodicity. Our generic approach favors storing periodicity in a separate field so that if changes are made, no changes to the data model are needed. Alternatively, you can provide separate domains for Monthly and Quarterly dates.

Another issue that arises with dates is possible restriction of ranges for a particular date. Range checks on date domains should be based on the system date, so that the ranges don't become out of date. For example, if you were using birth dates of employees, you might want to use SYSDATE – 100 years. Even this could be problematic if you maintain historical information about employees for companies in business a long time. Never assume that this system won't be in use 40 years from now. Who would have envisioned that systems created in the '60s would still be in use in 2000?

You may want to create date ranges based on specific named start dates. For example, for birth date, you may want to use the earliest birth date for someone in your system. For transaction dates, the range should be from the earliest transaction date currently in the system up through the system date, or the system date plus some time period for logging new transactions. For example, in a system involving project planning with milestones, the appropriate domain for milestones is the earliest date for information migrated from the legacy system through the system date plus 20 years, because the client was preparing long range plans.

Storing years (fiscal or tax) usually doesn't involve date fields. Years are stored in a 4-character field. We recognize that in the year 10,000, someone will have to deal with this problem as well. But it won't be any of us.

For storing dates, we suggest using the domains shown in Table 6-5.

We strongly urge using validation ranges whenever possible for dates and times to ensure that incorrect transaction dates cannot be entered (for example, Year 02).

The first date domain would require a database trigger to perform the truncation of the date value. If an application were using SYSDATE as the default value, the inserted value would store the time at which the transaction took place. If this information is not appropriate, then you can remove it through a database trigger that performs a TRUNC on that column.

Name	Type	Length	Precision	Min	Max	Values	Default
Date	Date					Truncate to midnight	
Month	Date					Truncate to lowest month	
Qtr	Date					Truncate to lowest quarter	
Time	Date						
Year	Number	4		1900	Sysdate year + 30		
Birth date	Date			1900	sysdate		
Emp Birth date	Date			1900	Sysdate – 15 years		
Tran date	Date			1970 or earliest transaction date	Sysdate + max lead time		Sysdate
Plan date	Date			1970	Sysdate + 30 years		

TABLE 6-5. *Suggested Domains for Dates*

The domain object type would simply be as follows in Code Example 6-6:

```
CREATE OR REPLACE TYPE DATE_MIDNIGHT AS OBJECT (
COL          DATE)
/
```

Code Example 6-6

Notice that we have not gained anything from the database perspective by defining this domain object type, as we could have simply defined the datatype of the column as DATE. However, this implementation is similar to the Boolean implementations from earlier in the chapter, in that the corresponding Oracle Designer domains would be more flexible than the database domains. The domain name indicates that there is additional validation attached to this domain, though it is physically attached to the columns, not to the members of the object type.

The following example uses the DATE_MIDNIGHT object type and a database trigger to ensure that the transaction date only records the month, day, and year of the transaction as shown in Code Example 6-7.

NOTE

Database Triggers do not support Object or Collection Type :NEW columns to be modified as of Oracle8i. The syntax shown in the following examples is correct, but is not yet supported.

```
--***Example_06_06 is prerequisite
CREATE TABLE TRANS (
TRANS_ID      NUMBER (10) NOT NULL PRIMARY KEY,
TRANS_DATE    DATE_MIDNIGHT NOT NULL)
/

CREATE OR REPLACE TRIGGER BIU_TRANS
BEFORE INSERT OR UPDATE
ON TRANS
FOR EACH ROW
BEGIN
:NEW.trans_date.col := trunc(:new.trans_date.col);
END;
/
```

Code Example 6-7

Note that Oracle Designer will not generate this trigger for you. You will most likely store this rule as part of the domain description in Oracle Designer, and then create the trigger during physical implementation.

The DATE_MONTH and DATE_QUARTER datatypes can essentially be created in the same way as the DATE_MIDNIGHT datatype. The syntax is provided below. Note that the date-based columns will still store a value for the entire date format, regardless of whether you choose to utilize each and every component. For example, the DATE_QUARTER domain would return a value of '01-JUL-1998' when it performs the following TRUNC. Unfortunately, we cannot attach default login to the domain to perform TRUNK automatically. Instead, we must write the code.

```
TRUNC('18-AUG-1998,'Q')
```

It does not return a numeric value indicating the quarter (i.e., '1' for the period covering January – March, '2' for the period covering April – June, etc.). See Code Examples 6-8 and 6-9.

Date Truncated to first day of month

```
CREATE OR REPLACE TYPE DATE_MONTH AS OBJECT (
COL          DATE)
/
CREATE TABLE TRANS (
TRANS_ID      NUMBER (10) NOT NULL PRIMARY KEY,
TRANS_DATE    DATE_MONTH NOT NULL)
/

CREATE OR REPLACE TRIGGER BIU_TRANS
BEFORE INSERT OR UPDATE
ON TRANS
FOR EACH ROW
BEGIN
:NEW.TRANS_DATE.COL := TRUNC(:NEW.TRANS_DATE.COL,'MON');
END;
/
```

Code Example 6-8

Date Truncated to first day of quarter

```
CREATE OR REPLACE TYPE DATE_QUARTER AS OBJECT (
COL          DATE)
/
CREATE TABLE TRANS (
TRANS_ID      NUMBER (10) NOT NULL PRIMARY KEY,
TRANS_DATE    DATE_QUARTER NOT NULL)
/

CREATE OR REPLACE TRIGGER BIU_TRANS
BEFORE INSERT OR UPDATE
```

```
ON TRANS
FOR EACH ROW
BEGIN
:NEW.TRANS_DATE.COL := TRUNC(:NEW.TRANS_DATE.COL,'Q');
END;
/
```

Code Example 6-9

Time

The Time Domain is the same as the DATE data type, in that there is no restriction applied to it. Again, you will create object types that directly correspond with the domains in Oracle Designer primarily because of default values and additional data checks. In this case, we may want to create two domains, one that defaults to SYSDATE, and another that does not. The two domains will be identical in every aspect except name, though the columns that reference them may contain a default value based upon the Oracle Designer version of the domain.

```
CREATE OR REPLACE TYPE DATE_TIME AS OBJECT (
COL        DATE)
/

CREATE OR REPLACE TYPE DATE_TIME_SYSDATE AS OBJECT (
COL        DATE)
/

CREATE TABLE PERSON (
EMP_ID         NUMBER (10) NOT NULL PRIMARY KEY,
ENAME          VARCHAR2 NOT NULL,
HIRE_DATE      DATE_TIME,
CREATED_DATE   DATE_TIME_SYSDATE NOT NULL,
MODIFIED_DATE  DATE_TIME SYSDATE NOT NULL)
/
```

Code Example 6-10

Year

The year domain would be implemented as NUMBER(4). You might also want a check constraint to ensure that the value is BETWEEN 1900 AND

2100. This way, you can be sure that the year entered will fall within an acceptable range.

```
CREATE OR REPLACE TYPE YEAR AS OBJECT (COL          number (4),
MAP MEMBER FUNCTION YEAR_MAP RETURN NUMBER)
/

CREATE OR REPLACE TYPE BODY YEAR IS
MAP MEMBER FUNCTION YEAR_MAP RETURN NUMBER IS
BEGIN
RETURN COL;
END;
END;
/

CREATE TABLE SEMESTER (
CLASS_YEAR          YEAR NOT NULL CHECK (CLASS_YEAR.COL BETWEEN 1900
AND 2100),
SEMESTER_CD        VARCHAR2 (5))
/

CREATE OR REPLACE TRIGGER BIU_SEMESTER
BEFORE INSERT OR UPDATE
ON SEMESTER
FOR EACH ROW
DECLARE
INVALID_YEAR    EXCEPTION;
BEGIN
IF :NEW.CLASS_YEAR.COL BETWEEN 1900 AND 2100
THEN NULL;
ELSE RAISE INVALID_YEAR;
END IF;
EXCEPTION
WHEN
INVALID_YEAR THEN
raise_application_error('-20001','CLASS_YEAR IS NOT A VALID YEAR
BETWEEN 1900 AND 2100.');
END;
/
```

Code Example 6-11

Date of Birth

For the Date of Birth (DOB) domain, we will only require the creation of the domain and then a check constraint on each column instantiated upon that domain. The following code represents the birth date domain and an instantiation of the domain, including a check constraint.

```
CREATE OR REPLACE TYPE DOB AS OBJECT (
COL           DATE)
/

CREATE TABLE EMP (
EMP_ID        NUMBER (10) NOT NULL PRIMARY KEY,
NAME_TX       VARCHAR2 (60) NOT NULL,
BIRTH_DATE    DOB CHECK (BIRTH_DATE.COL > SYSDATE-5475,
'DD-MON-YYYY'))
/
```

Code Example 6-12

   Note that the check constraint deducted 5,475 days, or 15 years, from SYSDATE. The idea is that we are absolutely sure that we will not have any employees younger than 16 years old.

Transaction Date

The transaction date domain will require an object type and a BEFORE INSERT database trigger for each instantiation of the domain. The reason this check cannot be performed within a check constraint is that it requires validation against the transaction date of the earliest recorded transaction. This means that we must perform a query against the table to determine the low end of the transaction range. The reason we only create a BEFORE INSERT trigger is that we will not permit transaction dates to be updated.

```
CREATE OR REPLACE TYPE TRAN_DATE AS OBJECT (
COL              DATE,
MAP MEMBER FUNCTION TRAN_DATE_MAP RETURN DATE)
/

CREATE OR REPLACE TYPE BODY TRAN_DATE IS
MAP MEMBER FUNCTION TRAN_DATE_MAP RETURN DATE IS
BEGIN
RETURN COL;
```

```
END;
END;
/

CREATE TABLE TRANS (
TRANS_ID        NUMBER (10) NOT NULL PRIMARY KEY,
TRANS_DATE      TRAN_DATE NOT NULL)
/

CREATE OR REPLACE TRIGGER BI_TRANS
BEFORE INSERT
ON TRANS
FOR EACH ROW
DECLARE
CURSOR C1 IS
SELECT MIN(TRANS_DATE) FIRST_TRAN
FROM TRANS;
INVALID_DATE EXCEPTION;
V_DATE   DATE;
BEGIN
FOR C1_REC IN C1 LOOP
V_DATE := C1_REC.FIRST_TRAN.COL;
 IF :NEW.TRANS_DATE.COL BETWEEN V_DATE AND SYSDATE + 3650 T
HEN
NULL;
ELSE RAISE INVALID_DATE;
END IF;
END LOOP;
EXCEPTION
WHEN INVALID_DATE THEN
raise_application_error('-20001','TRANSACTION DATE MUST BE
BETWEEN '
                                ||TO_CHAR(V_DATE)||' AND
'
                                ||TO_CHAR(SYSDATE + 3650)
||',');
END;
/
```

Code Example 6-13

This trigger ensures that the newly entered transaction date falls between the date of the first recorded transaction and three years from the current date.

Financial Transaction Domain

The financial transaction domain shown in Code Example 6-14 would be exactly the same as the transaction domain defined earlier, except the allowable future transaction range would probably go as far as 30 years or more into the future.

```
DROP TABLE FIN_TRANS;
DROP TYPE FIN_TRAN_DATE;
CREATE OR REPLACE TYPE FIN_TRAN_DATE AS OBJECT (
COL             DATE,
MAP MEMBER FUNCTION DT_MAP RETURN DATE)
/

CREATE OR REPLACE TYPE BODY FIN_TRAN_DATE IS
MAP MEMBER FUNCTION DT_MAP RETURN DATE IS
BEGIN
RETURN COL;
END;
END;
/

CREATE TABLE FIN_TRANS (
TRANS_ID        NUMBER (10) NOT NULL PRIMARY KEY,
TRANS_DATE      FIN_TRAN_DATE NOT NULL)
/

CREATE OR REPLACE TRIGGER BI_TRANS
BEFORE INSERT
ON FIN_TRANS
FOR EACH ROW
DECLARE
CURSOR C1 IS
SELECT MIN(TRANS_DATE) FIRST_TRAN
FROM FIN_TRANS;
INVALID_DATE EXCEPTION;
V_DATE    DATE;
BEGIN
FOR C1_REC IN C1 LOOP
V_DATE := C1_REC.FIRST_TRAN;
 IF :NEW.TRANS_DATE BETWEEN FIRST_TRAN AND SYSDATE + 10950 THEN
NULL;
ELSE RAISE INVALID_DATE;
END IF;
END LOOP;
```

```
EXCEPTION
WHEN INVALID_DATE THEN
RAISE_APPLICATION_ERROR('-20001','TRANSACTION DATE MUST BE
BETWEEN'||TO_CHAR(V_DATE)||
                          ' AND '||TO_CHAR(SYSDATE + 10950)||'.');
END;
/
```

Code Example 6-14

Number

Numbers are the most difficult domains to determine. There are many different levels of validation and precision necessary when you're using numbers. For example, Number includes all of the following:

- Counts (integers)
- Continuous measurements including percentages
- Currencies

For number fields, we not only have to worry about minimum and maximum length, but also level of precision, namely number of places after the decimal point. Typically, many different number ranges and precision domains are needed. Originally, we believed that restricting domains to positive numbers was a good idea, but in practice, this rarely seems to happen. For example, you would think that counts for inventories would be positive; however, backordered items may be recorded as negative. The most common place to use a positive restriction is on numbers that are primary keys being populated with a sequence so that a constraint is irrelevant. Using our generic approach, you typically do not need to specify ranges on numbers, because the range is implied in the field length.

Money

Currency is one of the most interesting items to contend with. For people in the United States, it is easy to use NUMBER 14,2 for the currency datatype. There are several problems with this strategy. Foreign currencies may require more or fewer digits. For example, systems storing transactions in Japanese yen usually do not require numbers beyond the decimal. Italian lira or Russian rubles may require higher maximum values. Even for U.S. currency, numbers may not need to be tracked to the penny. You may be tracking only to the dollar or thousands of dollars.

Another complication is that you may have currency figures within the database where calculating numbers beyond two places after the decimal is required, such as the values of some financial instruments.

You cannot automatically assume that currency amounts may not be negative. Therefore, you may want to allow negative numbers to support transactions and net negative balances on accounts.

The following domains might be appropriate for supporting U.S. currency:

- N6_2   NUMBER 6,2

- N14_2   NUMBER 14,2

```
CREATE OR REPLACE TYPE N6_2 AS OBJECT (
COL                      NUMBER (6,2))
/

CREATE OR REPLACE TYPE N14_2 AS OBJECT (
COL                      NUMBER (14,2))
/
```

Code Example 6-15

Depending upon the specific system, you might also want the same two domains restricted with more or fewer significant digits past the decimal point. You can even specify that values must be in intervals greater than integers. For example, NUMBER (6,-3) forces values to be stored in intervals of 1000. This may be useful for international currencies requiring at least 1000:1 exchange rates. This means that to support all international currencies, the following domains should be used:

- N10_2   NUMBER 10,2

- N20_2   NUMBER 20,2

Use Code Example 6-16 for this purpose.

```
CREATE OR REPLACE TYPE N10_2 AS OBJECT (
COL                      NUMBER (10,2))
/

CREATE OR REPLACE TYPE N20_2 AS OBJECT (
COL                      NUMBER (20,2))
/
```

Code Example 6-16

Suggesting domains for currency is completely system specific. The appropriate domains for a large New York brokerage house would be different from the currency domains for a small retailer.

A list of currency domains we have used is shown in the following Table 6-6. It would be unusual if all of them were needed by any one system. Again, you will find some overlap between the structure of these datatypes and the more generic datatypes listed above. It might look like unnecessary overhead today, but it will embrace upcoming features seamlessly. These domains can easily be created following the syntax noted throughout this chapter.

Name	Type	Length	Precision	Min	Max	Values	Default
Small amt.	Number	10	2				
Large amt.	Number	14	2				
Small amt. precise	Number	16	6				
Large amt. precise	Number	18	6				
Intl small amt.	Number	12					
Intl large amt.	Number	16					
Intl small amt. precise	Number	16	4				
Intl large amt. precise	Number	20	4				

TABLE 6-6.   *Currency Domains*

Percents

Percents have many of the same complications as money. It is easy to think of them as a 2,0 field. However, depending upon the application, you may want a much higher degree of precision. There is no reason to believe that percents greater than 100 are impossible. Typically, most applications will only require 1 percent domain. Using 5,2 or 6,2 is usually safe—unless you are dealing with a financial institution, in which case, 10,5 or 15,10 may be necessary. The percent domains we use are shown in the following Table 6-7.

```
CREATE OR REPLACE TYPE SMALL_PCT AS OBJECT (
COL              NUMBER (5,2))
/

CREATE OR REPLACE TYPE LARGE_PCT AS OBJECT (
COL              NUMBER (6,2))
/

CREATE OR REPLACE TYPE SMALL_FIN_PCT AS OBJECT (
COL              NUMBER (10,5))
/

CREATE OR REPLACE TYPE LARGE_FIN_PCT AS OBJECT (
COL              NUMBER (15,10))
/
```

Code Example 6-17

Name	Type	Length	Precision	Min	Max	Values	Default
Pcnt	Number	3		-100	100		
Big pcnt	Number	5					
Pcnt precise	Number	5	2	-100	100		
Big Pcnt precise	Number	7	2				
Finance pcnt	Number	15	5				

TABLE 6-7. *Percent Domains*

Other Numbers

We need to have several domains to support numbers in general. To avoid confusion, percent and currency domains should not be used for noncurrency or percent numbers. The following domains are used for numbers:

SMALL_INT	Number 5
LARGE_INT	Number 10
SMALL _NR	Number 10,5
LARGE_NR	Number 10

Scientific applications may require greater precision and will need additional domains. Code Example 6-18 shows the code for these domains.

```
CREATE OR REPLACE TYPE SMALL_INT AS OBJECT (
COL              NUMBER (5))
/

CREATE OR REPLACE TYPE LARGE_INT AS OBJECT (
COL              NUMBER (10))
/

CREATE OR REPLACE TYPE SMALL_NR AS OBJECT (
COL              NUMBER (10,5))
/

CREATE OR REPLACE TYPE LARGE_NR AS OBJECT (
COL              NUMBER (10))
/
```

Code Example 6-18

Other Datatypes

Datatypes other than the ones mentioned here are rare enough not to merit a domain. Long text, OLE text, pictures, movies, and files can usually be supported without domains.

Conclusion

The list of domains that we have presented in this chapter should support most business systems. You should not apply domains without thought. You may want to use a slightly larger or slightly smaller list of domains. Given any particular system, you may need more domains to support higher levels of precision (for example, for scientific applications), but we have found this list to be adequate for most business systems.

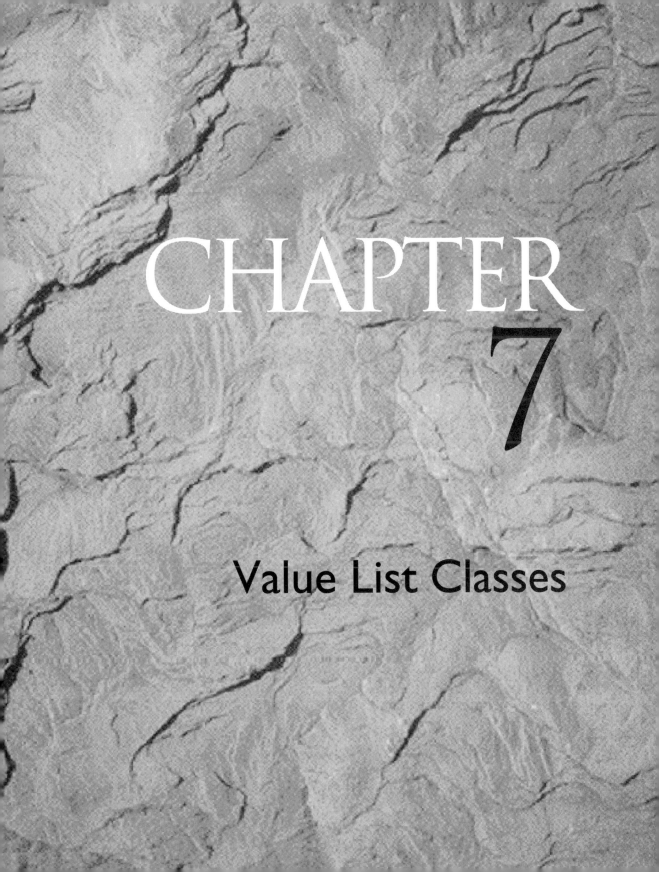

CHAPTER
7

Value List Classes

e discussed value lists briefly in Chapter 4. However, more detail is needed, because value list classes are an important aspect of database design. A *value list class* supports one or more attributes in one or more object classes. These classes store a valid list of values within the system. The objects in a value list class do not correspond to real-world objects of interest. They are merely valid values for other attributes.

With the advent of object-relational modeling, as we overload and genericize more tables, we will have main table object classes that must be typed in order to determine the type of each object in the object class. By use of the techniques described in this book, it is likely that over half of the object classes in a data model will be value list classes.

What are we trying to accomplish with a data model? We are trying to store information about an organization. But we need to store the correct information. There are usually many business rules that define the valid values for fields. A large portion of data modeling is attempting to incorporate as many of these rules as possible in the data model. One of the most efficient ways to do this is through *domain validation* of field values, which means determining a list of valid values for each field.

Object Class or Value List Class?

Often it is difficult to determine whether a given set of items should be designated as a regular object class or a value list class. For example, in a class storing a list of countries for address information, you could argue whether this should be an object class or a value list class. Clearly, countries are things of interest in the real world. However, for most systems, this is an external, static list that rarely changes.

We say that a class is a *value list class* if it meets one or more of the following criteria:

1. The class is composed of items that do not represent any particular object in the real world. Examples include Gender and Primary Colors.

2. The class is composed of valid values that are a matter of choice. An example would be valid car colors for a given car manufacturer.

3. The class is composed of values that are completely external to the system but represent real things that are changeable. We may only be interested in a subset of these values. Examples include counties, states, provinces, postal codes, and telephone exchanges.

4. The class is composed of artificial internal groupings of values that are relatively stable. Examples include geographic regions or, for a retail store, designating certain apparel model numbers as "Spring" or "Fall."

What makes a value list class different from any other object class? Functionally, value list classes are maintained through a centralized administrative function. They tend to be more stable than primary classes. The notion of value list classes must include intent on the part of the users. Is this something that is of interest in its own right, or is its only function in the system to validate another field? Even with intent, two users may differ in their opinions. Fortunately, there should be no real cost to misclassifying an object class as a value list class. There is nothing to prevent a core data table from having the same structure and being maintained the same way as a value list class. You could argue against the need to use value list classes at all. However, they are a useful way to divide the object classes, although there is no one, clear, concise definition to determine, in every case, whether a given object class is a value list class.

A word of caution: We worked on a system where a number of core data tables were misspecified as value list classes. This resulted in an automatic assumption that little, if any, analysis would be necessary on these structures. Unfortunately, a great deal of analysis was overlooked, and development of major portions of the system was delayed.

What Goes into a Value List Class?

Once we have defined a value list class, we need to decide what attributes should go into it. Appropriate attributes for a value list class include the following:

- *Code* This is a two- to ten-character short descriptive identifier of the object class. Typically, you should have such a short description, particularly in reports where space is a consideration.

- *Value Name* This is a 40- to 80-character description of the value list object.

- *Active_YN* This is an indicator to allow for the deletion of objects from the value list class while still allowing the object to exist so that it can be attached historically. This indicator is not usually necessary in a data warehouse.

- *Order* A number that is used to provide a logical sort order for the values.

    You can also add standard system auditing columns such as CREATE_DT, CREATE_BY, MOD_DT, and MOD_BY.

The following table maintains status values for Purchase Orders (i.e., PO). Notice the prefix "VL_". This prefix indicates that the object class is a Value List object class. Also note that the name of the table (i.e., PO) that will reference the objects in this value list class is included in the name of the value list class (i.e., VL_PO_STATUS) as shown in Code Example 7-1.

```
CREATE TABLE VL_PO_STATUS (
STATUS_CD       VARCHAR2(2) NOT NULL PRIMARY KEY,
NAME_TX         VARCHAR2(40) NOT NULL,
ORDER_NR        NUMBER,
ACTIVE_YN       CHAR(1) default 'Y' NOT NULL ,
CREAT_BY        VARCHAR2 (30) NOT NULL,
MOD_BY          VARCHAR2 (30),
CREAT_DT        DATE NOT NULL,
MOD_DT          DATE)
/
```

Code Example 7-1

In more tightly controlled systems, you may want to have START_DT and END_DT fields to show the period for which that value is valid. This means that a value may become invalid for a period and can later be reactivated. However, we would have no way of historically storing periods of invalidity. We have never encountered a requirement to store these types of historical changes in reference tables. However, if such a requirement were to exist, we could support it through one of the generic history structures as discussed in Chapter 15.

Overloading Value List Classes

A single domain validation can be used to validate the values for multiple attributes in different object classes. This commonly occurs in status tables. Typically, statuses include values such as Pending, Initial, Cancel, and Close. In a particular system, most status values are common to multiple objects. But one class of object may use a slightly different list of valid values than another. In this event, you can add indicator attributes in the value list class. We only recommend applying this technique for closely associated object classes. For example, we can have a status for a purchase order (PO) as well as a status for a purchase order detail. For a PO, the appropriate statuses are Initial, Pending, Approved, Completed, and Canceled. For a PO Detail, the appropriate statuses are Initial, Pending, Back Ordered, Completed, and Canceled.

There is some overlap between the two lists, but each has status values pertaining to only that object type. We want to store these statuses together. The initial status has the same semantic meaning in both contexts and should be stored in a single same place in the database. Using a traditional approach, we would store the valid status values independently. Physically, they would be stored either in separate reference tables, or in the same general reference table with the table and attribute identifier to indicate which table/attribute each code validated, or as two independent check constraints.

All of these traditional methods of handling the two status lists violate the premise that all information should only be stored in one place in the database. The approach we advocate can be implemented using the structure shown in Table 7-1.

Status STATUS_CD	NAME_TX	For PO	For PO_DTL
Init	Initial	T	T
Pend	Pending	T	T
Comp	Completed	T	T
Canc	Canceled	T	T
Appr	Approved	T	F
Back	Back Ordered	F	T

TABLE 7-1.   *Example of Value List Table*

Overloading value list classes is not done merely for expediency. To do otherwise would result in a denormalized structure. A more complex structure using generalization could be used, but the overloading strategy is the easiest and cleanest way to model. You could argue that if we are including different status classes in a system, they should be stored as independent classes even though they have overlapping values. This is wrong because the same value would be stored in two different places. This means that you are storing the same object twice in the database. You may wish to implement these as separate value list classes, but you should recognize that anytime you have the same value stored in two different value list classes with exactly the same semantics, these are the same object. To be theoretically correct in a relational or object-relational database, objects should only be stored once.

Let's assume that both PO and PO_DTL only require the status values listed in Table 7-1. Notice that the lists are identical. The most common implementation would be to create a single reference table, VL_PO_STATUS, and to create foreign keys from both PO and PO_DTL to VL_PO_STATUS as shown in Code Example 7-2.

```
CREATE TABLE VENDOR (
VENDOR_ID       NUMBER (10) NOT NULL PRIMARY KEY,
DESCR_TX        VARCHAR2 (40))
/


CREATE TABLE ITEM (
ITEM_ID         NUMBER (10) NOT NULL PRIMARY KEY,
DESCR_TX        VARCHAR2 (40))
/

CREATE TABLE VL_PO_STATUS (
STATUS_CD       VARCHAR2 (4) NOT NULL PRIMARY KEY,
DESC_TX         VARCHAR2 (40) NOT NULL,
ACTIVE_YN       CHAR (1) DEFAULT 'Y' NOT NULL ,
CREAT_BY        VARCHAR2 (30) DEFAULT USER NOT NULL ,
MOD_BY          VARCHAR2 (30),
CREAT_DT        DATE DEFAULT SYSDATE NOT NULL ,
MOD_DT          DATE)
/

INSERT INTO VL_PO_STATUS (STATUS_CD, DESC_TX) VALUES ('INIT','INITIAL');
INSERT INTO VL_PO_STATUS (STATUS_CD, DESC_TX) VALUES ('PEND','PENDING');
```

```
INSERT INTO VL_PO_STATUS (STATUS_CD, DESC_TXX) VALUES ('CANC','CANCELED')
INSERT INTO VL_PO_STATUS (STATUS_CD, DESC_TX) VALUES ('COMP','COMPLETED');

CREATE TABLE PO (
PO_ID    NUMBER (10) NOT NULL PRIMARY KEY,
VENDOR_ID  NUMBER (10)  NOT NULL REFERENCES VENDOR (VENDOR_ID),
STATUS_CD  VARCHAR2 (4) NOT NULL REFERENCES VL_PO_STATUS (STATUS_CD))
/

CREATE TABLE PO_DTL (
PO_ID       NUMBER (10) NOT NULL REFERENCES PO (PO_ID),
PO_DTL_ID  NUMBER (3) NOT NULL,
ITEM_ID     NUMBER (10) NOT NULL REFERENCES ITEM (ITEM_ID),
QTY         NUMBER   (10,2) NOT NULL,
STATUS_CD VARCHAR2 (4) NOT NULL REFERENCES VL_PO_STATUS (STATUS_CD),
PRIMARY KEY (PO_ID,PO_DTL_ID))
/
```

Code Example 7-2

This structure works as long as the status value class lists remain identical across the two object classes. However, things get significantly more complicated when the two value class lists begin to deviate, as shown in Table 7-2.

Status STATUS_CD	NAME_TX	For PO	For PO_DTL
Init	Initial	T	T
Pend	Pending	T	T
Apprv	Approved	F	T
Comp	Completed	T	T
Canc	Canceled	T	T
Prog	In Progress	T	F
Bkord	Back Ordered	F	T

TABLE 7-2.   *Overloaded Value List Classes*

Notice that by using these value lists, we can identify codes that are only valid for one of the classes. We typically create independent status tables based upon subdividing the scope of the business areas. The VL_PO_STATUS table just shown is a clear-cut example of creating a single status value list class to serve a specific object class.

However, there is a case to be made that status objects for PO and PO_DTL objects are very similar, if not identical in nature. There may be statuses that apply to one and not the other, such as the status shown earlier for "In Progress," which only applies to PO objects, and "Back Ordered," which only applies to PO_DTL objects. But in the end, the majority of the statuses (i.e., Initial, Pending, Approved, Completed, Canceled) are truly the same objects.

Therefore, creating two independent value list classes as in Code Example 7-3, one for PO statuses and another for PO_DTL statuses, would be a denormalization.

```
CREATE TABLE VL_PO_STATUS (
STATUS_CD        VARCHAR2 (5) NOT NULL PRIMARY KEY,
DESC_TX          VARCHAR2 (40) NOT NULL,
ACTIVE_YN        CHAR (1) DEFAULT 'Y' NOT NULL ,
CREAT_BY         VARCHAR2 (30) DEFAULT USER NOT NULL ,
MOD_BY           VARCHAR2 (30),
CREAT_DT         DATE DEFAULT SYSDATE NOT NULL ,
MOD_DT           DATE)
/

INSERT INTO VL_PO_STATUS (STATUS_CD, DESC_TX) VALUES ('INIT','INITIAL');
INSERT INTO VL_PO_STATUS (STATUS_CD, DESC_TX) VALUES ('PEND','PENDING');
INSERT INTO VL_PO_STATUS (STATUS_CD, DESC_TX) VALUES ('CANC','CANCELED');
INSERT INTO VL_PO_STATUS (STATUS_CD, DESC_TX) VALUES ('COMP','COMPLETED');
INSERT INTO VL_PO_STATUS (STATUS_CD, DESC_TX) VALUES ('PROG','IN PROGRESS');

CREATE TABLE VL_PO_DTL_STATUS (
STATUS_CD        VARCHAR2 (5) NOT NULL PRIMARY KEY,
DESC_TX          VARCHAR2 (40) NOT NULL,
ACTIVE_YN        CHAR (1) DEFAULT 'Y' NOT NULL ,
CREAT_BY         VARCHAR2 (30) DEFAULT USER NOT NULL ,
MOD_BY           VARCHAR2 (30),
CREAT_DT         DATE DEFAULT SYSDATE NOT NULL,
MOD_DT           DATE)
/
```

```
INSERT INTO VL_PO_DTL_STATUS (STATUS_CD, DESC_TX) VALUES ('INIT','INITIAL');
INSERT INTO VL_PO_DTL_STATUS (STATUS_CD, DESC_TX) VALUES ('PEND','PENDING');
INSERT INTO VL_PO DTL_STATUS (STATUS_CD, DESC_TX) VALUES ('APPRV','APPROVED');
INSERT INTO VL_PO DTL_STATUS (STATUS_CD, DESC_TX) VALUES ('CANC','CANCELED');
INSERT INTO VL_PO_DTL_STATUS (STATUS_CD, DESC_TX) VALUES ('COMP','COMPLETED');
INSERT INTO VL_PO_DTL_STATUS (STATUS_CD, DESC_TX) VALUES ('BKORD','BACK ORDER');
```

Code Example 7-3

If at some time a decision were made to change the "Pending" status to "Retained," this change would have to be performed in both of the value list classes, requiring the following UPDATE statements shown in Code Example 7-4.

```
--example_07_03 is prerequisite
UPDATE VL_PO_STATUS SET STATUS_CD = 'RET',
                        DESC_TX   = 'RETAINED',
                        MOD_BY    = USER,
                        MOD_DT    = SYSDATE
            WHERE       STATUS_CD = 'PEND'
/

UPDATE VL_PO_DTL_STATUS SET STATUS_CD = 'RET',
                            DESC_TX   = 'RETAINED',
                            MOD_BY    = USER,
                            MOD_DT    = SYSDATE
                WHERE       STATUS_CD = 'PEND'
/
```

Code Example 7-4

If there is any chance that these value lists may change, though a subset of their values remains synonymous, then the preceding design should be waived in lieu of the following structure, again using PO and PO_DTL statuses as Code Example 7-5 shows

```
DROP TABLE VL_PO__PO_DTL_STATUS;
CREATE TABLE VL_PO__PO_DTL_STATUS (
STATUS_CD      VARCHAR2 (5) NOT NULL PRIMARY KEY,
DESC_TX        VARCHAR2 (40) NOT NULL,
ACTIVE_YN      CHAR (1) DEFAULT 'Y' NOT NULL ,
CREAT_BY       VARCHAR2 (30) DEFAULT USER NOT NULL ,
MOD_BY         VARCHAR2 (30),
CREAT_DT       DATE default SYSDATE NOT NULL,
```

```
MOD_DT          DATE,
PO_YN           CHAR (1) DEFAULT 'Y' NOT NULL ,

PO_DTL_YN       CHAR (1) DEFAULT 'Y' NOT NULL )
/

INSERT INTO VL_PO__PO_DTL_STATUS (STATUS_CD, DESC_TX, PO_YN, PO_DTL_YN)
VALUES ('INIT','INITIAL','Y','Y');
INSERT INTO VL_PO__PO_DTL_STATUS (STATUS_CD, DESC_TX, PO_YN, PO_DTL_YN)
VALUES ('PEND','PENDING','Y','Y');
INSERT INTO VL_PO__PO_DTL_STATUS (STATUS_CD, DESC_TX, PO_YN, PO_DTL_YN)
VALUES ('APPRV','APPROVED','N','Y');
INSERT INTO VL_PO__PO_DTL_STATUS (STATUS_CD, DESC_TX, PO_YN, PO_DTL_YN)
VALUES ('CANC','CANCELED','Y','Y');
INSERT INTO VL_PO__PO_DTL_STATUS (STATUS_CD, DESC_TX, PO_YN, PO_DTL_YN)
VALUES ('COMP','COMPLETED','Y','Y');
INSERT INTO VL_PO__PO_DTL_STATUS (STATUS_CD, DESC_TX, PO_YN, PO_DTL_YN)
VALUES ('BKORD','BACK ORDER','N','Y');
INSERT INTO VL_PO__PO_DTL_STATUS (STATUS_CD, DESC_TX, PO_YN, PO_DTL_YN)
VALUES ('PROG','IN PROGRESS','T','F');
```

Code Example 7-5

We propose using this single table structure to accommodate value list classes for closely associated object classes. There is an overlap of status objects for POs and PO_DTLs. Using this structure, you would identify the different statuses, and set the PO_YN and PO_DTL_YN indicators to "Y," if the respective object class were to utilize the status.

Using this structure, changing the "Pending" status to "Retained" would only require a single update. Adding status values does not affect development. Applications are prebuilt with WHERE clauses that filter based upon the PO_YN and PO_DTL_YN indicators, so applications will automatically pick up any value list changes.

The same status table can be easily modified to validate additional status attributes in other tables by adding additional indicator columns, though we strongly advocate limiting the exposure of a given status table to, at most, one business area.

You could argue that what should be done is to have a list of possible tables and a list of attributes, and to create an association between the two to validate which codes are appropriate for which attributes. However, this is a more complex structure requiring a more complex application to maintain. Using this reference table to validate other status attributes requires a modification to the database anyway. Therefore, we believe that the easiest way to implement this construct is with the method outlined earlier.

Order

What happens if you have a reference table and you want to display items in a non-alphabetical order? For example, for Valid Statuses (Initial, Pending, Completed, Canceled), users want to see the pop-up list in this order. There may be no column in the table to sort on to achieve the desired result. We solve this problem by adding an order column to every reference table. In code, to access reference tables, you sort by the Order column first, and then the Name or the Code column is sorted second. If you end up not using the Order column, you will sort by the next most logical attribute.

The following VL_PO_STATUS value list class in Code Example 7-6 has been modified to include an ORDER_NR column. The insert statements that follow set the ORDER BY flag to list the statuses in the order Initial, Pending, Approved, Completed, Canceled, In Progress, Back Ordered. Note that the ORDER_BY values are incremented by 5. This is to allow ample room for the adjustment of ordering based upon the addition of status values in the future.

```
DROP TABLE VL_PO__PO_DTL_STATUS;
CREATE TABLE VL_PO__PO_DTL_STATUS (
STATUS_CD       VARCHAR2 (5) NOT NULL PRIMARY KEY,
DESC_TX         VARCHAR2 (40) NOT NULL,
ACTIVE_YN       CHAR (1) DEFAULT 'Y' NOT NULL ,
ORDER_NR        NUMBER (3),
CREAT_BY        VARCHAR2 (30) DEFAULT USER NOT NULL ,
MOD_BY          VARCHAR2 (30),
CREAT_DT        DATE DEFAULT SYSDATE NOT NULL,
MOD_DT          DATE,
PO_YN           CHAR (1) DEFAULT 'Y' NOT NULL ,
PO_DTL_YN       CHAR (1) DEFAULT 'Y' NOT NULL )
/
INSERT INTO VL_PO__PO_DTL_STATUS (STATUS_CD, DESC_TX, ORDER_NR, PO_YN, PO_DTL_YN)
VALUES ('INIT','INITIAL',1,'Y','Y');
INSERT INTO VL_PO__PO_DTL_STATUS (STATUS_CD, DESC_TX, ORDER_NR, PO_YN, PO_DTL_YN)
VALUES ('PEND','PENDING',2,'Y','Y');
INSERT INTO VL_PO__PO_DTL_STATUS (STATUS_CD, DESC_TX, ORDER_NR, PO_YN, PO_DTL_YN)
VALUES ('APPRV','APPROVED',3,'N','Y');
```

```
INSERT INTO VL_PO__PO_DTL_STATUS (STATUS_CD, DESC_TX, ORDER_NR, PO_YN, PO_DTL_YN)
VALUES ('CANC','CANCELED',5,'Y','Y');
INSERT INTO VL_PO__PO_DTL_STATUS (STATUS_CD, DESC_TX, ORDER_NR, PO_YN, PO_DTL_YN)
VALUES ('COMP','COMPLETED',4,'Y','Y');
INSERT INTO VL_PO__PO_DTL_STATUS (STATUS_CD, DESC_TX, ORDER_NR, PO_YN, PO_DTL_YN)
VALUES ('BKORD','BACK ORDER',7,'N','Y');
INSERT INTO VL_PO__PO_DTL_STATUS (STATUS_CD, DESC_TX, ORDER_NR, PO_YN, PO_DTL_YN)
VALUES ('PROG','IN PROGRESS',6,'T','F');
```

Code Example 7-6

Also note that only one ORDER_NR column is required, even though
there are multiple object classes sharing this value list class, because a
subset of these statuses will still maintain the exact ordering, give or take a
few additional status values.

Recursive Value List Tables

In many cases, you need to classify some type of object with a domain
reference. For example, all of these projects are of a particular type. The
project types themselves may fall into categories. The standard model for
this is shown in Figure 7-1, followed by the DDL shown in Code Example
7-7 to create these tables.

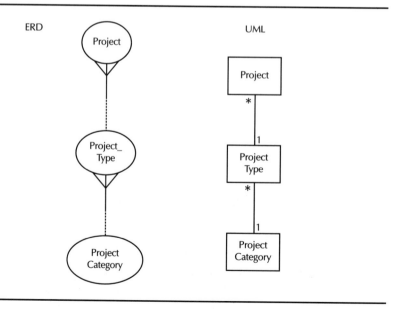

FIGURE 7-1. *Candidate for recursion*

```
CREATE TABLE PROJ_CTGY (
    PROJ_CTGY_CD        VARCHAR2 (2) NOT NULL PRIMARY KEY,
    DESCR_TX            VARCHAR2 (40) NOT NULL,
    ACTIVE_YN           CHAR (1) DEFAULT 'Y' NOT NULL ,
    ORDER_BY            NUMBER (3),
    CREAT_BY            VARCHAR2 (30) DEFAULT USER NOT NULL ,
    MOD_BY              VARCHAR2 (30),
    CREAT_DT            DATE DEFAULT SYSDATE NOT NULL,
    MOD_DT              DATE)
/

CREATE TABLE PROJ_TYPE (
    PROJ_TYPE_CD        VARCHAR2 (2) NOT NULL PRIMARY KEY,
    PROJ_CTGY_CD        VARCHAR2 (2) NOT NULL REFERENCES PROJ_CTGY (PROJ_CTGY_CD),
    DESCR_TX            VARCHAR2 (40) NOT NULL,
    ACTIVE_YN           CHAR (1) DEFAULT 'Y' NOT NULL ,
    ORDER_BY            NUMBER (3),
    CREAT_BY            VARCHAR2 (30) DEFAULT USER NOT NULL ,
    MOD_BY              VARCHAR2 (30),
    CREAT_DT            DATE NOT NULL,
    MOD_DT              DATE)
/

CREATE TABLE PROJECT (
    PROJECT_ID          NUMBER (10) NOT NULL PRIMARY KEY,
    PROJ_TYPE_CD        VARCHAR2 (2) NOT NULL REFERENCES PROJ_TYPE (PROJ_TYPE_CD),
    DESCR_TX            VARCHAR2 (40) NOT NULL,
    ACTIVE_YN           CHAR (1) DEFAULT 'Y' NOT NULL ,
    ORDER_BY            NUMBER (3),
    CREAT_BY            VARCHAR2 (30) DEFAULT USER NOT NULL ,
    MOD_BY              VARCHAR2 (30),
    CREAT_DT            DATE NOT NULL,
    MOD_DT              DATE)
/
```

Code Example 7-7

Although this structure works perfectly well, it is the beginning of a hierarchical rollup of categorization terms. This is an unstable model. First, we have typed objects. Second, we categorize the types. It is not absurd to think that we may want to categorize categories. Such multi-level structures are not uncommon in real-world systems such as the Dewey Decimal System, SIC codes, and, for manufacturing firms, the Parts and Inventory lists. For example, in a Parts Inventory table, we have an engine. It is categorized as an "Acme Co. Model 401b" which rolls up to "10HP Diesel

Engines/Diesel Engines/Engines/Power Train Component", etc. We do this so we can aggregate Sales, Repair Costs, and Purchase Prices at any of these levels. Levels that go this deep are unstable, because more levels can always be added. The model is made much more complex because behaviors or objects may be attached at one or more levels. In performing project specification of parts, we may only be able to specify one level, but will need associations with every level in the hierarchy. At this point, there would be five to six reference tables in a class with all associated references in addition to association classes for each one. Adding another level will cause the model to change significantly.

For all of these reasons, creating each level as its own class is not a good idea. Instead, we can create a model as shown in Figure 7-2. The DDL shown in Code Example 7-8 will only be shown in relational syntax.

```
--****example_07_07 prerequisite
DROP TABLE PROJECT;
DROP TABLE PROJ_TYPE;

CREATE TABLE PROJ_TYPE (
PROJ_TYPE_CD        VARCHAR2 (2) NOT NULL PRIMARY KEY,
PROJ_TYPE_CD_REF   VARCHAR2 (2) REFERENCES PROJ_TYPE (PROJ_TYPE_CD),
DESCR_TX            VARCHAR2 (40) NOT NULL,
ACTIVE_YN      CHAR (1) DEFAULT 'Y' NOT NULL ,
ORDER_BY       NUMBER (3),
CREAT_BY       VARCHAR2 (30) DEFAULT USER NOT NULL ,
MOD_BY         VARCHAR2 (30),
CREAT_DT       DATE DEFAULT SYSDATE NOT NULL,
MOD_DT         DATE)
/

CREATE TABLE PROJECT (
PROJECT_ID     NUMBER (10) NOT NULL PRIMARY KEY,
PROJ_TYPE_CD   VARCHAR2 (2) NOT NULL REFERENCES PROJ_TYPE (PROJ_TYPE_CD),
DESCR_TX        VARCHAR2 (40) NOT NULL,
ACTIVE_YN      CHAR (1) DEFAULT 'Y' NOT NULL ,
ORDER_BY       NUMBER (3),
CREAT_BY       VARCHAR2 (30) DEFAULT USER NOT NULL ,
MOD_BY         VARCHAR2 (30),
CREAT_DT       DATE DEFAULT SYSDATE NOT NULL,
MOD_DT          DATE)
/
```

Code Example 7-8

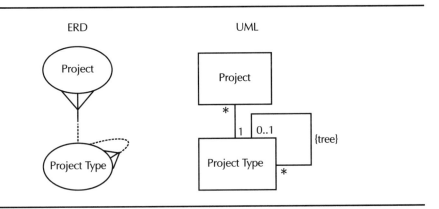

FIGURE 7-2.   *Models showing hierarchy*

This model is not entirely equivalent to the earlier model. There are several things wrong with this model:

1. We don't know what is a category and what is a type.

2. There is no way to enforce that only types get attached to projects in this model.

3. In the original model shown in Figure 7-1, there is a business rule that types roll up to categories. This model does not include that business rule.

4. There are only two levels in the tree in the first model. This cannot be discerned in the second model or stored in the data when the system is implemented using the second model.

To solve these problems, we will need another domain class pointing to the Project Type domain class. This takes care of determining whether something is a Type or a Class. Next, we need to enforce that types roll up to categories. We will place a recursive 0..1/ 0..1 on the Project Type Level class. This allows us to store the business rule that Types roll up to Classes and enforces the business rule of how many levels are allowed. We can then draw an association between the two recursive relationships to indicate that the Project Type recursion is consistent with the Project Type Level recursion. Finally, to enforce the rule that only Project Types are allowed to be associated with projects, we will add indicator columns to the Project Type Level table to indicate which levels of Project Types may be attached

to Projects. The new model is shown in Figure 7-3 with accompanying
Code Example 7-9.

```
CREATE TABLE PROJ_TYPE_LVL (
PROJ_TYPE_LVL_CD        VARCHAR2 (2) NOT NULL PRIMARY KEY,
PROJ_TYPE_LVL_CD_REF  VARCHAR2 (2)
  REFERENCES PROJ_TYPE_LVL (PROJ_TYPE_LVL_CD),
DESCR_TX           VARCHAR2 (40) NOT NULL,
ACTIVE_YN      CHAR (1) DEFAULT 'Y' NOT NULL ,
ORDER_BY       NUMBER (3),
CREAT_BY       VARCHAR2 (30) DEFAULT USER NOT NULL ,
MOD_BY         VARCHAR2 (30),
CREAT_DT       DATE DEFAULT SYSDATE NOT NULL,
MOD_DT         DATE,
CONSTRAINT ProUniqCons UNIQUE(PROJ_TYPE_LVL_CD, PROJ_TYPE_LVL_CD_REF))
/

CREATE TABLE PROJ_TYPE (
PROJ_TYPE_CD        VARCHAR2 (2) NOT NULL PRIMARY KEY,
PROJ_TYPE_CD_REF  VARCHAR2 (2) REFERENCES PROJ_TYPE (PROJ_TYPE_CD),
PROJ_TYPE_LVL_CD       VARCHAR2 (2) NOT NULL,
PROJ_TYPE_LVL_CD_REF  VARCHAR2 (2) ,
DESCR_TX           VARCHAR2 (40) NOT NULL,
ACTIVE_YN      CHAR (1) DEFAULT 'Y' NOT NULL ,
ORDER_BY       NUMBER (3),
CREAT_BY       VARCHAR2 (30) DEFAULT USER NOT NULL ,
MOD_BY         VARCHAR2 (30),
CREAT_DT       DATE DEFAULT SYSDATE NOT NULL,
MOD_DT         DATE,
FOREIGN key  (PROJ_TYPE_LVL_CD, PROJ_TYPE_LVL_CD_REF)
  REFERENCES PROJ_TYPE_LVL (PROJ_TYPE_LVL_CD, PROJ_TYPE_LVL_CD_REF))
/

CREATE TABLE PROJECT (PROJECT_ID     NUMBER (10) NOT NULL PRIMARY KEY,
PROJ_TYPE_CD   VARCHAR2 (2) NOT NULL
  REFERENCES PROJ_TYPE (PROJ_TYPE_CD),
DESCR_TX           VARCHAR2 (40) NOT NULL,
ACTIVE_YN      CHAR (1) DEFAULT 'Y' NOT NULL ,
ORDER_BY       NUMBER (3),
CREAT_BY       VARCHAR2 (30) DEFAULT USER NOT NULL ,
MOD_BY         VARCHAR2 (30),
CREAT_DT       DATE DEFAULT SYSDATE NOT NULL,
MOD_DT         DATE)
/
```

Code Example 7-9

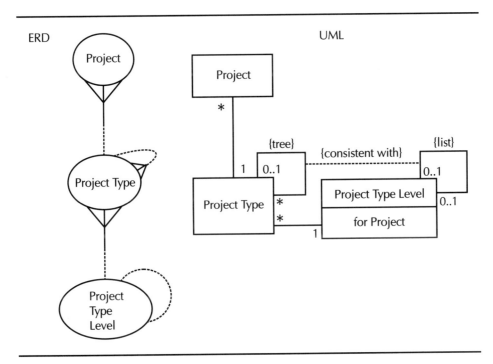

ERD   UML

FIGURE 7-3.   *Association of recursive structures*

A common extension to this design is requiring that an object can be rolled up using more than one categorization scheme. For example, we might want to model a 101A Engine through our Parts list or through a hierarchical structure such as the technical requirements to maintain it. The motor might roll up to a midlevel mechanic, mechanic, maintenance worker, etc.

We can now duplicate the same structure several times. However, in the preceding example, these structures have no overlap, so we have created a structure supporting any number of hierarchies. We may now have to attach a particular engine to more than one type with an adjustment to the model as shown in Figure 7-4 and Code Example 7-10.

```
CREATE TABLE PROJ_TYPE_LVL (
PROJ_TYPE_LVL_CD        VARCHAR2 (2) NOT NULL,
PROJ_TYPE_LVL_CD_REF  VARCHAR2 (2) REFERENCES PROJ_TYPE (PROJ_TYPE_CD),
DESCR_TX           VARCHAR2 (40) NOT NULL,
ACTIVE_YN        CHAR (1) NOT NULL DEFAULT 'Y',
```

```
ORDER_BY        NUMBER (3),
CREAT_BY        VARCHAR2 (30) NOT NULL DEFAULT USER,
MOD_BY          VARCHAR2 (30),
CREAT_DT        DATE NOT NULL,
MOD_DT          DATE
PRIMARY KEY (PROJ_TYPE_LVL_CD, PROJ_TYPE_LVL_CD_REF))
/

CREATE TABLE PROJ_TYPE (
PROJ_TYPE_CD        VARCHAR2 (2) NOT NULL PRIMARY KEY,
PROJ_TYPE_CD_REF  VARCHAR2 (2) REFERENCES PROJ_TYPE (PROJ_TYPE_CD),
PROJ_TYPE_LVL_CD      VARCHAR2 (2) NOT NULL,
PROJ_TYPE_LVL_CD_REF  VARCHAR2 (2) ,
DESCR_TX            VARCHAR2 (40) NOT NULL,
ACTIVE_YN       CHAR (1) NOT NULL DEFAULT 'Y',
ORDER_BY        NUMBER (3),
CREAT_BY        VARCHAR2 (30) NOT NULL DEFAULT USER,
MOD_BY          VARCHAR2 (30),
CREAT_DT        DATE NOT NULL,
MOD_DT          DATE
FOREIGN KEY PROJ_TYPE__PROJ_TYPE_LVL_R (PROJ_TYPE_LVL_CD, PROJ_TYPE_LVL_CD_REF)
REFERENCES PROJ_TYPE_LVL (PROJ_TYPE_LVL_CD, PROJ_TYPE_LVL_CD_REF))
/

CREATE TABLE PROJECT (
PROJECT_ID      NUMBER (10) NOT NULL PRIMARY KEY,
 DESCR_TX           VARCHAR2 (40) NOT NULL,
ACTIVE_YN       CHAR (1) NOT NULL DEFAULT 'Y',
ORDER_BY        NUMBER (3),
CREAT_BY        VARCHAR2 (30) NOT NULL DEFAULT USER,
MOD_BY          VARCHAR2 (30),
CREAT_DT        DATE NOT NULL,
MOD_DT          DATE)
/
CREATE TABLE PROJECT__PROJ_TYPE (
PROJECT_ID      NUMBER (10) NOT NULL REFERENCES PROJECT (PROJECT_ID),
PROJ_TYPE_CD  VARCHAR2 (2) NOT NULL REFERENCES PROJ_TYPE (PROJ_TYPE_CD),
CREAT_BY        VARCHAR2 (30) NOT NULL DEFAULT USER,
MOD_BY          VARCHAR2 (30),
CREAT_DT        DATE NOT NULL,
MOD_DT          DATE
PRIMARY KEY (PROJECT_ID, PROJ_TYPE_CD, CREAT_DT))
/
```

Code Example 7-10

ERD

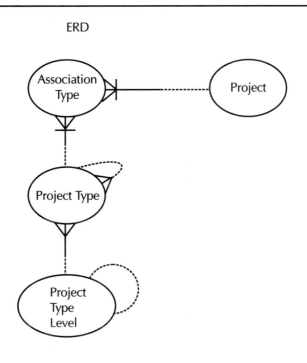

UML

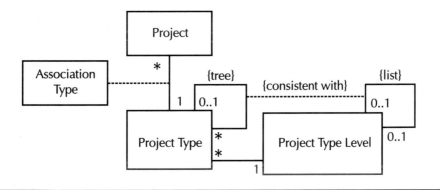

FIGURE 7-4. *Example of structure supporting multiple types*

If we want to support changes to our hierarchy over time, all of our recursive relationships become many-to-many relationships and we need to create association tables as shown in Figure 7-5.

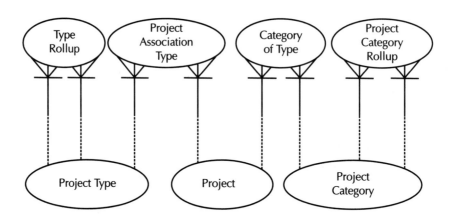

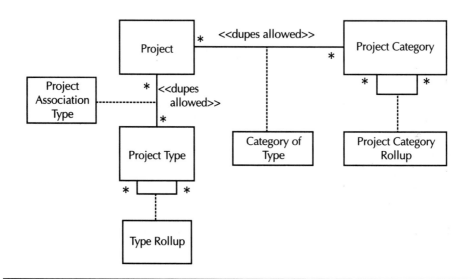

FIGURE 7-5. *Example of hierarchy with association tables*

The final generalization we may want to use for categorization is not only multiple independent hierarchies, but also multiple overlapping hierarchies. Fortunately, the model in Figure 7-5 is flexible enough to support that requirement as well.

PART III

Basic Modeling

CHAPTER

8

Relationships:
Association

ust as with ER diagramming, in object modeling it is crucial to identify and construct appropriate interactions or relationships between classes. In UML we have a richer language for describing these relationships than in ERDs.

Association is one of the most common relationship types encountered, and should be familiar to ER modelers. To some extent, the association relationship is the relationship of last resort. Using an association relationship between two classes does not indicate how the classes interact, but merely represents the fact that these two classes have something to do with each other. This does not say anything about the type of relationship, but simply that one exists.

This notion of "typing" a relationship will be somewhat difficult for most ER modelers, because the types of relationships in ER modeling are quite limited. ER modelers should be careful not to fall into the trap of using UML to simply draw their ERDs with a different notation. There are other, more precise relationships (composition, aggregation, and generalization) that will be discussed in later chapters. In this chapter, we will only discuss the basic cardinality relationship types.

Cardinality

What is meant by cardinality? In different classes, there are multiple objects. *Cardinality* refers to creating *association sets* that will relate one or more objects in the first class to one or more objects in the second class. An association set can be defined as any subset of the first class (not necessarily proper) and any subset from the second class. The whole concept of an association set does not fit the traditional way that relational modelers have had to think about cardinality, because we didn't have a notation flexible enough to demand that level of conceptualization. With cardinality relationships, we are defining data-related business rules that restrict the way association sets are built.

The simple example from ER modeling of a 1-to-many relationship between Department and Employee may clarify this point. For each department, there are one or more employees. The structure of the data is as shown in Table 8-1:

- Accounting (Acct) department has employees Al, Bel, Cil
- Finance (Fin) department has employees Del, Ed
- Management (Mgmt) department has employees Fil, Gil, Hal

Dept

DeptNo	Dname
10	Acct
20	Fin
30	Mgmt

Emp

DeptNo	EmpNo	EName
10	1	Al
10	2	Bel
10	3	Cil
20	4	Del
20	5	Ed
30	6	Fil
30	7	Gil
30	8	Hal

TABLE 8-1. *Department/Employee Data Structure*

In this case, the three defined object associations in terms of DeptNo values to EmpNo values are

- {10} , {1, 2, 3}
- {20} , {4, 5}
- {30} , {6, 7, 8}

The rules of cardinality relationships limit the size of the two defined subsets. For example, a 1-to-1 relationship would require there to be exactly one element in each object association.

In UML, a number placed on each side of the relationship represents the cardinality associated with objects in that class. Allowable values are single integers (for example, "1"), a list of integers (for example, "0,1,2"), a range of integers (for example, "0..2"), or a combination (for example, "2,4,6,10..20"). However, such complex cardinality rules are extremely rare. To represent that any number of objects are allowed in the association, the symbol "*" is used. "*" refers to any nonnegative integer. "1..*" refers to any positive integer.

For your convenience, Figure 8-1 defines how each of the standard ER modeling relationship notations translates into UML notation.

Even more interesting and complex business rules can be represented using UML. The following is an example:

> "All committees must have at least three and no more than 20 members. However, people need not be assigned to committees. At most, a person may be on two committees."

In UML syntax, this is drawn as shown here:

Complex UML cardinality relationship

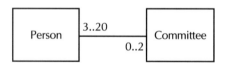

Note that such complex cardinality relationships are quite rare. Almost all associations that a designer normally encounters can be described with the cardinalities 0, 1, 0..1, 1..*, and *.

As you can see from the previous example, determining the appropriate cardinalities of relationships can be more complicated than it appears. A good way to approach this is to think of an individual object in one of the classes and ask: "How many objects from the other class might it be associated with?" Then reverse the process using an example from the other class. It is important to carefully determine the cardinality on each side of the relationship individually.

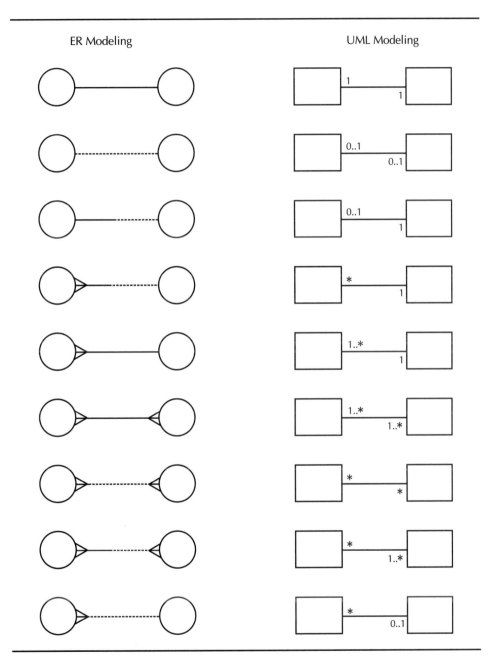

FIGURE 8-1.   *UML equivalents of basic ER modeling relationships*

Optional and Mandatory Relationships

One of the common confusions with UML diagramming is whether to place a "1" or a "0..1" on a given side of a relationship. An example is shown here:

Basic mandatory relationship

The "1" next to Class B in this illustration indicates that every object from Class A must be involved in the association. This is the same as making the ERD relationship mandatory for that object. For example, if a PO must always have at least 1 PO detail, then the cardinality on the PO Detail side would be 1..*. Since each PO detail must be associated with a PO, a 1 is placed next to the PO , because every PO detail is associated with exactly 1 PO. For Departments and Employees, if an employee were allowed to be unassigned, then 0..1 would be placed next to Dept. However, if employees were always assigned to a department, a 1 would be placed next to Dept. This system may seem backwards to designers who are used to the ERD notation. Care must be used with UML syntax so as not to make errors in specifying association cardinality.

There is similar confusion about when to use a "*" (meaning 0 to N) and a "1..*." "*" alone means that not necessarily every object in the class with which it is associated is involved in the relationship. "1..*" means that the association is mandatory. For example, in a PO-PO Detail association, if a PO must have at least one PO detail, the PO Detail cardinality would be 1..*, as shown here:

Example of mandatory association
on both PO and PO detail

Frequently, the workflow of an organization prevents many seemingly logical mandatory relationships from being implemented in the database. For example, it is easy to say that every department has at least one employee. The relationship is shown here:

Example of mandatory optional 1-to-many relationship

However, what happens when a new department is created? This rule would not allow the creation of a department unless an employee were immediately assigned to it. If every employee were removed from the department (perhaps for the purposes of a reorganization), the department would have to be deleted.

Even for situations where it seems particularly appropriate to use a mandatory association, such as between PO and PO detail, it is easy to see that insisting that every PO must have a PO detail, as shown below, is probably overly restrictive. One alternative for implementing such a rule is to use Oracle8 deferred constraints. A discussion of deferred constraints can be found in Chapter 1.

Example of mandatory 1-to-many relationship

What happens if a PO is opened but the person opening it is not sure what is being purchased, or wants to create headers for 18 different purchase orders all at once and then add details later? What if a PO is created with no details and the employee wishes to go to lunch? Another problem with this cardinality relationship may occur if a PO is opened and the user attempts to add a PO detail, but the item to be purchased is not stored in the system. The PO cannot be added, because the item is not available. All work completed up to that point would be wasted effort.

Keep in mind that the notational differences between "0..1 and 1" and "* and 1..*" may seem subtle. However, from the perspective of implementing the data structure, the implications of selecting one or the other are significant.

If you want to think of a logical data model as being separate from the physical data model (that is, changing data-related business rules as the system moves closer to implementation), you may want to use the 1 and 1..* notations more frequently in the logical data model. These constraints can be relaxed somewhat as you move closer to implementation. We do not recommend adopting this strategy. In our experience, placing only implementable business rules into the data model as early as possible greatly simplifies the database design process.

Contingent Constraints

Much of the confusion in the examples earlier arises from a business rule we will call a *contingent constraint*. A contingent constraint is enforced under certain conditions (for example, when an attribute has a certain value) but not at all times. This is an important concept in modeling. Many business rules are conditional.

Contingent constraints are frequently found wherever there are workflow-related rules. Here are a few examples:

- Purchase orders over $80,000 must be approved by the Director of Purchasing.

- Unless a project has been approved, it can't receive funding or be assigned a project manager.

- A purchase order cannot be approved by the person who requested it.

Contingent constraints can also be found in nonworkflow systems, as evidenced by the following examples:

- Salary increases may be no greater than 20 percent per year.

- Purchase orders must have at least one item to be approved.

- Departments must have at least one employee to receive funding.

- Basketball teams must have at least eight members to register for a tournament.

No explicit modeling convention for contingent constraints currently exists within UML or ERDs. However, there are two ways to model such constraints. One way is to place notes in the data model to describe the contingent constraints as shown here:

Example of note describing contingent constraint

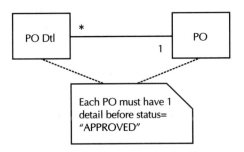

The other way to include such rules in the data model is to build a business rule engine right into the data model. Then the business rules are stored and implemented at run time. A compromise strategy is to build enough of the business rule engine to store the requirements but to code them by hand before implementation. Business rule development is discussed in Chapter 17.

Examples of Association Relationships

To clarify the concept of cardinality, each type of association relationship will be discussed in the context of a specific example.

Example 1: 1-to-1 Relationship, Mandatory on Both Sides In Example 1, shown next, both classes represent the employee. Information that is visible to all users is stored in the Employee class, and sensitive information (such as Social Security number and Salary) is stored in the Secure Employee class. This construct is infrequently used. An argument could be made for making both Employee and Secure Employee a single class called Employee. But in systems where security is of great concern, a structure similar to the one shown in the illustration might actually be used.

1-to-1 relationship—mandatory on both sides

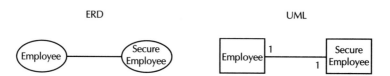

Example 2: 1-to-1 Relationship, Mandatory on One Side   Example 2, illustrated next, shows how we used to represent the object-oriented notion of generalization using ERDs when the only available representation was cardinality. Here we have modeled that some persons may be lawyers. This structure will rarely be used in UML, not because it is no longer valid, but because there is a more precise way to describe this type of relationship between classes. This concept of generalization will be discussed in more detail in Chapter 14.

1-to-1 relationship—mandatory on one side

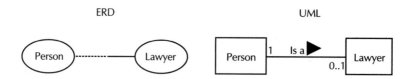

Example 3: 1-to-1 Relationship, Optional on Both Sides   Example 3, illustrated next, shows a 1-to-1 relationship between two classes where objects from one class need not be associated with objects from the other class. Usually we are interested in the history of such relationships, so 1-to-1 relationships frequently turn into many-to-many relationships. This construct is rarely used.

1-to-1 relationship—optional on both sides

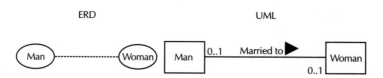

Example 4: 1-to-Many Relationship, Optional on Both Sides   If you are not interested in employment history, the method shown in Example 4, illustrated next, is the best way to represent the Employment relationship (with optionality on both sides). A department need not have any

employees, and an employee need not be attached to a particular department. When modeling this relationship in a real system, the relationship is usually many-to-many, because employees may change departments over time. However, for illustrative purposes, this is a useful example. This relationship involves two classes, each of which can exist without the other, but may have an association.

1-to-many relationship—optional on both sides

Example 5: 1-to-Many Relationship, Mandatory on "1" Side, Optional on "Many" Side   The diagram shown next represents a very unusual relationship. We don't know of any case where we've ever needed to use this relationship in ERD modeling. We couldn't even think of a good example for this relationship. If this were the cardinality for an Employment relationship, it would mean that each department must have at least one employee, but employees need not be assigned to any department. Such a relationship is not logically false, but is not encountered often in the real world.

1-to-many relationship, mandatory on "1" side,
optional on "many" side

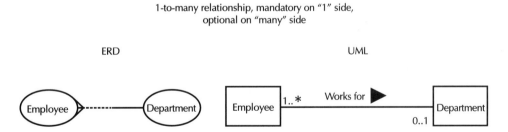

Example 6: 1-to-Many Relationship, Optional on the "1" Side and Mandatory on the "Many" Side   Shown below is one of the most common cardinalities encountered, namely an optional/mandatory, 1-to-many relationship. The relationship between any primary class such as Product and a value list class such as Product Type or between Project and Project Status illustrates this relationship. In the example earlier, each product must be associated with a particular type, and each type may have any number of products associated with it.

Example of 1-to-many relationship, optional/mandatory

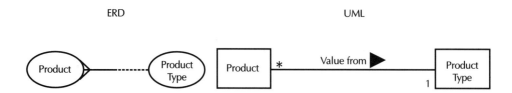

Example 7: 1-to-Many Relationship, Mandatory on Both Sides   The UML diagram in Example 7, illustrated next, corresponds to a 1-to-many relationship, mandatory on both sides, in ERD notation. The standard example of PO and PO Detail has been discussed earlier in this chapter. If you are trying to capture business rules, this seems like a logical relationship. However, because of workflow requirements, it is a relatively rare structure in the real world. If we could indicate that the constraint would be valid at some point in time, but not necessarily at record creation (a contingent constraint), this could be a much more common construct.

Example of 1-to-many relationship, mandatory on both sides

All of the previous examples had direct correlates to ERD notation, as shown in Figure 8-1. The following are some examples of relationships that are not easily represented in ER modeling.

Example 8: Complex Association 1   The diagram shown next represents the rule "Students may take any number of Course Offerings. The maximum number of students in any one class is 20."

UML representation of complex association 1

Example 9: Complex Association 2   The diagram shown next represents the rule "To be eligible for an intramural basketball league, you must have at least eight players on your team but no more than ten players. An individual must belong only to one team."

UML representation of complex association 2

Example 10a: Complex Association 3   Example 10a, shown next, represents the rule "A marriage (in most places in the world) is made up of exactly two individuals."

UML representation of complex association 3

Note that in this example, there is no way to instantiate which person is the husband or wife in the relationship. If this business rule needs to be represented so that a distinction can be made between husbands and wives in the database, we would need to have two relationships between marriage and person, as shown in the next example.

Example 10b: Complex Association 3   Note that, in Example 10b, shown next, we are still not enforcing gender in the database. To do this would require generalization, a concept that will be discussed in Chapter 14. In the diagram shown in Example 10a, the marriage must be between two different people. Perhaps even more distressing is that there is nothing in Example 10b to prevent an individual from being married to him- or herself. The limitations of this example point out that care must be taken in modeling business rules in UML. The flexibility in UML syntax makes it easy to incorrectly model relationships.

UML representation of complex association 3b

Notes on UML Conventions Notation

Naming relationships in UML is quite different from naming relationships in ERDs. The conventional wisdom with ERDs is to name the relationships with phrases. For example, the Employment relationship between Person and Department is "Employer for" or "Employed by," depending upon the direction. This notation was widely supported (but not widely followed), owing to the fact that creating such phrases to express the relationship often proved difficult. Modelers like David Hay and Ulka Rodgers seem to have little trouble determining appropriate relationship names. However, many modelers spend hours trying to come up with good, descriptive phrases only to end up with generic relationship names such as "associated with" or "relates to." The UML proponents have a formal, more elegant standard.

First, we will describe the UML rules, including some examples where these naming conventions work well. Then we will provide guidelines for implementing the UML standard.

UML Naming Rules

In ERDs there are two sides of a relationship to name. In UML there are not only object role names attached to each side of the relationship, but we also have the option of placing a name and a direction on the relationship itself. The ends of the relationship are called *association roles.* As mentioned in *The UML Notation Guide,* the end of the relationship indicates "the role played by the class attached to the end of the path near the role name" (p. 84). This concept of a role works well in many cases. For example, between Department and Person, for the employment relationship between the two using the full UML notation, we would write:

UML diagram showing roles

This diagram reads as follows: "The department acting as employer may employ any number of persons as employees." However, we could just as easily have written the same relationship with the arrow going the opposite direction, as shown next, from the Employee's perspective and calling the relationship "works for."

UML diagram showing roles

Linguistically, the UML notation includes the role that each object in the class is assuming in the relationship expressed with a noun on each side. The relationship itself is expressed with a verb and preposition. This notational scheme holds up fairly well. However, sometimes it is difficult to determine the appropriate word to describe the roles of the objects. Also, if you are creating abstract models where the same relationship might represent more than one type of association, the naming becomes somewhat more complex.

There are times when the same ERD verb phrases that we used on relationships still work well with UML models. For example, the relationship between Person and Committee classes (on p. 17 of *The UML Notation Guide,* Version 1.1, September 1, 1997) is named "member of" with no role descriptors on the ends of the relationship at all. To use full UML syntax with this example, we would write

Example of full UML syntax

Which naming of the relationship would make the most sense in this case? *The UML Guide* suggestion with the simple "member of" name seems much clearer than using the full notational standard shown earlier. On one hand, we do want to apply a consistent set of standards and to name our relationships consistently. On the other hand, the purpose of naming the relationships is to effectively communicate the data-related business rules. The ultimate test of whether a relationship is adequately named is whether the diagram communicates the relationship accurately to whomever is working with it.

We recommend using a *relationship phrase* consisting of a noun or verb followed by a preposition. Additionally, if required to enhance the clarity of the diagram, use roles on the relationship ends. Note that in using this relationship phrase in the case of a 1-to-many relationship, it is usually more descriptive to name the relationship going from the child (many) side to the parent (one) side of the relationship. For example, to describe the Dept/Emp example, "works for" usually seems easier to understand than "employer of."

In the case of value list reference tables, the phrase "value from" can be used to describe the relationship between child and parent. This should be used in lieu of incorporating the name of the class in the relationship. For example, for the relationship between Project and Status, the most natural name would be "status for." Even though this name would clearly define the relationship, if, at a later time, the name of the status class is changed, the relationship name would also have to be changed. For this reason, we will use "value from" for all value list classes, except where an alternate name would significantly enhance the readability of the diagram.

Extending UML: Stereotypes, Constraints, and Notes

The UML designers allowed for the possibility that UML might not be able to satisfy the modeling needs of everyone. Because UML was designed to support object-oriented programmers, it sometimes falls short in supporting object-relational database modeling. Fortunately, UML provides three mechanisms to extend the UML notation: stereotypes, constraints, and comments.

Stereotypes and *constraints* are keywords that can be attached to any UML element to alternate meaning or functionality. Stereotypes designated by «guillemets» extend or redefine an element. There are pre-defined stereotypes such as "Abstract" for class. However, users can also create their own stereotypes to alter or extend the semantics of UML.

Constraints designated with curly set brackets { } limit the functionality of the UML object. There are native constraints defined by UML such as the "Or" constraint on an association between relationships. However, additional constraints may be defined by the user.

In the class diagram, Notes are graphically represented text objects that can be attached to any UML object. Notes are depicted as shown next in a text box that resembles the old flow chart symbol for punch card:

UML Notes symbol

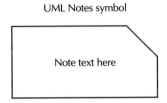

Note text here

Notes are useful for declaring data-related business rules that could not be represented otherwise. It is often difficult to determine whether a keyword should be designated as a stereotype or a constraint. Keep in mind that if you are limiting existing behavior or functions, a constraint should be used. If you are redefining or extending behavior, then a stereotype is appropriate.

Do Crows Still Fly South?

Within the Oracle community, there has been relatively strong adherence to ensuring that the "many" side of all relationship ends be placed on the top or left, the so-called "crows fly south and east rule." Such a convention has merit. Conforming to this standard enforced a certain amount of uniformity in the way diagrams were laid out, grouping the entities with the most rows (usually the most important ones) in the upper-left corner of the diagrams. Most of the reference tables (which we call *value list classes*) were grouped along the bottom or right side of the diagram. We recommend adopting the same standard in UML. Thus, for all relationships, the side of the relationship with the highest cardinality will appear on the top or left. For example, in laying out the Dept/Person relationship, the Person class would appear above or to the left of the Dept class. Of course, it is not always possible to do this. Sometimes, there will be so many classes and relationships between them that some relationships will have to be drawn in the wrong direction.

Other Guidelines for Creating UML Drawings

Clear and understandable drawings are just as important when you're using UML as they are with ERDs. Many of the same guidelines apply:

- Try to avoid crossing lines.

- Avoid having lines with many bends.

- Lines should all be perfectly horizontal or perfectly vertical.

- If you do need to violate the "crows fly south" rule, we find it useful to put those relationship lines on a slight angle to make them stand out. This strategy is also useful for crossed lines.

- Making a class tall and thin or short and wide can simplify a diagram and eliminate crossed or bent lines.

- Judicious use of white space can make diagrams more readable. Classes that are clearly associated should be physically closer to each other, so they can be grouped more easily.

- Color or shade certain groups of classes, such as value list classes, core classes that drive applications (Employee, Dept., Project), and classes shared from other schemas. Coloring can be useful for different purposes at different times, so there is no one consistent standard to use. Coloring should be done carefully, so the diagram doesn't look too confusing.

- Class diagrams may consist solely of all of the classes needed to support a particular screen module or report. We include such diagrams as part of the system documentation.

- It is important to take into account the audience for the diagrams when they are created.

- An enterprisewide data diagram is usually only useful for systems professionals. Diagrams for user discussions should be simple enough to fit on a single 8½" by 11" page. There should be no more than 10 to 15 classes per page.

- Simplified class diagrams can be useful in discussions with users. We frequently create diagram versions with the value list classes taken out to show users.

- A useful way to present diagrams to users is to start with a blank white board and build the diagram, explaining it as you go along.

- When you're discussing a diagram, a report with descriptions of all relevant classes and attributes should be available to facilitate the discussion.

Many-to-Many Relationships

Frequently, the relationship between two classes is *..*. However, the same many-to-many relationship issues arise when either or both sides are 1..*, or anytime that the cardinality on both sides of the relationship is potentially greater than one. Often, when this occurs, there is another class of interest worth explicitly modeling. The classic example is the many-to-many relationship between Student and Course Offering. In this case, there is a need for another class, because the act of a student taking a course offering is, in itself, something of interest. To recognize the need for this additional class, ask: "In what class would we place the student's grade?" The grade cannot be stored in the Student class, because each student could then only have one grade. Likewise, the grade cannot be stored in the Course Offering class, because every student in a class cannot have the same grade. What is needed is a third class, called an *association class.* In this case, the association class would be "Enrollment." Using the ERD style of modeling, the only way to represent this is to break the many-to-many relationship into two 1-to-many relationships as shown here:

"ERD"–style representation of many–to–many relationship

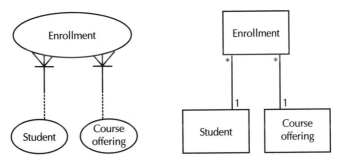

However, in UML, we don't need to break apart the relationship. Instead, we can leave the logical and descriptive relationship intact, showing the association class associated with the relationship itself as it should be. The syntax for this is shown here:

UML representation of many–to–many relationship

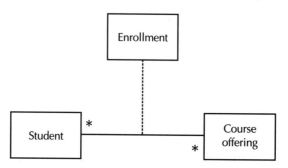

This is a far superior syntax that provides for a much cleaner implementation of the many-to-many relationship than is afforded by the ERD syntax. Unfortunately, in UML this intersection entity can only be used in precise circumstances. The primary key of the intersection class is logically a concatenation of the primary keys of the two main classes. This effectively means that there is, at most, one object in the intersection class for each pairing of the main classes. In this example, a student may be enrolled in a particular course offering no more than one time. This is a reasonable restriction for the Student/Class example. However, this is not a reasonable restriction in many other cases. For example, in most real organizations, the association between Dept and Employee is a many-to-many (*..*) relationship, because, over time, an employee may change departments and can be associated with several departments.

If we modeled this relationship with the UML association class, the restriction would mean that if an employee were to change departments and then return to the original one, such a move would violate the rule, because we would need to show that the employee had been associated with the same department twice. In this example, it is necessary is to add Start Date to the primary key for the Enrollment class. However, that is not what the UML syntax means.

In real database systems, association classes that do not require uniqueness are more common than the intersections that are limited to a

Cartesian product of the primary classes. Oracle's Object Database Designer does not yet support the intersection class notation.

   We will add an additional class to support an employee working for the same department several times. The example to support employment is shown here:

UML representation of intersection class

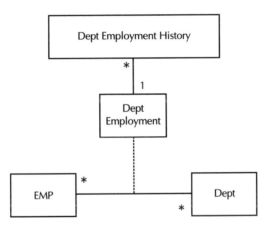

   Actually, the relationship between Dept Employment and Dept Employment History should be a *composition* relationship. Composition relationships will be covered in Chapter 9.

   We also have the ability to use stereotypes to extend UML. Because we will frequently need to allow pairings in many-to-many relationships, we can add the stereotype keywords «dupes allowed» on the relationship phrase between Course and Student as shown here:

UML representation of intersection class using stereotypes

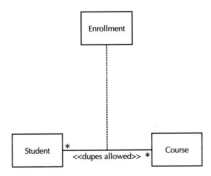

This method has the advantage of concise syntax but we are changing the meanings of the UML syntax. People reading the diagram will need to become accustomed to the semantics of the stereotypes or they may be confused or misled.

Implementing Relationships

Relationships, a common construct in both RDBMS and OODBMS, are implemented slightly differently in traditional ERDs versus object-oriented models. The following sections will explain how to physically implement relationships in both environments.

Relational Implementation

A *relationship* is the means by which Oracle7 enforces data integrity between a child and a parent table. These relationships are physically implemented through the use of foreign key constraints. Foreign keys of child tables reference the primary key, or unique identifier of the parent table. The primary key of the parent table must be defined before the creation of a foreign key that refers to it.

Primary Keys

The first step in defining physical relationships requires that a table have a unique identifier declared, which we refer to as the primary key. The syntax for declaring unique identifiers is as follows, using the STATE and CITY tables as shown in Code Example 8-1:

```
CREATE TABLE STATE
(STATE_CD   VARCHAR2(8) NOT NULL PRIMARY KEY,
DESCR_TX    VARCHAR2(40) )
/

CREATE TABLE CITY
   (CITY_CD    VARCHAR2(8) NOT NULL PRIMARY KEY,
    DESCR_TX   VARCHAR2(40) NOT NULL)
/
```

Code Example 8-1

Now we have identified the STATE_CD column as containing the values that uniquely identify (UID) each object in the STATE table and the CITY_CD column as the UID for the CITY table. A primary key must exist on the table that you plan to reference via a foreign key, in order for the foreign key to be successfully created. We will review the syntax for foreign keys in the next section. The goal will be to relate the city of Newark to the state of NJ, as shown in this table:

CITY

CITY_ID	DESCR_TX	STATE_CD
1	Newark	NJ

Foreign Keys

There are various methods for implementing foreign keys. The next few sections will review a number of examples of relationships and the constraints that support them, using both relational and object-relational syntax.

Mandatory 1-to-Optional Many—1-to-*

In relational syntax using the CITY and STATE example, we created two tables, one per entity. The relationship between the CITY and STATE tables declares that a state may contain one or more cities, but a city must exist in one and only one state. This relationship would be implemented via a foreign key constraint. A foreign key constraint is what ties the city of Newark to the state of NJ. The way we would model this relationship in both ERD terms and corresponding UML terms is as shown here:

Fragment of **CITY** table showing State-City relationship
using traditional relational foreign key

ERD   UML

Using the same method, we would create a foreign key on the CITY table, which would point to the STATE table for the purpose of validation. In this manner, a city could not be defined unless it was attached to a valid state. The modification to the CITY table from the Code Example 8-1 in the Primary Key section shown in Code Example 8-2 demonstrates the correct syntax for ensuring that each CITY record must relate to a valid STATE record:

```
--****EXAMPLE_08_01 IS PREREQUISITE
DROP TABLE CITY
/
CREATE TABLE CITY
   (CITY_ID       VARCHAR2(8) NOT NULL PRIMARY KEY,
    DESCR_TX      VARCHAR2(40) NOT NULL ,
    STATE_CD      VARCHAR2(8) NOT NULL REFERENCES STATE (STATE_CD) )
/
```

Code Example 8-2

The basic Insert syntax described earlier also applies to the foreign key Code Example 8-1 in Oracle7, as shown next in Code Example 8-3:

```
--****EXAMPLE_08_02 IS PREREQUISITE
INSERT INTO STATE (STATE_CD, DESCR_TX)
VALUES ('NJ','NEW JERSEY')
/
INSERT INTO CITY (CITY_ID, DESCR_TX, STATE_CD)
VALUES (1, 'Newark', 'NJ')
/
```

Code Example 8-3

However, note that the SELECT syntax has become more complex, because we now have to access two tables from one statement. SQL does not assume the connection path between the two tables. You must manually specify the join condition as shown by the WHERE clause in Code Example 8-4 next:

```
--****EXAMPLE_08_03 IS PREREQUISITE
SELECT S.DESCR_TX, C.DESCR_TX
FROM STATE S, CITY C
WHERE S.STATE_CD = C.STATE_CD
/
```

Code Example 8-4

This requires additional effort on the part of the programmer and almost seems unnecessary, because the join condition is essentially the structure of the foreign key and therefore should be resolved by the parser.

Object-Relational Implementation

In object-relational syntax, the concept of relational integrity can take on one of two different forms:

- Traditional foreign key
- Object reference

We will use the same STATE/CITY classes example, and apply Oracle's object-relational syntax. Let us assume that each STATE object may be linked to one or more CITY objects, and each CITY object must be linked to one and only one STATE object. We will introduce the object-relational syntax for implementing object references (OIDs) in this section. In the following section we will describe the implementation of traditional referential integrity using object-relational syntax.

Object Reference (OID) Example

First, we must create the STATE object type as follows in Code Example 8-5:

```
CREATE OR REPLACE TYPE STATE_TYPE
AS OBJECT(
STATE_CD  VARCHAR2(8),
DESCR_TX  VARCHAR2(40))
/
```

Code Example 8-5

Second, we define the STATE object table, based upon the object type we just defined, declaring the STATE_CD column as the primary key of the STATE object class. Notice that we specify that the STATE_CD column is mandatory in the CREATE TABLE statement, not in the CREATE TYPE statement. Although it is an attribute of the column, you may need to set this attribute differently depending upon the object class you are building, as shown in Code Example 8-6:

```
--****EXAMPLE_08_05 IS PREREQUISITE
CREATE TABLE STATE
OF STATE_TYPE(
```

```
STATE_CD   NOT NULL PRIMARY KEY,
DESCR_TX   NOT NULL)
/
```

Code Example 8-6

Next, we define the CITY object table. When defining the CITY object type, we define an Object Reference that points to the STATE table. This Object Reference essentially replaces the functionality of the foreign key. The following Code Example 8-7 shows the CITY_TYPE object type with a reference to the STATE class, followed by the CITY class defined based upon the CITY_TYPE object type.

```
--EXAMPLE_08_06 IS PREREQUISITE
CREATE OR REPLACE TYPE CITY_TYPE
AS OBJECT(
CITY_ID   VARCHAR2(8),
STATE_CD REF STATE_TYPE)
DESCR_TX VARCHAR2(40),
/

CREATE TABLE CITY
OF CITY_TYPE(
CITY_ID NOT NULL PRIMARY KEY,
STATE_CD NOT NULL,
DESCR_TX NOT NULL)
/
```

Code Example 8-7

A general observation of SQL syntax differences between the relational and object-relational formats is that INSERT statements tend to be more complex in object-relational syntax, while SELECT statements tend to be simpler as compared with the pure relational syntax. This is illustrated in Code Example 8-8, using the CITY object class.

```
--EXAMPLE_08_07 IS PREREQUISITE
INSERT INTO STATE(STATE_CD, DESCR_TX)
            VALUES('NJ','NEW JERSEY')
/

INSERT INTO CITY (CITY_ID,
                  DESCR_TX,
                  STATE_CD)
```

```
VALUES ('4',
        'Washington',
        (SELECT REF(S)
        FROM STATE S
        WHERE STATE_CD = 'NJ'));

SELECT C.DESCR_TX, C.STATE_CD.DESCR_TX
FROM CITY C;
```

Code Example 8-8

Notice that while the INSERT statement now includes the REF command, the SELECT statement no longer requires a join to retrieve both the names of the state and city for each record.

It is important to note that object references are not entirely perfect. Early versions of Oracle8 do not enforce integrity. For example, after referencing the object NJ from the STATE class by the Newark object of the CITY object class, the NJ object could be deleted, resulting in a dangling object reference in the CITY object class. Oracle8i has included a constraint to prevent dangling references, but was not available for us to review.

Dangling references are similar to the issue of orphaned child records, where one object had a relationship to another object that no longer exists. We would be required to write all of the necessary triggers or methods to enforce integrity between object references, a feature that we already have at no cost through standard primary key/foreign key referential integrity. The object-relational examples throughout this book will utilize foreign keys as opposed to OIDs, unless specifically intended to exemplify OIDs.

The other drawback to object references is the storage overhead required. Oracle has developed an algorithm that ensures uniqueness of OIDs across instances. This algorithm generates a unique identifier similar to the ROW IDs we have used in relational implementations. The issue with OIDs is that they are 36 bytes long. This is a sizable increase in overhead, considering that OIDs add 36 bytes to each object or row in any given table, including references. Note that *Scoped references* are much smaller, adding only 16 bytes. Oracle8i will allow user-defined OIDs, i.e. FKs as REFs, which means that any storage penalty vanishes.

Traditional Referential Integrity in Object-Relational Syntax

We can still define referential integrity constraints within the state and city object types as we did in the example earlier, with the exception of the ref in the CITY_TYPE. Instead, the CITY type would contain a column called STATE_CD, and the CITY table based upon the CITY_TYPE would define the foreign key to the STATE table as in Code Example 8-9.

```
--EXAMPLE_08_07 IS PREREQUISITE
DROP TABLE CITY
/

CREATE OR REPLACE TYPE CITY_TYPE
AS OBJECT(
CITY_ID    VARCHAR2(8),
DESCR_TX   VARCHAR2(40),
STATE_CD   VARCHAR2 (8))
/

CREATE TABLE CITY
OF CITY_TYPE(
CITY_ID NOT NULL PRIMARY KEY,
STATE_CD NOT NULL
   REFERENCES STATE (STATE_CD),
DESCR_TX NOT NULL)
/
```

Code Example 8-9

Using this style, we have essentially utilized the best of both the relational and object-relational capabilities. The object-relational syntax provides us with the ability to genericize the structure of our table, while the relational syntax provides us with the assurance of referential integrity across classes.

With PK-based REFs, we maintain all the benefits of PK/FK and in addition provide navigational access (both in SQL and in 3GLs like C++ or Java).

Optional 1-to-Optional Many—0..1-to-*

The next example will provide the syntax for implementing the relationship between EXPENSE and REIMBURSEMENT in a hypothetical expense tracking system. A Reimbursement may satisfy any number of expenses, although a specific Expense can be satisfied by only one Reimbursement, if at all. The illustration next displays the diagramming techniques to support this relationship in both ERD and UML diagrams.

1–to–many relationship, optional on both sides

ERD   UML

Relational Implementation

Using the relational approach, we would create two tables, one for
EXPENSE and one for REIMBURSEMENT, as follows in Code Example 8-10:

```
CREATE TABLE REIMBURSEMENT(
REIMBURSEMENT_ID  NUMBER(10) NOT NULL PRIMARY KEY,
DESCR_TX          VARCHAR2(1000)),
AMOUNT_NR         NUMBER (6,2) NOT NULL)
/
CREATE TABLE EXPENSE (
EXPENSE_ID        NUMBER(10) NOT NULL PRIMARY KEY,
DESCR_TX          VARCHAR2(1000) NULL,
REIMBURSEMENT_ID NUMBER(10) NULL
REFERENCES REIMBURSEMENT (REIMBURSEMENT_ID),
AMOUNT_NR         NUMBER (6,2) NOT NULL)
/
```

Code Example 8-10

The key to implementing an optional 1-to-many relationship is to declare
the columns in the dependent table that form the primary key to be NULL,
or to allow objects to be processed, without values for the dependent
columns. This can be observed via the REIMBURSEMENT_ID column in
the EXPENSE table. The REIMBURSEMENT_ID column of the EXPENSE
table REFERENCES via a foreign key the REIMBURSEMENT_ID of the
REIMBURSEMENT table. The critical point here is that the
REIMBURSEMENT_ID column in EXPENSE is NULL(able), indicating
that an EXPENSE can exist, independent of a REIMBURSEMENT. We do not
recommend storing the total value of each reimbursement redundantly
within the reimbursement table, though we realize that this is not an
uncommon practice.

More details about the implementation of denormalization techniques
will be provided in Chapter 18. In this case, it would appear that we could
create a database trigger on the EXPENSE table. The objective of this trigger

would be to compare the total value of expenses allocated to a specific reimbursement with the total value of the reimbursement itself. Unfortunately, this proposed implementation would give rise to the mutating table dilemma.

Object-Relational Implementation

Using the object approach, we might create two object types and object classes, one of each for EXPENSE and REIMBURSEMENT, as shown in Code Example 8-11:

```
CREATE OR REPLACE TYPE REIMBURSEMENT_TYPE
AS OBJECT(
REIMBURSEMENT_ID  NUMBER(10),
DESCR_TX          VARCHAR2(1000),
AMOUNT_NR         NUMBER (6,2))
/
CREATE OR REPLACE TYPE EXPENSE_TYPE
AS OBJECT(
EXPENSE_ID        NUMBER(10),
DESCR_TX          VARCHAR2(1000),
REIMBURSEMENT_ID REF REIMBURSEMENT_TYPE
AMOUNT_NR         NUMBER (6,2))
/
CREATE TABLE REIMBURSEMENT
OF REIMBURSEMENT_TYPE(
REIMBURSEMENT_ID NOT NULL PRIMARY KEY)
/
CREATE TABLE EXPENSE
OF EXPENSE_TYPE(
EXPENSE_ID        NOT NULL PRIMARY KEY,
REIMBURSEMENT_ID NULL)
/
```

Code Example 8-11

The only difference between the CITY/STATE example and the EXPENSE/REIMBURSEMENT example is that the referencing column is NULL in the case of EXPENSE.REIMBURSEMENT_ID, which means that an expense may exist without being associated with a reimbursement, whereas a city cannot exist unless a state has been designated. This holds true in both the ERD and UML approaches.

Note that the decision to implement object types should not be made lightly. Object types should only be created when we can cite at least two instances of object tables that will be spawned from the given object type.

Optional Many-to-Many—0..*-to-*

The following example will explain how to implement an optional many-to-many relationship in both ERD and UML terminology, based upon the modeling example shown here:

Many–to–many relationship diagrams

ERD   UML

Many-to-many relationships are typically resolved by creating an intersection table and relating it to each of the two tables on either side of the relationship. Therefore, the many-to-many relationship between the PROJECT and CLIENT tables would actually require the creation of the following three tables in relational notation, as shown in Code Example 8-12:

```
CREATE TABLE PROJECT
(PROJECT_ID NUMBER (10)      NOT NULL PRIMARY KEY,
 STATUS_TX  VARCHAR2 (100)   NOT NULL,
 DESCR_TXS  VARCHAR2 (40)    NOT NULL,
 DESC_TXL   VARCHAR2 (1000)  NULL,
 COMPL_PCT  NUMBER (3)       NOT NULL,
 START_DT   DATE             NULL,
 END_DT     DATE             NULL)
/
CREATE TABLE CLIENT
(CLIENT_ID  NUMBER (10)      NOT NULL PRIMARY KEY,
 DESCR_TX   VARCHAR2 (40)  NOT NULL,
 ACTIVE_YN  CHAR (1)         NOT NULL)
/
CREATE TABLE PROJECT_ASSOCIATION(
PROJECT_ID NUMBER (10) NOT NULL
  REFERENCES PROJECT (PROJECT_ID),
CLIENT_ID  NUMBER (10) NOT NULL
REFERENCES CLIENT (CLIENT_ID),
PRIMARY KEY (PROJECT_ID, CLIENT_ID))
/
```

Code Example 8-12

Notice the definition of the primary key of the PROJECT_ASSOCIATION table, which is the combination of the foreign keys from the PROJECT and CLIENT tables. This essentially means that the association of a CLIENT and a PROJECT is static. In other words, this implementation could not track that a CLIENT broke away from a project, only to rejoin it at a later date. The relationship either exists, or does not exist. This model does not provide the ability to track project associations over time. To allow for such ability, we would add two columns to the PROJECT_ASSOCIATION table, START_DATE and END_DATE, as follows in Code Example 8-13:

```
--EXAMPLE_08_12 IS PREREQUISITE
DROP TABLE PROJECT_ASSOCIATION;

CREATE TABLE PROJECT_ASSOCIATION(
PROJECT_ID NUMBER (10) NOT NULL
  REFERENCES PROJECT (PROJECT_ID),
CLIENT_ID  NUMBER (10) NOT NULL
REFERENCES CLIENT (CLIENT_ID),
START_DATE DATE NOT NULL,
END_DATE   DATE,
PRIMARY KEY (PROJECT_ID, CLIENT_ID, START_DATE))
/
```

Code Example 8-13

Next, we would add the START_DATE column to the primary key, as shown earlier. Lastly, our application would require logic to ensure against overlapping client/project relationships.

Object-Relational Implementation

The object-relational syntax is quite similar to the relational syntax, where we create three independent objects and use object references to relate them as shown in Code Example 8-14. Again, please note that careful thought must be applied prior to defining Object Types.

NOTE
You cannot create constraints on members of a REF to a multi-column type, even in Oracle8i. Expect a future release to allow the following PRIMARY KEY example in the PROJECT_ASSOCIATION table.

```
--***************************
--object reference as PK component generating error
--*****************************************
CREATE OR REPLACE TYPE PROJECT_TYPE
AS OBJECT(
PROJECT_ID  NUMBER(10),
STATUS_TX   VARCHAR2 (100),
DESCR_TX    VARCHAR2 (40),
DESC_TX     VARCHAR2 (1000),
COMPL_PCT   NUMBER (3),
START_DT    DATE,
END_DT      DATE)
/
CREATE OR REPLACE TYPE CLIENT_TYPE
AS OBJECT(
CLIENT_ID  NUMBER (10),
DESCR_TX   VARCHAR2 (40),
ACTIVE_YN  CHAR (1))
/
CREATE OR REPLACE TYPE PROJECT_ASSOCIATION_TYPE
AS OBJECT(
PROJECT REF  PROJECT_TYPE,
CLIENT  REF  CLIENT_TYPE)
/
CREATE TABLE CLIENT
OF CLIENT_TYPE(
CLIENT_ID  NOT NULL PRIMARY KEY)
/
CREATE TABLE PROJECT
OF PROJECT_TYPE(
PROJECT_ID NOT NULL PRIMARY KEY)
/
CREATE TABLE PROJECT_ASSOCIATION
OF PROJECT_ASSOCIATION_TYPE(
PROJECT NOT NULL,
CLIENT  NOT NULL,
PRIMARY KEY (PROJECT.PROJECT_ID, CLIENT.CLIENT_ID))
/
```

Code Example 8-14

1-to-1 Mandatory on Both Sides

The following diagrams show the mandatory 1-to-1 relationship in both ERD and UML format:

1-to-1, mandatory on both sides, relationship diagrams

ERD   UML

     We will use Example 1 from the "Examples of Uses of Association Relationships" section earlier in this chapter. This example associates two object classes, EMPLOYEE and SECURE_EMPLOYEE. As explained in the example, the purpose of this design is to protect certain employee-specific data from unwanted access. It must be noted that this relationship is rarely implemented in the real world, because these classes are mutually exclusive. The traditional approach to implementing this example would be to enforce one side of the relationship but not both. Although the examples that follow will demonstrate that data structures can be created to enforce this relationship, you will most likely find that building applications to work with these structures is challenging.

Relational Implementation

In relational notation, we would be tempted to create two tables, EMPLOYEE and SECURE_EMPLOYEE, and incorrectly relate them to each other through the use of two foreign keys, one in each table referring to the other, as shown in Code Example 8-15.

```
CREATE TABLE EMPLOYEE(
EMPLOYEE_ID          NUMBER   (10)   NOT NULL PRIMARY KEY,
LNAME                VARCHAR2 (30)   NOT NULL,
FNAME                VARCHAR2 (30)   NOT NULL,
SECURE_EMPLOYEE_ID NUMBER     (10)   NOT NULL)
/
CREATE TABLE SECURE_EMPLOYEE(
SECURE_EMPLOYEE_ID  NUMBER (10) NOT NULL PRIMARY KEY,
EMPLOYEE_ID          NUMBER (10) NOT NULL
  REFERENCES EMPLOYEE (EMPLOYEE_ID),
```

```
SSN                   VARCHAR2 (9)  NOT NULL,
SALARY                NUMBER (9,2) NOT NULL)
/
ALTER TABLE EMPLOYEE
ADD FOREIGN KEY (SECURE_EMPLOYEE_ID)
REFERENCES SECURE_EMPLOYEE (SECURE_EMPLOYEE_ID)
/
```

Code Example 8-15

The reason we need to add one of the two foreign keys after the fact using the ALTER command is that creating a mandatory 1-to-1 relationship forces us into a circular reference—does EMPLOYEE come before SECURE_EMPLOYEE? Obviously, the 1-to-1 mandatory relationship declares that they both most be instantiated simultaneously. Mandatory 1-to-1 relationships are not widely used in production systems.

When dropping one or both of these tables, we must either disable the foreign keys first, or use the Cascade Constraints option. The reason is that we have effectively created a circular reference between the two tables, making them entirely dependent upon one another.

Object-Relational Implementation

A similar circularity issue arises in object-relational syntax, only we resolve it in a different manner. The object-relational command set does not include an ALTER command for tables based upon object types. Instead, we can compile both object types, and then compile the first one again. The first time we compile EMPLOYEE_TYPE, we will receive an error, because it is attempting to reference the SECURE_EMPLOYEE_TYPE object type, which does not exist yet. The second time we compile, EMPLOYEE_TYPE will follow the compilation of SECURE_EMPLOYEE_TYPE, and it will therefore succeed. The syntax is as shown in Code Example 8-16:

```
CREATE OR REPLACE TYPE EMPLOYEE_TYPE
AS OBJECT(
EMPLOYEE_ID           NUMBER (10),
LNAME                 VARCHAR2 (30),
FNAME                 VARCHAR2 (30),
SECURE_EMPLOYEE_ID  REF SECURE_EMPLOYEE_TYPE)
/
CREATE OR REPLACE TYPE SECURE_EMPLOYEE_TYPE
AS OBJECT(
```

```
SECURE_EMPLOYEE_ID NUMBER (10),
EMPLOYEE_ID        REF EMPLOYEE_TYPE,
SSN                VARCHAR2 (9),
SALARY             NUMBER (9,2))
/
CREATE OR REPLACE TYPE EMPLOYEE_TYPE
AS OBJECT(
EMPLOYEE_ID        NUMBER (10),
LNAME              VARCHAR2 (30),
FNAME              VARCHAR2 (30),
SECURE_EMPLOYEE_ID  REF SECURE_EMPLOYEE_TYPE)
/
```

Code Example 8-16

When you create the EMPLOYEE_TYPE object type, you will receive a compilation error, because it refers to the SECURE_EMPLOYEE_TYPE object type, which you have not yet created. When creating two object types that relate to each other through object references, you will have to re-create the first one you compile, after you compile the second.

To make the earlier example work, you must first compile the EMPLOYEE_TYPE object type, then compile the SECURE_EMPLOYEE_TYPE object type, and lastly recompile the EMPLOYEE_TYPE. You will then be able to create the following tables shown in Code Example 8-17 based upon the preceding object types, following the steps discussed earlier.

```
--EXAMPLE_08_16 IS PREREQ
CREATE TABLE EMPLOYEE
OF EMPLOYEE_TYPE(
EMPLOYEE_ID NOT NULL PRIMARY KEY,
SECURE_EMPLOYEE_ID NOT NULL)
/
CREATE TABLE SECURE_EMPLOYEE
OF SECURE_EMPLOYEE_TYPE(
SECURE_EMPLOYEE_ID NOT NULL PRIMARY KEY,
EMPLOYEE_ID NOT NULL)
/
```

Code Example 8-17

As suggested earlier, we propose creating the two tables with a single, mandatory foreign key from the SECURE_EMPLOYEE table to the EMPLOYEE table, as shown in Code Example 8-18:

```
CREATE TABLE EMPLOYEE(
EMPLOYEE_ID        NUMBER   (10) NOT NULL PRIMARY KEY,
LNAME              VARCHAR2 (30) NOT NULL,
FNAME              VARCHAR2 (30) NOT NULL,
SECURE_EMPLOYEE_ID NUMBER   (10) NOT NULL)
/
CREATE TABLE SECURE_EMPLOYEE(
SECURE_EMPLOYEE_ID NUMBER (10)  NOT NULL PRIMARY KEY,
EMPLOYEE_ID        NUMBER (10)  NOT NULL
  REFERENCES EMPLOYEE (EMPLOYEE_ID),
SSN                VARCHAR2 (9) NOT NULL,
SALARY             NUMBER (9,2) NOT NULL)
/
```

Code Example 8-18

This is an example of where we might choose to soften our stand on a relationship during physical implementation. Though it makes logical sense to present a mandatory relationship between these two object classes, it might not be worth the cost of implementation.

1-to-0..10

Here is an example of a business rule that cannot be represented using ERD notation based upon two object classes, TEAM and PLAYER. Each team may have between 0 and 10 active players, and each player must be associated with one and only one team. The correct UML notation is shown here:

UML Team/Player relationship diagram

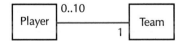

Although we cannot effectively model this relationship in ERD notation, the business rule can be physically implemented in relational syntax, as well as in object-relational syntax, as shown in the next two sections.

Relational Implementation

In Oracle7, we would create two tables and a database trigger, as follows in Code Example 8-19:

```
CREATE TABLE TEAM(
TEAM_ID   NUMBER (10)   NOT NULL PRIMARY KEY,
NAME      VARCHAR2 (30) NOT NULL)
/
CREATE TABLE PLAYER(
PLAYER_ID    NUMBER (10) NOT NULL PRIMARY KEY,
TEAM_ID      NUMBER (10) NOT NULL
  REFERENCES TEAM (TEAM_ID),
LNAME        VARCHAR2 (30) NOT NULL,
FNAME        VARCHAR2 (30) NOT NULL,
PLAYER_NBR   VARCHAR2 (2))
/
CREATE OR REPLACE TRIGGER BI_TRIGGER
BEFORE INSERT ON PLAYER
REFERENCING OLD AS OLD NEW AS NEW
FOR EACH ROW
DECLARE
CURSOR C1 IS
SELECT COUNT (*) + 1 CNT FROM PLAYER
WHERE TEAM_ID=:NEW.TEAM_ID;
C1_REC C1%ROWTYPE;
TOTAL_PLAYERS_ERR      EXCEPTION;
BEGIN
OPEN C1;
FETCH C1 INTO C1_REC;
CLOSE C1;
IF C1_REC.CNT NOT BETWEEN 0 AND 10 THEN
RAISE TOTAL_PLAYERS_ERR;
 END IF;
EXCEPTION
WHEN TOTAL_PLAYERS_ERR THEN
RAISE_APPLICATION_ERROR ('-20001',
  'ONLY 0 TO 10 PLAYERS ALLOWED PER TEAM.');
END;
/
```

Code Example 8-19

In Code Example 8-19, a BEFORE INSERT trigger is created on the PLAYER table, which performs a player count for the team that the new player record is being inserted into. The first step would be to insert a TEAM record into the TEAM table, as follows in Code Example 8-20:

```
--EXAMPLE_08_19 IS PREREQ
CREATE SEQUENCE TEAM_SEQ;

INSERT INTO TEAM (TEAM_ID, NAME)
VALUES (TEAM_SEQ.NEXTVAL,'MUSTANGS');
```

Code Example 8-20

Next, we need to insert rows into the PLAYER table. The following statement shown in Code Example 8-21 generates UIDs for each new player record and prompts you to input the last name, first name, and player number each time you execute it.

```
--EXAMPLE 08_21 IS PRERE

CREATE SEQUENCE PLAYER_SEQ;

INSERT INTO PLAYER (PLAYER_ID,
                    TEAM_ID,
                    LNAME,
                    FNAME,
                    PLAYER_NBR)
           VALUES(PLAYER_SEQ.NEXTVAL,
                  1,
                  '&LNAME',
                  '&FNAME',
                  &PNO);
```

Code Example 8-21

If this statement is executed 11 times, the last record will fire the application error –20001, which delivers the following message:

ONLY 0 TO 10 PLAYERS ALLOWED PER TEAM.

Note that this implementation does not prevent a player from being reassigned to a team and it thus violates the constraint. Writing the trigger to prevent this action involves avoiding a complex mutating table problem and is beyond the scope of this book.

Object-Relational Implementation

The only difference in implementing this example using object-relational syntax is the way you decide to implement the object tables. You can create the PLAYER and TEAM object tables based upon object types if you wish, but the core to making this relationship work is the database trigger. Unfortunately, neither Oracle Designer nor ODD generates database triggers to support such complex business rules. Instead, you must write the program logic manually.

In later chapters we will discuss more specific relationship types that further define the nature of the interaction among classes. These types of relationships include

- Composition

- Aggregation

- Generalization

Each of these relationships is more precise than simple association, and so should be used where appropriate in place of association.

CHAPTER
9

Composition and Aggregation: "Close Associations"

o far, we have only discussed associations where objects are linked to other objects. An association tells us that one object has something to do with another object. It doesn't tell us anything about the nature of that relationship. Sometimes it is useful to model a tighter relationship between objects. We might want to be able to say that one object is part of another, or that an object is almost defined by its relationships to other objects. This chapter will discuss these closer associations, namely composition and aggregation relationships.

Modeling and Implementing Close Associations

From a modeling perspective the relationship between a purchase order and a purchase order detail is quite different from the relationship between a project and an employee who is acting as project manager. In the purchase order/purchase order detail case, we can say that it doesn't make sense to have a purchase order detail without a purchase order. The detail is part of the parent object. A purchase is, to some extent, defined by its details. The details tell us what was purchased. Without the details, the purchase order has little meaning. Details on purchase orders never move from purchase order to purchase order.

The relationship between a project and the project manager is quite different. Projects are independent objects. They are of interest to the organization independent of who manages them. A project is not defined by who the manager is, and managers can easily be replaced on projects. Similarly, project managers are simply employees who, as one of their roles, can act as a manager of a project. An employee can also have other roles. An employee need not even be associated with any project and can manage several projects at once.

Logically, we can see that some relationships have very different meanings from other relationships. We say that the relationship between a purchase order and its purchase order details is an example of a *close association.* From an implementation perspective, close associations are of interest because we have different requirements for items that are close associations. We usually want to retrieve closely associated objects together, so we want them stored in such a way that retrieval of those objects is efficient. Once an object is close associated, we may want to prevent the changing of that link. We may want to create, update, and delete close associated objects together, so having them stored as some kind of grouped object would be desirable.

UML provides for two kinds of close association: aggregation and composition. *Composition* and *aggregation* are new relationships for ER modelers and will require careful explanation. The difference between these two constructs is not clear to many people in the object-oriented community either, so careful attention should be paid to the following discussion.

First, we will review the kind of close association that we can model in entity relationship modeling. In entity relationship modeling, when we need to talk about one entity being closely related to another, we can use the dependent relationship represented by a UID bar on the relationship, as shown in Figure 9-1.

A *dependent* relationship is used when we want to say that the child object (in this case the purchase order detail) is dependent on the parent object (in this case the purchase order). "Dependent" means that the child object has no meaning outside of the context of the parent object.

Dependent relationships are primarily used in two contexts. The first is illustrated by the Purchase Order–PO Detail example. Anytime we have a line item on a document (or something similar), we model it with a dependent relationship, as shown in Figure 9-1.

The second place that such relationships are frequently used is with intersection entities that arise from many-to-many relationships. Instances of intersection entities have no meaning without their parent objects, so a dependent relationship is appropriate. It doesn't make any sense to talk about an enrollment of a student in a course offering without knowing who the student is and what course he or she is taking. This relationship is shown in Figure 9-2. Note from the earlier example that an entity may be dependent on more than one parent entity.

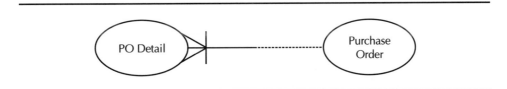

FIGURE 9-1.   *Dependency relationship*

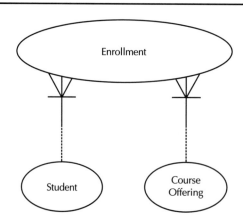

FIGURE 9-2. *ERD showing intersection entity*

The way that the dependence relationship is typically implemented is by making the primary key of the master table (for example, Purchase Order in Figure 9-1) part of the primary key of the detail table (PO Detail). Logically, this means that the PO Detail is "dependent" on the PO. In other words, a PO Detail has no meaning outside of the context of its master, the PO. It makes no sense to talk about a PO Detail that is not attached to a PO.

Because of the traditionally unchangeable nature of primary keys, this meant that, not only was the detail table always attached to the master table, but that it could also never change which master it was attached to. In our experience, this has been a confusing concept for data modelers. Many modelers never use the dependent construct at all. When it is used, it is usually only thought of in terms of its physical implementation. There was a failure to recognize the strong logical relationship between the two entities.

Unfortunately, in UML, this relationship is even more complex. Now there are two different types of close association between object classes:

■ Aggregation

■ Composition (sometimes called "strong aggregation")

We will discuss each concept separately.

Aggregation

In the UML aggregation relationship, objects from one class collectively define the objects in the aggregation class. The classic example of this kind of relationship is the association between committee and person, in that a committee is made up of the people on the committee. A committee can be defined as a collection of people.

NOTE

Aggregation   *Class A is said to be an aggregation of class B if an object in class A is defined as a collection of objects from class B. Objects from class B need not be attached to any object from class A.*

Aggregation does not correspond to any concept in entity relationship diagramming. This is a new concept that is much weaker than the dependency relationship. All aggregation says is that the two classes are more strongly related than a simple association, but they can still exist independently.

In the relational dependency relationship, the child object cannot be thought of outside the context of its parent. In aggregation, the parent cannot be thought of outside the context of its children. Some archetypal examples of aggregation relationships are shown using both ERD and UML formats in Figure 9-3.

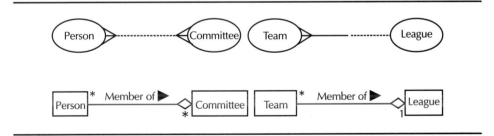

FIGURE 9-3.   *Common aggregation relationships*

The other aspect of an aggregation relationship is that the details (Person and Team in the examples earlier) have relevance outside of the context of their masters (Committee and League).

So, what does aggregation tell us? Aggregation is not purely a logical notation. With aggregated classes, we know that we will usually be working with the detail objects at the same time we work with the parent object. It makes sense for us to store the classes together in the database. It also makes sense for us to have a special access method that allows us to quickly retrieve the child objects when looking at the parent object.

With the relational implementation, there is little that would need to be done to support aggregation. We should store aggregated classes as clustered tables, but no changes to the table structures are needed. With an object-relational implementation, we can implement the association using a table of references. We will discuss this method in more detail at the end of the chapter.

Sometimes, aggregation is used because of a unique workflow. In one system, we encountered some government contract change requests. These requests came in individually over an extended period and were eventually bundled together into a contract modification, as shown in Figure 9-4.

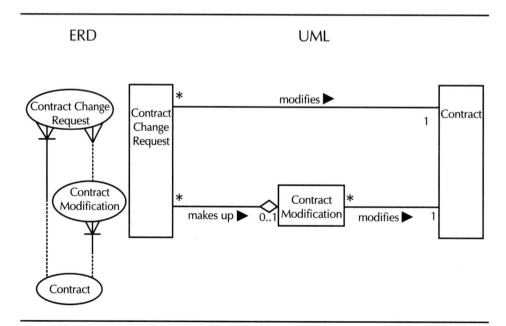

FIGURE 9-4. *Aggregation examples*

The structure shown in Figure 9-4 can be used in another similar situation. A system must be versioned, and system enhancement requests are received over time. These must be prioritized and associated with a particular system version. The appropriate model is shown in Figure 9-5. Note that it is still important to show cardinality in using aggregations.

Composition

Composition (sometimes called "strong aggregation") is similar to aggregation, although the physical implementations of these structures may be very different. Close association is one of the places where it is clear that UML was developed by programmers and not by database designers.

The composition definition, as described in UML, cannot be effectively used by object-relational designers. The formal rule in UML is that the detail *can* exist independently of the master until it is attached to a master. However, from that point forward, the detail must *always* be associated with some master. This distinction is more in keeping with how C++ works. The

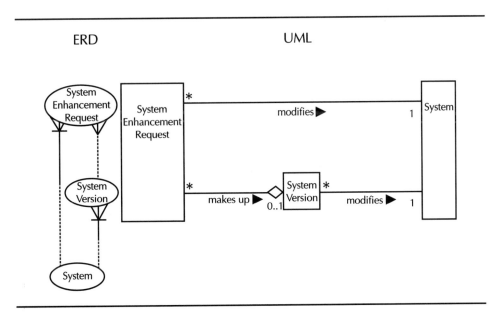

FIGURE 9-5.   *System enhancement request model*

distinction that we are suggesting between aggregation and composition is a more restrictive condition than required by the formal UML syntax, but is more logically clean and consistent with the way databases interact with these constructs.

We will define composition to be similar to the dependency relationship in ERDs, but a bit more restrictive than ERD dependency.

NOTE

Composition   Class A is said to be a composition of class B if each object of class B is a part of an object of class A. Objects of class B may not exist unless they are part of a specific object from class A. Class B objects may not exist independently. An object from class B may not be a composition child of more than one object at a time, whether it is from class A or another class.

In an aggregation relationship, the master is composed of its details, but the details can be independent of the master. In a composition relationship, the master is still composed of the details, but these details cannot be thought of outside the context of the master.

Our old dependency examples of PO and PO Detail can be used to illustrate this, as shown in the UML diagram in Figure 9-6.

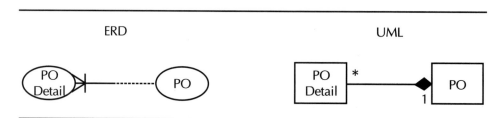

FIGURE 9-6.   *Composition relationship*

In this book, composition will only be used to indicate that objects in the detail object class always belong to one and only one master and have no independent meaning apart from that master. Therefore, a composition relationship is something like a PO/PO Detail relationship.

Composition in UML is slightly more restrictive than dependency in an ERD. For example, in an ERD you might want to say that a Course at a university is dependent on the Department where it is offered. Furthermore, specific Offerings of this course would be dependent on the Course, as shown in Figure 9-7.

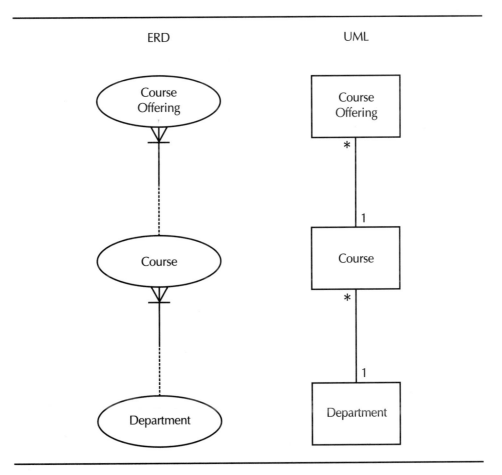

FIGURE 9-7. *ERD dependencies do not always translate to UML composition*

Notice how the UML equivalent in Figure 9-7 uses simple association. Actually, using composition in this case would not violate the composition definition in UML, nor does it violate our more restrictive definition. However, in practice, object-oriented designers only use composition when the composition detail objects are created and destroyed at the same time as the parent object. Because Courses and Course Offerings are created completely independently from their parents, composition should not be used in this situation.

When to Use Composition and Aggregation

Composition and aggregation are more precise relationships than simple association. They should be used whenever appropriate for the logical model. The strategy should be to use composition if it is appropriate, aggregation if composition is too restrictive, and to use simple associations if aggregation is too restrictive. Of course, you should not use these association types unless the situation warrants it, but designers should always use the most restrictive relationship possible.

When the model is refined as it moves toward implementation, the designer has to think about what the best structure would be with respect to implementation. Implementation has a big impact on which relationships to use. In relational modeling, you had to be very careful in the use of dependent relationships. Because dependent relationships are implemented as foreign keys that become part of the primary keys, some unintended side effects were possible. First, if there were several dependent relationships in a chain, primary keys could become very large. Second, if the dependent table were recursive, then the foreign key could be very complex. The problems with implementation are no less severe with the new object-relational structures. We will discuss how these structures are implemented later in the chapter.

Frequently, we have the option of representing the same situation as either a composition or an aggregation. For example, in our committee membership example shown in Figure 9-3, we can represent the same example as shown in Figure 9-8.

ERD   UML

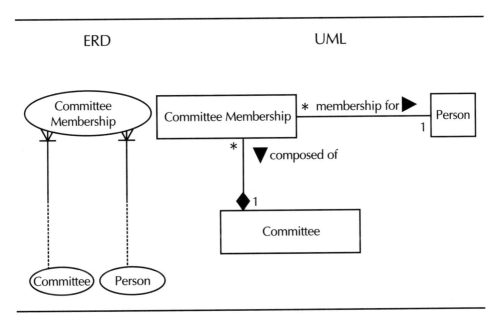

FIGURE 9-8.   *UML composition construct*

The first visible difference is the extra intersection class, but there is nothing to prevent you from using a similar structure in the aggregation example as shown in Figure 9-9. The ERD for each of these examples (Figures 9-8 and 9-9) would be the same.

Using aggregation as shown in Figure 9-9, the focus is placed on the relationship between committee and person with the committee membership arising from that relationship. Using composition to represent this relationship as shown in Figure 9-8, committee membership is given greater emphasis.

In this case, we believe that the aggregation construct makes the most sense. However, a professional association, for which memberships are critical, might view the composition diagram as being the most appropriate to represent their business rules. Therefore, there is no one correct answer to this modeling problem. Both versions accurately represent the business rules. The composition representation focuses attention in one direction, while the second aggregation representation focuses attention in a different direction.

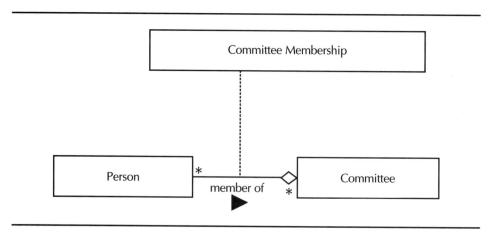

FIGURE 9-9. *UML aggregation construct*

To summarize, we have discussed three kinds of relationships so far. It is important to clarify when to use each of these:

- **Composition**   The detail object must belong to a master. It is not meaningful to discuss the detail out of context of the master. If the master is deleted, all details would logically have to be deleted. Best example: PO – PO Detail.

- **Aggregation**   The master is made up of (and to some extent defined by) the details. However, it is relevant to talk about details outside the context of the master. Best example: a committee made up of a number of people.

- **Simple Association**   This relationship type is used to represent every other type of relationship between object classes. The implication is that if you can use one of the other three types (Composition, Aggregation, or Generalization), you should.

The models used for physical implementation may change somewhat because of the way we implement these associations. We will now discuss the physical implementations of the close associations and then conclude the chapter with a few examples of both the best logical and the best physical model uses of close relationships.

Physical Implementation of Associations

Until Oracle8 was released, the only options available for implementing associations were integrity constraints and clusters. Integrity constraints provided the ability to associate rows between two tables, but did not provide functionality specifically aimed at enhancing overall data manipulation/retrieval performance. Several examples of associations were provided in Chapter 8. Clusters were developed not only to provide a mechanism for closely associating data between tables, but also specifically to maximize efficiency of data manipulation/retrieval.

Oracle8 now offers two additional techniques for closely associating rows between two object classes. These two techniques are nested tables and VARRAYs. Nested tables are based on object types and do not store their data in the same location as the master table. Nested tables appear to have more performance benefits than VARRAYs, because a full scan of a table including a VARRAY must scan the contents of the VARRAY, while querying a table that contains a nested table would not require scanning of the nested table itself. On the other hand, data stored within a VARRAY is stored in the same location as the data of the master table, resulting in maximum retrieval efficiency. More details regarding each of these options are available later in this chapter.

Clusters

Clusters may be used for storing data between closely associated tables. The purchase order and purchase order details scenario would be an example of a relationship between two tables that is so strong that in most cases we require access to the purchase order detail rows via the purchase order rows. Clusters store the rows of the tables they contain in an isolated area.

To implement a cluster, you must first issue the CREATE CLUSTER statement, as follows in Code Example 9-1:

```
CREATE CLUSTER PO_CLUSTER
(PO_ID NUMBER (10))
/
```

Code Example 9-1

The column reference to PO_ID is called the *cluster key*. The cluster key contains the column(s) that is used to join the clustered tables. The next step would be to create the tables within the PO_CLUSTER as shown in Code Example 9-2.

```
--EXAMPLE_09_01 IS PREREQ
CREATE TABLE PO (
PO_ID       NUMBER (10) NOT NULL,
VENDOR_ID   NUMBER (10) NOT NULL,
CREATE_DATE DATE NOT NULL,
EMP_ID      NUMBER (10) NOT NULL)
CLUSTER PO_CLUSTER (PO_ID)
/

CREATE TABLE PO_DTL (
PO_ID       NUMBER (10) NOT NULL,
LINE_NBR    NUMBER (3)  NOT NULL,
ITEM_ID     NUMBER (10) NOT NULL,
QTY         NUMBER (10,2) NOT NULL)
CLUSTER PO_CLUSTER (PO_ID)
/
```

Code Example 9-2

The critical component to the cluster's enhanced performance is known as the *cluster index*. A cluster index must be created before inserting data into the cluster tables. You do not have to specify the components of a cluster index, because they are automatically defined based upon the components of the cluster key. An example of creating a cluster index is shown in Code Example 9-3:

```
--EXAMPLE_09_02 IS PREREQ
CREATE INDEX PO_CLUSTER_IDX
ON CLUSTER PO_CLUSTER
/
```

Code Example 9-3

As rows are inserted into the clustered tables, the key values of PO_ID are only stored once, as a unique set of values within the cluster key. The rows of both of these tables are actually stored together in the same physical location, as though the tables were nested.

Index Organized Tables

Oracle8 supports a form of table organization called *Index Organized Tables* (IOTs). In IOTs, the table data is organized as an index on the primary key of the table. That is, in these tables, rows are physically clustered (and ordered) on the primary key. This can be quite useful in modeling composition (parent-child relationships). In the example, the PO_DTL table could be organized as an Index Organized Table with primary key as (PO_ID, LINE_NBR). This guarantees that all the lines of a purchase order (for a given PO_ID) will be physically clustered together as shown in Code Example 9-4:

```
CREATE TABLE PO_DTL (
        PO_ID       NUMBER (10) NOT NULL,
        LINE_NBR   NUMBER (3) NOT NULL,
        :
        :
        PRIMARY KEY (PO_ID, LINE_NBR)
) ORGANIZATION INDEX;
```

Code Example 9-4

Oracle8 allows for nested tables to be created as Index Organized Tables. Therefore, for a given parent row, its child rows are physically clustered together. So, when a parent row is accessed all its children rows can be efficiently retrieved. When only parent rows are accessed, this can also be done efficiently as the children rows are not intermixed with the parent rows. Also, for large child-sets, parent and a reference to the child-set can be returned so that the children rows can be accessed on demand; the child-sets can also be filtered. This avoids unnecessary transporting of children rows for every parent.

Clusters Versus Index Organized Tables

Clusters and Index Organized Tables are similar in the sense that both mechanisms physically cluster related rows. However, cluster tables can cluster rows from multiple table whereas Index Organized Tables store rows of a single table. These differences have pros and cons. If a parent-child relationship (composition) is implemented using the Index Organized Table option, it is efficient to perform operations (scans, filtering) on the parent table; since the parent table does not store children rows, the number of I/Os will be smaller. Also, large child-sets can be returned efficiently using Index Organized Tables.

While cluster tables may seem to offer better parent/children row retrieval, the performance benefits are nominal over Index Organized Tables. In addition, cluster tables have the following limitations:

- Clusters cannot be partitioned

- Parallel operations are limited

- Clusters cannot contain LOB columns

Overall, Index Organized Tables are preferred over cluster tables both for single table clustering as well as for parent-child relationships. Clustering should be used for storing greater than two related tables and their data.

Examples

We will conclude this chapter with several examples that illustrate when to use each kind of relationship.

Example 1: Keyword Association   Frequently, we want to be able to attach keywords to various objects. For example, with movies, we might want to describe a movie as both romance and comedy, as exemplified by the film *When Harry Met Sally,* or as action, drama, and romance for *Gone with the Wind.*

Even though we could use a close association to model this situation, the simple intersection class shown in Figure 9-10 provides the clearest model. For the best physical implementation we might want to use the model shown in Figure 9-11 to reflect that we are mainly interested in keywords when we are manipulating a movie object, and that movie keywords are part of the movie object.

Example 2: Document/Document Detail   Let's say we are modeling a retail organization. We have sales to customers. Cash sales might not be attached to a customer, but if we know the customer, we will attach the sales to the

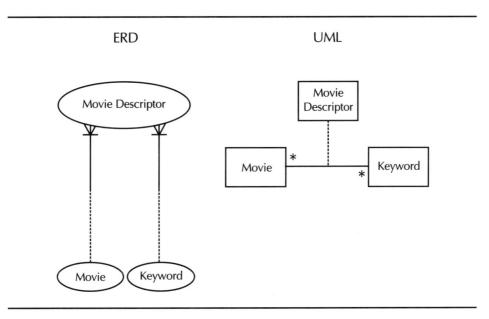

FIGURE 9-10. *Association/intersection example*

customer. A sale may involve any number of inventory items. The correct model is shown in Figure 9-12.

The model in Figure 9-12 is what we would expect to solve this problem with the possible exception of the optional-optional relationship between

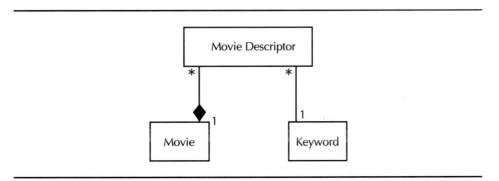

FIGURE 9-11. *Best physical implementation model using intersection*

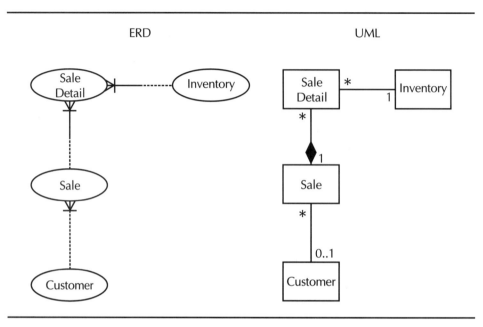

ERD · UML

FIGURE 9-12. *Retail Sales model*

Customer and Sale. The optionality is there to support the cash sales. In the UML model we are able to show Sale Details as part of Sale.

Example 3: Workflow Event   On many objects there are various actions that affect the object. Such events are usually performed by someone and are of a particular type. For the example shown in Figure 9-13, let's say we are modeling the approval process of a purchase order. Approval takes place for each line item, not for the whole order. The correct model is shown in Figure 9-13.

Relational Support for Composition Relationships

We will use the Committee Membership model from Figure 9-8 as the basis for our Composition Relationship example. The model shows three independent object classes: Committee Membership, Person, and

ERD   UML

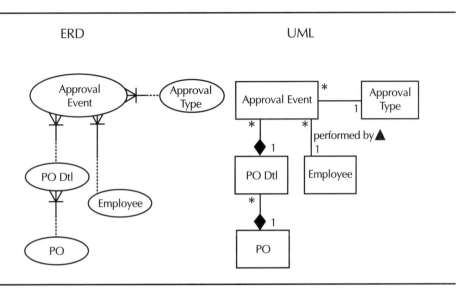

FIGURE 9-13. *Workflow model*

Committee. The following DDL shown in Code Example 9-5 is required, although the columns are hypothetical.

```
CREATE TABLE PERSON (
PERSON_ID            NUMBER (10) NOT NULL PRIMARY KEY,
LNAME                VARCHAR2 (40) NOT NULL,
FNAME                VARCHAR2 (40) NOT NULL)
/

CREATE TABLE COMMITTEE (
COMMITTEE_ID         NUMBER (10) NOT NULL PRIMARY KEY,
DESCR_TXT            VARCHAR2 (25) NOT NULL,
START_DATE           DATE NOT NULL,
END_DATE             DATE)
/

CREATE TABLE COMM_MBR (
PERSON_ID            NUMBER (10) NOT NULL
  REFERENCES PERSON (PERSON_ID),
COMMITTEE_ID              NUMBER (10) NOT NULL
  REFERENCES COMMITTEE (COMMITTEE_ID),
```

```
COMM_MBR_IND          VARCHAR2 (1) DEFAULT 'S' NOT NULL
    ,
START_DATE            DATE DEFAULT SYSDATE NOT NULL

    ,
END_DATE              DATE,
PRIMARY KEY (PERSON_ID, COMMITTEE_ID, START_DATE))
/
```

Code Example 9-5

Notice that the primary key of the COMM_MBR table is the combination of the foreign keys from PERSON and COMMITTEE. In addition, the START_DATE of the Committee Membership is also a component of the primary key. The idea here is that it does not make sense to think of a committee membership outside of the scope of the committee.

Object-Relational Composition Example

As in previous examples, we might implement three object types, each spawning a table that would correspond to the PERSON, COMMITTEE, and COMM_MBR object classes as shown in Code Example 9-6.

```
CREATE OR REPLACE TYPE PERSON_T
AS OBJECT(
PERSON_ID             NUMBER (10),
LNAME                 VARCHAR2 (40),
FNAME                 VARCHAR2 (40))
/
CREATE OR REPLACE TYPE COMM_T
AS OBJECT(
COMM_ID               NUMBER (10),
DESCR_TXT             VARCHAR2 (25),
START_DATE            DATE,
END_DATE              DATE)
/

CREATE OR REPLACE TYPE COMM_MBR_T
AS OBJECT(
PERSON_ID             NUMBER (10),
COMM_ID               NUMBER (10),
COMM_MBR_IND          VARCHAR2 (1),
START_DATE            DATE,
END_DATE              DATE)

/
```

```
CREATE TABLE PERSON
OF PERSON_T(
PERSON_ID              NOT NULL PRIMARY KEY,
LNAME                  NOT NULL,
FNAME                  NOT NULL)
/
CREATE TABLE COMM
OF COMM_T (
COMM_ID                NOT NULL PRIMARY KEY,
DESCR_TXT              NOT NULL ,
START_DATE             NOT NULL)
/

CREATE TABLE COMM_MBR
OF COMM_MBR_T (
PERSON_ID              NOT NULL
  REFERENCES PERSON (PERSON_ID),
COMM_ID                NOT NULL
  REFERENCES COMM (COMM_ID),
COMM_MBR_IND           DEFAULT 'S' NOT NULL ,
START_DATE             DEFAULT SYSDATE NOT NULL,
PRIMARY KEY (PERSON_ID, COMM_ID, START_DATE))
/
```

Code Example 9-6

Object-Relational Support for Composition Relationships

Oracle8 provides two new techniques that can be used in place of one another in support of a composition relationship. The first technique is a nested table, which actually creates a table that is physically stored with the master table. The second technique is called a VARRAY, which is an array that can be stored within the master table, itself.

Nested Tables

Nested tables are the logical equivalent of clustered tables, although they are not implemented in the same way. The following example will be presented in object-relational syntax for nested tables. This example creates a nested table for Purchase Order Details (PO_DTL), which is embedded in the master table, Purchase Order (PO). We must create three object types, one of which is of type TABLE. Then, we create the PO table, which has the PO_DTL table embedded within it as a nested table.

Since nested tables are only available in object-relational syntax, there is no relational example. To implement this type of relationship in relational syntax, you would create two tables with the appropriate foreign key constraint associating them, or use the cluster example from the previous section.

Aggregations can be implemented by use of the nested table approach, though they are typically implemented using the 0..1-to-* method. An example of implementing this method is available in Chapter 8.

INDEX ORGANIZED NESTED TABLES VS. CLUSTERS   Nested tables can be stored in Index Organized Tables. The nested tables stored in Index Organized Tables will perform as well as clusters; in addition, unlike clusters, there is no loss in functionality (i.e. parallel operations, LOB columns, etc.). The following syntax illustrates the use of Index Organized Table for nested table storage (Code Example 9-5 can be modified as follows in Code Example 9-7):

```
CREATE TABLE PO of PO_TYPE(
     PO_ID NOT NULL PRIMARY KEY,
     DESCR_TX  NOT NULL,
     VENDOR_ID  NOT NULL REFERENCES VENDOR (VENDOR_ID))
     NESTED TABLE PO_DTL STORE AS DTL (
       (PRIMARY KEY (NESTED_TABLE_ID, ITEM_ID))
       ORGANIZATION INDEX COMPRESS);
```

Code Example 9-7

In the above Code Example 9-7, the PO_DTL nested table is stored in DTL, which is an Index Organized Table; all the details of a given purchase order are physically clustered together. In addition, the COMPRESS clause factors out the PO_ID key of the parent PO row. That is, the PO_ID is not repeated in every line item in Code Example 9-7, thus providing significant storage savings over the Code in Example 9-8:

```
CREATE OR REPLACE TYPE PO_DTL_TYPE
AS OBJECT(
ITEM_ID  VARCHAR2 (5),
QTY      NUMBER (5))
/
CREATE OR REPLACE TYPE PO_DTL_TABLE_TYPE
AS TABLE OF PO_DTL_TYPE
/
```

```
CREATE OR REPLACE TYPE PO_TYPE
AS OBJECT(
PO_ID      VARCHAR2 (5),
DESCR_TX   VARCHAR2(40),
VENDOR_ID      VARCHAR2 (5),
PO_DTL PO_DTL_TABLE_TYPE)
/
CREATE TABLE PO
OF PO_TYPE(
PO_ID      NOT NULL PRIMARY KEY,
DESCR_TX   NOT NULL,
VENDOR_ID NOT NULL)
NESTED TABLE PO_DTL STORE AS PO_DTL
/
```

Code Example 9-8

The following statement shown in Code Example 9-9 can be used to insert one Purchase Order object and associate two PO detail objects to the Purchase Order object:

```
--EXAMPLE_09_08 IS PREREQ
INSERT INTO PO (PO_ID,
                DESCR_TX,
                VENDOR_ID,
                PO_DTL)
VALUES (        '1000',
                'NEW OFFICE EQUIPMENT',
                '10',
PO_DTL_TABLE_TYPE (
                PO_DTL_TYPE ('04569', 5),
                PO_DTL_TYPE ('32834', 1)))
/
```

Code Example 9-9

To select the item numbers of the items in ascending order for Purchase Order 1000, we could use the following statement shown in Code Example 9-9:

```
--EXAMPLE_09_08 IS PREREQ
SELECT ITEM_ID, QTY
FROM THE (SELECT PO_DTL
          FROM PO
```

```
            WHERE PO_ID = '1000')
ORDER BY ITEM_ID
/
```

Code Example 9-9

To add another item to Purchase Order 1000, you could use the following statement shown in Code Example 9-10:

```
EXAMPLE_09_09 IS PREREQ
INSERT INTO THE (SELECT PO_DTL
                FROM PO
                WHERE PO_ID = '1000')
        VALUES ('92845', 4)
/
```

Code Example 9-10

VARRAYs

A VARRAY is a new data type that provides the ability to support multivalue or repeating groups. VARRAYs can be implemented as domains through an object type, but note that VARRAYs, like nested tables, cannot be nested, themselves. VARRAYs can contain one or more columns, and are stored in the same segment as the master object, if space is available. We will show how to implement a VARRAY of temperatures taken at time intervals. Code Example 9-11 will define a new domain of type VARRAY, supporting hourly temperature samples.

```
CREATE OR REPLACE TYPE TEMP_ARGS
AS OBJECT(
TEMPERATURE  NUMBER (5,2),
SAMPLE_DATE  DATE)
/

CREATE OR REPLACE TYPE HOURLY_TEMP
AS VARRAY (24) OF TEMP_ARGS
/
```

Code Example 9-11

After we have created the object types, we can utilize them in the definition of a table that tracks the days studied, as follows in Code Example 9-12:

```
--EXAMPLE_09_11 IS PREREQ
CREATE TABLE DAYS(
DAYS_ID  NUMBER NOT NULL PRIMARY KEY,
SAMPLE   HOURLY_TEMP)
/
```

Code Example 9-12

Nested Tables Versus VARRAYs

Both nested tables and VARRAYs have limitations. Objects within a VARRAY are stored directly with the master record, achieving optimal performance. Objects within nested tables are actually stored independent of the master table, and therefore require an index for optimal retrieval. The syntax of object-relational SQL used to retrieve data from nested tables has also grown quite complicated, as noted in the earlier example.

VARRAYs cannot be accessed independent of the master record. However, if you are striving for the perfect approach to storing purchase order details and require the ability to quickly count the total number of widgets ordered in a specified time frame, only nested tables can be applied. Oracle8i provides syntax for unnesting nested tables to satisfy queries such as, "Show me a count of widgets ordered by all customers."

Figure 9-12 might be a perfect example of requiring multiple levels of nesting, with one minor change to the model. If the relationship between SALE and CUSTOMER required that a SALE must be tied to a CUSTOMER, then you could argue for the ability to nest CUSTOMER, SALE, and SALE DETAIL all together. Unfortunately, the current version of Oracle8 only permits one level of nesting, so you could nest CUSTOMER and SALE, or SALE and SALE DETAIL, but not all three.

Aggregation Example—Relational Syntax

Aggregations can be implemented by use of the nested table approach, although they are typically implemented using a foreign key. We will build an example from Figure 9-4, and additional examples of implementing this

technique are available in Chapter 8. The contract change request model
requires three tables: CONTRACT, CONTRACT_CHANGE_REQ, and
CONTRACT_MOD. There are three mandatory 1-to-many relationships: one
from CONTRACT_MOD to CONTRACT, one from CONTRACT_CHANGE_
REQ to CONTRACT_MOD, and one from CONTRACT_CHANGE_REQ to
CONTRACT. The following DDL shown in Code Example 9-13 would be
used to implement this model.

```
CREATE TABLE CONTRACT (
CONTRACT_ID NUMBER (10) NOT NULL PRIMARY KEY,
DESCR_TXT    VARCHAR2 (40) NOT NULL,
START_DATE   DATE NOT NULL,
END_DATE     DATE)
/

CREATE TABLE CONTRACT_MOD (
CONTR_MOD_ID   NUMBER (10) NOT NULL PRIMARY KEY,
CONTR_MOD_TXT VARCHAR2 (10) NOT NULL,
START_DATE     DATE NOT NULL,
CONTRACT_ID    NUMBER (10) NOT NULL
  REFERENCES CONTRACT (CONTRACT_ID))
/

CREATE TABLE CONTRACT_CHANGE_REQ (
CONTRACT_CHANGE_REQ_ID NUMBER (10) NOT NULL PRIMARY KEY,
CONTRACT_ID             NUMBER (10) NOT NULL
  REFERENCES CONTRACT (CONTRACT_ID),
CONTRACT_MOD_ID         NUMBER (10) NOT NULL
  REFERENCES CONTRACT_MOD (CONTR_MOD_ID),
DESCR_TXT               VARCHAR2 (2000) NOT NULL,
START_DATE              DATE NOT NULL)
/
```

Code Example 9-13

In aggregation relationships such as the one between CONTRACT_
CHANGE_REQ and CONTRACT_MOD, it would make sense to talk about
change requests independent of the contract modification that would
implement them. For example, we might assign separate individuals to
investigate change requests independent of others. Therefore, it would be
appropriate to generate a list of change requests without concern for the
contract modification that they are assigned to.

It is also important to note that the foreign key from the
CONTRACT_MOD is not a component of the primary key of the
CONTRACT_CHANGE_REQ table. This means that a change request can
easily be reassigned from one contract modification to another, without
requiring a modification to the primary key value.

Object Relational Aggregation Example

The key difference in implementing this model via object-relational syntax is
the availability of domains and OIDs. The structure of the tables does not
change as shown in Code Example 9-14:

```
CREATE OR REPLACE TYPE ID AS OBJECT (
COL      NUMBER (10))
/
CREATE OR REPLACE TYPE VC2_40 AS OBJECT (
COL     VARCHAR2 (40))
/

CREATE OR REPLACE TYPE VC2_10 AS OBJECT (
COL     VARCHAR2 (10))
/

CREATE TABLE CONTRACT (
CONTRACT_ID  ID NOT NULL,
DESCR_TXT    VC2_40 NOT NULL,
START_DATE   DATE NOT NULL,
END_DATE     DATE,
PRIMARY KEY (CONTRACT_ID.COL))
/

CREATE TABLE CONTRACT_MOD (
CONTR_MOD_ID  ID NOT NULL,
CONTR_MOD_TXT VC2_10 NOT NULL,
START_DATE    DATE NOT NULL,
CONTRACT_ID   ID NOT NULL,
FOREIGN KEY (CONTRACT_ID.COL)
  REFERENCES CONTRACT (CONTRACT_ID.COL),
PRIMARY KEY (CONTR_MOD_ID.COL))
/

CREATE TABLE CONTRACT_CHANGE_REQ (
CONTRACT_CHANGE_REQ_ID ID NOT NULL,
CONTRACT_ID            ID NOT NULL,
```

```
  FOREIGN KEY (CONTRACT_ID.COL)   REFERENCES CONTRACT
(CONTRACT_ID.COL),
CONTR_MOD_ID         ID NOT NULL,
  FOREIGN KEY (CONTR_MOD_ID.COL)   REFERENCES CONTRACT_MOD
(CONTR_MOD_ID.COL),
DESCR_TXT                VC2_40 NOT NULL,
START_DATE               DATE NOT NULL,
  PRIMARY KEY (CONTRACT_CHANGE_REQ_ID.COL))
/
```

Code Example 9-14

Note that nested tables can be accessed independently using "unnesting" syntax. The following Code Example 9-15 demonstrates this technique:

```
SELECT d.item_id
FROM PO p, TABLE(P.PO_DTL) d
WHERE d.qty > 30;
```

Code Example 9-15

In the above query, since no PO table columns are accessed in the select list or in the where clause, the detail table (DTL) is independently accessed. The query optimizer is capable of performing this optimization implicitly.

CHAPTER
10

Recursive Structures

recursive relationship occurs when you have an association between an object class and itself. Recursive relationships are useful for modeling many interesting structures. Most commonly, they are used for hierarchical structures, such as the organizational structure of a company. However, in addition to modeling hierarchical relationships, recursive relationships can also be used to model linked lists, networks, rings, and pairings. Although recursive relationships are not often used in traditional modeling, we believe that this is a mistake. Recursive relationships are very powerful, allowing modelers to greatly simplify structures while making models more robust and stable with respect to unanticipated changes to business rules. This chapter will discuss the different types of recursive relationships and how these can best be modeled.

In this chapter, we will outline each of the different recursive structures from a business perspective and then discuss how to model and support each of them.

Types of Recursive Structures

There are nine types of recursive structures that we will discuss:

- **Multi-network** This type of structure is used to keep track of the general interactions among objects. The reason it is called a multi-network is because this structure can contain any number of independent networks. Any particular object can have any number of parents and any number of children. An example would be tracking relationships among people in an organization.

- **Network** Single networks are slightly more restrictive than multi-networks, because all items must be connected through one network. This means that, given any two objects in the network, a series of relationships to get from one object to another must exist. This structure could be used for a network of locations for a regional airline. A single network would support the business rule that you can get from any one location in the network to any other location.

- **Multi-tree** This type of structure is used for storing strict hierarchical relationships. Any object may have any number of children and, at most, one parent. In addition, there is a stipulation that there is exactly one object in each tree (called the *root object)* that has no parent. The term "multi-tree" is used to allow for multiple independent tree structures. This is a very common recursive structure that can be used to model situations such as parts explosion in specific identification inventories (what parts exist as components of other parts).

■ **Tree**   Tree structures are similar to multi-tree structures, except that they are restricted to support only one tree. Exactly one object in the class would have no parent, and all other objects would have exactly one parent. This is a common structure used for situations such as departmental or reporting structures in an organization.

■ **Multi-linked list**   A multi-linked list is an open chain of objects where each element has, at most, one parent and, at most, one child. In each chain there exists an element with no parent (top) and an element with no child (bottom). These structures are useful for tracking items such as versions of contracts.

■ **Linked list**   Linked lists are restricted to a single linked list object within the structure. Examples are the name of a single company in a single company system, or the version number of the production database system.

■ **Multi-ring**   Multi-ring structures are linked lists with no bottom or top. Every element has both a parent and a child. The entire structure is made of closed loops. This would be useful for tracking locations associated with round-trip tickets in an airline reservation system, business trips for an organization, or planned routing for a piece of equipment that must be returned.

■ **Ring**   This is a structure containing a single cycle. An example is a retailer storing fashion seasons such as spring, summer, back-to-school, fall, holiday, and winter, which continually repeat the same cycle.

■ **Pairs**   Pairs of objects are equivalent to a two-element multi-linked list. This structure is useful in modeling pairings of individuals, such as identifying married employees.

There are other possible structures that can be supported, including trees that loop back on themselves, trees of finite height, B-trees, classes that may support more than one recursion type simultaneously, and multi-networks that support exactly two or exactly three networks. However, our list encompasses all the recursive structures we have seen and used in practice. One of these structures could be easily modified to support any other recursive structure.

Representing Network Structures

In a hierarchy, each object in an object class has at least one parent and any number of children. In a network, any object in an object class can have any number of children and any number of parents. This is particularly useful in situations where structures are similar to the following manufacturing example typified by a component (carburetor) of an engine, which itself is made up of many component types. In this case, "carburetor" refers to the plans to make a carburetor and not a specific carburetor. This "carburetor type" can be used in the manufacture of many engines or types of engines. This could be modeled based on the object class "Engine Component" as shown in Figure 10-1.

This representation supports the network structure, but there is nothing to prevent an object from being declared to be a component of itself. Another

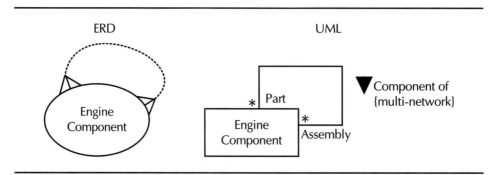

FIGURE 10-1. *Network relationship*

problem is that this structure could represent a cycle that says, "A is a component in B which is in turn a component in A." Even though this is the best representation we have for a network, it is not perfect. Cardinality on both sides of the relationship for a network is * and not 1..*. If either side is 1..*, you are forcing loops to be part of the network. Notice that the cardinality of the network relationship is * to *. A relationship of * to * with two object classes typically generates an association object class as discussed in Chapter 3. It is important to represent this association class, because this is where you need to place the attribute that declares the quantity of components used in a particular assembly type as shown in Figure 10-2.

Throughout the discussion of recursive relationships, we have noted that the UML diagrams are often imprecise. One way to improve the precision with which the relationships are represented is by adding stereotype keywords to describe them more fully. UML supports our ability to add

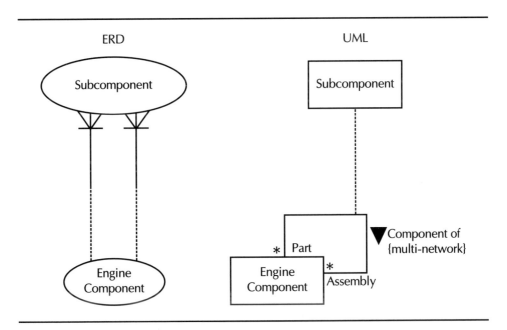

FIGURE 10-2.   *UML representation of association class*

additional keywords to UML constructs (called *constraints)* to extend the UML notation. Note that in Figure 10-2 we identified the relationship as "multi-network" through the use of a constraint.

Representing Tree Structures

The most common use for recursion is for representing a tree or hierarchical structure. Consider a hierarchical management structure as shown with the following individuals:

Hierarchical structure

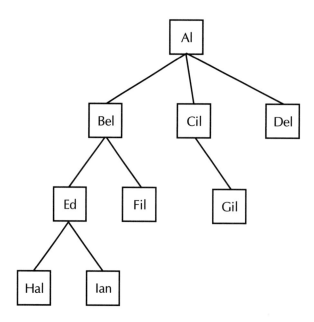

This structure is modeled as shown in Figure 10-3.

It may not be clear that this structure can be used to store a hierarchy. Let us assume simple relational implementation of this structure and store

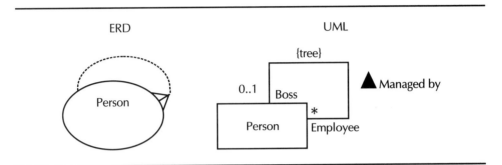

FIGURE 10-3.   *ERD and UML representation of hierarchy*

the hierarchy from the hierarchy illustration in a Person table. This result is shown in Table 10-1.

Person

Person ID	Person	Manager
1	Al	
2	Bel	1
3	Cil	1
4	Del	1
5	Ed	2
6	Fil	2
7	Gil	3
8	Hal	5
9	Ian	5

TABLE 10-1.   *Hierarchical Table*

A recursive 1-to-many model supports a hierarchical structure, but does not restrict us to that structure. We declare that this represents a hierarchy by using the constraint {tree}. Without explicitly declaring that we are trying to represent a hierarchy, we should recognize that a simple recursive structure does not enforce a strict hierarchical model. Here are the different ways that we could violate a hierarchical structure using a recursive model:

1. In the same object class, you may place more than one independent hierarchical structure. This means that you could have more than one item that has no parent. There may be times that you want to use this structure. If storing multiple hierarchies in the same structure is your intent, then we suggest that you use the constraint <<multi-tree>> to make clear your business rule. This comes in handy if your model must support more than one organizational structure.

2. An object can be linked to itself. In the example earlier, an individual could be his or her own manager. This is a relatively easy problem to detect, but it must be watched for.

3. You may have a closed loop in your data, as shown in Figure 10-4, where Al's manager is represented as Ed. In this case, a true hierarchy no longer exists, because there is no top level.

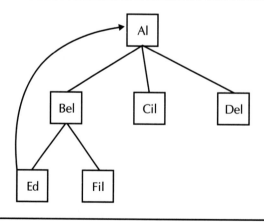

FIGURE 10-4. *Recursive closed loop*

If what you are trying to model allows any of these other types of relationships, there is no problem. When you draw a recursive 0..1 to * relationship to support a hierarchical structure, you need to recognize that you haven't fully captured this business rule in your model. Your model allows the creation of objects that violate the hierarchical business rule.

Notice that cardinality on either side of the hierarchical relationship is optional (0 is an allowable value). Many people find this confusing. Often the relationship is inaccurately modeled as 0..1 to 1..*. This is incorrect. That relationship indicates that every record in the object class must be linked to a parent record, effectively forcing data to look like the closed loop in Figure 10-4 management structure, where Al is also managed by Ed. The confusion arises because of a failure to recognize that recursion entails overloading the object class so that one object class has both parent and child records within it. The fact that every child record has a parent leads to the false conclusion to use 1..*. However, this ignores the fact that there are also parent records in the object class. Anytime you are trying to represent a hierarchical relationship, it should be modeled as 0..1 to *.

Representing Linked List Structures

Another common type of business rule supported with recursion is a linked list. A *linked list* includes chains of elements, each of which is hooked together. This is frequently used for version control. For example, contracts often have several versions. Linked lists can be represented in two ways:

A) 0..1 to 0..1   This way of representing a linked list is shown in Figure 10-5.

The ERD and UML representations for this type of linked list structure are shown in Figure 10-6.

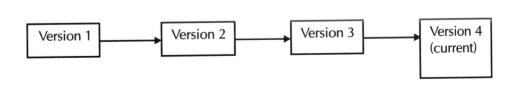

FIGURE 10-5.   *Linked list diagram A*

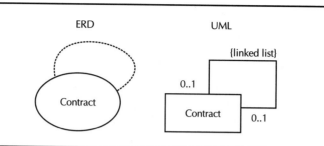

FIGURE 10-6. *Linked list diagram B*

B) Another way to represent this is 0..1 to * with the keyword "ordered" as shown in Figure 10-7. Figure 10-7 models the situation represented in Figure 10-8.

The constraint keyword "ordered" is used to indicate that there is a relevant ordering of the objects in the object class. Either of the representations in Figures 10-6 and 10-7 supports linked lists; however, neither is without flaws. As in the earlier hierarchy example, many of the same problems of * to 0..1 representations apply. 0..1 to 0..1 allows for reflexivity, meaning that a contract can be a version of itself or create a ring structure, allowing version 4 to be the parent of version 1.

Of the two options of representing linked lists, 0..1 to 0..1 is preferable. Using this description for the relationship is more precise in that it completely supports the linked lists and allows for fewer types of erroneous data to be entered into the structure. Another advantage to this representation is that 0..1 to * usually represents a hierarchy. If, in your

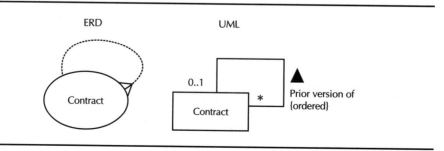

FIGURE 10-7. *Linked list with keyword*

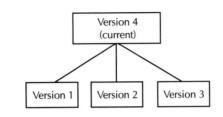

FIGURE 10-8. *Ordered linked list*

modeling conventions, 0..1 to * consistently represents hierarchies and 0..1 to 0..1 represents linked lists, it will be easier for people to understand these diagrams.

Despite the problems of imprecise modeling and more difficult concepts, for both hierarchical structures and linked lists, recursive relationships are still the best way to model these structures. The alternative is to have an object class for each level in the hierarchy. In the manager example, we would need four separate object classes, one for each level, as shown in Figure 10-9.

In the linked list example, we would need a separate object class for each possible version of the document. Relationships should never be modeled in either of these ways for several reasons:

- The number of object classes greatly increases. Not only are additional object classes needed for levels or versions, but intersection object classes are also needed to represent the * to * (many-to-many) relationship with every level.

- The relationships themselves become much more complex. Any single object class relationship is present at each of the levels.

- The structure is inherently unstable. What happens if four levels or versions are modeled, and an additional level or version is added? This is another good reason to think carefully about the abstractions of object classes inherent to the organization.

- From a physical implementation perspective, applications must be written against many more structures.

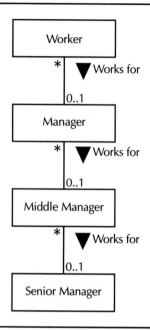

FIGURE 10-9.   *Hierarchy class*

There are two possible objections to using recursive structures. The first is that they are somewhat more complex to work with than the traditional inflexible structures. More expertise is required to implement recursive structures. Developers must learn to use the CONNECT BY command in SQL. Some added thinking is required to generate applications to support recursive structures out of Oracle Designer. This is a fair criticism. If you are working with a junior development team, explicit training will be needed to teach developers how to effectively use recursive structures.

Because you are placing information that would traditionally have been placed in several object classes into a single object class, when implementing recursive structures, the single object class might conceivably generate a very large table. This may affect performance. There are ways to get around this problem. Performance degrades proportionally to LN (table size), assuming that accesses are done using B-tree indexes. This is a solution dependent upon the skill of the developers. A second solution to the performance problem of large tables is to partition the tables using Oracle8's ability to physically partition a table.

Representing Ring Structures

To represent a ring structure such as A=>B=>C=>A, the appropriate relationship is 1-to-1. Every element has exactly one parent and exactly one child. In business systems, this is a very rare construct, but could be used to model a state transition diagram for simple ring-structured process flows. An example would be an internal control that passes administrative control periodically from one organization unit to another, eventually passing control back to the original unit. This process repeats in a way that's similar to determining the dealer in a poker game. This would be modeled as a 1-to-1 relationship as shown in Figure 10-10.

As in earlier examples, there is nothing to prevent an organization unit from passing control to itself. There is no way in UML to specify a minimum or maximum size of the ring. If it is important to do this, you need to model the ring as its own object class and represent the business rule as shown in Figure 10-11.

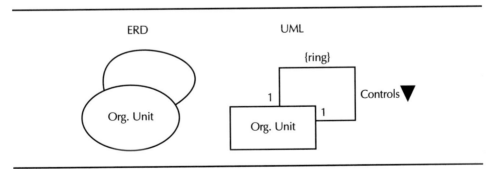

FIGURE 10-10. *Ring relationship*

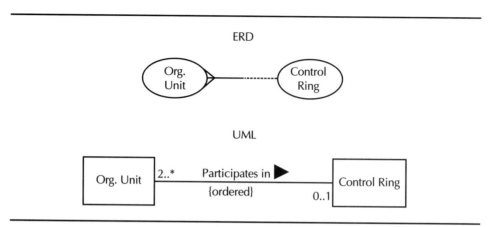

FIGURE 10-11. *Adding a keyword*

In Figure 10-11, we require that the ring has at least two organization units participating in it, and their sequence in the ring will be tracked because of the {ordered} keyword on the relationship.

If the organization only has one ring, it seems pointless to create an object class to support it, but the judgment about how to handle this must be made on a case by case basis. We would never make a control ring object class unless we were creating more than one ring. If not every organization unit participates in the ring, then the relationship should be 0..1 to 0..1. However, using the 0..1 to 0..1, you are not enforcing that the rings are closed, because this is the same structure we use for linked lists.

Representing Pairing Structures

Recursion can also be used to support the pairing of objects for a variety of uses. For example, if you were running a couples retreat, you might create a model that looks like Figure 10-12.

The problem here is that we are using the same structures that can be used for a ring. Instead, we can use the same method as in Figure 10-11,

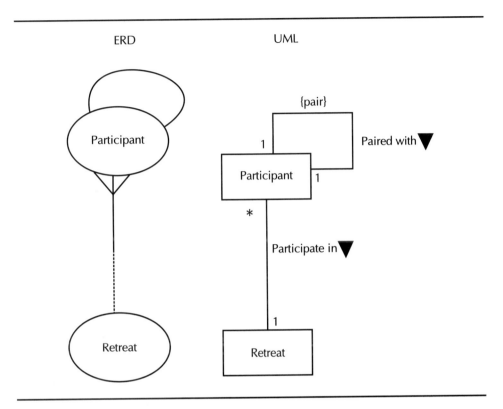

FIGURE 10-12.   *Representation of pairing A*

namely to determine whether it is worthwhile to have the overhead of an extra object class to define, or to be satisfied with the imprecision of the recursive relationship. In this case, we would opt not to use the recursive structure and add the "Couple" object class as shown in Figure 10-13.

This makes a cleaner representation of the relationship being modeled. In other circumstances, we might opt not to build the extra object class. As expressed earlier, modeling is an art. There is no hard and fast rule about the optimal way to model a given system.

ERD   UML

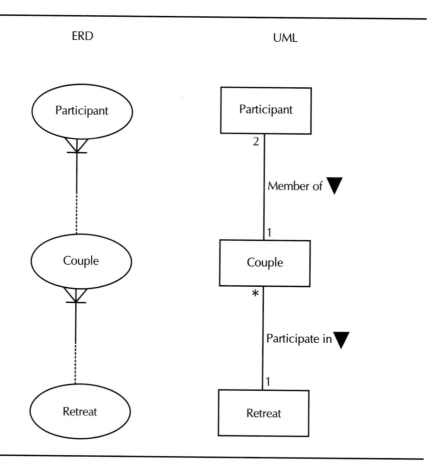

FIGURE 10-13.   *Representation of pairing B*

Implementing Recursive Structures

The following sections will explain the guidelines we follow in creating recursive data structures. An example will be provided in both relational and object-relational syntax.

Recursive data structures are a key component to the design of flexible systems. Many different modeling approaches can be used to satisfy the same requirement. Recursive data structures are not a mandatory component of a successful data model. The issue is the means by which we evaluate the model itself.

For example, when a team completes the strategy phase of the systems development life cycle, has any mention been made of the system's proposed longevity, or has the primary requirement been to satisfy the needs of today's users? If the latter is true, this is not an entirely bad thing. Many systems have a rather rigid set of business rules that do not change often. These types of systems do not require architectures that are as flexible as those that are more volatile. The level of development is certainly simplified by an order of magnitude when a rigid approach is used. However, what happens when our organization goes through a restructuring some time after the system has been implemented? If we followed the rigid approach, we would have to make substantive changes to both the data model and the applications.

Recursive structures allow us to build more flexible systems by enabling us to capture certain business rules in *data,* as opposed to *structure.* The physical implementation of recursive relationships tends to be quite uniform. The additional validation code you develop (i.e., database triggers) will be the means by which you differentiate recursive relationships. The remainder of this chapter will provide examples of implementing the four types of recursive techniques (i.e., hierarchy, network, ring, pairing) as defined earlier in the chapter, using both relational and object-relational syntax.

Network Structures

Network structures are the most flexible implementation of recursive structures, in that an object class can have any number of children and any number of parents.

- **Multi-network** To implement a multi-network, set up the recursive many-to-many table and place no restrictions on it.

- **Single network** You need to make sure that there is only one network by doing a recursive search through the network starting at the node you are manipulating. Recursively walk through the network, counting the number of objects to which you are connected. This count should equal the number of objects in the table. The constraint checking to see if there is only one network should only be a warning. Otherwise, you could prevent appropriate editing of the structure.

Relational Implementation

Let's take the example shown in Figure 10-1. This example would spawn two tables, as follows in Code Example 10-1:

```
CREATE TABLE PART (
PART_ID   NUMBER         NOT NULL PRIMARY KEY,
NAME_TX       VARCHAR2 (40) NOT NULL)
/
CREATE TABLE COMPONENT (
PART_ID       NUMBER         NOT NULL REFERENCES PART (PART_ID),
PART_ID_REF  NUMBER NOT NULL   REFERENCES PART (PART_ID),
PRIMARY KEY (PART_ID, PART_ID_REF))
/
```

Code Example 10-1

The PART table is the structure in which we define the parts that are referred to as components within other parts. For example, we might create two objects in the PART table: Carburetor and Engine. To include the Carburetor as a component of the Engine, we would create a record in the COMPONENT table, with a PART_ID that refers to the Engine PART, and a PART_ID_REF that refers to the carburetor.

Notice that we did not create a traditional recursive structure in this example (i.e., one table with a foreign key relating to itself). Rather, we created a second structure (COMPONENT), with two foreign keys back to the first (PART). In this manner, we can support the * to * relationship. Unfortunately, there is nothing in this structure to prevent you from making the Engine a component of itself. If appropriate to the system being designed, this business rule would have to be written in PL/SQL (i.e., database trigger).

Object-Relational Implementation

The object-relational structures to support this example might include two row types, PART_T and COMPONENT_T, and two column types, ID and SHORT_TXT. Two object tables, PART and COMPONENT, would be created based upon the PART_T and COMPONENT_T row types. OIDs are automatically generated for each PART and COMPONENT row, and the PART and PART_ID_REF columns on COMPONENT serve as pointers to OID values from PART, as shown in Code Example 10-2.

```
CREATE OR REPLACE TYPE ID AS OBJECT
(COL            NUMBER (10))
/

CREATE OR REPLACE TYPE SHORT_TXT AS OBJECT
(COL            VARCHAR2 (30))
/

CREATE OR REPLACE TYPE PART_T AS OBJECT (
PART_ID        ID,
NAME_TX        SHORT_TXT)
/

CREATE OR REPLACE TYPE COMPONENT_T AS OBJECT (
PART_ID        REF PART_T ,
PART_ID_REF    REF PART_T )
/

CREATE TABLE PART OF PART_T (
PART_ID        NOT NULL ,
NAME_TX        NOT NULL)
/

CREATE TABLE COMPONENT OF COMPONENT_T (
PART_ID        NOT NULL ,
PART_ID_REF    NOT NULL )
/
```

Code Example 10-2

Hierarchical (Tree) Structures

Hierarchical relationships are probably the most commonly used recursive technique found in data modeling. The management structure of an organization is typically hierarchical, because each employee is generally assigned a manager. The advantage to modeling this complex relationship using a recursive structure is that if/when your organizational management structure changes, there are no programmatical changes required. You need only modify the definition of the organization management structure, as defined by a series of rows related to each other in a recursive structure, such as ORGANIZATION.

■ **Multi-tree** Set up a recursive 1-to-many relationship, and then ensure that no cycles have been included. To detect cycles, recursively walk the structure up to the top of the tree or return to the start (fail). Another way to do this is to initiate a CONNECT BY query starting with the object you are manipulating. If the query returns an error, then a cycle has been detected.

■ **Tree** Implementation is similar to multi-tree, except that there must be only one object in the table with no parent. However, if this fails, you may only give a warning, or you won't be able to change the root of the tree.

Relational Implementation

Suppose we were to define a recursive structure to accommodate the earlier example on the subset of data defined in Figure 10-3, using Oracle7 relational syntax as shown in Code Example 10-3.

```
CREATE TABLE PERSON (
PERSON_ID          NUMBER            NOT NULL PRIMARY KEY,
PERSON_ID_REF      NUMBER                 REFERENCES PERSON
(PERSON_ID),
NAME_TX            VARCHAR2 (40)  NOT NULL)
/
```

Code Example 10-3

Using the preceding structure, we could create a record for Al, where he has no manager declared, and rows for each of the other people with each of their managers declared respectively. This model is assuming that all managers are considered equal. In other words, this model does not allow for multiple levels within the management structure, such as Department Managers reporting to Division Managers. The only information gathered here is that someone may or may not report to someone else.

If we were to add a POSITION_TYPE TABLE and relate it to the PERSON table as follows, we would be able to assign each person to a specific position. The syntax for adding such a reference is as follows in Code Example 10-4:

```
CREATE TABLE POSITION_TYPE (
POSITION_TYPE_CD   VARCHAR2 (5)     NOT NULL    PRIMARY KEY,
NAME_TX            VARCHAR2 (40)    NOT NULL)
```

```
/
ALTER TABLE PERSON ADD POSITION_TYPE_CD REFERENCES POSITION_TYPE
(POSITION_TYPE_CD)
/
```

Code Example 10-4

Although we can now capture the positions of both the person managed and the manager for any given object, we do not have the ability to define the valid management structure. In other words, there is nothing in this model to prevent one from creating "Matt" who is a Mailroom clerk, and assigning him as the manager of "Jim" the CEO. This scenario exemplifies what we call a *ring structure,* and will be discussed in further detail later in this chapter.

To enforce the hierarchical nature of the preceding example and prevent a ring structure from occurring, we might create a Before Insert/Update trigger on the PERSON table. This trigger would perform a generic CONNECT BY query, to ensure that a loop does not exist within the data. The trigger might be written as shown in Code Example 10-5:

```
CREATE OR REPLACE TRIGGER BIU_PERSON
BEFORE INSERT UPDATE
ON PERSON
FOR EACH ROW
DECLARE
RING_ERR              EXCEPTION;
CURSOR C1 IS
SELECT LPAD(' ',6*(LEVEL-1))||PERSON_ID_REF
NAME_TX
FROM PERSON
START WITH PERSON_ID = :NEW.PERSON_ID
CONNECT BY PERSON_ID_REF = PRIOR PERSON_ID;
C1_REC  C1%ROWTYPE;
V_NAME_TX    PERSON.NAME_TX%TYPE;
BEGIN
FOR C1_REC IN C1 LOOP
V_NAME_TX := C1_REC.NAME_TX;
END LOOP;
EXCEPTION
WHEN OTHERS THEN
RAISE_APPLICATION_ERROR(-20001,
' - Invalid entry caused loop.  Please ensure '||
' hierarchy is not violated by the manager of '||
v_name_tx);
```

```
END;
/
```

Code Example 10-5

This trigger will execute a query that climbs the recursive tree of data. As long as the loop is open, meaning there exists a row that does not have an assigned manager, then the trigger condition will be satisfied, and the new insert or update will complete successfully. On the other hand, if the loop is closed, an error will be generated, and the trigger will fail the requested operation.

Object-Relational Implementation

To implement this same hierarchical example in object-relational syntax, we might create two object types and two object classes, as follows in Code Example 10-6:

```
CREATE OR REPLACE TYPE POSITION_T
AS OBJECT
(POSITION_TYPE_CD VARCHAR2 (5) ,
 NAME_TX          VARCHAR (40) )
/

CREATE TYPE PERSON_T AS OBJECT
(PERSON_ID  NUMBER (10) )
/

CREATE OR REPLACE TYPE PERSON_T AS OBJECT
(PERSON_ID  NUMBER (10) ,
 PERSON_ID_REF     NUMBER (10) ,
NAME_TX      VARCHAR2 (40) ,
POSITION     VARCHAR2 (5) )
/
CREATE TABLE POSITION OF POSITION_T
(POSITION_TYPE_CD NOT NULL UNIQUE,
 NAME_TX NOT NULL)
/
CREATE TABLE PERSON OF PERSON_T
(PERSON_ID NOT NULL UNIQUE,
 PERSON_ID_REF REFERENCES Person(person_id),
 NAME_TX NOT NULL,
 POSITION REFERENCES position(position_type-cd) )
/
```

Code Example 10-6

While this example used foreign keys to link the tables, object references would also have been a viable option, as shown in Code Example 10-2.

Linked List Structures

Linked list structures can be modeled in the same way as hierarchical structures (i.e., 0..1 to *), as shown earlier. Using the 0..1 to * approach has a number of flaws that were described earlier in this chapter and provides more flexibility than a linked list requires. Therefore the 0..1 to * approach is not recommended for linked lists.

The suggested modeling approach to linked lists is represented in Figure 10-6. This figure demonstrates a 0..1 to 0..1 relationship, allowing any version of an object class to be related to, at most, one object of another object class. The 0..1 to 0..1 approach is clearly the most robust and exercises the most control over the entry of erroneous data.

However, the physical implementation will still create the same recursive structure as in the hierarchical example. The difference in the code would be the addition of a BEFORE-INSERT trigger, which would enforce the correct ordering of versions. For example, we may wish to generate the version numbers automatically, and perhaps even generate each new version object upon a modification of the prior version object. Another rule we can enforce in a BEFORE-INSERT trigger is that a given document version precedes, at most, one other version. This enhancement would enforce the desired linked characteristic.

- **Multi-linked list**   Use a recursive 1-to-1 tree structure. All of the CONNECT BY queries on any manipulated element should succeed.

- **Linked list**   This structure is similar to a multi-tree structure in that there should only be one element in the database with no parent. Again, only a warning should be issued.

Figure 10-6 would result in the following table shown in Code Example 10-7:

```
CREATE TABLE CONTRACT (
    CONTRACT_ID           NUMBER (10) NOT NULL PRIMARY KEY,
    CONTRACT_ID_REF       NUMBER (10) REFERENCES CONTRACT (CONTRACT_ID),
    CONTRACT_TXT          VARCHAR2 (10) NOT NULL,
    DESCR_TXT             VARCHAR2 (100),
    START_DATE            DATE NOT NULL,
    END_DATE)
```

Code Example 10-7

Ring Structures

We can expand upon the example from the hierarchical section to provide an example of a ring structure. We must change the POSITION_TYPE object class into a recursive structure, which we use to define the valid personnel structural components. In other words, we would use the POSITION_TYPE table to declare that Department Managers manage Project Leaders, Project Leaders manage Technicians, etc., as shown in Code Example 10-8.

- **Multi-ring** This is a recursive 1-to-1 structure where all CONNECT BY queries fail by use of a warning.

- **Ring** Recursively walk the cycle to ensure that the size of the cycle is equal to the size of the table. This must be done with a warning; otherwise, developers would need to be very careful about the algorithm used to insert objects.

Relational Implementation

Code Example 10-8 uses three tables, a unique constraint, and a database trigger to ensure that each person can be assigned to one and only one manager.

```
CREATE TABLE POSITION_TYPE (
POSITION_TYPE_ID        NUMBER NOT NULL PRIMARY KEY,
POSITION_TYPE_ID_REF NUMBER
  REFERENCES POSITION_TYPE(POSITION_TYPE_ID),
NAME_TX                 VARCHAR2 (40) NOT NULL)
/
CREATE TABLE PERSON (
PERSON_ID               NUMBER          NOT NULL PRIMARY KEY,
NAME_TX                 VARCHAR2 (40)  NOT NULL,
POSITION_TYPE_ID        NUMBER          NULL
  REFERENCES POSITION_TYPE (POSITION_TYPE_ID))
/


CREATE TABLE MGT_RELATIONSHIP (
PERSON_ID_MGR           NUMBER (10) NOT NULL
  REFERENCES PERSON (PERSON_ID),
PERSON_ID_EMP           NUMBER (10) NOT NULL
  REFERENCES PERSON (PERSON_ID) ,
PRIMARY KEY (PERSON_ID_MGR, PERSON_ID_EMP))
/
```

```
CREATE OR REPLACE TRIGGER BIU_MGT_RELATIONSHIP
BEFORE INSERT OR UPDATE
ON MGT_RELATIONSHIP
FOR EACH ROW
DECLARE
CURSOR C5 IS
SELECT POSITION_TYPE_ID
FROM PERSON
WHERE PERSON_ID = :NEW.PERSON_ID_MGR;
V_POSITION_TYPE_ID_MGR    POSITION_TYPE.POSITION_TYPE_ID%TYPE;
V_POSITION_TYPE_ID_EMP    POSITION_TYPE.POSITION_TYPE_ID%TYPE;
CURSOR C10 IS
SELECT POSITION_TYPE_ID
FROM PERSON
WHERE PERSON_ID = :NEW.PERSON_ID_EMP;
CURSOR C15 IS
SELECT '1'
FROM POSITION_TYPE
WHERE POSITION_TYPE_ID = V_POSITION_TYPE_ID_EMP
AND    POSITION_TYPE_ID_REF = V_POSITION_TYPE_ID_MGR;
C15_REC C15%ROWTYPE;
INVALID_MANAGER  EXCEPTION;
BEGIN
IF :NEW.PERSON_ID_MGR IS NOT NULL THEN
  FOR C5_REC IN C5 LOOP
       V_POSITION_TYPE_ID_MGR := C5_REC.POSITION_TYPE_ID;
    FOR C10_REC IN C10 LOOP
       V_POSITION_TYPE_ID_EMP := C10_REC.POSITION_TYPE_ID;
      OPEN C15;
      FETCH C15 INTO C15_REC;
        IF C15%NOTFOUND THEN
          RAISE INVALID_MANAGER;
        END IF;
      CLOSE C15;
    END LOOP;
  END LOOP;
END IF;
EXCEPTION
WHEN INVALID_MANAGER THEN
RAISE_APPLICATION_ERROR(-20001,'Selected Manager is invalid.');
END;
/
```

Code Example 10-8

The primary keys of both the PERSON and POSITION_TYPE tables remain the same. The additional table, MGT_RELATIONSHIP, must be created to break out the management structure from the PERSON structure. This is done to avoid the mutating table error. The BEFORE INSERT OR UPDATE trigger, BIU_MGT_RELATIONSHIP, validates the management relationship. The first step the trigger performs is to retrieve the position type of the manager person row and the employee person row. Then, the trigger validates the management relationship between these two roles in the POSITION_TYPE table.

Notice that the position relationship can be specified for all employees, without assigning them to a manager. This is a business choice made prior to defining the appropriate implementation. Leaving the recursion within the PERSON table would have forced a mutation error on updates to a person's manager assignments.

This design is not perfect, however. It only works for environments where you only care about an employee's current manager assignment. If your system required complete history of an employee and their manager assignments throughout their career with the organization, this would not work.

We restrict an employee to be assigned one and only one manager by the UNIQUE constraint on the PERSON_ID_EMP column of the MGT_RELATIONSHIP table, above. This constraint allows a maximum of one management relationship at any given time, per employee.

Implementing Paired Structures

To construct a paired structure, use a recursive 1-to-1 structure and include a trigger that forces the value of the ID to be less than the recursive foreign key (when it exists). Place a unique index on the ID together with the recursive foreign key. An example of these structures could be two tables: RETREAT and PARTICIPANTS. The PARTICIPANTS table is a simple recursive structure with a unique index on the recursive foreign key and a database trigger, which ensures that the value of the primary key is less than the value of the recursive foreign key, as shown in Code Example 10-9.

```
CREATE TABLE RETREAT(
RETREAT_ID     NUMBER(10) NOT NULL PRIMARY KEY,
NAME_TX        VARCHAR2(40) NOT NULL,
START_DATE     DATE NOT NULL,
END_DATE       DATE NOT NULL)
/
```

```
CREATE TABLE PARTICIPANTS(
PARTICIPANT_ID   NUMBER(10) NOT NULL PRIMARY KEY,
PARTICIPANT_ID_RFK NUMBER(10)
 REFERENCES PARTICIPANTS (PARTICIPANT_ID),
RETREAT_ID    NUMBER(10)NOT NULL
 REFERENCES RETREAT(RETREAT_ID),
UNIQUE(PARTICIPANT_ID_RFK))
/

CREATE OR REPLACE TRIGGER BIU_PARTICIPANTS
BEFORE INSERT OR UPDATE
ON PARTICIPANTS
FOR EACH ROW
DECLARE
INVALID_RELATIONSHIP EXCEPTION;
BEGIN
IF :NEW.PARTICIPANT_ID<= :NEW.PARTICIPANT_ID_RFK THEN
RAISE INVALID_RELATIONSHIP;
EMD IF;
EXCEPTION
WHEN INVALID_RELATIONSHIP THEN
RAISE_APPLICATION_ERROR(-20001,'INVALID PAIR.
PLEASE SELECT AGAIN.');
END;
/
```

Code Example 10-9

Other Implementation Issues

Of course, there are other drawbacks to the implementation of recursive structures besides their complexity. For example, the volume of data is no longer distributed across multiple tables. Therefore, data retrieval may be hampered significantly.

In Oracle7 the general approach to enhance performance is to regulate data access paths in order to utilize indexes. However, this solution degrades as the size of the table increases.

In Oracle8 we have the ability to partition tables. This means that we can dictate where each record is physically stored, giving us the ability to group rows logically by the manner in which they are generally accessed. Partitioned tables are discussed in more detail with accompanying examples in Chapter 1.

Conclusion

The way to approach whether to model a relationship with recursion is not to ask the question "Does the object class relate to itself in a 1-to-1, 1-to-many, or many-to-many relationship?" Instead, determine the pattern of how the object classes relate to each other (hierarchy, network, ring, pairing). The nature of the data structure will determine the cardinality of the recursive relationship.

CHAPTER
11

Or and *N-ary* Relationships

here are several complex relationships that require a little more careful thinking and consideration in modeling and implementation. These include so-called *Or* and *N-ary* relationships, which will be discussed in this chapter.

Or Relationships

Frequently, when you have relationships in a UML data modeling diagram, you encounter a situation where one or another relationship is appropriate, but never both. For example, a contract can be agreed to by exactly one party, either a person or organization, but not both. We can model this relationship as shown in Figure 11-1.

In this case, the diagram indicates that a contract may be between a person, an organization, or neither. If we want to specify that the contract must be an agreement with exactly one party, it can be done as shown in Figure 11-2 next. If there were no dotted line, this would mean that the contract would have to be with both person and organization simultaneously. The cardinality indicated by the "1" next to both Person and Organization combined with the dotted line indicates that the contract must be with either one person or one organization.

This is one of the few places where ERD notation works better than UML notation. In a large, complex diagram where classes are far apart, the dotted line will be near the contract; but the only way to see whether the *Or* relationship requires a value is to follow the cardinality lines to the base of

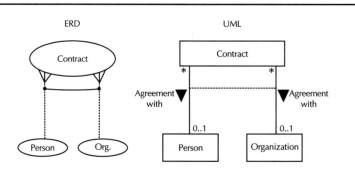

FIGURE 11-1. *Representation A of* Or *relationship*

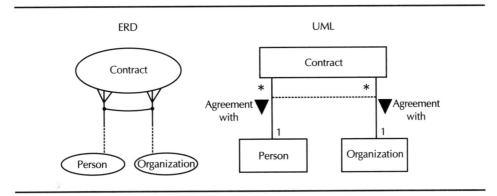

FIGURE 11-2. *Representation B of* Or *relationship*

both Person and Organization. In ERDs, the arc is placed where the optional-mandatory relationship occurs and is easier to see clearly.

In using an *Or* structure, the cardinality of all of the relationships on the *Or* must be exactly the same on the end of the relationship farthest from the dotted line (Person, Organization). On the Contract side, the cardinality may be different. We have not seen an instance where this occurred, but it is logically possible. For example, an artificial rule may be created for Persons only, allowing a maximum of ten contracts, but no such restriction would apply to Organizations. In this case, the cardinality on the contract side of the Person/Contract relationship would be 0..10 and the Organization/Contract relationship would remain *. To be precise, the only cardinality that must be the same is that on the Person/Organization side. If you allow 0 on one relationship, then both must allow 0, otherwise the relationship pair makes no logical sense. *Or* relationships are often used in modeling. In an enterprisewide data model of 100 to 200 classes, there may be between two and ten *Or* relationships.

By use of generalization (UML) or subtypes (ERDs), *Or* relationships can usually be avoided. Generalization will be discussed in Chapter 14.

N-ary **Relationships**

Infrequently, you may have a single association among three or more classes. In such circumstances, it is sometimes useful to represent this relationship individually. For example, an auto insurance policy can be represented in at least two ways in UML. Both syntaxes are allowed. The question is whether you want to reflect that the insurance policy is a result of the relationship among Person, Car, and Coverage as shown in Figure 11-3 or is better represented in another way.

This relationship can also be redrawn as an *N-ary* relationship as shown in Figure 11-4.

In this example, there is no reason to use the *N-ary* relationship. As of this writing, we have not seen an example where the *N-ary* syntax is obviously clearer than the other representation.

Other Association Relationships

The dotted line connecting two associations indicates that one or the other relationship is used. Since we are constraining the relationship, curly brackets { } will also be needed to modify the relationship between the associations. Since "exclusive or" is the most common constraint, we don't need to show {or} on the relationship.

This same notation can be used to indicate other types of relationship interactions. For example, if we have Committee and People classes, people belong to committees and one person on the committee is designated as chairperson. This can be modeled as shown in Figure 11-5. Note that we are able to place an arrow on a UML relationship to indicate directionality when necessary.

Chapter 10 demonstrated that this syntax is also useful for declaring that the organization reporting structure must be consistent with the structure of the organization itself, as shown in Figure 11-6.

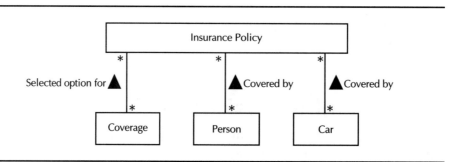

FIGURE 11-3. *UML representation of association among three classes*

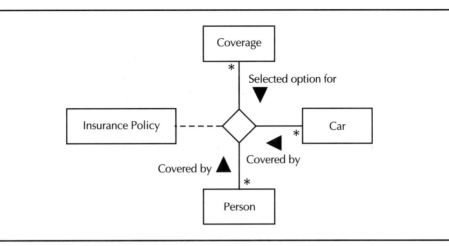

FIGURE 11-4. *UML representation of* N-ary relationship

Implementing *Or* and *N-ary* Relationships

The *Or* relationship actually documents a contingency between two or more relationships. Figure 11-1 describes an object class called Contract, which can be agreed to by either a Person or an Organization, but not both. The

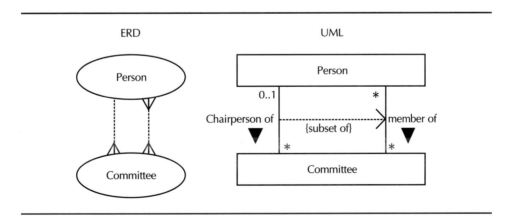

FIGURE 11-5. *Subset constraint between relationships*

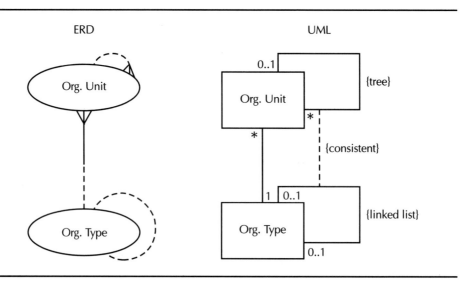

ERD   UML

FIGURE 11-6. *Recursive org unit structure*

physical implementation of this example is provided next, using both
Oracle7 Relational syntax and Oracle8 Object-Relational syntax.

Relational Implementation

The Contract example would require the creation of three tables, Contract,
Person, and Organization. The Contract table would have two foreign keys,
relating to Person and Organization, respectively. The syntax for creating
these three tables is described next in Code Example 11-1:

```
CREATE TABLE PERSON (
PERSON_ID   NUMBER  (10)  NOT NULL PRIMARY KEY,
LNAME_TX    VARCHAR2 (30) NOT NULL,
FNAME_TX    VARCHAR2 (30) NOT NULL)
/
CREATE TABLE ORGANIZATION (
ORGANIZATION_ID NUMBER (10)   NOT NULL PRIMARY KEY,
NAME_TX         VARCHAR2 (60) NOT NULL)
/
CREATE TABLE CONTRACT (
CONTRACT_ID     NUMBER (10)       NOT NULL PRIMARY KEY,
```

```
DESCR_TX          VARCHAR2 (100)     NOT NULL,
PERSON_ID          NUMBER (10)
  REFERENCES PERSON (PERSON_ID),
ORGANIZATION_ID  NUMBER (10)
  REFERENCES ORGANIZATION (ORGANIZATION_ID))
/
```

Code Example 11-1

Figure 11-1 declares that a contract can be defined whether or not it is agreed to by either a person or an organization. However, this is not the entire reason for the components of both foreign keys to be optional. By definition, the *Or* relationship states that a contract can only be agreed to by a person or an organization.

Even if the cardinality were to change to say that a contract must be an agreement with either a person or an organization, as shown in Figure 11-2, the physical data structures would still remain the same. The difference would be in the definition of the database trigger on the CONTRACT table. This trigger would define the PL/SQL to enforce the *Or* relationship.

While you can also code this validation step in your client applications, defining the rule in the server means that it will always be enforced. The following database trigger shown in Code Example 11-2 would be applied to the CONTRACT table, to support Figure 11-1, where the relationships to PERSON and ORGANIZATION are optional, but both together cannot be associated with a given CONTRACT.

```
CREATE OR REPLACE TRIGGER PERSON_OR_ORGANIZATION
BEFORE INSERT or UPDATE
ON CONTRACT
For each row
DECLARE
OPTIONAL_PARTY    EXCEPTION;
BEGIN
IF :NEW.PERSON_ID IS NOT NULL
AND :NEW.ORGANIZATION_ID IS NOT NULL THEN
RAISE OPTIONAL_PARTY;
END IF;
EXCEPTION
WHEN OPTIONAL_PARTY THEN
RAISE_APPLICATION_ERROR('-20001',' A SINGLE CONTRACT CANNOT BE'||
                  ' AGREED TO BY BOTH A PERSON'||
```

```
                              ' AND AN ORGANIZATION.  PLEASE'||
                              ' SELECT EITHER A PERSON,'||
                              ' ORGANIZATION, OR NEITHER.');
END;
/
```

Code Example 11-2

To enforce the example in Figure 11-2, we would add an additional ELSIF condition to this database trigger, which would require that either a PERSON or an ORGANIZATION has been identified as agreeing to the CONTRACT as shown in the following Code Example 11-3.

```
CREATE OR REPLACE TRIGGER PERSON_OR_ORGANIZATION
BEFORE INSERT or UPDATE
ON CONTRACT
For each row
DECLARE
TWO_PARTY  EXCEPTION;
NO_PARTY   EXCEPTION;
BEGIN
IF :NEW.PERSON_ID IS NOT NULL
AND :NEW.ORGANIZATION_ID IS NOT NULL THEN
RAISE TWO_PARTY;
ELSIF :NEW.PERSON_ID IS NULL
AND :NEW.ORGANIZATION_ID IS NULL THEN
RAISE NO_PARTY;
END IF;
EXCEPTION
WHEN TWO_PARTY THEN
RAISE_APPLICATION_ERROR('20001',' A SINGLE CONTRACT CANNOT BE'||
                        ' AGREED TO BY BOTH A PERSON'||
                        ' AND AN ORGANIZATION.  PLEASE'||
                        ' SELECT EITHER A PERSON,'||
                        ' ORGANIZATION, OR NEITHER.');
WHEN NO_PARTY THEN
RAISE_APPLICATION_ERROR('20001',' A SINGLE CONTRACT MUST BE
AGREED'||
                        ' TO BY EITHER A PERSON OR AN'||
                        ' ORGANIZATION.  PLEASE SELECT EITHER'||
                        ' A PERSON, ORGANIZATION, BUT NOT BOTH.');
END;
/
```

Code Example 11-3

Object-Relational Implementation

The contract with either a person or an organization example can be implemented in Oracle8 using three object types, three object classes, and a single member method. The syntax for this example follows in Code Example 11-4:

```
CREATE OR REPLACE TYPE PERSON_TYPE
AS OBJECT (
PERSON_ID         NUMBER (10),
LNAME_TX          VARCHAR2 (30),
FNAME_TX          VARCHAR2 (30))
/
CREATE OR REPLACE TYPE ORGANIZATION_TYPE
AS OBJECT (
ORGANIZATION_ID  NUMBER (10),
NAME_TX          VARCHAR2 (60))
/
CREATE OR REPLACE TYPE CONTRACT_TYPE
AS OBJECT (
CONTRACT_ID       NUMBER (10),
DESCR_TX          VARCHAR2 (100),
PERSON_ID                 REF PERSON_TYPE,
ORGANIZATION_ID           REF ORGANIZATION_TYPE,
MEMBER FUNCTION CONTRACT_PARTY RETURN NUMBER,
STATIC PROCEDURE INSERT_CONTRACT (P_DESCR_TX IN VARCHAR2,
                                  P_PERSON_ID IN NUMBER,
                                  P_ORGANIZATION_ID IN NUMBER),
PRAGMA RESTRICT_REFERENCES(CONTRACT_PARTY,RNDS,WNDS,RNPS,WNPS))
/


CREATE OR REPLACE TYPE BODY CONTRACT_TYPE AS
MEMBER FUNCTION CONTRACT_PARTY
  RETURN NUMBER IS
BEGIN
IF PERSON_ID IS NULL
AND ORGANIZATION_ID IS NULL

  THEN RETURN 0;
ELSIF PERSON_ID IS NOT NULL
AND ORGANIZATION_ID IS NOT NULL
  THEN RETURN 2;
ELSE RETURN 1;
END IF;
END;
```

```
STATIC PROCEDURE INSERT_CONTRACT (P_DESCR_TX IN VARCHAR2,
                                  P_PERSON_ID IN NUMBER,
                                  P_ORGANIZATION_ID IN NUMBER)
IS
TWO_PARTY  EXCEPTION;
NO_PARTY   EXCEPTION;
V_CONTRACT      CONTRACT_TYPE;
V_CONTRACT_ID   NUMBER(10);
REF_PERSON      REF PERSON_TYPE := NULL;
REF_ORG         REF ORGANIZATION_TYPE := NULL;
VAR             NUMBER;

BEGIN
 BEGIN
  EXECUTE IMMEDIATE 'SELECT REF(p) FROM PERSON p WHERE p.PERSON_ID = :1'
  INTO REF_PERSON USING P_PERSON_ID;
 EXCEPTION
  WHEN OTHERS THEN NULL;
 END;
 BEGIN
  EXECUTE IMMEDIATE 'SELECT REF(o) FROM ORGANIZATION o
   WHERE o.ORGANIZATION_ID = :1' INTO REF_ORG USING
P_ORGANIZATION_ID;
 EXCEPTION
  WHEN OTHERS THEN NULL;
 END;

SELECT CONTRACT_SEQ.NEXTVAL INTO V_CONTRACT_ID FROM DUAL;

V_CONTRACT := CONTRACT_TYPE(V_CONTRACT_ID,
                            P_DESCR_TX,
                            REF_PERSON,
                            REF_ORG);

VAR := V_CONTRACT.CONTRACT_PARTY();

IF var = 0
  THEN RAISE NO_PARTY;
ELSIF var = 2
  THEN RAISE TWO_PARTY;
ELSE
    EXECUTE IMMEDIATE 'INSERT INTO CONTRACT VALUES (:1)' USING V_CONTRACT;
END IF;

END;
END;
```

```
/

CREATE TABLE PERSON
OF PERSON_TYPE (
PERSON_ID  NOT NULL PRIMARY KEY,
LNAME_TX   NOT NULL,
FNAME_TX   NOT NULL)
/

CREATE TABLE ORGANIZATION
OF ORGANIZATION_TYPE (
ORGANIZATION_ID  NOT NULL PRIMARY KEY,
NAME_TX          NOT NULL)
/

CREATE TABLE CONTRACT
OF CONTRACT_TYPE (
CONTRACT_ID NOT NULL PRIMARY KEY,
DESCR_TX    NOT NULL)
/
```

Code Example 11-4

This example created a method INSERT_CONTRACT, which would be used as the main method for inserting contract records.

The problem with methods versus database triggers is that developer access to objects is not limited through methods. Therefore, methods are currently no more than suggested data access/manipulation approaches, whereas database triggers are directly attached to tables and will fire every time a row is inserted, updated, or deleted, for every application written against a given table.

N-ary Relationships

The concept of the *N-ary* relationship is more of a logical modeling technique. We tend to implement *N-ary* relationships as a series of foreign keys to an intersection table, rather than creating an intersection of the dependent relationships and then relating this intersection to the actual object of interest.

In Figures 11-3 and 11-4, we discussed how an Insurance Policy is composed of a compound relationship among a Coverage, a Person, and a Car. The physical implementation of both of these models would require four tables, COVERAGE, PERSON, CAR, and INSURANCE POLICY.

The only additional value that Figure 11-4 provides in comparison to Figure 11-3 is that it clearly defines the relation between COVERAGE, PERSON, and CAR as being something of interest (indicated by the center diamond), to which we assign an INSURANCE POLICY. The physical implementation would not create a fifth table representing the COVERAGE/ PERSON/ CAR relationship, primarily because the INSURANCE POLICY entity documents it.

Relational Implementation

The following table definitions support the Insurance Policy example using relational syntax as shown in Code Example 11-5:

```
CREATE TABLE COVERAGE (
COVERAGE_ID NUMBER (10)    NOT NULL PRIMARY KEY,
NAME_TX      VARCHAR2 (50)  NOT NULL)
/
CREATE TABLE PERSON (
PERSON_ID   NUMBER (10)     NOT NULL PRIMARY KEY,
LNAME_TX    VARCHAR2 (30)   NOT NULL,
FNAME_TX    VARCHAR2 (30)   NOT NULL)
/
CREATE TABLE CAR (
VIN             VARCHAR2 (50)      NOT NULL PRIMARY KEY,
MAKE            VARCHAR2 (20)      NOT NULL,
MODEL           VARCHAR2 (20)      NOT NULL,
YEAR            VARCHAR2 (4)       NOT NULL,
COLOR           NUMBER (20))
/
CREATE TABLE INSURANCE_POLICY (
POLICY_ID    NUMBER (10)    NOT NULL PRIMARY KEY,
COVERAGE_ID NUMBER (10)     NOT NULL
  REFERENCES COVERAGE (COVERAGE_ID),
PERSON_ID   NUMBER (10)     NOT NULL
  REFERENCES PERSON (PERSON_ID),
VIN          VARCHAR2 (50) NOT NULL
  REFERENCES CAR (VIN))
/
```

Code Example 11-5

Coverage, Person, and Car are connected to Insurance Policy using mandatory foreign keys. These relations assert that an insurance policy is composed of the association of one coverage, one person, and one car.

Object-Relational Implementation

This example could be implemented in Oracle8 using four object types and four object references, as follows in Code Example 11-6:

```
CREATE OR REPLACE TYPE COVERAGE_TYPE
AS OBJECT (
COVERAGE_ID   NUMBER (10),
NAME_TX       VARCHAR2 (50))
/
CREATE OR REPLACE TYPE PERSON_TYPE
AS OBJECT (
PERSON_ID   NUMBER (10),
LNAME_TX    VARCHAR2 (30),
FNAME_TX    VARCHAR2 (30))
/
CREATE OR REPLACE TYPE CAR_TYPE
AS OBJECT (
VIN    VARCHAR2 (50),
MAKE   VARCHAR2 (20),
MODEL VARCHAR2 (20),
YEAR   VARCHAR2 (4),
COLOR NUMBER (20))
/
CREATE OR REPLACE TYPE INSURANCE_POLICY_TYPE
AS OBJECT (
POLICY_ID     NUMBER (10),
COVERAGE_ID   REF COVERAGE_TYPE,
PERSON_ID     REF PERSON_TYPE,
VIN           REF CAR_TYPE)
/

CREATE TABLE COVERAGE
OF COVERAGE_TYPE(
COVERAGE_ID NOT NULL PRIMARY KEY,
NAME_TX       NOT NULL)
/
CREATE TABLE PERSON
OF PERSON_TYPE (
PERSON_ID   NOT NULL PRIMARY KEY,
```

```
LNAME_TX    NOT NULL,
FNAME_TX    NOT NULL)
/
CREATE TABLE CAR
OF CAR_TYPE (
VIN      NOT NULL PRIMARY KEY,
MAKE     NOT NULL,
MODEL    NOT NULL,
YEAR     NOT NULL)
/
CREATE TABLE INSURANCE_POLICY
OF INSURANCE_POLICY_TYPE (
POLICY_ID       NOT NULL PRIMARY KEY,
COVERAGE_ID  NOT NULL,
PERSON_ID    NOT NULL,
VIN          NOT NULL)
/
```

Code Example 11-6

We can replicate the core of this functionality in Oracle7 as well. This can be accomplished by creating functions and procedures that are the intended data access and manipulation paths. However, just as with Oracle8 objects, there is no way to limit data access to these stored program units.

CHAPTER
12

Cyclical Structures

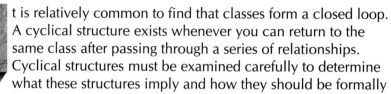

t is relatively common to find that classes form a closed loop. A cyclical structure exists whenever you can return to the same class after passing through a series of relationships. Cyclical structures must be examined carefully to determine what these structures imply and how they should be formally modeled. The simplest case of this is *recursion,* where one class is hooked to itself. The specifics of this special type of cyclical relationship are discussed in greater detail in Chapter 10. Here, we will discuss several common examples of cyclical structures.

Some modelers will go to great lengths to avoid using cyclical structures. IDEF modeling declares cyclical structures to be illegal. However, cyclical structures cannot be easily avoided. In fact, to not use them in a data model precludes many data-related business rules from being modeled.

Because of the generic approach advocated in this book and discussed more fully in Chapter 16, you will find cyclical structures occurring frequently in our examples. In this chapter, we will discuss the problems raised by cyclical structures, and how these problems can be dealt with most effectively.

Implications of Cyclical Structures

Figure 12-1 illustrates a classic example of Courses offered through Departments in a college or university setting. Particular class offerings at a particular date and time are then assigned to a Professor. The Professor is employed by one or more Departments. There is nothing wrong with this model; but it is important to recognize the business rules that it implies. This model structure implies that any professor can teach any class for any department. Should this be the case? The reason that the question of the appropriateness of the business rule arises is due to the cyclical structure of the model. Notice how there are two dependencies between Department and Offering—one through Course and one through Employment. This structural redundancy should lead us to question the nature of the relationship between Department and Course Offering. As stated earlier, the model implies that the two relationships are completely independent. Therefore, any Professor can teach any class.

ERD   UML

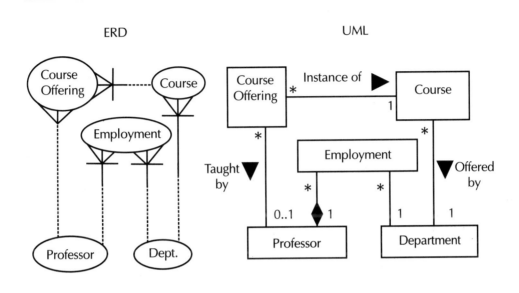

FIGURE 12-1.   *Simple cyclical structure*

    To enforce a more restrictive business rule such as "Professors are only
allowed to teach courses for the Department for which they are currently
employed," would require a trigger to be written.
    Such a trigger could be placed on the Course Offering table to enforce
this business rule. In Oracle, there are several ways to implement this. If we
change the model to look like Figure 12-2, then DeptNo, the primary key of
the Department table, would come into the Course Offering table through
both paths. We could then add a simple constraint that the two Department
numbers would have to be equivalent.
    This model could also be supported through only having a single
Department Number column in the Course Offering table shared by both
constraints. However, then we would be unable to enforce this through the
traditional referential integrity but instead through triggers.
    Once you use the cycle to inspire you to ask questions, you may end up
changing the data model. A university might take the approach of enforcing

ERD   UML

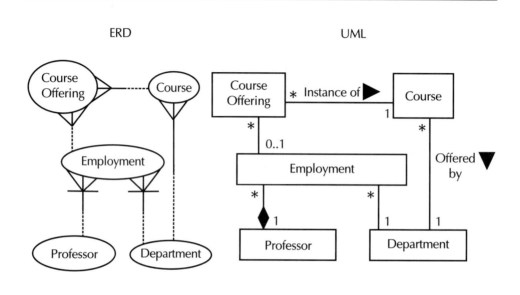

FIGURE 12-2. *Professor/Course model*

the business rule that professors must either teach within their departments or have specific authorization to teach a course outside of their department. If this business rule were true, then we would be inclined to redo the data model as shown in Figure 12-3.

With this structure, a Professor is assigned to a course explicitly through his or her employment in the Department or through a teaching authorization. We still need triggers to resolve the cycle problems (to ensure that authorization to teach the course is correct). If authorization is through the department, we must ensure that the right department is authorizing the course. Using this structure does make it possible to capture the business rules effectively. UML actually has syntax for capturing such complex constraints, largely through text boxes attached to classes by dotted lines. No product is currently attempting to actually generate such constraints to code as of this writing; and it does not seem likely that any will be developed in the near future. If a UML product supported such syntax, it would be useful to include the constraints in the data model. Otherwise, your data model will only represent a subset of the data-related business rules.

ERD

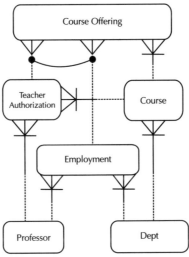

UML

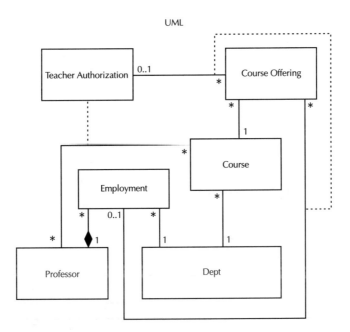

FIGURE 12-3. *Modified Professor/Course model*

Using Object IDs (OIDs)

Object IDs (OIDs) provide a much cleaner implementation of business rules than foreign keys as shown in Figure 12-4.

In this model, we have Insurance Companies with General Agents. A General Agent may represent several Insurance Companies. When a policy is issued, it is done either directly from the Insurance Company or through the General Agent. With a traditional relational implementation, the Insurance Company Identifier would make its way to the Policy via both paths. Using OIDs, the Identifier would be hooked either to the Insurance Company Record or to the Agent Affiliation Record. Using a traditional relational implementation, we would remodel Figure 12-4 as shown in Figure 12-5.

In this case, the Insurance Policy always comes directly from the Insurance Company and optionally from a General Agent. You then need a constraint on the Insurance Policy to enforce that the General Agent has an

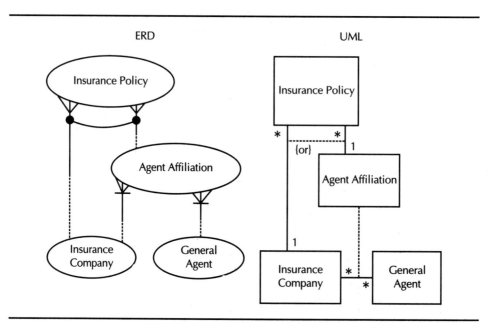

FIGURE 12-4. *Object-relational implementation of insurance agent example*

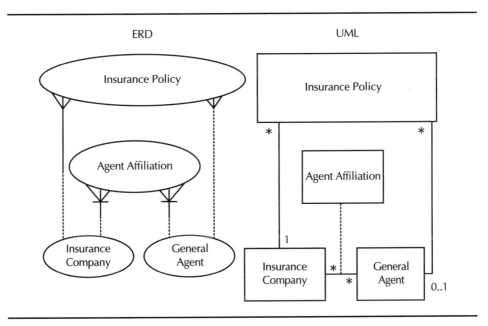

FIGURE 12-5. *Traditional relational implementation of insurance agent example*

affiliation with the Insurance Company. There is some appeal to this model, because if you are using OIDs, there is a direct link back to the Insurance Company. With the first model, there are two paths to worry about. Therefore, we believe that the best model in this case is shown in Figure 12-6.

From a physical implementation perspective, this third model is best for OIDs. A Policy must be associated with an Insurance Company and optionally to an Agent Affiliation. Which of these models is best depends upon your goals:

■ The first (Figure 12-4) is the most logically correct.

■ The second (Figure 12-5) is the model that can be best implemented physically for a relational database.

■ The third model (Figure 12-6) is best when you're using OIDs.

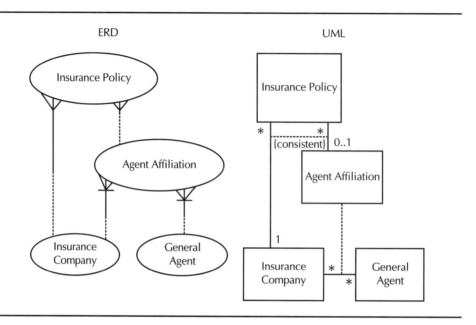

FIGURE 12-6. *Optimal object-relational implementation of insurance agent example*

You might start with the first model in Analysis and have the model evolve into either of the other two models depending upon your implementation choices.

Genericization with Cyclical Structures

Sometimes, genericization can lead to interesting cyclical structures. In a model that includes Loans and Payments as shown in Figure 12-7, normally there are simple payments on a loan. Each loan has many payments in a traditional system. However, there were special cases where a company would pay off many loans simultaneously.

The left model shows the logical structure of the information. Since, other than this relationship, simple and group payments were the same, the physical implementation followed the model on the bottom. The triggers to enforce this were complex. We needed to ensure that only one of these relationships was in force at any one time.

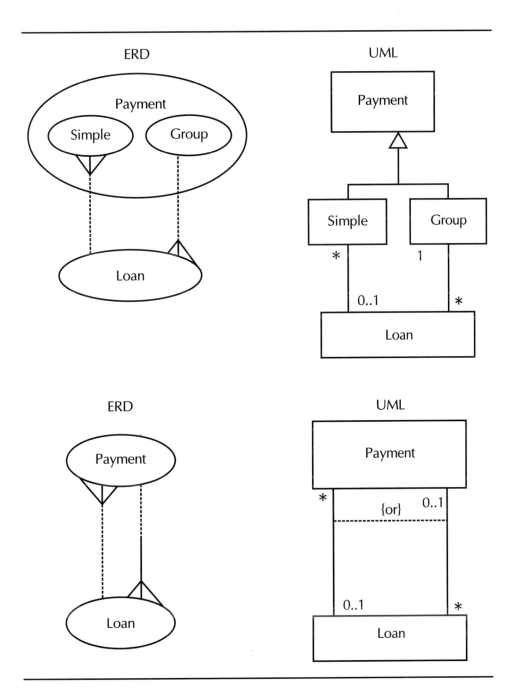

FIGURE 12-7. *Cyclical models*

Implementation of Cyclical Structures

If the intent of Figure 12-2 was to require the professor's department be equivalent to the department that is offering the class, then you might assume that it would only require the addition of a check constraint that would verify that the two separate DeptNo columns had equivalent values. However, check constraints are not allowed to reference other columns. Therefore, the following trigger shown in Code Example 12-1 is required, based upon the given data structures.

```
CREATE TABLE DEPT (
DEPTNO      NUMBER(10) NOT NULL PRIMARY KEY,
DESCR_TXT  VARCHAR2(20) NOT NULL)
/
CREATE TABLE COURSE (
COURSENO   NUMBER (10) NOT NULL,
DEPTNO     NUMBER (10) NOT NULL
  REFERENCES DEPT(DEPTNO),
DESCR_TXT  VARCHAR2 (100) NOT NULL
PRIMARY KEY (COURSENO,DEPTNO))
/
CREATE TABLE PROF (
PROFNO      NUMBER (10) NOT NULL PRIMARY KEY,
LNAME       VARCHAR2 (30) NOT NULL,
FNAME       VARCHAR2 (30) NOT NULL)
/
CREATE TABLE EMPLY(
DEPTNO      NUMBER (10) NOT NULL
  REFERENCES DEPT(DEPTNO),
PROFNO      NUMBER (10) NOT NULL,
START_DATE DATE NOT NULL,
END_DATE    DATE
PRIMARY KEY (DEPTNO,PROFNO))
/
CREATE TABLE OFFRNG(
OFFNO            NUMBER (10) NOT NULL PRIMARY KEY,
COURSENO   NUMBER (10) NOT NULL,
DEPTNO_COURSE NUMBER (10) NOT NULL,
PROFNO          NUMBER (10) ,
DEPTNO_EMPLY  NUMBER (10),
START_DATE    DATE    NOT NULL,
```

```
END_DATE        DATE
FOREIGN KEY (COURSENO,DEPTNO_COURSE)
  REFERENCES COURSE(COURSENO,DEPTNO)
FOREIGN KEY (PROFNO,DEPTNO_EMPLY)
  REFERENCES EMPLY(PROFNO,DEPTNO))
/
CREATE OR REPLACE TRIGGER BIU_COURSE_OFFERING
BEFORE INSERT UPDATE ON
COURSE_OFFERING
FOR EACH ROW
DECLARE
PROF_DEPTNO_ERR     EXCEPTION;
BEGIN
IF :NEW.DEPTNO_COURSE != :NEW.DEPTNO_EMPLY THEN
RAISE PROF_DEPTNO_ERR;
END IF;
EXCEPTION
WHEN PROF_DEPTNO_ERR THEN
RAISE_APPLICATION_ERROR
  (-20005, 'Professor must be employed'||
          ' by Department offering Course.');
END;
/
```

Code Example 12-1

If we chose to extend the preceding example to ensure that the Professor is currently employed by the Department offering the Course, then the trigger would look as shown in Code Example 12-2:

```
--EXAMPLE_12_01 IS PREREQ
CREATE OR REPLACE TRIGGER BIU_COURSE_OFFERING
BEFORE INSERT OR UPDATE ON
OFFRNG
FOR EACH ROW
DECLARE
PROF_DEPTNO_ERR     EXCEPTION;
PROF_EMPLOY_ERR     EXCEPTION;

CURSOR C1 IS
SELECT START_DATE
FROM EMPLY EMP
WHERE EMP.PROFNO = :NEW.PROFNO
AND EMP.DEPTNO = :NEW.DEPTNO_EMPLY
```

```
AND EMP.START_DATE <= :NEW.START_DATE
AND (END_DATE = NULL
  OR END_DATE >=:NEW.END_DATE);

EMPLOYMENT_REC C1%ROWTYPE;

BEGIN
IF :NEW.DEPTNO_COURSE != :NEW.DEPTNO_EMPLY THEN
RAISE PROF_DEPTNO_ERR;
ELSE
OPEN C1;
FETCH C1 INTO EMPLOYMENT_REC;
IF C1%NOTFOUND THEN
RAISE PROF_EMPLOY_ERR;
END IF;
CLOSE C1;
END IF;
EXCEPTION
WHEN PROF_DEPTNO_ERR THEN
RAISE_APPLICATION_ERROR (-20005, 'Professor must be'||
            ' employed by Department offering Course.');
WHEN PROF_EMPLOY_ERR THEN
RAISE_APPLICATION_ERROR (-20006, 'Professor must be'||
            ' employed by Department offering Course'||
            ' prior to the Courses START_DATE.');
END;
/
```

Code Example 12-2

We cannot enforce date ranges through integrity constraints, because constraints are based on the premise of equality, not ranges. They allow us to enforce *column1 = column2*. Ranges, whether they be dates or alphanumeric, require coding for enforcement.

Insurance Policy Example

The relational implementation of the insurance policy example would be developed in much the same way as the Class Offering example. In both cases, the table INS_PLCY exists with two separate references to the INS_CO table. One reference is a direct foreign key from INS_PLCY to INS_CO. The second is an indirect reference, which is a foreign key to the AGENT_AFFIL table, whose primary key is the combination of the foreign keys from INS_CO and AGENT_AFFIL.

Had both constraints been mandatory, we would only need one occurrence of the column from the referenced table. However, in light of one of the constraints being optional, we must create two separate column references for INS_CO_ID, and a trigger to ensure that their values equate when not null.

You will have to create a database trigger on the Insurance Policy table that queries the Agent Affiliation table for an active affiliation between the given Insurance Company and General Agent. As shown in Code Example 12-3, this query must validate that the date of the INS_PLCY falls within the Agent Affiliation date range, where appropriate.

```
CREATE TABLE GEN_AGENT(
GEN_AGENT_ID      NUMBER (10) NOT NULL PRIMARY KEY,
DESCR_TX          VARCHAR2 (40) NOT NULL)
/
CREATE TABLE INS_CO(
INS_CO_ID         NUMBER (10) NOT NULL PRIMARY KEY,
DESCR_TX          VARCHAR2(40) NOT NULL)
/
CREATE TABLE AGENT_AFFIL(
GEN_AGENT_ID      NUMBER (10) NOT NULL,
INS_CO_ID         NUMBER (10) NOT NULL,
START_DATE        DATE NOT NULL,
END_DATE          DATE,
PRIMARY KEY (GEN_AGENT_ID,INS_CO_ID),
FOREIGN KEY  (INS_CO_ID)
  REFERENCES INS_CO (INS_CO_ID))
/
CREATE TABLE INS_PLCY(
INS_PLCY_ID          NUMBER (10) NOT NULL PRIMARY KEY,
INS_CO_ID__INS_CO  NUMBER (10) NOT NULL
  REFERENCES INS_CO(INS_CO_ID),
GEN_AGENT_ID         NUMBER (10),
INS_CO_ID__AGENT_AFFIL NUMBER (10),
START_DATE        DATE DEFAULT SYSDATE NOT NULL,
END_DATE          DATE,
FOREIGN KEY (GEN_AGENT_ID,INS_CO_ID__AGENT_AFFIL)
  REFERENCES AGENT_AFFIL (GEN_AGENT_ID,INS_CO_ID))
/
```

```
CREATE OR REPLACE TRIGGER BIU_INS_POLICY
BEFORE INSERT or UPDATE ON
INS_PLCY
FOR EACH ROW
DECLARE
AGENT_AFFIL_ERR        EXCEPTION;

CURSOR C1 IS
SELECT START_DATE
FROM AGENT_AFFIL
WHERE  GEN_AGENT_ID = :NEW.GEN_AGENT_ID
AND INS_CO_ID = :NEW.INS_CO_ID__AGENT_AFFIL
AND START_DATE <= :NEW.START_DATE
AND (END_DATE >= :NEW.START_DATE
  OR END_DATE IS NULL);

C1_REC C1%ROWTYPE;
BEGIN
IF :NEW.GEN_AGENT_ID IS NOT NULL THEN
OPEN C1;
FETCH C1 INTO C1_REC;
IF C1%NOTFOUND THEN
RAISE AGENT_AFFIL_ERR;
END IF;
END IF;
CLOSE C1;
EXCEPTION
WHEN AGENT_AFFIL_ERR THEN
RAISE_APPLICATION_ERROR (-20005, 'General Agent must'||
          ' be Affiliated with Insurance Company in'||
          ' order to provide Policy.');
END;
/
```

Code Example 12-3

This trigger will only verify the Agent Affiliation if a General Agent has been identified on the Insurance Policy. In this scenario, the trigger will determine whether the START_DATE of the insurance policy falls within the effective date range of the Agent Affiliation. If there is no corresponding Agent Affiliation, then the AGENT_AFFIL_ERR exception will be issued.

Object-Relational Implementation

This model is a poor example for implementing OIDs. The intent is to have the insurance policy object be able to point to either an insurance company object or a general agent object, without having multiple insurance company references and ensuring that there is an affiliation between a supplied general agent and an insurance company.

The only way to refer to two separate data sets through the same OID is when both structures were created based upon the same object type. Object references point to object types, which indirectly point to object classes.

The dilemma arises with the relationship between an agent and an insurance company. We cannot create additional columns in a table that is based upon an object reference. Therefore, we cannot add a foreign key to the agent table that points to the insurance company table, because the column does not exist in the object type that both tables were based upon.

We could add a pseudo-column to the object type, and use it in the agent table as a foreign key to the insurance company table; however, that would confuse the intent of the object type definition.

In short, OIDs do not provide specialized functionality to avoid the dual reference to Insurance Company from Insurance Policy.

Loan Payments Example

This scenario tends to represent a far more complicated modeling issue than a physical implementation issue. It is intriguing to consider the rule that a company might only make a blanket payment if they were closing multiple loans. However, it would make more sense to loosen this rule to allow companies to make blanket payments at any time. This would be implemented through a basic, many-to-many relationship. The physical implementation of such a relationship traditionally spawns three tables. In this case, we would have the LOAN, PAYMENT, and PAYMENT_DTL tables as shown in Code Example 12-4.

```
CREATE TABLE LOAN (
LOAN_ID        NUMBER (10) NOT NULL PRIMARY KEY,
AMT            NUMBER (10,2) NOT NULL,
START_DATE     DATE NOT NULL,
END_DATE       DATE)
/
```

```
CREATE TABLE PAYMENT (
PAYMENT_ID        NUMBER (10) NOT NULL PRIMARY KEY,
AMT               NUMBER (10,2) NOT NULL,
RECEIVED_DATE     DATE,
CHECK_TXT         VARCHAR2 (10))
/
CREATE TABLE PAYMENT_DTL (
LOAN_ID           NUMBER (10) NOT NULL
  REFERENCES LOAN (LOAN_ID),
PAYMENT_ID        NUMBER (10) NOT NULL
  REFERENCES PAYMENT (PAYMENT_ID),
AMT               NUMBER (10,2) NOT NULL,
PRIMARY KEY (LOAN_ID, PAYMENT_ID))
/

CREATE TABLE MIR_PAYMENT_DTL (
LOAN_ID           NUMBER (10) NOT NULL
  REFERENCES LOAN (LOAN_ID),
PAYMENT_ID    .   NUMBER (10) NOT NULL
  REFERENCES PAYMENT (PAYMENT_ID),
AMT               NUMBER (10,2) NOT NULL,
PRIMARY KEY (LOAN_ID, PAYMENT_ID))
/
```

Code Example 12-4

In this example, we created a fourth table, MIR_PAYMENT_DTL, that mirrors the PAYMENT_DTL table.

The primary key of the PAYMENT_DTL table ensures that a specific payment can be associated to a specific LOAN for a specific dollar amount. However, there is an additional check that must occur. In light of the requirement of applying portions of a single payment to multiple loans, we must write a database trigger to verify that the amount we have allocated is equal to the amount that was received.

Unfortunately, we are once again confronted by the legendary mutating table dilemma. In this example, we created a second table, MIR_PAYMENT_DTL, which is a mirror image of the PAYMENT_DTL table as shown in Code Example 12-5.

```
--EXAMPLE_12_04 IS PREREQ
CREATE OR REPLACE TRIGGER BIU_PAYMENT_DTL
BEFORE INSERT or UPDATE
ON PAYMENT_DTL
```

```
FOR EACH ROW
DECLARE
CURSOR C1 IS
SELECT SUM(AMT) SUB_AMT
FROM MIR_PAYMENT_DTL
WHERE PAYMENT_ID = :NEW.PAYMENT_ID;
c1_rec c1%ROWtype;
CURSOR C2 IS
SELECT AMT
FROM PAYMENT
WHERE PAYMENT_ID = :NEW.PAYMENT_ID;
c2_rec c2%ROWtype;
TOTAL_AMT  NUMBER (10,2);
INVALID_AMT_ERR EXCEPTION;
BEGIN
FOR C1_REC IN C1 LOOP
 TOTAL_AMT := C1_REC.SUB_AMT + :NEW.AMT;
  FOR C2_REC IN C2 LOOP
   IF TOTAL_AMT > C2_REC.AMT THEN
    RAISE INVALID_AMT_ERR;
   END IF;
  END LOOP;
END LOOP;
EXCEPTION
WHEN INVALID_AMT_ERR THEN
RAISE_APPLICATION_ERROR (-20005, 'You only have
'||to_char(c2_rec.amt-c1_rec.sub_amt)||' left to allocate.');
END;
/
```

Code Example 12-5

This trigger will determine whether the user is attempting to overallocate funds from a specific payment, and fire the INVALID_AMT_ERR exception handler in the event of a violation. While the addition of the mirrored table satisfies our requirements, it also appears as a less than elegant solution.

Conclusion

Anytime you have a structure where one entity leads back to the starting point entity, you need to closely examine what the business rules really are, in order to determine the best model. Typically, the model created in Analysis will clearly represent the business rules. However, this is not always the case. Sometimes, all of the business rules cannot be represented. In the Course and Professor example, you cannot necessarily infer what all of the business rules are. This is a good example of a situation where you cannot get all of the business rules into the data model using UML notation. However, there is usually a diagrammatic depiction that closely approaches an accurate representation of the business rules.

For physical implementation, as demonstrated by the Insurance example, the best representation may change. This change will depend upon how you choose to physically implement the model. It is not our intent to discourage the reader from using cyclical structures. There are many cases where cyclical structures are clearly the best way to represent something. Anytime you have a cyclical structure, it should be viewed as a warning flag to carefully examine the business rules to determine the best logical model and its eventual evolution into a workable physical model.

CHAPTER
13

Methods

he most compelling criticism of ER modeling and the relational database community in general is the lack of attention paid to process. One of the reasons that we end up with bad data models is that the design process is driven by the ERD. Frequently, only after the ERD is substantially complete is any thought given to process. Even then, process-related information is usually given much less attention than the data model and is often only fully specified as the applications are designed. When the Process Modeling tool was added to Oracle Designer, this enabled us to model processes within Oracle Designer. However, it remains an underutilized feature of the tool.

This separation between data and process within the database community is perhaps its greatest weakness. Object classes within a data model do not exist in isolation from their business processes. What we do with the information and how it functions in an organization is just as important as the information itself.

Operations Versus Methods

According to *UML Semantics* (v. 1.1, 1 Sept, 1997, Rational Software et al.), an *operation* is "a service that can be requested from an object to effect behavior" (p. 155) and a *method* is "the implementation of an operation. It specifies the algorithm or procedure that effects the results of an operation" (p. 154). From these definitions, we might be inclined to conclude that operations are logical constructs and methods are physical constructs. However, the distinction is not quite so clear cut. "Operations" refer to the specifications, whereas the "method" refers to the actual algorithm of code.

The reason for carefully distinguishing between the two is to allow for overloading. Operations can be overloaded and used by different classes and mean different things in each of those classes. Unless you are in a situation where you are overloading an operation, operations and methods are the same. Developers working on a system that does not overload any operations may use the terms interchangeably. In this book, we will always use the term "method," unless we are referring to an operation that will be inherited and overloaded.

It is helpful to understand the concept of generalization to clarify the distinctions between operations and methods. In Chapter 14, we will discuss generalization and classes that inherit properties and methods from other classes, along with the correct UML notation.

A View of Methods

Methods are associated with object classes and describe the legal operations associated with a particular object class. For example, in an Employee object class, valid methods might be Hire, Fire, Assign/Unassign Office, and Change Demographic Information. Methods may serve a number of different purposes. First, methods can be viewed as similar to logical functions in the traditional CASE method or in CADM (CASE Application Development Method). Such functions can provide a place to store required functions with their primary object classes, helping to organize and clarify the logical model. With such an approach, there is no expectation that these methods would necessarily be instantiated in the physical representation (tables) of these object classes. Instead, the methods would simply act as tags to guide developers in building applications associated with these object classes.

Another way to view methods is from the perspective of a traditional object-oriented designer. In this instance, you would exhaustively define all operations associated with an object class through methods, and then restrict access to the object class solely through its associated methods. This provides an absolutely clean approach. The interfaces to an object are fully defined by its methods. However, the problem in this way of doing development is that more work will need to be done with current products. We have a long tradition within the relational community of having applications hook directly to tables. This provides us with sophisticated functionality very quickly.

Methods can be an important part of data hiding. The relational practice of hooking applications directly to tables breaks applications anytime tables change. This makes relational systems relatively fragile. Well-designed method interfaces help isolate developers from such changes.

Methods provide server functionality. The relational equivalents of methods are functions and packages. Clearly, many relational applications use functions and packages extensively to get very important server-based behavior. The benefit of methods over functions and packages is that they are packaged with the data, so they are easier to use and maintain.

The tools to support this are still in their infancy. At this writing, Oracle Developer support for Oracle8 objects is very recent and still evolving. We can probably foresee that within months products will be developed that automate the process of method construction. Development tools will help build graphical front-ends to attach to objects through their methods. However, until such tools exist, it will probably not be practical to completely specify all of the methods necessary to provide interaction with an object class.

For example, in a recent project, we were building a commercial off-the-shelf package that would be sold and distributed to many clients. We wanted our development team to have access to the complete tables, but to provide only limited access to the tables to the client developers. In this case, the primary applications can be built using traditional relational techniques while simultaneously publishing the implemented methods as an API for outside developers. This is one of the key differences between entities and object classes. Entities do not directly support any process information.

Within the Oracle environment, we traditionally build the database and then determine the appropriate functions. This has led to a database-centric orientation to system design. Data-centric analysts focus on what we are trying to capture information about and are largely unconcerned with the underlying processes. However, it is critical to recognize that paying attention to processes can influence the design of the data model.

Consider the following example of a manufacturing model. (This example has been oversimplified to illustrate our point.) In representing manufacturing items such as Inventories, Assemblies, and Finished Goods, there is a strong temptation to represent all items in a single class. In all cases, inventory, assemblies, and finished goods are parts of the manufacturing process. However, in thinking about process information, these three items may be viewed differently. Inventory items are purchased and then used in manufacturing. Assemblies are collections of inventory items that have undergone some amount of manufacturing, but are neither bought nor sold directly. Finished goods are the only items that are sold and, in general, are neither bought nor used as assemblies in other finished goods.

The real world is not nearly this simple. Some inventory items may be purchased and sold without any modifications. Some assemblies may periodically be available from outside sources. Finished goods may occasionally act as assemblies for other finished goods. How can we effectively model such a complex environment? One attempt at modeling this in UML is shown in Figure 13-1.

```
                    ┌─────────────────────┐
                    │       Mfg. Item      │
                    ├─────────────────────┤
                    │        Item #        │
                    │       Item name      │
                    ├─────────────────────┤
                    │        Buy ( )       │
                    │        Sell ( )      │
                    │        Mfg ( )       │
                    └─────────────────────┘
```

FIGURE 13-1.   *Methods manufacturing model A*

Having a single object class is not completely accurate, because not all items are subject to each of the three identified methods. A second way of representing this Manufacturing model is shown in Figure 13-2.

This model is inadequate because the object classes are not distinct. An individual object could be bought and/or manufactured and/or sold. Any individual object may be inventory, assembly, or finished good. There is no clean way to accurately represent this. In ERD modeling in the past, we have represented this example as shown in Figure 13-3.

This representation indicates that any individual manufacturing item may act as an inventory, assembly, or finished good. Without methods, this structure would be adequate. However, we want to be able to add the additional step of methods. These are operations appropriate for all types of

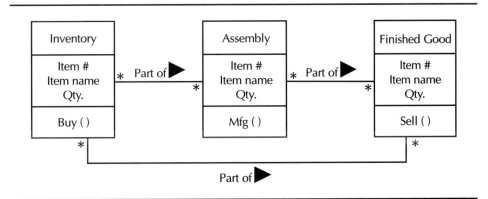

FIGURE 13-2.   *Methods manufacturing model B*

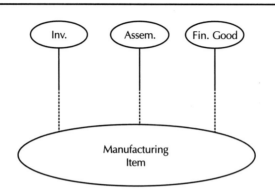

FIGURE 13-3. *ERD representation of manufacturing model*

manufacturing items, such as testing or discarding. If we only used the normal cardinality relationship in UML, the model would be drawn as shown in Figure 13-4.

This diagram still does not satisfy our requirements. There is no clear representation that you are allowed to test or discard a finished good. UML

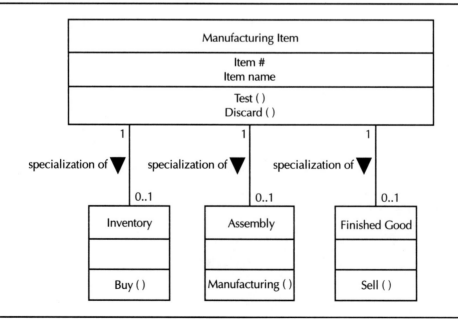

FIGURE 13-4. *Normal cardinality in UML*

uses a different syntax that helps to better represent this situation. This will be solved using the concept of generalization, which will be discussed in Chapter 14.

Using Methods to Define Attributes

If we completely encapsulate a class with methods, then we also have the ability to alter the attributes for the class. The only way to access a method is by passing parameters to it. The union of all these parameters effectively defines the visible attributes for the developer. We may have one set of attributes associated with the actual class, but the developers need not be aware of what these attributes are. The strength of this approach can be illustrated by the example of a birth date or age. In the data model within a Person class, we might want to have the attribute "Date of Birth" (DOB). However, for retrieving and perhaps even entering information, it might be easier to work with two fields: Age and birthday. A developer could have methods that would allow him or her to store, retrieve, or otherwise manipulate age and birthday, but never be aware that within the class, the information is being stored in a single field called "DATE_OF_BIRTH."

In many systems we can have calculated fields that could be manipulated independent of the class attributes. Using this approach, we can have methods that allow input into a Sales table by Total Price and Quantity. The class would store the information as Quantity and Unit Price. There are two ways to implement this. The first is through methods, as discussed earlier. The second way involves a similar effect that can be achieved through views and INSTEAD OF triggers. INSTEAD OF triggers replace the normal Oracle functionality for Insert/Update/Delete and allow the database developer to carefully control what Insert, Update, and Delete mean. For the age and birthday example, we can create a view on the Person table with age and birthday as attributes. When an insert is made into this view, the DATE_OF_BIRTH can be calculated, and the appropriate traditional insert statement can be built and executed.

What Are the Appropriate Methods for a Given Class?

This is a difficult question to answer. Determining the appropriate set of methods for a given class implies that we know how we would be building our applications against the object tables. As of this writing, the primary method for accessing tables is Oracle Developer. At this point, Oracle Developer is still evolving the means to support object tables and methods. In the short run, development will probably occur most efficiently by hooking data blocks directly to object tables as we have done in the past with methods only used for complex coding. It will take some time before complete method-based database interaction will compete with traditional development methods. However, probably within one to two years, there will be effective development shops performing all database access through methods.

Implementing Methods

Methods define the paths through which data can be reported and/or manipulated for object classes. Methods are associated with a specific object class and can be used to operate on other object classes based upon the same object types. There are four types of methods available:

- Constructor
- Member
- Order
- Map

Each will be described separately.

Constructor Methods

Constructor methods are automatically created for object classes based upon their object type. This type of method is used in DML statements to create new object rows for the given object class. The constructor method assumes the name of the object type that it is based upon. You do not have to reference the constructor method explicitly in DML statements for row types. Code Example 13-1 inserts a row into the EMP object table, which is constructed from the PERSON_T type.

```
CREATE OR REPLACE TYPE PERSON_T AS OBJECT
(PERSON_ID              NUMBER
 LAST_NAME              VARCHAR2 (50) ,
 FIRST_NAME             VARCHAR2 (50) ,
```

```
  BIRTH_DATE              DATE,
  GENDER_mf               CHAR (1)0
/

CREATE TABLE EMP OF PERSON_T (
PERSON_ID  NOT NULL PRIMARY KEY,
LAST_NAME  NOT NULL,
FIRST_NAME NOT NULL,
BIRTH DATE NOT NULL,
GENDER_MF  NOT NULL)
/

INSERT INTO EMP (PERSON_ID
                LAST_NAME,
                FIRST_NAME
                BIRTH_DATE,
                GENDER_MF)
     VALUES  (1,
              ' SMITH',
              'ED',
              SYSDATE,
              'M')
/
```

Code Example 13-1

Notice that this INSERT statement did not declare the PERSON_T type in the VALUES clause. It is not required for row types. However, you must reference column types in DML statements. Code Example 13-2 defines the FIRST_NAME and LAST_NAME columns with the NAME_T type. The NAME_T type is a column type and must therefore be referenced within the VALUES CLAUSE of the INSERT statement.

```
CREATE OR REPLACE TYPE NAME_T AS OBJECT(
COL       VARCHAR2(50))
/

CREATE OR REPLACE TYPE PERSON_T AS OBJECT
  (PERSON_ID              NUMBER,
   LAST_NAME              NAME_T,--VARCHAR2  (50),
   FIRST_NAME             NAME_T,--VARCHAR2  (50),
   BIRTH_DATE             DATE,
   GENDER_MF              CHAR (1))
/
```

```
CREATE TABLE EMP OF PERSON_T (
PERSON_ID    NOT NULL PRIMARY KEY,
LAST_NAME    NOT NULL,
FIRST_NAME   NOT NULL,
BIRTH_DATE   NOT NULL
GENDER_MF    NOT NULL
/
INSERT INTO EMP   (PERSON_ID,
                   LAST_NAME,
                   FIRST_NAME,
                   BIRTH_DATE,
                   GENDER_MF)
         VALUES(1,
                   NAME_T('SMITH'),
                   NAME_T('ED'),
                   SYSDATE,
                   'M')
/
```

Code Example 13-2

If you try the preceding INSERT statement without referencing the NAME_T type for the LAST_NAME and FIRST_NAME columns, you will receive the following error:

```
INSERT INTO EMP   (PERSON_ID,
                   LAST_NAME,
                   FIRST_NAME,
                   BIRTH_DATE,
                   GENDER_MF)
         VALUES  (1,
                   'SMITH',
                   'ED',
                   SYSDATE,
                   'M')
/
ORA-00932: inconsistent datatypes
```

Constructor methods cannot be restricted in any way. This is a significant limitation, because it prevents encapsulation. However, a future release of Oracle8 will support user-defined constructor methods. This feature will allow developers to define constructor methods for specific DML activities, such as INSERT PERSON for the earlier example.

Today we can create member methods (discussed in the next section) that simulate this functionality. But to do so, we must either hard-code the name of the table in a DML statement embedded within the member method, or use dynamic SQL. In the end, neither option supports encapsulation. So how should we implement encapsulation? Code Example 13-3 is intended to define a PERSON object class with the following members encapsulated:

- BIRTH_DATE

- GENDER_MF

- EMP_YN

```
CREATE OR REPLACE TYPE NAME_T AS OBJECT(
COL        VARCHAR2(50))
/

CREATE OR REPLACE TYPE PERSON_T AS OBJECT
  (PERSON_ID          NUMBER,
   LAST_NAME          NAME_t, --VARCHAR2 (50),
   FIRST_NAME         NAME_t, --VARCHAR2 (50),
   BIRTH_DATE         DATE,
   GENDER_MF          CHAR (1),
   SALARY                 NUMBER (10,2),
   EMP_YN                 CHAR (1)0
/

CREATE TABLE PERSON OF PERSON_T (
PERSON_ID    NOT NULL PRIMARY KEY,
LAST_NAME    NOT NULL,
FIRST_NAME   NOT NULL,
BIRTH_DATE   NOT NULL,
GENDER_MF    NOT NULL,
EMP_YN          NOT NULL)
/

CREATE OR REPLACE TYPE EMP_T AS OBJECT (
EMP_ID                   NUMBER (10),
LAST_NAME            NAME_T,
FIRST_NAME           NAME_T,
SALARY                   NUMBER (10,2))
/

CREATE OR REPLACE VIEW OV_EMP OF EMP_T WITH OBJECT OID (EMP_ID)
AS SELECT PERSON_ID EMP_ID, LAST_NAME, FIRST_NAME, SALARY
FROM PERSON
WHERE EMP_YN = 'Y'
/
```

```
CREATE OR REPLACE TRIGGER IOU_EMP
INSTEAD OF UPDATE
ON OV_EMP
FOR EACH ROW
BEGIN
UPDATE PERSON SET LAST_NAME=:NEW.LAST_NAME,
                  FIRST_NAME = :NEW.FIRST_NAME,
                  SALARY     = :NEW.SALARY
             WHERE PERSON_ID  = :NEW.EMP_ID;
END;
/
```

Code Example 13-3

The first object type we defined was the NAME_T column type. The NAME_T type was used in the creation of the PERSON_T row type. The PERSON table was created from the PERSON_T row type. A constructor method is automatically created to allow DML operations against all columns of the PERSON table, but we want to hide the BIRTH_DATE, GENDER_MF, and EMP_YN fields. To encapsulate these fields, we need to create an object view. To create an object view, we must first create the object type that it will be based upon. The type we created is called EMP_T. The OV_EMP object view will contain the IDs LAST_NAME, FIRST_NAME, and SALARY of employees only.

To create the DML, we could define an INSTEAD OF trigger on the OV_EMP view. The IOU EMP (Instead Of Update Emp) trigger defers UPDATE statements against the OV_EMP view to update rows within the PERSON table.

This is the best option available today; however, we can expect much more flexibility via user-defined constructor methods in the future. We could have created a member method in the PERSON_T type to update the person's name and/or salary, but this would not have accomplished the desired encapsulation.

Member Methods

Member methods are user-defined access paths that declare the valid reporting and data-manipulation guidelines for a specific object class. Member methods are physically implemented as PL/SQL procedures and/or functions, defined as part of the object type specification.

Member methods are intended for data retrieval activity. Although DML statements can be embedded within member methods, Oracle does not suggest using this strategy. User-defined constructor method capability is being planned for future Oracle8 releases. If you intend to embed DML statements within member methods, you can do so either explicitly by naming the table within the DML statement, or by issuing the DML statement using dynamic SQL. The member method shown in Code Example 13-4, AGE, will return the age of each person stored in any table based upon the PERSON_T type.

```
CREATE OR REPLACE TYPE PERSON_T AS OBJECT
 (PERSON_ID               NUMBER,
  LAST_NAME               VARCHAR2  (50),
  FIRST_NAME              VARCHAR2  (50),
  BIRTH_DATE              DATE,
MEMBER FUNCTION AGE RETURN NUMBER)
/

CREATE OR REPLACE TYPE BODY PERSON_T IS
MEMBER FUNCTION AGE RETURN NUMBER IS
BEGIN
RETURN  (SYSDATE - BIRTH_DATE)  /  365  ;
END;
END;
/

CREATE TABLE PERSON OF PERSON_T  (
PERSON_ID   NOT NULL PRIMARY KEY,
LAST_NAME   NOT NULL,
FIRST_NAME  NOT NULL,
BIRTH_DATE  NOT NULL)
/
```

Code Example 13-4

To execute the AGE method, we could use the PL/SQL block shown in Code Example 13-5.

```
DECLARE
AGE NUMBER
CURSOR C1 IS
SELECT *
FROM PERSON;
BEGIN
FOR C1_REC IN C1 LOOP
```

```
AGE := PERSON_T.AGE(NULL);
DBMS_OUTPUT.PUT_LINE(TO_CHAR(AGE));
END LOOP;
END:
/
```

Code Example 13-5

This procedure fetches each row from the PERSON table and calculates the age by calling the AGE member method of the PERSON_T type.

Order/Map Methods

Order and map methods are used to compare and/or sort data of the same object type. You must, in fact, define either a map or order method within your object type specification in order to perform nonequality comparisons.

To implement a map method for the PERSON object class, you would declare the map member function in the definition of the object type, as follows in Code Example 13-6:

```
CREATE OR REPLACE TYPE PERSON_TYPE AS OBJECT (
PERSON_ID             NUMBER (10),
LNAME_TX              VARCHAR2 (30),
FNAME_TX              VARCHAR2 (30),
MAP MEMBER FUNCTION PERSON_MAP RETURN VARCHAR2)
/
CREATE OR REPLACE TYPE BODY PERSON_TYPE (
MAP MEMBER FUNCTION PERSON-MAP RETURN VARCHAR2 IS
BEGIN
RETURN LNAME_TX || FNAME_TX;
END;
/
```

Code Example 13-6

Order methods require more complicated syntax to accomplish a very similar task. The same example is provided using an order method in Code Example 13-7:

```
CREATE OR REPLACE TYPE PERSON_TYPE
AS OBJECT (
PERSON_ID    NUMBER (10),
```

```
LNAME_TX      VARCHAR2 (30),
FNAME_TX      VARCHAR2 (30),
ORDER MEMBER FUNCTION PERSON_MAP
  (IN_PERSON PERSON_TYPE) RETURN INTEGER)
/
CREATE OR REPLACE TYPE BODY PERSON_TYPE IS
ORDER MEMBER FUNCTION PERSON_MAP
  (IN_PERSON PERSON_TYPE) RETURN INTEGER IS
SELF_PERSON  VARCHAR2 (60) := SELF.LNAME_TX ||
                               SELF.FNAME_TX;
V_PERSON     VARCHAR2 (60) := IN_PERSON.LNAME_TX ||
                              IN_PERSON.FNAME_TX;
BEGIN
IF SELF_PERSON < V_PERSON THEN
RETURN -1;
ELSIF SELF_PERSON > V_PERSON THEN
RETURN 1;
ELSE RETURN 0;
END IF;
END;
END;
/
```

Code Example 13-7

When writing methods for object types, you have multiple
implementation choices—PL/SQL, C/C++, or Java. Of these, PL/SQL and
Java methods run within the address space of the server. C and C++
methods are dispatched as *external procedures* and run outside the servers'
address space.

It is possible to mix and match implementation choices for an
object—i.e., you can have one method in Java, another in PL/SQL, and a
third written as an external procedure in C.

The best implementation choice varies from situation to situation. The
following rules of thumb may be of help:

I. PL/SQL tends to offer the best price-performance for methods that
   are not computation intensive. If you are familiar with SQL, PL/SQL
   provides the cleanest integration between procedural operations and
   querying. PL/SQL is robust and stable, and perhaps the best
   understood. The other implementation options are typically favored
   over PL/SQL if you have a large body of code already implemented

in another language that you want to include in your application. This book has exclusively dealt with PL/SQL examples.

2. Java is a new implementation choice in Oracle, not only for object methods, but also for stored procedures, functions, etc. The advantage of Java is that it is open. It is suitable for web-based applications or those that need to be easily partitioned over networks.

3. A callout involving C or C++ is, in general, the fastest option available for computation-intensive methods. However, callouts incur the cost of dispatch, and in some cases, if the amount of processing done in C or C++ is not very large, this dispatch cost is greater than the performance benefit that C++ provides.

There are many architectural issues involved in deciding which language should be chosen for implementing what method. In this book, we discuss the logical aspects of modeling your data and application. You may want to refer to Oracle documentation for detailed discussion of the multiple implementation choices available to you.

CHAPTER
14

Generalization

here is often commonality between object classes. This commonality may arise through attributes, methods, or relationships. Whenever significant commonality among object classes exists, you should contemplate creating a generalization object class.

When you declare that one class is a generalization of another, one class is called the generalization class and the other is the specialization class. The specialization class inherits all attributes and methods from the generalization class. When you wanted to represent this type of relationship in an ERD, you would use a 1-to-1 optional/mandatory relationship between the generalization and specialization entities. The traditional description of this relationship is "is a." For example, the Person class is a generalization of the Employee class, meaning that an Employee inherits all of the attributes and methods from a Person.

The most common use for generalization is an analog for the relational notion of subtypes. For example, employees that are either hourly or salaried might be represented as shown in Figure 14-1.

Note that we can use either the "Or" solution or the tree structure as shown in Figure 14-1. The UML diagrams in Figure 14-1 both represent the same situation. They are semantically equivalent. In both cases, the employee is either salaried or hourly. Differences are merely notational.

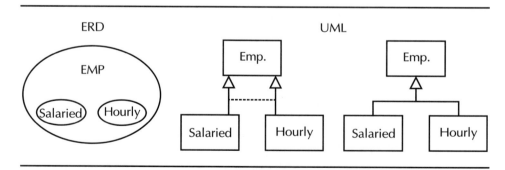

FIGURE 14-1. *UML representation of subtype generalization*

Concepts of Generalization

Using the generalization concept, we can declare that a manufacturing item is a generalization of inventory item, assembly, and finished good. The model is shown in Figure 14-2.

Generalizations in UML are somewhat more flexible than supertype/subtype relationships in ERDs. Each instance of a supertype must be instantiated as exactly one instance of exactly one of the subtypes. In UML, this is not the case. If you wish to denote that objects in the generalization class must be instantiated in one of the specialization classes, then you associate the stereotype «abstract» with the generalization class. This indicates that the generalization class does not really contain objects but acts as a template for the specification classes. Attributes and methods from the generalization class are then inherited by the specialization class, as shown in Figure 14-3.

With the «abstract» notation, the two diagrams in Figure 14-3 are semantically equivalent. If we have a person who can assume many roles such as a customer, employee, both, or neither, one way to represent this is shown in Figure 14-4.

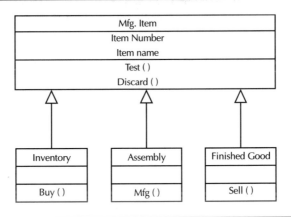

FIGURE 14-2. *Generalizations in UML*

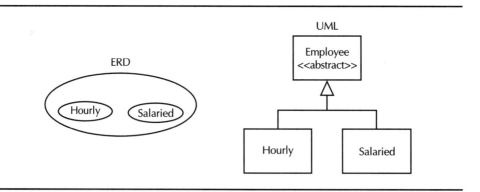

FIGURE 14-3. *Generalization with abstract stereotype*

The diagrams shown in Figure 14-4 are also semantically equivalent. In both cases, a person may be a customer, employee, both, or neither. For the person to be in the database, he or she must at least be a customer or an employee. In UML, we could represent this with the keyword «abstract» on the Person class. There is no way to represent this in an ERD. However, we can change the way we think about this model. Rather than saying that a person is an employee or a customer, we can say that a person has roles of a particular type and redraw the model as shown in Figure 14-5.

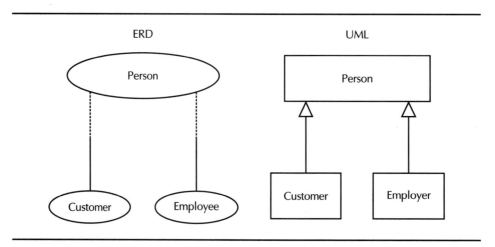

FIGURE 14-4. *Diagrams representing classes with multiple roles*

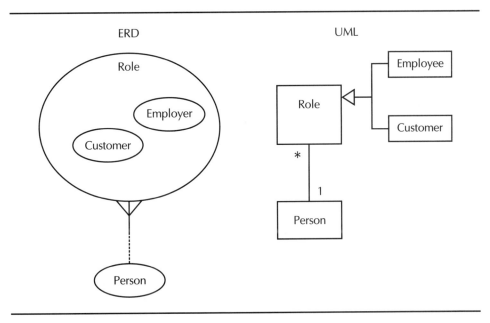

FIGURE 14-5.   *Alternate way of showing roles*

In this case, the two diagrams are semantically equivalent but there is a problem. There is nothing in these diagrams to prevent a single individual from having multiple Customer or Employer roles. You will need to decide on a case-by-case basis which model better represents your business rules.

If you have multiple generalizations of the same class, keep in mind that even if you declare the generalization class to be abstract, only one of these generalizations is required. If you want all of the generalizations to be required, then you should use the stereotype keyword «mandatory» on those generalizations as shown in Figure 14-6.

We did not place the mandatory stereotype on the fixed price/time and materials generalization because when the contract is instantiated, we might not know the financial details of the contract.

Dynamic Generalization

By default, once an object has been assigned to a given specialization class (for example, an Employee object is designated as Hourly or Salaried) as in Figure 14-7, it cannot be subsequently changed (e.g. a salaried

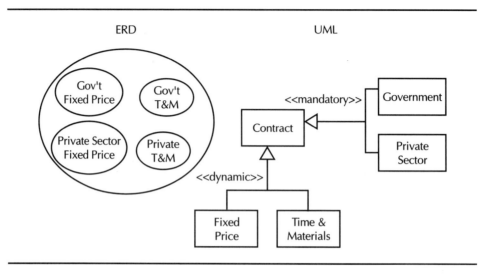

FIGURE 14-6. *Mandatory generalizations*

employee cannot be changed to an hourly employee). This is the same as calling a foreign key relationship nontransferable in ERD notation.

Transferability of a relationship is a concept from relational theory that is rarely used. Oracle Designer provides the capability to declare that relationships are nontransferable but we have seen very few design teams take advantage of this feature.

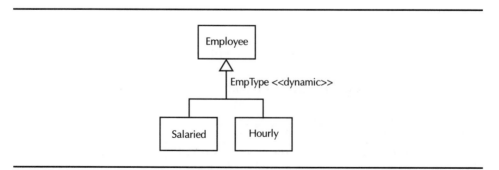

FIGURE 14-7. *Dynamic generalization*

Designers should use great caution before declaring that a relationship is not dynamic (nontransferable in ERD notation). Once a relationship is marked as non-dynamic, as soon as the object is instantiated, you can never change its type. In a relational database, this means that the foreign key is not updatable. In order to denote that your generalizations are updatable for a particular object, you need to place the keyword «dynamic» on the generalization.

In our Contract example, once a contract is designated as Government or Private Sector, this would not change. However, the contract could change from fixed price to time & materials as shown in Figure 14-6. Note that "dynamic" is denoted as a stereotype for the generalization because we are relaxing the UML constraint of nontransferability.

Inheritance

Generalization means much more than a simple association relationship since it implies the notion of inheritance. Object classes that are specializations of other object classes automatically inherit both the attributes and the methods of the generalization class. For example, in Figure 14-2, Item Number and Item name would be attributes that apply to all four object classes. Similarly, the operations "Test" and "Discard" would also apply to all of the object classes. However, the inheritance does not work in the other direction. The operation "Buy" only applies to inventory objects. If you want "Test" to mean something different for Inventory Items rather than Assemblies or Finished Goods, you would show the method "Test" in the Inventory Object class. This would provide that "Test" would mean something different, "overriding" the Test operation inheritance from the Manufacture Item object class. This notion of inheritance of both attributes and methods is key to the object-oriented approach.

Complex Generalization

Generalization need not be particularly simple. For example, the diagram in Figure 14-8 is a model to support security on a web access system. Note that Account Requesters can be one of five different types: External Organization, External Person, External EDI, Internal Person, and Internal Software Process. It makes sense to generalize these to "Account Requester" in order to apply common attributes such as Account ID or common methods such as Grant/Revoke account. Note also that there can be

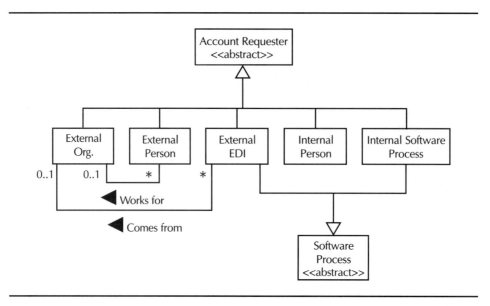

FIGURE 14-8. *Complex generalization*

relationships between the specialization object classes and other object classes or among the specialization object classes themselves.

Multiple Generalization

There need not be only one generalization structure from a given object class, as shown in Figure 14-9—the example of a consulting contract, which can be Time & Materials or Fixed Cost and independently classified as Government or Private.

Abstract Object Classes

The concept of generalization includes the notion of an abstract object class. An abstract class has no objects of its own, but is only used to provide a template for refinement object classes based upon the generalization. For example, since value list classes may all share a similar structure, we can declare that structure once and declare each value list class to be a

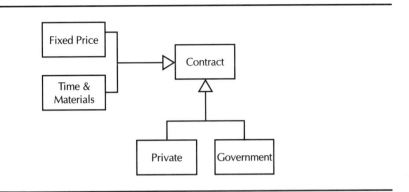

FIGURE 14-9. *Multiple generalization*

specialization of that abstract class. We denote this with the keyword "Abstract" beneath the name of the object class, as in the diagram shown in Figure 14-10.

Figure 14-10 indicates that each status object class has the same structure but each has its own independent objects.

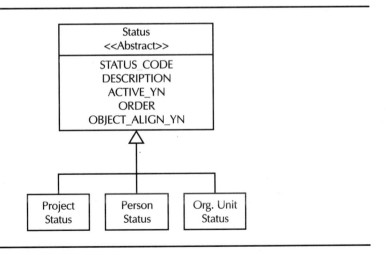

FIGURE 14-10. *Abstract object class*

Implementing Generalization

Implementing generalization is a difficult problem for the designer of an object-relational database. We may have a clear sense of what we are modeling in the real world and how we will represent it using generalization. However, it is not always clear how even our "ideal object-relational product" would handle generalization. We have encountered the same problem in relational databases.

Simulating Inheritance

We have been modeling supertypes and subtypes for years without any type of explicit structure to support them. These were implemented in a variety of ways. These same techniques can be applied to generalization. In fact, with the object-oriented features in Oracle8i, we may be able to implement generalization better than subtypes in relational databases.

Using the classic Hourly/Salaried Employee example shown in Figure 14-3, the following techniques can be used to simulate inheritance. In this case, since we are describing the same situation as subtyping, all of the workarounds used in relational modeling can be used here as well:

- Place all attributes and methods from the generalization and specialization classes and put everything in one table. Using this strategy, there will be both attributes and methods applicable to only one or the other specification class (subtype).

- Implement the structure as two tables—one for salaried and one for hourly employees. Then, copy all of the attributes from the Employee class to the tables for the subclasses.

- Implement the structure as three tables, storing the appropriate attributes in each table. Either foreign keys (relational) or object pointers (object-relational) link objects in the Employee class to their associated objects in the Salaried or Hourly class. To implement this structure relationally, the pointer implicitly goes in either direction. To implement this with object references, you will need to select the direction of the pointer. It is also possible to have the pointers go in both directions—from Employee to Salaried/Hourly and vice versa. This strategy means that we are storing redundant information. We do not believe this is a good solution. We have never implemented it this way, but it should work (in theory).

None of these strategies provide true inheritance. However, they do allow us to take generalization elements from our models and effectively implement them in the database.

Classifying Generalization Relationships

Generalization relationships can be divided into four classifications:

- Subtype generalizations

- Multiple generalizations

- Abstract generalizations

- Overlapping generalizations

We will discuss these separately and provide examples for each classification.

Subtype Generalizations

The Salaried/Hourly Employee Subtype Generalization in Figure 14-1 can be implemented as one or more tables. If we were to implement this example using one table, we would create a table called EMPLOYEE, as shown in Code Example 14-1.

```
CREATE TABLE EMPLOYEE (
EMPLOYEE_ID NUMBER (10) PRIMARY KEY,
LNAME_TX    VARCHAR2 (30),
FNAME_TX    VARCHAR2 (30),
SALARIED_YN VARCHAR2 (1),
PAY_AMT     NUMBER (10,2))
/
```

Code Example 14-1

We would implement this example as a single table since there is only a single attribute (i.e., PAY_AMT), which describes the pay relationship of the employee to the employer. If there were dozens of attributes that describe salaried employees and dozens of other attributes used to describe hourly employees, we would most likely create three tables, as shown in Code Example 14-2.

```
CREATE TABLE EMPLOYEE (
EMPLOYEE_ID NUMBER (10)    NOT NULL PRIMARY KEY,
LNAME_TX    VARCHAR2 (30) NOT NULL,
FNAME_TX    VARCHAR2 (30) NOT NULL)
/
CREATE TABLE SALARY (
SALARY_ID    NUMBER (10)    NOT NULL PRIMARY KEY,
EMPLOYEE_ID  NUMBER (10)    NOT NULL
  REFERENCES EMPLOYEE (EMPLOYEE_ID),
PAY_AMT      NUMBER (10,2) NOT NULL,
SALARY1      VARCHAR2 (10),
--…
SALARY99     VARCHAR2 (10))
/
CREATE TABLE HOURLY (
HOURLY_ID    NUMBER (10)    NOT NULL PRIMARY KEY,
EMPLOYEE_ID  NUMBER (10)    NOT NULL
  REFERENCES EMPLOYEE (EMPLOYEE_ID),
PAY_AMT      NUMBER (10,2) NOT NULL,
HOURLY1      VARCHAR2 (10),
--…
HOURLY99     VARCHAR2 (10))
/
/
```

Code Example 14-2

Creating three tables allows us to separate the attributes of each pay relationship into independent structures, simplifying reporting by Hourly relationship as separate from Salary. However, doing it this way increases the overall size of the data model by two additional tables.

Another reason for physically implementing subtypes relates to performance. If we expect to create substantially more hourly than salaried employees, we may wish to break that data set into two separate tables, provided that reporting is typically performed on one subset or the other, but not both simultaneously. We could also implement a single table and partition it by Pay Type.

Multiple Generalizations

An object class can also be classified in more than one way. For example, Figure 14-6 describes a typical consulting contract, which can be generalized in two different ways. The first method of generalization is to declare the contract as either Fixed Price or Time & Materials. A second method of generalization could be used to declare the contract as pertaining to the Government or Private Sector. This example of multiple generalizations could be implemented with as few as one to as many as five tables.

To implement the multiple generalization using one table, we would define each of the two generalizations as indicator columns, as shown in Code Example 14-3.

```
CREATE TABLE CONTRACT(
CONTRACT_ID     NUMBER (10)      NOT NULL PRIMARY KEY,
DESCR_TXT       VARCHAR2 (50)    NOT NULL,
FIXED_PRICE_YN CHAR (1)          NOT NULL,
PRICE_AMT       NUMBER (10,2),
PRIVATE_YN      CHAR (1)         NOT NULL)
/
```

Code Example 14-3

Each generalization can be determined through the two indicators on the Contract table. It makes sense to implement the contract example using one table because the two generalizations each have a maximum of two valid values (i.e., FIXED_PRICE_YN can either be 'Fixed Price' or 'Time and Materials'). Two value generalizations are easily represented by Boolean flags, thereby requiring fewer tables to be built. If either of the generalizations contained more than two valid values, it would make sense to define the refinement object classes as separate tables referenced by the CONTRACT object class.

The appropriate implementation strategy would be determined in a similar way to the method described for subtype generalizations. If we expect large volumes of data, it might be appropriate to subset the data into multiple tables in Oracle7.

Using Oracle8 partitioning, we could achieve the same performance benefit while keeping our data model as simple as possible. Of course, at least one more table would be required to complete this model, namely, one that maintained information about the parties that can participate in a given contract. The example above ignores the relationships from CONTRACT to PERSON and ORGANIZATION, as described in Figure 10-1 in Chapter 10.

Abstract Generalizations

Abstract generalizations define the template upon which specific object classes are declared. Abstract generalizations are implemented as object types. Figure 14-7 would result in the creation of one object type and three object classes, as shown in Code Example 14-4.

```
CREATE OR REPLACE TYPE STATUS_TYPE
AS OBJECT (
STATUS_CD   VARCHAR2 (5),
DESCR_TX    VARCHAR2 (20),
ACTIVE_YN   VARCHAR2 (1),
ORDER_BY    NUMBER (5))
/
CREATE TABLE PROJECT_STATUS
OF STATUS_TYPE (
STATUS_CD NOT NULL PRIMARY KEY,
DESCR_TX  NOT NULL,
ACTIVE_YN NOT NULL)
/
CREATE TABLE PERSON_STATUS
OF STATUS_TYPE (
STATUS_CD NOT NULL PRIMARY KEY,
DESCR_TX  NOT NULL,
ACTIVE_YN NOT NULL)
/
CREATE TABLE ORG_UNIT_STATUS
OF STATUS_TYPE (
STATUS_CD NOT NULL PRIMARY KEY,
DESCR_TX  NOT NULL,
ACTIVE_YN NOT NULL)
/
```

Code Example 14-4

These three tables all maintain data with similar structures and can therefore be defined based upon one common object row type.

Overlapping Generalizations

Overlapping generalizations provide multiple methods for logically grouping objects, where those objects may belong to one or more of those generalizations. Using the Manufacturing Item example in Figure 14-2, the three different types of manufacturing items (i.e. Inventory, Assembly, and

Finished Good) share a common data type. In fact, a given manufacturing item may be an inventory item, an assembly, and a finished good simultaneously.

This model could be implemented using one or four tables. If we were to create one table, it would be defined as shown in Code Example 14-5.

```
CREATE TABLE MANUFACTURING_ITEM (
ITEM_NBR    NUMBER (10)    NOT NULL PRIMARY KEY,
NAME_TX     VARCHAR2 (50)  NOT NULL,
TEST_YN     CHAR (1)       NOT NULL,
DISCARD_YN  CHAR (1)       NOT NULL,
BUY_YN      CHAR (1)       NOT NULL,
MFG_YN      CHAR (1)       NOT NULL,
SELL_YN     CHAR (1)       NOT NULL)
/
```

Code Example 14-5

Using this structure, any manufacturing item could be defined as being an Inventory Item, an Assembly, or a Finished Good item, or any combination of the three.

Once again, we may choose to implement this example using four separate tables, based upon expected data volume or the quantity of dependent attributes (i.e., attributes that only pertain to a subset of item types). Notice that all flag/indicator columns (i.e., BUY_YN, TEST_YN, etc.) are mandatory. Given the Boolean nature of the data that will be stored in these fields, a default value would be assigned for these fields guaranteeing that a value will be supplied. This allows the specification to declare that the fields are mandatory.

Summary of Methods Implementation

Though Oracle8 methods are certainly a step in the direction of object-oriented development (OOD), it is important to note that Oracle8 objects are not completely encapsulated. It is possible to encapsulate Oracle8 objects, if absolutely necessary. The fullest encapsulation occurs (if you need it) when the data for an object is stored without structure in a LOB so that it is opaque to SQL. Methods are provided as part of the object to interpret this LOB and pick out data members. Obviously, you get this kind of encapsulation only at a price: the loss of many operations that need to know the structure of the data. Nonetheless, this approach is feasible, although we do not recommend it. The less strict implementation of encapsulation is to say that the attributes are not opaque to SQL, but the applications voluntarily use method interfaces to access data. In other words, the automatic generation of constructor methods opens the door to data manipulation as defined by the developer. True OOD would eliminate constructor methods and require manual design and development of an encapsulated set of member methods that define the available data manipulation access paths.

We can replicate the core of this functionality in relational databases as well. This can be accomplished by creating functions and procedures that are the intended data access and manipulation paths. However, just as with object-relational structures, there is no easy way to limit data access to these stored program units unless data is stored as LOBs.

Conclusion

Generalizations should be used frequently in a model. They can greatly simplify the complexity of a diagram. In the Account Requester example, we took very disparate object classes (Persons, Organizational Units, Software) and generalized these to an "Account Requester." Object classes need not have a lot in common to be candidates for generalization. They only need to have something in common. It is necessary to want to use object classes in similar ways or identify some key aspect in order to justify generalization. However, just because two object classes have something in common does not mean that you should necessarily construct a generalization. The key test should be the answer to the question: "Does the generalization make the model clearer and easier to work with?"

It is also possible to overgeneralize and unnecessarily add many generalizations that contribute nothing to the model. There may be a temptation to create a generalization where it does not make sense to do so. For example, many different object classes might have a quantity attribute. This doesn't mean that we should remove the quantity attribute and generalize all of these to an abstract object class called "things that can be counted." It may also appear to be useful to generalize for physical implementation purposes and create an abstract object class merely for the purpose of propagating attributes. But such a generalization represented in a logical diagram adds complexity with no value whatsoever.

PART
IV

Time Related Modeling: Tracking History

CHAPTER
15

Time-Related Modeling

B ecause data continually changes, special care must be taken in data models that include time-related information. To track information over time, several strategies can be used. When data changes, there are some circumstances where we want to track those changes and others where only current values are required. A person changing his or her name, or a person receiving a raise, are both examples of data changes that usually need to be tracked over time. There are also changes necessary because of data entry errors. Do we need to historically track data that was changed to correct an earlier mistake? When you are dealing with large sums of money, as in a banking system, high-security systems, or in working with legal documents such as contracts, any and all changes may need to be meticulously tracked, regardless of the reasons for the changes. In other cases, you may only need to track current information.

When thinking about tracking historical information on a particular class, you need to evaluate (on an attribute-by-attribute level) what information will be tracked. In addition to deciding what information must be tracked, you must decide how that history information will be accessed. For example, do you want a history log on an object class, or is it important to be able to re-create and display an object class as of an earlier date?

History logs are easy to implement because they may be as simple as comments attached to an object. Re-creating an earlier image of an object is much more storage intensive and, in general, somewhat more difficult to code. For example, in some contracting systems, you must be able to go back to earlier decisions and report on the database at any point in time. Here is an example where restating of old information requires meticulous tracking of errors versus real changes. For example, suppose on January 1 a client sends a contract for purchasing a good for $1,000, and the data entry person mistakenly types $10,000. When we mail the contract to the client, the error is noticed, and on January 10 we correct it and change it back to $1,000. On February 1, the client renegotiates the contract down to $500. On March 1 we dispute what was originally agreed to. When restating the facts of the contract, we need to be able to show that on January 1, the cost was really $1,000 and not $10,000, even though $10,000 showed as the "correct" amount. From the auditor's perspective, it is important to know what the legal obligation was and how it was represented in the system. This creates a complex situation to distinguish between the errors and changes and how this historical information is reported on earlier restatements of the system.

Modeling Time-Related Data and Tracking History

Even though the tracking of history often involves extra object classes, we do not always represent those object classes in the data model, because this often makes the model too complex. One of the possibilities for handling this (as discussed in more detail in the "Implementing History" section of this chapter) is to have a separate history object class for most of the primary object classes in the diagram.

To indicate that history will be tracked on a given object class, we can employ user-defined *stereotypes*. Using the example of tracking changes to a contract, we would use two stereotypes—history error and history change—as shown in the following illustration:

```
Contract
<<history error>>
<<history change>>
```

History can also be directly modeled in the class diagram. For example, in an Employee database, if you wanted to know what department a person worked in, you could have a simple relationship between Department and Person. However, if the person could change departments over time, you need to break this information into its own object class, as shown in Figure 15-1.

In this example, the date would have to become part of the primary key for Employment History, because a person could conceivably work for the same department twice over his or her entire career.

Including time-related tables in a system can be complicated. In any system where time is part of a candidate key, you are tracking history. The following are some warnings about time-related tables:

- Don't make end dates mandatory, because you will not always know this information when the record is created.

- If you are in a relational environment, be careful about making the start date a part of the formal primary key, because of the difficulty of changing primary key fields in Oracle.

■ In a situation where a date field is part of the primary key and might change, you should use the system-generated primary key.

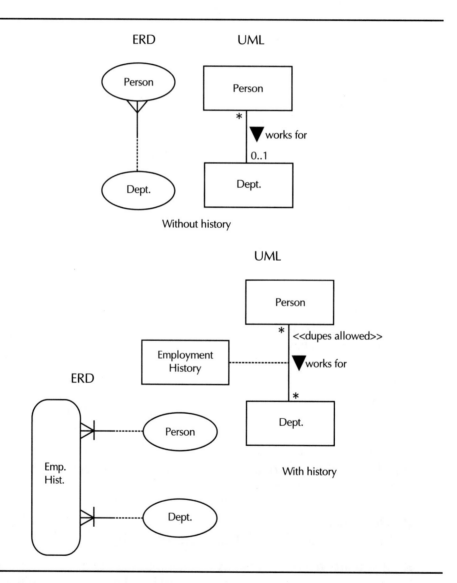

FIGURE 15-1. *Employment history*

Methods of Tracking History

There are six principal ways to accommodate history in any system:

1. Breaking out history information to an intersection table

2. Adding attributes to handle history

3. Maintaining a transaction log

4. Duplicating classes

5. Storing objects and their histories in the same class

6. No explicit handling—history is an inherent part of the model

Each of these methods will be discussed separately.

1. Using an Intersection Table

Figure 15-1 is an example of breaking out history to an intersection table. This is one of the most common ways of handling history information. The idea is that you are taking a 1-to-many relationship and changing it to a many-to-many relationship with allowable duplicates in order to determine what the historical values were. This occurs because the relationship between department and employee is *dynamic,* meaning that the relationship may change over time. (This is called *transferable* in relational database terminology.) By use of this method, a person could work for the Accounting department, transfer to the Finance department, and then transfer back to the Accounting department and still be accurately tracked by the system.

This method is useful when it is important to track the associated history information. However, since we are adding an association class each time we break out history to an intersection table method, this method is not without cost. It is easy to fall into the trap of using many history association tables within a model without recognizing that the value of the information stored in these tables is far less than the complexity that they add to the applications and the additional costs of developing the system. For example, we were brought in to audit one model where there were approximately 50 value list classes (actually reference tables, since this was a relational system). The previous developers had asked the users if they needed to track historical changes in the values for these tables. Users answered that they believed that tracking changes was useful. The developers then generated 50 additional association tables. Upon further analysis, it was determined that users didn't really need this history-tracking capability. They had no idea of the impact that their request would have on the user interface and of the additional complexity required in the applications to support history tracking. After this was explained, the users decided that the information was not important enough to justify the impact of changes to the model.

Using an intersection table is an extremely reliable method to use, providing perfect historical tracking of the specified information. However, the decision to use this method must be carefully weighed against the additional costs and complexities that result.

2. Tracking History by Adding Attributes

When history can be supported through simply adding attributes or relaxing constraints, this is a cheap and easy way to accomplish history tracking. No significant changes to the data model or applications are necessary.

Simply adding an attribute to an existing class can sometimes provide us with history. This is especially true when we are dealing with an association class. For example, suppose we are tracking committee membership as in Figure 15-2. By simply adding start and end dates to the Committee Membership class and by stereotyping the relationship to allow for duplicates, this alone gives us history about who was on each committee and when. It even allows us to assign people to a committee on future dates.

Figure 15-1 shows the breaking out of an Employment History object class to track history explicitly. History can also be explicitly accounted for through attribution. For example, in the situation with committee membership shown in Figure 15-2, without the attributes of Start Date and End Date, this model would only track current membership.

This ability to track future membership is a useful modeling device. In the example shown in Figure 15-3, there are project milestones that can be created when the project is created.

In this case, we can establish project milestones long before they actually occur. Note that we have left optional the "Performed by" relationship to Person, because when the milestone object is created, no person is necessarily associated with it.

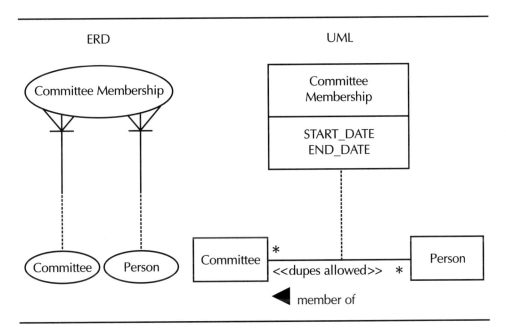

FIGURE 15-2. *Tracking history using additional attributes*

3. Maintaining a Transaction Log

Another strategy for handling history is to store all history for all object classes in one omnibus History object class. This would be a transaction log approach where, in the History object class, we track everything necessary about a transaction, to be able to report or potentially re-create that transaction. This ability to have a single object class generically hook to numerous other object classes will be discussed in Chapter 16.

If you build a generic, flexible structure to track the history of an object once, it can be used for your entire system. We could use the structure shown in Figure 15-4 to create a generic transaction log.

The domain class assists us in writing the applications. It specifies the data type of the event details. Each history event is associated with a particular object. We know what object table it is associated with because of its relationship with the table class, but we also need to know what

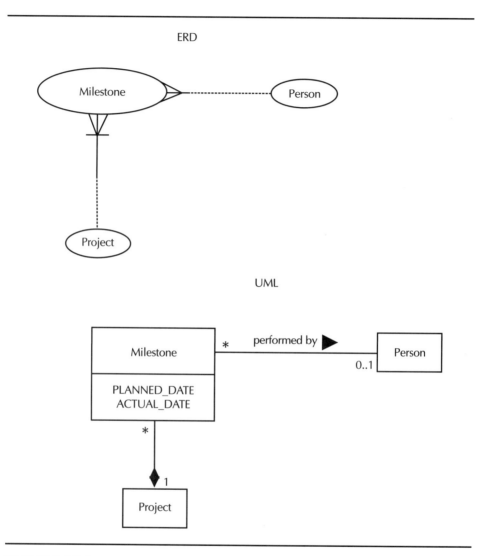

FIGURE 15-3. *Project milestones*

particular object we are storing history about. To do this requires that either the OID or primary key (in a relational model) be stored in the History Event class as attributes. For relational systems, we have used a single-column numeric primary key to link back. This technique is discussed in more detail

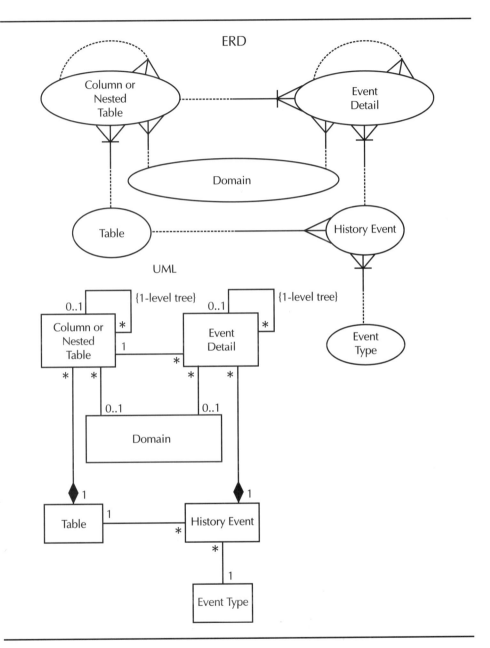

FIGURE 15-4. *Data structure for a generic, history transaction log*

in Chapter 16. The 1-level tree recursion on the Column and Event Detail classes supports Oracle8 nested table structures. A 1-level tree is needed because, currently in Oracle8, you can't have nested tables within other nested tables. To be technically correct, the precise diagram for Columns or Nested Tables is as shown in Figure 15-5.

With this structure, we then place triggers on all of the tables in the database to automatically populate records into the structure every time a record is updated or deleted. When a record is updated, only columns where values change are stored in the History Event Detail Table. When a record is deleted, its entire structure is copied into the history tables. No action is required for insertion of records. This method of storing history, although clumsy, provides the ability to retrieve and view every record in the database and re-create its values at any point in time. If you don't want history on all tables, you don't need the archiving log triggers on every table in the database.

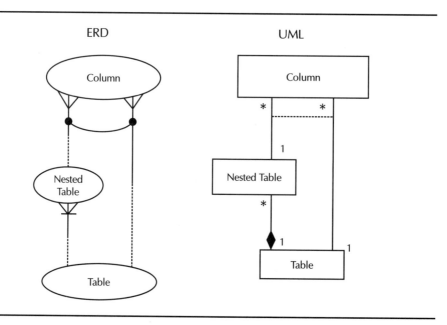

FIGURE 15-5.   *Nested tables*

It is also possible to use the same idea but not implement it as rigorously by creating a single simple history table so that when a record is modified or deleted, a text field describing the change to the table is automatically generated. For example, if in a Person table, a salary were to change from $1,000 to $1,500 and the commission change from $0 to $500, you might generate the following description:

SALARY:1000, 1500; COMMISSION 0, 500

This type of text field allows users to look at the history table and detect what changes were made, assuming that they understand the data structure. However, it is virtually impossible to roll back the values of objects to an earlier time using this structure. For example, we cannot take a contract and show what it looked like a year ago—but we can show all the changes made in the last year.

We highly recommend this generic transaction log approach to tracking history. Even if we have history built into other places in the model, a clear, easy-to-read transaction log is useful for the entire database. If you are not concerned about storage space, you can change the algorithm to store the full structure of an object at insertion rather than deletion. This provides a full transaction log for every event in the database. To facilitate reconstruction of the database back to an earlier time, whether you are using the single table structure or a more complex structure, you can store the text of the Data Manipulation Language (DML) statements right in the History Event class table.

If you are using the more complex structure shown in Figure 15-4, then the DML statements can be created on the fly. You will get a much faster rollback of an object by storing the actual DML text.

4. Duplicating Classes to Create History

This method involves making an exact duplicate of the class we want to track history about. For example, to create history about a project, we must duplicate the entire project class and add two attributes, Start Date and End Date, which identify the term for which these values of the attributes are valid. For every class you want to track history on with this method, you would have to make an additional history class. The primary data class and the history class are associated with a 0..1-to-* relationship. The primary key of the history class is the same as the primary key of the original data class, except that the history class start date must be included in the primary key. Before each change to any record in the primary class, the record is duplicated and inserted into the history class with the appropriate start date. The previous history record for that object is retrieved, and the end date is updated.

This method can be used only with a subset of all the attributes in the class. You need to externally modify all of your applications and reports to access these separate history structures. This was a common approach in the past, but very painstaking. Since we can now partition tables and the price of disk space continues to plummet, it is difficult to envision a situation where this approach would still be useful. In a very large system where tables have tens if not hundreds of millions of records, this approach might still have merit.

5. Storing Objects and Their Histories in the Same Class

Using this method, we are creating a simple recursive linked list to show objects and their histories. This modeling concept was discussed in more detail in Chapter 10. As an example, for tracking the history of a contract, we would place a recursive relationship on the contract. Anytime we wanted to version the contract, we could duplicate all of the contract information and then link the old contract to the new contract. For performance reasons, we use a current indicator to quickly find current versions of contracts.

This method has some problems. It clutters up your tables with historical records. In addition, the code required to support this structure is complex, because there is more relevant information in the Contract object than just what is stored in a single class. When we version the contract, in addition to duplicating the contract record, we also duplicate all of its associated details. For example, using the structure in Figure 15-6, you will also need to duplicate all of the detail records.

Decisions can be made about duplicating the detail records in the detail classes or what should be stored historically. This strategy provides good control over history. The disadvantage is that you are duplicating a lot of information that does not change. If you want to track all history—anytime that any field in the object or any field in any of its details changes—you need to version the entire structure. This can genereate thousands if not millions of objects with no information content. At the application level, this provides an easy way of looking at the system at a given time.

We used the example of a contract because with contracts or similar objects with many versions, this type of approach makes the most sense. Changes to contracts often require looking at an entire replication of the

ERD

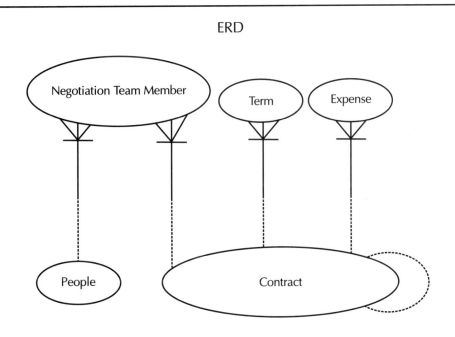

UML

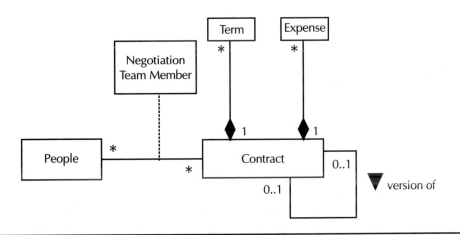

FIGURE 15-6. *Recursive linked list structure*

contract at an earlier time. In this way, historical contracts are stored in exactly the same way as a current contract. To look at an earlier version, you simply need to point to that version. Now that we can partition tables in Oracle8, large tables are no longer a problem. However, you do not want to make separate views unless they are needed for warehousing purposes. The strength of the approach of storing objects and their histories together is that you can retrieve a historical object as easily as a current one, so you will want to use the same access method for both.

When using this approach, you need to be careful that, for most reports, you only look at different contracts. For example, if you wanted to count the number of contracts with which a person is associated, you would need to join back to the Contract class to ensure that you are only looking at negotiation team members on current contracts. This structure does somewhat increase the complexity of application development, even though the data model is not more complex.

6. No Explicit Handling of History

Sometimes, simply by the nature of the model, history is tracked automatically. History may already be incorporated into a data model without explicit effort. For example, repair events on a project may already be tracked by the day the event occurred, start/end time, and associated costs. These together constitute the complete event history. Before explicitly trying to include history, analysis should be done to see if it might already have been implicitly included.

Time Zones

When an organization has business that spans multiple time zones and you are dealing with time-related information, you must be able to display transaction information from various perspectives. The idea is that all time-related information is dependent upon the time zone in which you want the information represented. For a transaction, the problem is that the time at which the transaction occurred from the perspective of the local business unit may be a relevant date. It is probably also relevant to be able to know what time that transaction occurred from the perspective of any specified time zone. Usually, this is limited to two perspectives, the head office and the local office. However, it is just as easy to store the date once, and then to display and manipulate it based on the specific time zones. This can be quite complex, particularly with financial transactions. Calculations must take place based on local time. Close of the banking transaction day may be 3 P.M. local time. Tracking daily interest must be done based on days in the local office, not the head office. The difference may only be fractions of pennies, but for a very large bank or brokerage organization, accounts must balance to the penny.

In various parts of the world, times are offset by various time adjustments, such as daylight saving time. The shifts are made differently in each local time zone. Even in the continental United States, where the shift is made at the same time in most places, it is not really the same time, because 2 A.M. is not the same in each zone. To handle this, you need to model Time Zone as a class, and then use sufficient attributes to model the various behaviors. Knowing what time zone a particular time value is associated with, you can then convert it to the correct time through a function that uses the information in the time zone class.

In dealing with time zones, we recommend that with each time attribute you also store the relevant time zone. This effectively means that there is an association between the Time Zone class and every other class that has a time-based attribute. The structure of the Time Zone class is as shown in Table 15-1.

The function to convert time from another time zone is as follows:

```
FUNCTION F_TIME_ZONE_TM
       (IN_SOURCE_TIME_ZONE_CD VARCHAR2,
        IN_DEST_TIME_ZONE_CD VARCHAR2,
        IN_TIME_TM)   RETURN DATE
```

Time Zone

TIME_ZONE_CD

NO_HOURS_DIFFERENT_NR

DAYLIGHT_SAVE_TM

STANDARD_TM

TABLE 15-1.   *Time Zone Class Structure*

Implementing History

This section will demonstrate implementations of some of the four methods mentioned earlier in relational syntax. Each example can be implemented by use of object-relational syntax, with very little modification.

In general, the purpose of capturing history about an object is to be able to view the evolution of that object over its lifetime. For example, we may need to review the employment history of a given person within our organization. During the relationship between the employee and the organization, the employee may have worked for multiple departments over time. This example is presented diagrammatically in Figure 15-1.

History in a Transaction Log

Maintaining history in a transaction log is not nearly as common as the first two approaches. Instead of capturing snapshots of records in a point-in-time manner and storing them in a static table, we would actually create a table to store the changes in the form of DML statements. The advantage to this method is that we could reapply the transactions from this log, should they need to be reversed.

With this method, we can also store who made the add/change and when they performed it. This information can be gathered with any of the examples we will demonstrate in this book, but it is especially important to capture this type of information in such volatile environments where the choice would be to implement a transaction log. To decide to reverse a transaction based upon user request, we would probably want to validate that the user requesting the reversal is either the same user that performed the original transaction, or that person's superior.

For records that were inserted into a given table, we would generate delete transactions and insert them into the transaction log as shown in Code Example 15-1. For records that were modified, we would generate update statements and insert them into the transaction log. Each transaction would be time-stamped as to the exact time the original transaction occurred. These time stamps provide the audit trail in the order that each transaction must be applied, in order to properly reverse a given transaction.

```
CREATE TABLE TRANS_LOG (
    TRANS_ID            NUMBER (10) NOT NULL PRIMARY KEY,
    TABLE_NAME          VARCHAR2 (30) NOT NULL,
```

```
ROW_ID              VARCHAR2 (200) NOT NULL,
DESCR_TXT           VARCHAR2 (2000) NOT NULL,
TRANS_DATE          DATE NOT NULL)
/
```

Code Example 15-1

This table will allow you to report the transactions that have occurred, by table. The transaction would be stored in the DESCR_TXT column. Triggers on each table can insert transactions into this structure for each transaction a user commits against a given table.

This sort of implementation can get quite complicated. Master-Detail inserts can cause the transaction log to become quite large, making the act of reversing what appears to be a single transaction significantly more complicated.

This structure would actually have to be extended to indicate dependencies of certain transactions, based upon other transactions. This could be implemented through a recursive relationship on the TRANS_LOG table, provided that the triggers on the dependent tables identified the transaction that a given transaction was dependent upon.

For example, you would not be able to reverse the insert of a record into the master if there were existing detail records, unless those detail records had already been reversed.

History in the Same Table

The model in Figure 15-1 could represent the tracking of employment history in the Person table. We would add two attributes to this table, START_DATE and END_DATE, which would be used to specify the outer parameters of a specific employment relationship as shown in Code Example 15-2.

Notice that this method overloads the Person table with additional rows generated by "Insertion Of" or "Modification To" an Employment Relationship. It does not track Persons outside of the scope of their Employment Relationship(s).

```
CREATE TABLE DEPT (
DEPT_ID             NUMBER (5) NOT NULL PRIMARY KEY,
DESCR_TXT           VARCHAR2 (50) NOT NULL)
/
```

```
CREATE TABLE PERSON (
EMP_ID          NUMBER (5) NOT NULL,
DEPT_ID         NUMBER (5) NOT NULL
  REFERENCES DEPT(DEPT_ID),
LNAME           VARCHAR2 (30) NOT NULL,
FNAME           VARCHAR2 (30),
START_DATE      DATE NOT NULL,
END_DATE        DATE NOT NULL,
PRIMARY KEY (EMP_ID, START_DATE, END_DATE))
/
```

Code Example 15-2

The Employment Relationship form will Insert a record into the Person table each time a new Employment Relationship is defined. The START_DATE will likely be defaulted to SYSDATE, and the END_DATE is optional.

Each time an existing Employment Relationship is modified, the END_DATE of the current Employment Relationship record will be set to SYSDATE and another row will be inserted into the Person table, reflecting the current information supplied in the Employment Relationship form. As a result, you have built a thorough log of every Employment Relationship Action that has ever been implemented.

There are two deterrents to implementing history within the same table: performance and the required coding. Clustering and/or Oracle8 partitioning are two RDBMS features that can eliminate most of the performance burden. Also, performance will most likely not be an issue in the example discussed earlier—although it would be in a securities environment that included keeping track of issues and who owns what, over time.

The second issue deals with the nuts and bolts of how we write the code to support this example. The cleanest way to implement such a strategy would be to create a database trigger on the Person table. This trigger would make the appropriate date/time stamping as well as insert the additional records into the Person table. The trigger would fire after updates and would look like Code Example 15-3:

```
--EXAMPLE_15_01 IS PREREQ

CREATE OR REPLACE TRIGGER AU_PERSON
AFTER UPDATE
ON PERSON
FOR EACH ROW
BEGIN
INSERT INTO PERSON (EMP_ID,
                    DEPT_ID,
                    LNAME,
                    FNAME,
                    START_DATE,
                    END_DATE)
          VALUES (:OLD.EMP_ID,
                  :OLD.DEPT_ID,
                  :OLD.LNAME,
                  :OLD.FNAME,
                  :OLD.START_DATE,
                  SYSDATE);
END;
/
```

Code Example 15-3

The Employment Relationship form would insert every new record into the Person table. The trigger shown earlier would insert a static record into the Person table tracking the last valid Employment Relationship before the modification.

The problem with this solution is that a database trigger cannot manipulate data (i.e., insert, update, delete) in the table that the trigger is defined upon. Notice that the trigger is created on the Person table and is attempting to do an insert into the Person table as well. Attempting to update a record in the Person table would cause the following error shown in Code Example 15-4:

```
--EXAMPLE_15_02 IS PREREQ
--MUTATING TABLE

INSERT INTO DEPT (DEPT_ID, DESCR_TXT)
VALUES (10,' Accounting')
/
```

```
INSERT INTO PERSON(EMP_ID,DEPT_ID,LNAME,FNAME,START_DATE,END_DATE)
VALUES (7934,10,'SMITH','JOE','12-DEC-1985','31-DEC-2002')
/

update person
set lname='Jones'
where emp_id=7934
```

Code Example 15-4

Therefore, the only way you could implement this operation would be by executing similar code from your form. This method requires much more coding because you lose the "old" and "new" system variables that the triggering method provides. Instead, you will have to define your own program-level variables to capture the point-in-time variables yourself. However, you can use triggers if you track history in a mirrored table.

History in a Mirrored Table

We can expand upon the previous example to demonstrate the tracking of history using a mirrored table. The mirrored table example is shown in the right-hand diagram in Figure 15-1. A third table would be created, PERSON_HIST, that would be defined exactly as the PERSON table is. Then a trigger would be created to insert into the new PERSON_HIST table, as opposed to the PERSON table. Also, the variables would be changed as shown in Code Example 15-5.

```
--EXAMPLE_15_03 IS PREREQ
CREATE TABLE PERSON_HIST (
EMP_ID            NUMBER (5) NOT NULL,
DEPT_ID           NUMBER (5) NOT NULL
  REFERENCES DEPT(DEPT_ID),
LNAME             VARCHAR2 (30) NOT NULL,
FNAME             VARCHAR2 (30),
START_DATE        DATE NOT NULL,
END_DATE          DATE NOT NULL,
PRIMARY KEY (EMP_ID, START_DATE, END_DATE))
/

create or replace trigger aiu_person
after insert or update
```

```
ON person
for each row
begin
insert into person_hist(emp_id,
                        dept_id,
                        lname,
                        fname,
                        start_date,
                        end_date)
             values(:new.emp_id,
                    :new.dept_id,
                    :new.lname,
                    :new.fname,
                    :new.start_date,
                    :new.end_date);
end;
/
```

Code Example 15-5

This is the cleanest method for coding history capture. The trigger will allow the most current Employment Relationships to be stored in the Person table, while the entire history of every Employment Relationship will be stored in the PERSON_HIST table. There will not be a performance hit when looking for the most current Employment information, because that is all the Person table contains. The only time you are forced to go through the entire history is when that is your specific request, at which time you would query the PERSON_HIST table instead.

Tracking history does tend to cause the overall size of a database to grow at seemingly alarming rates. Fortunately, we can cluster either by departments or people, or even partition with Oracle8.

CHAPTER
16

Generic Modeling

eneric modeling involves trying to make models flexible and sufficiently robust so that when new requirements inevitably arise, neither the model nor the applications have to change substantially. As we capture business rules, we build the data model to support not only those business rules, but also any similar rules. The added robustness of generic structures allows the models to support more business rules than were gathered initially. At some level, thinking along these terms makes analysis work simpler, because rather than exhaustively gathering all business rules, we need only gather the *structure* of the business rules. If the model supports this flexibility, then any additional business rules will fall into one of the already existing structures. Also, generic structures result in smaller models, which are easier to understand than ones with large numbers of entities.

The process of genericization is a way of thinking about data modeling. If you think along these lines, you will be likely to find many opportunities to genericize as you are building your models. Employed intelligently, the concept of genericization can greatly decrease the cost of a project. In this chapter, we will discuss the kind of thinking required to achieve the optimal genericization from very trivial modifications of traditional structures to very large and complex generic structures that can be dropped into many completely different systems.

In this chapter, we will describe a variety of techniques, some of which will be familiar and others of which will be complex from both a modeling perspective and from the fact that the forms to support them cannot be generated by Oracle Designer or any similar product. Even coding these structures by hand requires very skilled developers. To some extent, this is a criticism of the generic modeling approach in that it makes some models much more complex and difficult to implement. Another disadvantage of generic structures occurs when you're performing a legacy system redesign. The new generic structure will often be very different from the old structure, making the data migration mapping much more difficult. However, the advantages of generic modeling far outweigh the disadvantages, as long as you have very skilled modelers and developers on the development team. The techniques presented in this chapter will be organized from the simplest to the most complex.

Technique 1: Genericizing a Check Constraint to a Value List Class (Reference Table)

Frequently, attributes can be restricted to a list of valid values. This list can be implemented directly in the table through the use of a *check constraint.* The check constraint is used to restrict the values of a particular attribute to those in a given list. For example, we can restrict a gender attribute in a Person table to Male/Female, or a Boolean attribute to Yes/No, etc. However, many people use check constraints for status attributes such as the status of a project, which might be Initial, Approved, In Process, Complete, or Canceled. This is normally implemented in screen applications through a radio group, and we can generate elegant looking applications that work well. Unfortunately, we may want to refine our valid project statuses for a particular project. If this occurs, then we are forced to modify not only the check constraints (which is relatively easy to do), but also our applications to support the additional value(s). Often, this is not so simple. Usually, modifications to neither the database nor applications can be performed by users; they require DBA and/or developer talent.

The first genericization technique involves making a design decision to replace a check constraint with a value list class. An additional advantage to doing this is that there is no easy way to represent a check constraint in either an ER diagram or a UML class diagram. In either ERDs or UML, you can, however, show reference objects or value list classes. This is not to say that value list classes should be used all the time. There are still places where check constraints should be used. For example, the truth values of a Boolean field have been Y/N or T/F since logic systems were developed. Likewise, the list of valid genders (notwithstanding the talk show circuit) has remained similarly constant. The rule of thumb is that unless you are dealing with a list of valid values for an attribute that can never change, using a value list class rather than a check constraint is a safer and better choice. The world is an inherently dynamic place. Users will often claim that "we always use these five codes," but it has been our experience that the model and system eventually needed to be modified to support a sixth, seventh, eighth... code later.

Technique 2: Overloading Value List Classes

In many cases, value list classes contain similar information. You may end up having the same value list class appear in several different places in a model. The valid status example mentioned in the previous section is a good example here as well. Initial, Approved, In Process, Complete, and Canceled are common statuses for most projects or processes. Sometimes, one object may have extra possible statuses, but this list usually remains constant. We can create a single value list class for Status that can be used to support multiple structures. This technique was discussed in Chapter 7.

Technique 3: Tracking Historical Information

Frequently, in gathering requirements, users will say that they only need current information. For example, users will want to keep track of what department a person works in, but not where the person used to work. Be very careful about making a decision not to track historical information. This is not a simple decision, because tracking historical information in addition to single-point-in-time information is expensive. As discussed in Chapter 12, care must be taken in accepting point-in-time-only versus historical modeling. On a recent project, with grave misgivings and against our better judgment, we accepted the users' assurances that we didn't need to track historical information. This was a stand-alone system and the main personnel system for the organization did track employment history, which was stored elsewhere. There were no problems until we attempted to build a report showing information about a project. A simplification of the relevant data model is shown in Figure 16-1.

ERD

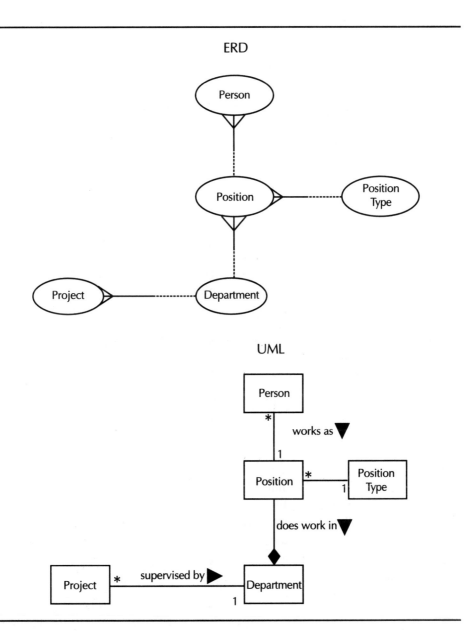

UML

FIGURE 16-1.   *Structure with no history*

We needed to track what were valid positions for a department and assign those positions to persons. Projects in this system were assigned to departments. When creating reports, we found a position for the Department called "Project Manager" assigned to the person who managed all projects. The problem arose when we needed to show who was the manager of a project. All that could be shown was the current project manager for the department. There was no way to track accountability back to the original project manager if the manager had moved on to another project.

The lesson learned here is that you should only limit your model to track current states of information when you are absolutely sure that you will never need to track history information. Rather than taking the user point-in-time requirement at face value, we should have recognized that historical information might also be relevant in this case. Including historical information in the model initially is not without cost, but the cost of not tracking it is unmet user requirements and the additional costs of changes to the data model and applications later. Modeling historical information is discussed more fully in Chapter 15.

Technique 4: Making a Relationship into a Class

There is often more than one relationship between two classes. When this occurs, you should determine whether this relationship is a good candidate for genericization. A good example is the relationship between Project and Department discussed in Technique 3. After we talked to a number of different users, we decided that there should be a 1-to-many relationship between Department and Project. When we designed prototype applications based upon this decision and showed them to all of the users in a Joint Application Development (JAD) session, we learned that the users were talking about two different types of relationships. One was the financial control of the project, and the other entailed administrative control of a project. For this organization, controls came from two different departments. We then needed to change the model to support two relationships as shown in Figure 16-2.

All was progressing smoothly until we discovered another relationship whereby a project was audited by a third department. At this point, we decided that genericization of the relationship between Project and

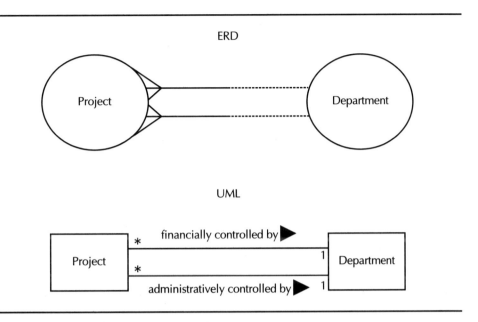

ERD

UML

FIGURE 16-2. *Multiple relationships between classes*

Department was appropriate. We modeled the relationship as shown in Figure 16-3.

With this model, any relationship between Project and Department can be added without having to change the model again. In this way, we have made a relationship into a class. This technique should always be used when more than two relationships exist between classes. Even when two relationships are discovered, you should carefully assess whether there may be more.

Technique 5: Creating Recursive Value List Classes

In many systems, it is common to need to go beyond simple typing of objects in order to implement some type of rollup structure. This technique is discussed in Chapter 7.

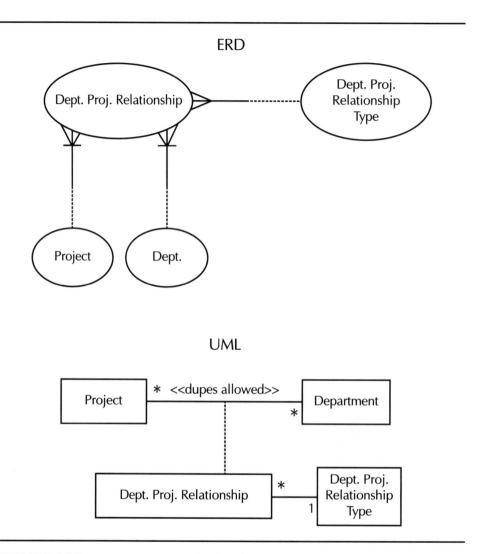

FIGURE 16-3. *Genericizing multiple relationships*

Technique 6: Storing Table Structures as Data

Traditional notions of generic modeling usually involve the storing of the whole structure of a table as data. This allows modifications to these "virtual tables" to occur through applications. Thus, users can make significant changes to these virtual tables without the support of a DBA or developer. Such virtual table structures are complex, difficult to understand and to code, and lead to terrible performance if the database is large. They also require expert developers and DBAs to maintain them properly. The advantage of these structures is that they support users directly making changes to the data model. This is potentially a great benefit. To clarify this idea, we will use a simple example that would never be implemented generically. Figure 16-4 shows a basic genericization for employees. Figure 16-5 shows the details of the full generic model.

In the full generic model shown in Figure 16-5, datatypes refer to the Oracle datatypes (VARCHAR2, DATE, NUMBER, etc.). Data Domains list the valid domains allowed to be used in this context. This is an idea borrowed from CASE tools to help us restrict allowable datatypes in the database. Using the Data Domains is essential to help simplify the development of the flexible applications necessary to support this structure. The Data Domains can include not only data length, but also formatting, default values, and check constraints. A table can also include a reference to an external PL/SQL function to support complex validation. Employee Type consists of the list of all possible types of employees—in this case, two would be included: Salaried and Hourly. Employee Attributes consist of all possible attributes used in this structure. The Valid Attributes class stores the information about which attributes are appropriate for which type of

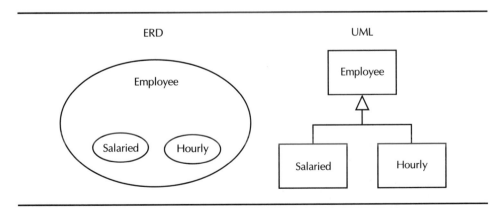

FIGURE 16-4.   *Simple employee generalization*

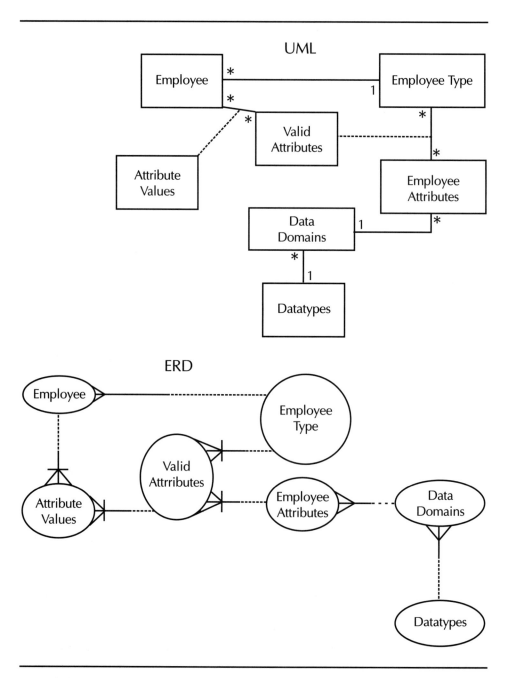

FIGURE 16-5. *Full generic model for employee types*

employee. The values of these attributes are stored in the Attribute Values class. The following points assist in comparing the two examples:

- The names of the specialization classes are stored in Employee Type.

- The names of the attributes in the specialization classes are stored in Employee Attributes.

- The declarations of which attributes are used in the specialization classes are stored in Attribute Values.

Therefore, a specific object from the Salaried class in Figure 16-4 would have each of its attributes stored as an individual object in the Attributes Values class in Figure 16-5.

If the number of attributes associated with different types of employees is large, there are many employees, or there is a high transaction volume, this structure becomes unusable, given current technology. For example, if there were 1,000 salaried and hourly employees with 50 specific attributes to be tracked, this would result in some 50,000 objects in the Attribute Values class.

This is still not an unworkable number. However, some thought must be given to the type of system for which this might be used and the potential performance impacts caused by the genericization. This type of structure is more likely to be used in the case of a pharmaceutical testing environment where scientists are given the ability to define their own tests and decide which attributes are appropriate for each test. If we assume that there is an average of ten attributes tracked for each test type and 1,000 different tests are run each day, over the course of a year, this would generate some 2 million objects in the Attribute Values class. This number of records makes performance tuning an important issue. Before creating a generic structure such as this, an impact analysis should be performed. Creating a generic structure for a high-volume financial system with hundreds, if not thousands, of transactions per second would be impossible given the current technology.

There are very few modelers with the skills to create effective generic structures. Even fewer of these have sufficiently skilled development teams to create the applications necessary to support such an effort. Often, explaining a generic model to a novice modeler or developer can be a challenging task. However, if you are in an environment with a highly skilled team and a performance burden that is not too heavy, judicious use of generic structures can greatly reduce the size and complexity of your data model.

Technique 7: Overloading Primary Data Classes

In Chapter 9 we discussed the appropriate structure for an Organization Unit. Rather than having separate classes for each Division/Department, we created a single class called Organization Unit. This is an excellent example of overloading a primary data class. Anytime a system includes the notion of objects contained in other objects such as Department/Division/Group, it is easy to recognize that these should be combined, because the definitions of these classes are all the same. In our Organization unit example, all different types of Organization Units can be defined as collections of people. It is also possible to combine structures that have quite dissimilar definitions if they have similar structures and/or overlapping information. In the retail system we discussed in Chapters 3 and 4, we had Sales, Purchases, and Receipt of Goods modeled as shown in Figure 16-6.

Note that all of these structures can be defined as a "movement or request for movement of some number of inventory items from one location to another." Thus, we combined all of these into a single, generic structure called "Merchandise Movement" as shown in Figure 16-7. Not only did this greatly reduce the complexity of the model, but later in the process when

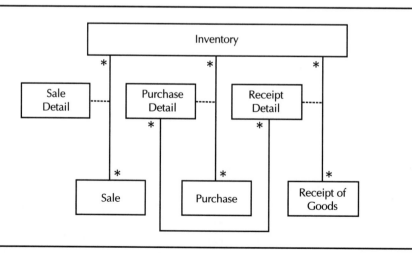

FIGURE 16-6. *Traditional retail system model*

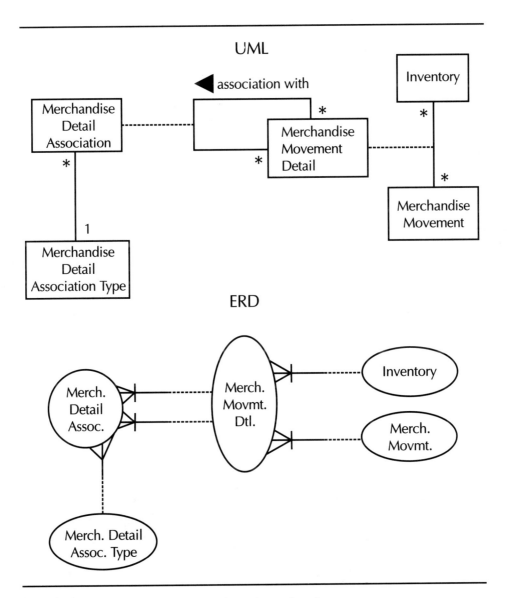

FIGURE 16-7. *Genericization of retail merchandise movement*

we uncovered previously unidentified merchandise movements such as a Sales Return, the generic model was flexible enough to accommodate the new transaction type without any changes.

Technique 8: Creating Large Complex Objects (COBs)

The next level of genericization involves reuse of the same or similar structures many times throughout the model. For example, suppose we have multiple kinds of comments associated with different structures—i.e., Persons may have comments concerning their job records, whereas Projects have comments attached regarding their feasibility. With either structure, it might be appropriate to have a generic remark. Traditionally, each different type of comment field is placed into the class itself. If comments of the same type can be applied by more than one person, they must be broken down into another detail class. These structures can be completely genericized so that they can be used seamlessly in any system. For example, using the techniques discussed earlier in this chapter, we transform the traditional structure shown in Figure 16-8 into the generic structure shown in Figure 16-9.

Notice how in the second diagram, we have not even attached Person and Project to Comment. We simply create a method called "Comment," which will create a comment for that class in the Comment structure. The rules determining what comment type is appropriate for which structure are stored in the Valid Comment Type class. We call this type of structure a *COB* (complex object). In its implementation, we include not only the classes and their implemented tables with appropriate triggers, but also their associated forms and reports. This allows us to reuse the structures not just within applications as shown here, but also across applications.

Implementing Generic Structures

Complex object development requires a highly skilled team, with extensive knowledge of PL/SQL. Stored Program Unit development (i.e., database triggers, packages, procedures, and functions) and DBMS_SQL are just two of the critical knowledge sets that are required to develop complex objects.

Building Complex Objects (COBs)

Complex objects (COBs) are not difficult to build once you have completed the first one. However, to build them, you need to understand and be able to use DBMS SQL.

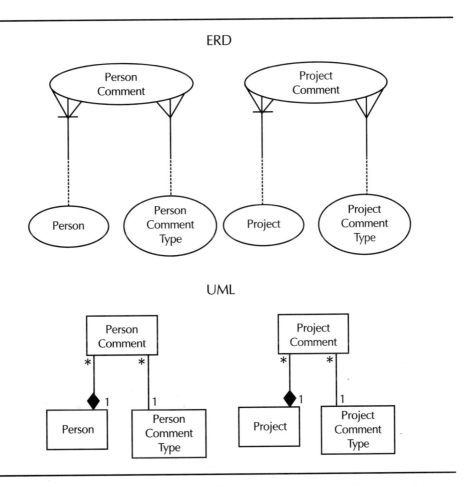

ERD

UML

FIGURE 16-8.   *Traditional comment field structure*

These structures can be quite complex. For example, the Workflow complex object we constructed not only stores workflow acts such as approval/denial, but also stores rules about who performs such actions. It requires ten to 16 tables and three multitab Forms modules to support it. COBs can also be very simple. For example, a Comments COB involves little more than a single table.

The remainder of this chapter will explain how to build the Comments COB. Once you see how one of these objects is built, you should be able to take the idea and build more structures on your own.

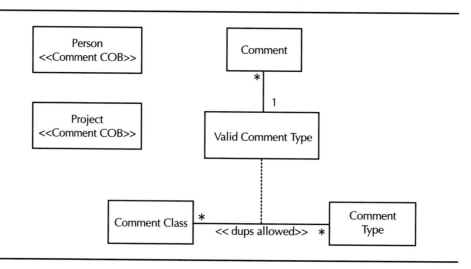

FIGURE 16-9. *Genericized comment field structure*

Before trying to build a COB, you should build the structure as a nongeneric object. For example, in this exercise, you should first build the Comments structure in the traditional way and then modify it to be a COB. If you have done a lot of template building in the past, you will probably feel comfortable going directly to the COB environment.

The basic table structure of the simple Comment COB is the comment table and a reference table that stores information about the objects that can be commented on. If we only want to allow commenting by people with a specific role, we need a few more tables. We will discuss the structure of each of the tables in turn.

Step 1: Building the COB Reference Table

We want to store the tables that will allow commenting. We need to do this so we can write database triggers to enforce the necessary pseudo-referential integrity. To do this, we build a reference table and store the commentable table names in it.

The reference table (COB_REF) is used for all COBs. For this simple structure, we need only one column to store the table name. However, we want to anticipate using more than one COB, so we will add a second column to indicate which tables will allow commenting.

To allow commenting on projects and purchase orders (at both the master and detail level), the appropriate reference table would be as shown in Table 16-1.

If we were to have more COBs in this application, we would simply add more indicator columns to the reference table. Of course, we could use a table that stores the names of the COBs and create an intersection table between table names and COBs. This is unnecessary because we have to make code changes to add a new COB anyway. Adding a column is painless, and it makes it easier to see quickly which table can use which COB.

Another useful factor in the Comments COB is to have a real name for this object to facilitate reporting from the table and to report more than the UID of the table. One way to support this is to put an extra VARCHAR2 (100) column in the comment table to store a character description of the object being commented on. For example, for Employees, use the employee name; for Inventory, use the name of the inventory item. However, if the name of the object changes, the linked comment field would not be automatically updated. To solve this problem, a display name column is added to the reference table.

This expression is usually just a column name. For the Employee table, it would be a concatenation of several columns with spaces or commas. It could also be a function of the table UID, which could return a character string, possibly requiring a query of its own.

Table Name	Display Name	Comment Y/N
PROJECT	'PROJECT: '||Project_name	Y
PO	'PURCH ORDER: ' ||To_char(PO_num) ||'-'|| to_char(approve_date, 'MM/DD/YYYY')	Y
PO_DTL	'PURCH ORDER DTL: '|| To_char(PO_num) ||'-'|| Item_name(item_id)	Y

TABLE 16-1.   *COB Reference Table*

For example, if someone were commenting on a purchase order detail line, when referencing that comment, it might be worthwhile to see the parent purchase order number, date, and vendor name. This might be a query involving a multitable join.

In the earlier example we have shown the following display names:

Project   The name of the project

Purchase Order   The PO number followed by the date the purchase order was approved (e.g., 21432 – 02/12/1998)

Purchase Order Detail   The PO number followed by the name of the item ordered. In this case the name of the item is returned through a function.

Step 2: Building the Comment Tables

In addition to a Comment table, we need a Comment Type table and an intersection table to validate which types of comments are appropriate for each table.

The COMMENT_TYPE table is a simple code description table.

VALID_COMMENT_TYPE is an intersection table between COB_REF and COMMENT_TYPE. Each row in this table represents an allowable type for a particular commentable table.

If you don't want to go to the trouble of genericizing the code (this is a bit annoying), instead you can have the user specify the comment type in the calling application, which is then passed as an additional user parameter. However, if you build a significant quantity of applications, genericizing the code will pay off in the long run and will be well worth the time and effort.

A simple Comments table is one where a user can log comments about any topic such as budgets, purchase order, manufacturing, etc. We can genericize all of these comments within a single table. The table structure is as follows in Code Example 16-1:

```
CREATE TABLE COMMENTS (
COMMENT_ID        NUMBER (10) NOT NULL PRIMARY KEY,
CREATE_DATE DATE NOT NULL,
   --Date and time comment was logged.
PERSON            VARCHAR2 (40) NOT NULL,
   --Name of person logging comment.
COMMENT TYPE      NUMBER (10) NOT NULL,
```

```
    -- Foreign key to the comment type table.
COMMENT_TX   VARCHAR2 (2000) NOT NULL,
  --Comment itself.
FK_TABLE          VARCHAR2 (30)   NOT NULL,
  --Name of the table on which the comment
  --is logged (This is a foreign key to the COB_REF table).
FK_LINK          NUMBER (10) NOT NULL)
  --Foreign key link. The key to the row on which the
  --comment was made. (This is an overloaded foreign
  --key that points to the table sited in the FK_TABLE column.)
/
```

Code Example 16-1

The first four columns contain all of the information we need about the comment. This table must now be linked to the object that the comment refers to. We need to make the table generic. The traditional way to do this would be by using an arced set of foreign keys (exclusive OR), which would require one foreign key column for every object that can be commented on. The disadvantage to this approach is that if we want to place commenting capability in a new system or to extend it to new objects, then data-model and programmatic changes to whatever modules are supporting comments would be required.

What is needed is a generic approach to link comments to any object. To support this, we added two columns to the comment table:

- The first additional column consists of the name of the table we are pointing to (FK_TABLE).

- The second is the UID for that table (FK_LINK). This imposes a minor limitation, namely that it forces us to use single-column primary keys in anything we need to link a generic object to. You can make this work with multicolumn primary keys; however, the coding is more difficult. In practice, we use system-generated numeric IDs only for columns that may require generic structures. In Oracle8 it may be possible to use the OID, but we have not been able to test this yet.

Step 3: Enforcing Referential Integrity
The FK_TABLE column is enforced through simple referential integrity. The FK_LINK column, however, is enforced through a BEFORE_INSERT trigger.

The trigger must enforce that the UID exists in the underlying table that we are trying to comment on.

This is where we need to use DBMS SQL, because the table name is being passed on the inserting row. The trigger does a lookup back to the underlying table to enforce the referential integrity.

You also need to add a BEFORE_DELETE trigger to each of the commentable tables to make sure that comments are not orphaned in the comment tables when commented-on objects are deleted.

To implement this, you have a few alternatives:

1. Do nothing. Creation of the comments is only through the comments application anyway. The trigger is difficult to write and is not necessary. Orphaning comments is not a big problem, because it won't happen much. Disks are cheap anyway.

2. Write the triggers by hand. As long as you are not using many COBs and don't have too many tables accessing them, this approach may be fine. However, if you are planning on writing a lot of systems, this becomes an arduous task.

3. Write utilities to create the triggers for you. If you are doing a lot of COB work, this will save you time in the long run.

Depending upon the system, each of these may be used. Surprisingly, the first alternative is not always as silly as it sounds. We worked on a system where few rows were ever deleted and all access to the COBs was through the applications. After much soul searching, we took the do-nothing approach.

Costs of Generic Implementation

While generic implementation leads to flexible systems, it also requires sacrifices. The two most critical are the performance implications that arise from combining similar but not homogeneous object sets into one common data structure known as *data migration*, and the way this generic strategy changes the scope of data migragion.

The costs of data migration tend to go unforeseen until far too late in the project schedule. The most common flaw in data migration planning is that not enough resources are invested in it. Many project schedules will list data migration as a single task in a development effort. By project's end, it will be evident that data migration was indeed an entirely separate project that was highly dependent upon several of the deliverables of the development project.

Therefore, for any project it is very important to plan ahead for data migration. This point is magnified, however, when genericization is the major thrust of the development effort. The key to this issue is that *data mapping,* or the process by which we gather the rules to transform one data set into a heterogeneous set of data structures, is heavily dependent upon the database design of the target system. As the target database design evolves, so must the data mappings.

Implementing generic data structures causes significantly more complex migration issues than traditional systems design. For example, a legacy system may contain two separate structures that store employee and customer information. We may choose to genericize these two structures into one structure called PERSON, upon which we indicate whether a given person is an employee, customer, or perhaps both.

Collisions

The first issue we will have to contend with is collisions. *Collisions,* or duplicate unique identifiers, typically do not occur in isolated data structures. However, when you extract the data from two independent data structures and merge them into one common data structure, all sorts of problems may arise. The legacy system may have used an internal numbering scheme to uniquely identify customers and employees, and there was no measure preventing the creation of both a customer and an employee, each being identified by ID='1'. The reason this was not an issue was because the two data sets were stored separately.

Merging these two data sets, however, requires one of two things. The first alternative would be to generate a new unique identifier for every record inserted into the generic structure (i.e., employee and customer records will receive new UIDs). This approach is only acceptable when the users of the system do not refer to these objects by their IDs.

The other alternative would be to add an indicator field called PERSON_YN to the PERSON table, which would indicate whether each object in the PERSON class was either a customer or an employee.

Performance

The second major implementation issue that generic design causes is the performance impact of consolidating multiple data structures in fewer structures with substantially more data. Fewer tables will mean fewer database applications accessing the same tables for multiple purposes. This inevitably leads to significant increases in I/O on the access of certain genericized tables.

Partitioning, as discussed in Chapter 9, can help resolve this problem. Simply partition the table in the same manner as you would have created separate tables (i.e., two partitions—CUSTOMER and EMPLOYEE). This way, your database requires one less table, though you are not losing out on performance. Unfortunately, this option is not available if you plan to implement using Oracle7.

Conclusion

Genericizing as much of a system as possible has both advantages and drawbacks. Determining what can and cannot be genericized and how best to model these structures requires a great deal of skill. Also, once they are modeled, implementing the generic structures takes an experienced development team. Performance considerations must always be taken into account as well. However, even with these negative aspects, the benefits of genericizing where appropriate are numerous. Genericized models are easier to read and provide the flexibility to cope with changes as they arise without making major changes to the data model or to the applications based upon the generic structures. Systems designed generically will have a longer lifespan and ultimately reduce the time and resources needed to keep up with ever-changing data and business rules.

CHAPTER
17

Implementing Business Rules

he automated support of business rules has been one of the hottest topics in the Oracle community for the last few years. The industry has tried using general business rule grammars (with no success), extending the Oracle Designer repository (with some success), and writing limited business rule generators (quite successfully).

Until recently, we were of the opinion that the quest for a general business rule generator was probably futile. There was no way that we would be able to get a reasonable set of business rules specified and generated. Business rules are too complex, and always require custom coding. After all, we already have a way of describing complex business rules; we call it PL/SQL.

At the same time, we have been building several limited business rule engines with great success. Each of these engines was more robust than the last, but none of them seemed to come anywhere close to something that we would want to use for trigger generation.

Implementing business rules within a database system is a challenging task. Traditionally, this has been handled by placing a small subset of the business rules into the database using a variety of techniques:

- Referential integrity

- Check constraints

- Datatypes

We have no illusion that all data-related business rules are easily supported within a data model. For example, there is no easy way to prevent loops in recursive structures when you are modeling hierarchical information. There is a whole other class of business rules that we traditionally handle through application logic. There has been much discussion of business rules in the last few years, but relatively little discussion of actual implementations of these rules. This chapter will present a few real-world implementations of storing application logic as data. There have been attempts at developing a grammar for business rules. We have not found any of these grammars to be particularly helpful in developing a data model to support the types of business rules described in this book.

There are several underlying principles to the approach we used in implementing business rules:

- Business rules, components of these rules, connections between these rules, and their impact on other entities in the data model are all "things of interest" just as Employees or Departments are of interest to most organizations. You can use the same data modeling skills to model these as any other item of interest.

- If you are accustomed to the idea of generic modeling, including storing column information as data, overloading entities, etc., the style of modeling described here will be easier to understand. Modeling business rules involves the modeling of abstractions.

- Once the business rules are stored in the database, you can drive programs using data from the tables. However, if you use this method, you may end up with terrible performance due to the high number of database accesses. You may also need to utilize DBMS SQL frequently in your program logic. The ability of PL/SQL to support this type of data driver program is somewhat limited since there are no C++-style pointers and only limited indirect variable referencing through COPY and NAME_IN commands. Therefore, one of the possible strategies is to have all data in the system and write a program to take data and build PL/SQL packages (limited code generator).

Supporting Database Business Rules

At the Lancaster County Tax Collection Bureau of Pennsylvania (LCTCB) we created a Revenue Acquisition and Distribution System (RADS) requiring a complex business rules engine. RADS involves management and processing of documents associated with tax collection. There is a complex workflow associated with these documents involving data validation, corrections of errors in the documents, and processing and distribution of funds.

There are aspects of RADS that make it particularly appropriate for using object-oriented structures. First, there are a number of different types of documents, such as individual and employer tax returns. Second, the types of operations performed on all of the documents are very similar. We must count on being in an environment where we support new documents—that is, monthly rather than quarterly employer reports or entirely different documents because of tax reform.

As part of the RADS project, we designed a rules engine to support validation of tax returns (e.g., to make sure that line1 + line2 = Line3 on your tax return). We built the code to parse rules and generate procedures. While writing up the system documentation for the engine design, it occurred to us that just as we could validate data in a document, we could validate data in a database.

We will not assert that the search for the ultimate business rule engine has ended. We are still only able to generate relatively simple business rules, though we can store and maintain the most complex rules in the system. We still don't think we can build the perfect business rule code generator, but we can get pretty close.

In the following sections, we will discuss the design of the Business Rule Information Generator (BRIG). First, the types of rules that we wanted to support will be discussed along with the other system requirements; then, the design will be described.

Rule Requirements

There are basically four different kinds of business rules that are commonly supported in systems that we design:

- Rules to validate a single column, requiring no reference to any other column. Simple check constraints fall into this category. However, we also need to support complex formatting rules for things like postal codes. For example, Canadian postal codes alternate letters and numbers in a six-character field that is supported by traditional check constraints.

- Rules that involve more than one column in the table being validated. For example, START_DATE < END_DATE.

- Rules requiring a reference to another table. For example, each EVENT_DATE on a project must be between the START_DATE and END_DATE for that project.

- Rules that are only enforced under certain circumstances (conditional constraints). For example, assume we have a customer table that holds both individuals and organizations. If the type of the record is 'PERSON', then the LAST_NAME field must not be null; if the record type is 'ORGANIZATION', then the field 'ORG_NAME' must not be null.

- Redundant columns. These are columns that are defined as being functions of other data in the database.

Other System Requirements

There were several requirements for the system:

- We wanted to be able to store the rules in a repository that could be maintained by the user, which would then generate the appropriate database triggers. We wanted there to be a minimum of programmer effort.

- We wanted the enforcement of those rules not to grossly affect the system performance.

- The system needed to be easy to use as there would potentially be hundreds of rules to maintain, and it could prove necessary to change the rules quickly.

- We needed the system to validate the syntax of the entered rules so that no invalid code would be generated.

- We didn't want to spend months building the system, so it needed to be relatively simple.

- The system needed to be able to support quite complex rules, and be able to grow over time.

The Design of the Business Rules Information Generator (BRIG)

The first debate occurred about whether or not to store our rules in a repository outside of Oracle Designer. By storing the rules in a separate repository, there were some trade-offs. On the positive side, rules could be stored in a complex structure not easily supported through user extensions. (We considered extending the repository to store the rules, but we wanted to have the system in production for a while before we made that decision.)

We were interested in writing very complex code against repository extensions for a first version. On the negative side, we would be storing many of our business rules outside of the Oracle Designer Repository. This would put our business rules in two places.

We decided to build a separate rules repository. The rationale was that our projects are not built to simply support a set of rules; rather, they are built to support a class of rules. That is to say, the flexible business rules are part of the implementation, not the design.

BRIG has had a profound impact on our design process. Now, business requirements are placed directly in the repository late in the Analysis phase. This tends to blur the line between analysis and development. As soon as rules are placed in the repository, they can be generated. No additional coding time is required.

The system has made us much more secure in our design process. If we decide that rules are too restrictive, they can be regenerated very quickly. Using BRIG, we can support a much larger percentage of our business rules without custom coding.

We made several key design decisions:

- Our solution for the system involved building a small repository to hold our rules with some simple forms to support rule maintenance.

- Rather than enforce the rules through lookups into the repository, we elected to use the repository to generate database triggers.

We noticed that if we supported rules that used custom functions that we could support arbitrarily complex rules through hand-coding some functions. Eventually, a function generator could be added to support generation of types of complex functions.

- We decided to build rules in two steps. First we would build elementary conditions, such as START_DATE < END_DATE, and then combine them using Boolean operators. Then we could simply refer to "RULE1 and RULE2".

The structure to hold the rules was rather complex, designed for nonintuitive data entry. To simplify this for users, we allowed them to enter the rules using normal programming syntax. We then wrote a parser to place their rules into the repository. (In practice, users wrote their rules in English and junior programmers entered the actual rules.)

We made an addition to the standard Boolean operators to support easier entry of rules. Specifically, we added an IF THEN ELSE structure to support conditional constraints (described above). "RULE1 => RULE2 else RULE3" would be interpreted as "(RULE1 and RULE2) or (not RULE1 and RULE3)". Similarly, "RULE1 => RULE2" would be interpreted as "(RULE1 and RULE2) or (not RULE1)".

We noted that rules fell into four categories for implementation:

- Simple check constraints
- Conditional triggers
- Redundant columns
- Recursive constraints

We had to support each type of constraint differently. Check constraints were limited to lists of values and ranges. Conditional triggers supported most complex rules. Redundant columns were supported with triggers (avoiding mutating tables was a significant problem). Recursive rules required a little different thinking.

Rule Storage

It is probably not obvious to the reader how rules are supported in a data structure. Note that we are storing rules using a parse tree. For example, the rule (Col1 + Col2)/2 < Col3 is represented in Figure 17-1.

Similarly, compound rules are stored in a separate (but similar) structure. The difference is that instead of combining parameters through operators, we are combining rules through Boolean operators. For example, the compound rule "(RULE1 and RULE2) or (not RULE3)" would be represented as shown in Figure 17-2.

Note that for rules, each element is either a function or a column. For compound rules, each element is either a Boolean operator or a rule.

Testing the depth of BRIG

The first test we set for BRIG was to see if it could support the complex data-related business rules for BRIG's own data structure. The following

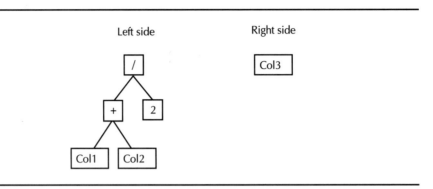

Left side   Right side

FIGURE 17-1.   *Sample rule parse tree*

business rules could not be supported through referential integrity and check constraints:

- In Compound Rule Details, there is a strict logical hierarchy in the way ANDs, ORs, and compound rules nest. There is nothing in the data model to enforce the structural syntax of a correct Boolean statement. The Rule Component structure has the same problem.

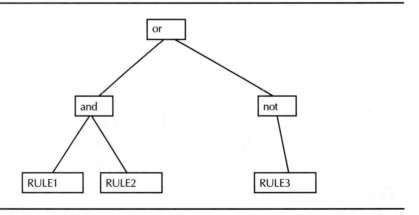

FIGURE 17-2.   *Sample compound rule*

- There is nothing in the model to enforce that the columns associated with the rule component must be from the same table that the rule is associated with.

- We cannot enforce that the function detail on a rule component is consistent with its parent function in the Rule Component recursion.

- When a Column is used in conjunction with a function detail, there is nothing to enforce that the data types are consistent.

Such rules can be entered into the system and generated. However, attempting to generate these rules points out the limitations in the rule engine. Each of these rules requires that we write a specific function to look up the correct data to make sure that model consistency is enforced. Some common functions such as summing up the details and storing them in a master (such as for a purchase order) can be classified and generated, but most other complex rules (such as ALL the complex rules for this system) still need custom coding. In applying the BRIG to a standard OLTP, the results are somewhat better. However, most complex rules require the writing of a custom function. BRIG works perfectly for almost all simple rules and helps in the maintenance of complex rules (though they still require some custom coding).

Our opinion hasn't changed that a generalized business rule engine that would support all rules can never be built. If someone can build a grammar that will allow generation of rules such as the ones required by the BRIG data structure itself, then we will gladly retire BRIG to the scrap heap. Until then, BRIG stands as a pretty good attempt at a generalized rule engine that generates 100 percent of the code for simple rules and helps to maintain complex rules.

Workflow Requirements

LCTCB has a very large volume of items to be processed. Currently, there are 250,000 tax returns processed annually. This, in itself, is not a very large volume. What makes LCTCB's situation unusual is that 90 percent of this workflow volume occurs in a 2–4 week period.

Because of the irregular periodicity of workflow volume, we need to have a flexible system that can accommodate low, medium, and high workflow volumes at different times. Certain specific portions of this process will still need to either be done manually or automated with lower precision. Since we are trying to maximize revenue, we may want to adjust the criteria for rejecting a tax return so that manual processing is required. These criteria may need to be changed on the fly. In order to evaluate all of these changes, we will need a sophisticated, flexible reporting system to measure the performance and costs of various events.

Creating an "Expert System"

There were many processes at LCTCB that were being performed manually that could have been automated. For example, all judgments regarding the detection of where errors occur in a return can and should be automated. In effect, we created an "expert system." However, from all of the work done in building expert systems, we know that first versions are often notoriously inefficient. In addition, in the case of RADS, we were providing automated functionality that did not exist in the legacy system.

The process that was used at LCTCB to process tax returns was not stable. No matter how well expert requirements are gathered, they will change in the new system. Therefore, RADS needed to be flexible in the way that the rules built into it are processed.

What we envisioned for the new system was to flexibly define documents on the fly; store instances of these generic, created on-the-fly documents; and process these documents using complex workflow-related rules. These rules will not only govern the tasks performed but also store, as data, what these tasks are and what impact they have on the documents in the system. In RADS, we effectively constructed an expert system to replicate the behavior of an expert tax return processor. The only behavior that we were unable to automate was the manual verification that the raw documents submitted (W-2s, letters, etc.) support the numbers on the tax return documents.

Evolution of the RADS

A great deal of careful analysis was needed for this system. Many portions of RADS evolved over time as our understanding of the LCTCB workflow and business rules deepened. The model we created was not the result of one short meeting. We first built one section that allowed us to think about how other portions of the system should be constructed. Early on, we recognized the need for generic documents requiring a structure such as the one shown in Figure 17-3.

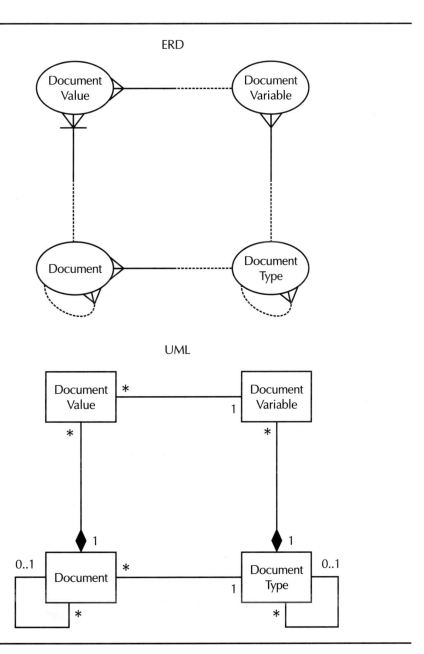

FIGURE 17-3.   *Generic document model*

In the Document Type and Document Variable entities, we define the document. For example, to define a W-2 tax form, we would create an object (W-2) in the Document Type class. Every line on the form would be represented as a separate variable in the Document Variable class. When a person files a W-2 and it is received by the system, we create one object in the Document table to represent the actual physical document and each value on the document becomes an object in the Document Value table. Each document value must be for a predefined variable in the Document Variable class.

The recursions of Document and Document Type are used in order to support repeating groups within documents. For example, on a tax form, you might have a list of business expenses and their associated amounts. We modeled this as if it were an embedded document; hence the recursion.

We also recognize that we needed a relatively sophisticated workflow system. We had built workflow systems in the past that were more basic, but this system required the implementation of full state transition diagrams.

For this system, the vision we had was that a document is always in a particular state. Based upon this state, there are one or more tasks that must be accomplished such as "Check a rule," "Execute a database procedure," or "Perform a manual task." As a result of performing these tasks, there will be an outcome. The outcome returns the document to another state. Diagrammatically, this process is shown in Figure 17-4.

This diagram conveys what we were trying to accomplish with our rules engine. In actually performing these operations, there can be many more tasks associated with a given state. The large boxes represent the states, with the tasks enclosed in the boxes. Lines represent the outcomes of the state boxes. Modeling these state transition diagrams in a relational database has gone through a number of iterations. The final result is shown in Figure 17-5.

In this diagram, a state is associated with a single task, which can be used by multiple states. It is the task that has various outcomes. Each of these outcomes results in a new state. With further analysis of this model, we discovered that the model didn't make sense. Notice that tasks have associated outcomes, each of which takes us to a new state. This is the definition of a state.

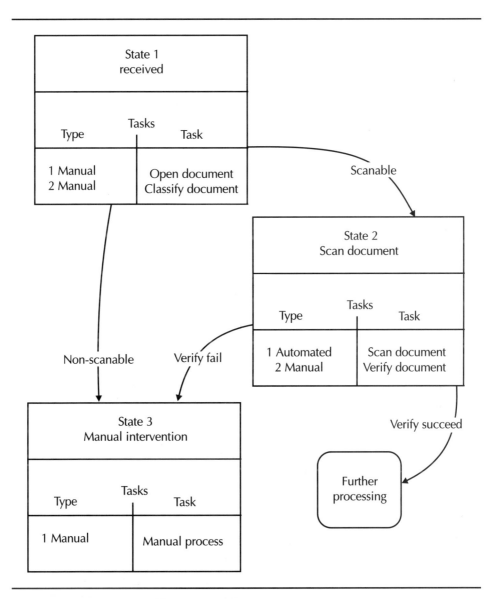

FIGURE 17-4.   *State transition diagram*

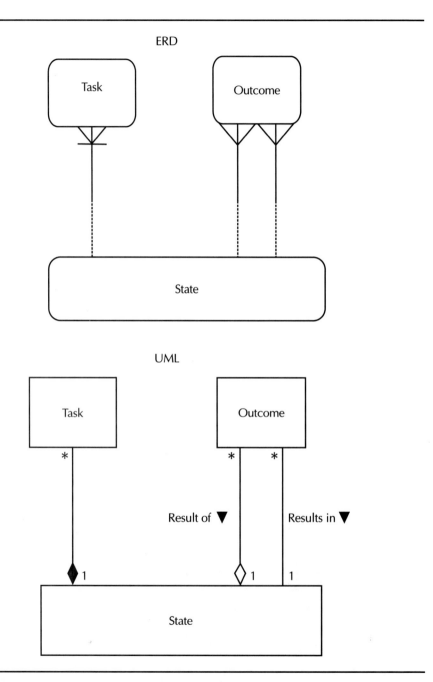

FIGURE 17-5. *Model of state transitions*

Validation Rules

For this system, we needed to support rules in the tax documents. Simple rules included ones such as "Line 15 (Total Gross Income) – Line 16 (Total Expenses) = Line 17 (Net Income)." However, other rules are more complex, requiring lookups to tax tables. Therefore, it was necessary to provide the ability to store any mathematical conditional statement that PL/SQL supports. We used a similar structure to the generalized business rule system discussed above.

Assignment Statements

The next requirement was to support assignment statements. Based on the detection of an arithmetic mistake, we might wish to assign that the value of one line on the form was equal to an arithmetic combination of other lines on the form. We noticed that the structure would also support assignment statements by merely restricting the rules for the assignment of equality operators. Therefore, the left-hand side of the rule must be a simple document variable, not a constant or a function. The right-hand side could be any mathematical expression. By including this requirement in the design, we were able to not only specify validation rules, but also assignment statements.

Compound Rules

As part of RADS, we wanted to be able to base an outcome on a Boolean combination of rules such as: "If Rule 1 and Rule 2 are true, but not Rule 3, this is the outcome." The structure of a compound rule is such that it uses rules as the components of the compound rule, but the structure looks like that of a rule. For rules, we used functions to combine elements. For compound rules, we used Boolean operators to combine structures. Because of the similarity in structure, we contemplated trying to incorporate rules and compound rules into the same structure. However, this made the model unworkable. Instead, we extended the model in the same way we did in the previous Business Rules example.

Comprehensive Rules Engine

The final model supports all of the rules engine requirements. Role and Required Role entities were added to this version of the model to control who is allowed to perform which manual tasks.

We made several very important observations about the completed model:

- First, we had generalized the system to such an extent that it became not simply a model to support validation of tax returns, but data validation of any document (tests, questionnaires, etc.).

- Second, we noticed that we had essentially built an expert system engine that would support the capture of the expert knowledge of tax return processors.

- Third, this model gave us the flexibility to change the rules whereby returns are processed very quickly and easily. For example, processing strategies could be changed and the system would include the ability to assess the impact of the change on the operation.

Building Applications to Support the Model

Most of the application development we used to support the RADS model is quite straightforward. There are two exceptions:

- Inputting rules
- Inputting compound rules

In both cases, forcing data input in a way that is consistent with the data model makes for a counterintuitive and user-hostile interface. To handle this, we built a parser to allow users to type in their business rules in a large text box. The parser takes a string such as "Line 1 + Line 2 = Line 3" as input, performs a syntax check, and automatically places that string into the structure. Then, within the structure, further validation is done to make sure that data types are consistent.

As we have described in this chapter, RADS should be able to automate all processing of a tax return with the exception of validating that numbers were entered correctly from the supporting documents. This is an excellent example of the power and efficiency of using generic structures coupled with an object-oriented approach. By applying object-oriented thinking to a very complex problem, we were able to represent the entire complex workflow of an organization and create a model flexible enough so that, over time, an organization can continually rearticulate its business functions without having to make substantial changes to the underlying data model.

Example: Automatic Setting of Record Status

This example involves the automatic setting of record status based upon various values in the database. The goal was to assign status to an audit report based upon the value of five different variables in the report itself.

In performing analysis, the users originally perceived the problems as a tree search, finding the value of the first variable, possibly looking at the second variable, etc., sequentially. This represented a very complex flow, making it difficult to code. Rather than trying to implement the entire Beyesian decision tree, we recognized that we merely needed to regard the flow as a function with five input values and one output value. Fortunately, in this case, each of the values was categorical and the number of values was very small. There were approximately 100 possible combinations. Therefore, we decided to drive the rules from a table.

We created a simple table with six columns in it—one for each of the independent variables and one for the dependent status variable. The actual data model is shown in Figure 17-6.

The table for the Status Rule model is as shown in Table 17-1.

RULE_ID	Number, PK
CATEGORY_ID	Varchar2 (10), FK
CLASS_CD	Varchar2 (10), FK
PAST_DUE_YN	Char (1)
SERIOUS_YN	Char (1)
REQUIRED_YN	Char (1)
STATUS_CD	Varchar2 (10), FK
START_DT	Date
END_DT	Date
ACTIV_YN	Char (1)

TABLE 17-1.   *Status Rule Table*

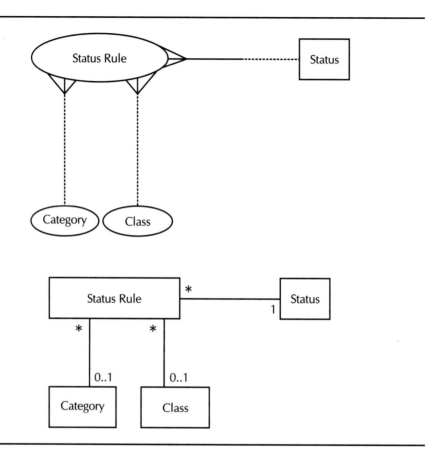

FIGURE 17-6. *Status rule data model*

In order to determine status, there are three categories, four different classes, and the _YN indicator variables for a total of 96 different independent variable combinations. However, we still did not want to enter 96 lines of data if we could avoid it. In this case, if the category were "CLOSED," then the status would automatically be CLOSED, thus making the status of the other variables irrelevant. This rule was enforced as "Category Closed = all other variables null." The null values indicate wild cards (any value is valid for that rule).

Using the wild-card notation meant that we had to be careful that the rules would never be inconsistent. For example, if we added the rule

"(Category = closed, class = small, all else = null) = status PENDING," this would be inconsistent with our first rule, which says that class is irrelevant if "Category = Closed." We needed to put a BEFORE_INSERT or BEFORE_UPDATE trigger on the rule table to prevent inconsistent rule specification.

The START_DT and END_DT fields serve to keep track of how the rules change over time. The ACTIV_YN indicator is a redundant column so that the active rules can be found without an inefficient search for a null end date.

In this particular system, rules did not change very often. We put a single index on all six of the independent variables so that when we needed to update the status of an audit report, it only required an indexed search of the database. This method provided adequate performance. We contemplated writing a program to generate a PL/SQL package that would assign the status. However, creating a code generator would have taken more time. Since this was unnecessary for performance reasons, we did not elect to do so. We did encapsulate a function that automatically set the status and stored it as a function in a PL/SQL package in the server. This is useful in that if we choose to rewrite the engine at a later time, the code will only be in one place.

CHAPTER
18

Denormalization

nce the data model for a system is complete and logically correct, we can implement it successfully as it stands and create applications. However, there is nothing to say that the design created is necessarily optimized for implementation. Also, there is no reason to say that the existing data model is necessarily inadequate.

TIP
You should usually keep your physical model
as close as possible to your logical model.

Back in the 1980s, it was very common to heavily denormalize data models. Detail records were brought into master records, whole structures collapsed into flat files, and clean, pristine, logical structures were moved into structures that would look familiar to COBOL/VSAM programmers. This was done because hardware was very expensive and relational database engines were quite slow. Consultants reported achieving, on average, improvements of a factor of ten in performance through massive denormalization. The conventional wisdom was that normalized models were fine in theory, but would not work in practice. We created normalized logical data models and built flat-file databases.

This strategy had disastrous results. When these systems went into production, they had the same problems as traditional flat-file systems. Specifically, they were inflexible and expensive to change. Any functionality not explicitly designed into the database could require very expensive modifications to the data structure. Towards the end of the 1980s, the database community began to realize the error of its ways in denormalizing the structures so severely. Despite the improved performance when the systems were first put into production, the cost of maintaining these systems was prohibitive.

However, there are denormalizations that can be done that do not greatly impact the ability of the system to respond to future requirements. In this chapter, we will outline a number of denormalization techniques that can be implemented without severely impacting the flexible nature of a quality data model.

Denormalization never exists without cost. In most cases, when performance is improved in one part of the system, it is degraded in other parts. Normalization is a style of modeling that is well understood by most data modelers. Denormalization is an idiosyncratic art. The more structures are denormalized, the more difficult it will be for other developers to work with them. This is a larger problem than it may appear. Developers come and go. Having a model that can be read and understood by future developers is important.

Denormalization should not be undertaken lightly. It may or may not improve performance. It will certainly make the model harder to read. Unless done very carefully, it will reduce the flexibility of the model. So why denormalize at all? There are several situations where it may become necessary:

- You must denormalize for performance reasons. You have a large, complex data model with tens of millions of rows in core tables. It may be that only through denormalization can you achieve acceptable performance.

- Use denormalization to simplify application logic. It may be that, to produce a particular report or screen, as many as 10–20 tables must be accessed in order to retrieve a particular piece of information. If we redundantly store it elsewhere in the database, we may be able to greatly reduce the complexity of the program logic.

If you are only denormalizing for the second reason, you should always contemplate using an updatable view rather than denormalizing. Instead of creating the redundant column, create a view showing that column. You must be careful with views since joining to views makes queries difficult to tune. However, if you can use a simple, single-table view with all additional columns created through embedded functions, you should be able to join to any nonfunction column in the view with no appreciable performance impact beyond that of function execution. Joining to views based upon multiple tables frequently results in unavoidable full table scans. This strategy should still be tried if the goal is to simplify application logic. If you can achieve adequate performance with views, then they should be used since they do not muddle the data model.

To denormalize, redundant attributes are frequently created. A redundant attribute is a function of other objects existing in an object class in the database. One example of this would be adding an Extended Price which = Existing Quantity x Existing Price. Another example is an UPPER (Name) where the uppercase values of a name are stored redundantly. This is quite common and used so that case-insensitive queries can be performed on the name field. The reason you cannot perform the query by merely putting the UPPER on the field at run time is because putting a function on a column in a WHERE clause defeats the index. The only time this technique is ever used is when it is necessary to index the redundant column.

Denormalization Techniques

We have identified 11 types of denormalization that may be necessary for ease of coding or performance reasons. We will describe each one and provide specific examples to illustrate these techniques.

Redundant Total Fields

The most common denormalization is to store the total of an amount in a detail column in the master table. For example, you can put an attribute in a purchase order that is the sum of the details. Such a column can be kept in synch either through triggers on the detail class or through batch updates. Theoretically, these details could also be kept in synch through application logic code. However, this makes the code unstable and is not recommended.

Denormalizing through redundant total fields enables you to see the totals without performing the join in aggregation. Another advantage to this technique is that you can index it. This is useful if you want to return purchase orders of a particular size range or retrieve the largest or smallest purchase orders. The only way to avoid a full table scan and calculation of every purchase order's details is through the creation of a redundant column. Aggregate columns such as this need not only be simple sums from the detail records. The amount owed on a customer account might also be useful, but may require a complex calculation. In general, if you are going to create a calculation column, it should be indexed so that it can be searched quickly.

Redundant Attribute Within the Row of a Table

Facilitating searches of text information as mentioned in the overview is typically handled by having a redundant column that is an uppercase transformation of the original data (UPPER). This is the most commonly used procedure. In a few cases, this can be a challenging problem, particularly with high volumes of data. One example involved matching addresses from one system to another. Extra spaces may be placed between number and street, abbreviations may be inconsistent. To solve this problem, use the following algorithm:

1. Convert the address to uppercase.

2. Remove all extraneous characters such as tabs, spaces, hard line returns, punctuation.

3. Force abbreviation of all words (i.e. West becomes wst or W).

4. Replace text like "1st" with "FIRST" to create consistency.

5. Take only the first 10 characters.

This algorithm allowed relatively accurate matching of addresses. In dealing with name and address searches in very large systems, you can store each word in its own column and index each column to efficiently search millions of records to find the appropriate information. Any of these methods can be easily supported through database triggers. The application developer need only use these columns if necessary. Since the trigger does not require any fetches to disk, the performance is quite fast.

This method is wasteful of disk space. However, the bottleneck in applications is usually not disk space but, rather, performance.

Extra Foreign Key Columns Where They Don't Belong

When you have a particularly long string of master-detail relationships that span several object classes, you may want to place a foreign key or an object pointer reference from one side of the chain to the other, as shown in Figure 18-1.

In this example, we might want to look at some subset of the claim details by name. Traditionally, we would have to join through several tables to accomplish this. Instead, if we place an object reference or foreign key in Claim Detail that points back to Group, this allows us to quickly retrieve the claim details that are associated with the group. This placing of redundant primary key columns can greatly simplify the coding of reports and applications.

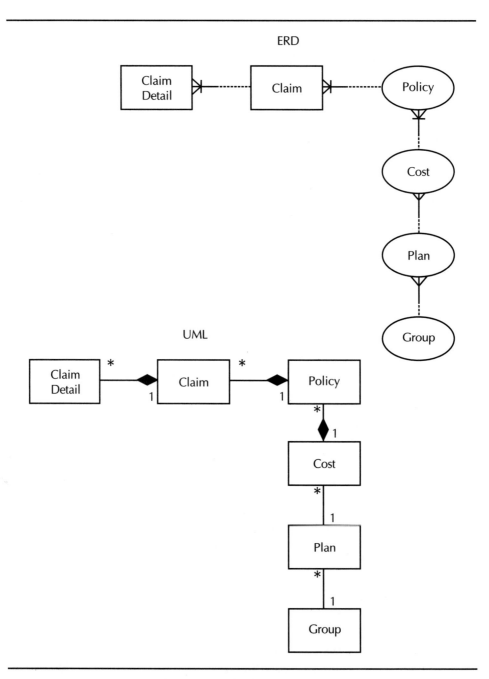

FIGURE 18-1. *Structure that requires foreign key columns*

Redundant Columns for History

Even though a model stores particular information, it may be relatively difficult to retrieve that information. For example, in the diagram shown in Figure 18-2, if we wanted to aggregate sales by department, we would have to join Sale to the Dept. only where the transaction date of the sale is between the start date and end date for when a particular employee was employed by that department. A normal join would double count all sales whenever an employee changed departments.

If you redundantly store an object reference or foreign key in the SALE table to indicate which department the employee worked for when the sale was made, then it is easy to aggregate sales by department. This technique can sometimes be used in lieu of actually tracking historical information. In the example above, the only reason to track employment history for an employee was so that credit for sales could be assigned to the proper department. If this is the only business requirement, then we might want to model the relationship as shown in Figure 18-3.

Using this structure means that we do not even need the Employment History class since all business relationships can be described by the additional relationship between Dept. and Sale. We will need to add a trigger so that when the sale is created, the Dept. reference is automatically populated.

This example is important since it demonstrates that we are trying to capture business rules in our data model. Very different models can both support the same business rules. However, such a simplification should only be done after careful consideration. In this case, we would not be inclined to simplify the model by removing the Employment History structure. To do this, you must be certain that the only reason employment history is being tracked is to support department rollup by Sale. Recently, we worked on a project where this situation arose. We argued strenuously that the employment history be maintained. Users assured us of the single purpose for tracking such history and we were overruled by the client. Before the system went into production, we discovered that several of the necessary reports could not be accurately produced without maintaining employment history.

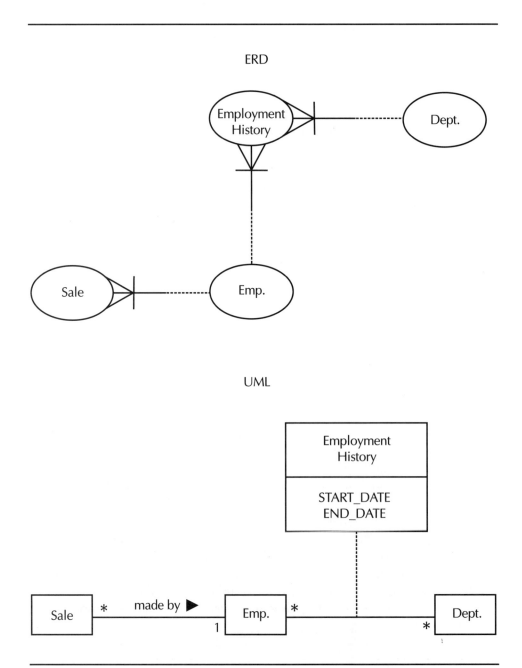

FIGURE 18-2. *Structure that could use redundant history columns*

ERD

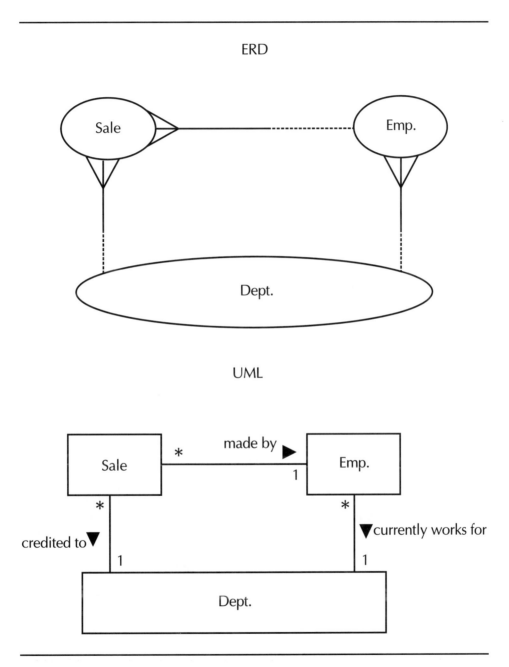

UML

FIGURE 18-3. *Alternative history tracking*

TIP
*The slight cost of modeling somewhat more
flexibly is usually much lower than later
modifying an entire system to accommodate a
new or unanticipated requirement.*

Recursion Level

In any recursive structures representing tree, network, linked list, etc. for
some applications, it is useful to know what level a given record is at in the
hierarchy. Using CONNECT BYs, level is available as a system column. If
CONNECT BYs are not used or if you are not starting on the top level of the
hierarchy, it may not be possible to determine the desired level or
inaccurate levels may be returned. There are not very many times that the
Level column is needed. However, it can be useful in debugging
applications as they are being written. The trigger to maintain this
functionality is cheap, requiring negligible space. The presence of the Level
column also alerts developers to the presence of a recursive structure. We
recommend adding Level as a redundant column in many recursive
structures.

Typing Master Tables

If a generalization class is not abstract (instantiated as a table), there is no
way to easily determine when looking at a row in the generalization table
what type each record is. It would be necessary to look through all of the
records in each of the specialization tables in order to determine where a
particular record exists. One solution to this problem is to store the name of
the applicable specialization table in the generalization. Thus, our standard
generalization example of hourly and salaried employees can be modified
as shown in Figure 18-4.

Using this structure, we have the employment type (salaried or hourly)
stored in the Employee table.

UML

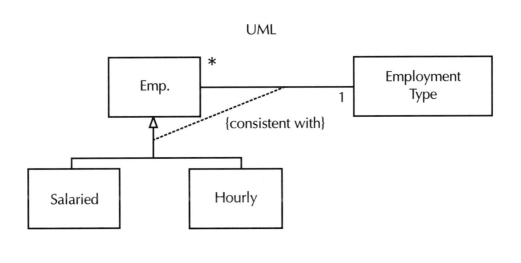

FIGURE 18-4. *Redundant table showing generalization*

Redundancy in COBS Development

As mentioned in Chapter 14, there are a few places in the development of complex objects (COBS) where redundant columns are used. More details can be found in Chapter 16.

Violations of First Normal Form

We do *not* recommend violating First Normal Form. However, we have considered it on several occasions. One instance involved a budget with associated budget details. Each budget detail had a portion of its fund allocated across four quarters. This could have been modeled as shown in Figure 18-5.

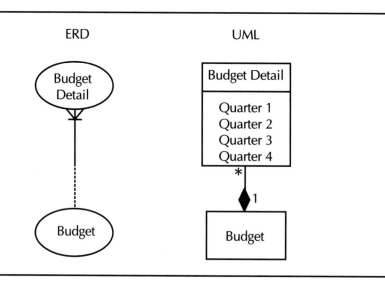

FIGURE 18-5. *Violating First Normal Form*

Using this structure, if the business rule ever changes and instead, semiannual or monthly allocations are needed, the model and all of the applications will need to be changed. By modeling this system as shown in Figure 18-6, we made the model somewhat more flexible to support budget apportionment across any time interval.

Such a structure requires more development time and results in poorer performance. If performance is of primary consideration, circumstances might justify a violation of First Normal Form. Keep in mind that using the first model will have severe implications if any changes are later necessary.

Overloaded Columns

Overloading columns can decrease the number of attributes that must be maintained in a table. We do *not* recommend using this strategy.

TIP
It is important that each attribute store one and only one type of information.

ERD

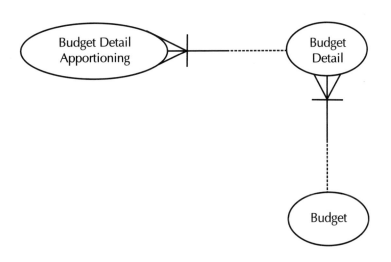

UML

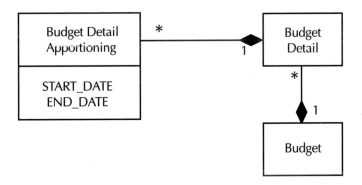

FIGURE 18-6. *Flexible budget*

The only exceptions to this rule may occur in full generic modeling where columns such as "value" are used. Each time different types of information are stored in the same column, problems inevitably arise. An example of difficulties with overloaded columns occurred in a system where contracts were put out for bid. At the detail level, there were materials and labor. For materials detail, the vendor bid on the price of the materials needed. For labor, the price was fixed and vendors bid the number of hours required. At the bid detail, the vendor bid a number representing a dollar amount or number of hours required depending upon what was being bid on. This way of modeling the structure decreased the number of attributes to maintain by one but cost dozens of hours in application development time to support this mistake in overloading a column. Do not confuse this error with a column used in genericization at the class level, which can be very helpful. For example, in a Demographics module, countries are divided into subunits for doing mailings that might be states, provinces, or some other unit names.

Typically, to handle this, we will have a single class for country and one for country subdivision that may represent a state, a province, etc. In this case, an attribute such as "name" in the subdivision refers to the name of the state or province. From a theoretical perspective, state names came from a different domain than province names, but they are used in the same way. From a system perspective, they are equivalent. Therefore, if the system uses the information in all circumstances in the same way, there is a case to be made for an overloaded column. If not, overloading the column will inevitably cause problems at some later time.

Multiattribute Columns

A relatively common strategy for fields such as Part Numbers or Contract Numbers is to embed information into the column. The only time this should ever be done is if nothing is ever done with any of the components of the field other than assembling them. For example, the year concatenated with a system-generated ID is always stored together. The components must never be altered in any way after the field is instantiated. If all of these conditions are met, then multiattribute columns could be used. It should still be recognized that this is bad modeling. System information inevitably changes. It is very rare that any field will never have any changes made to its underlying information.

Redundant History Tables

If we are tracking a ledger account, activity on a portfolio, or accounting expenses for a department, the volume of these transactions is fairly high and requires a complex structure. For reporting purposes, we are only interested in reporting at the aggregate level. To find out how much was spent or received during a given period of time, we need to aggregate all transactions occurring within that time period. Solving such a problem can be a performance nightmare. A redundant table can be used to store periodic information about a structure. This structure ends up as a composition class off of the structure for which history is being tracked, as shown in Figure 18-7.

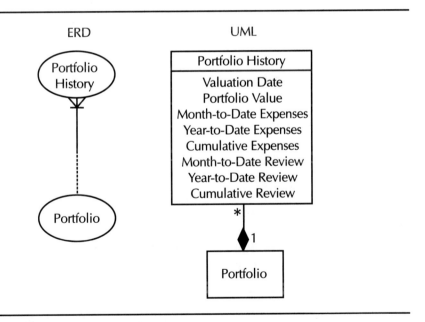

FIGURE 18-7. *Composition History class*

The fields in the History table are as follows:

- Valuation date (date that we are tracking history for)
- Actual value of portfolio on a given day
- Month-to-date revenue and expense figures
- Year-to-date revenue and expense figures

Rather than storing daily revenue and expenses, we use a "trick." If we stored daily expenses and wanted to determine total revenues over a period of time, we would have to sum the daily revenue for each column. Instead, by storing cumulative revenue and expenses since some arbitrary starting point to determine the number for revenue/expenses for any arbitrary period of time, only two records must be retrieved: beginning and end-of-time interval. Then we simply subtract the two values. This is much more efficient than summing across a large range. Such history tables can be used to greatly enhance performance and can frequently make building a separate data warehouse unnecessary.

Implementing Denormalization

This section will present examples of the 11 denormalization techniques described above. The question to keep in mind while reading this material is whether or not the benefits of denormalization truly outweigh the costs of additional coding and documentation. Most often, denormalization is conducted for performance benefits realized by reporting functions. However, we must take into account that denormalizing is reducing performance from the transaction processing perspective. Is quicker reporting from the OLTP worth slowing down the OLTP altogether?

Many organizations implement a reporting system that contains a snapshot of the OLTP database, which is refreshed periodically. This is a nice solution, providing that your organization does not truly need up-to-the-second information.

The ideal approach to denormalization is through triggering. If you can afford to wait for batch updates, then you can implement an OLAP for such reporting and not sacrifice the integrity of your OLTP design in the name of reporting performance. In our opinion, denormalization for performance should be saved for reporting systems.

Denormalization Techniques

We have identified 11 types of denormalization that may be necessary for ease of coding or performance reasons. We will describe each one and provide specific examples referring to the descriptions used in the first portion of the chapter to illustrate these techniques.

Redundant Total Fields

We will use the Purchase Order Header and Detail scenario for the Total field example. Unfortunately, this example brings up the mutating table issue unless we create a third table that mirrors the PO_DTL table. Assume we wanted to obtain split-second dollar amounts per purchase order. This requirement could be achieved by adding a column 'X_AMT' to the PO table. This column would be updated with the total dollar value of the PO by summing the individual dollar values of each PO_DTL associated with a given PO. For this example, we would create three tables, PO, PO_DTL, and X_PO_DTL, and a trigger AIU_X_PO_DTL to the X_PO_DTL table as shown in Code Example 18-1.

```
CREATE TABLE PO (
PO_ID                 NUMBER (10)    NOT NULL,
DESCR_TXT             VARCHAR2(100)  NOT NULL,
ADDR_ID_SHIP_TO       NUMBER (10)    NOT NULL,
ADDR_ID_BILL_TO       NUMBER (10)    NOT NULL,
CTCT_ID               NUMBER (10)    NOT NULL,
VENDOR_ID             NUMBER (10)    NOT NULL,
X_AMT                 NUMBER (10,2)  NOT NULL)
/
CREATE TABLE PO_DTL (
PO_ID                 NUMBER (10)    NOT NULL,
PO_DTL_ID             NUMBER (10)    NOT NULL,
ITEM_ID               NUMBER (10)    NOT NULL,
ORDR_QTY              NUMBER (10,2)  NOT NULL,
ORDR_PRC              NUMBER (10,2)  NOT NULL)
/
CREATE TABLE X_PO_DTL (
PO_ID                 NUMBER (10)    NOT NULL,
PO_DTL_ID             NUMBER (10)    NOT NULL,
ITEM_ID               NUMBER (10)    NOT NULL,
ORDR_QTY              NUMBER (10,2)  NOT NULL,
ORDR_PRC              NUMBER (10,2)  NOT NULL)
/
```

```
CREATE OR REPLACE TRIGGER AIU_PO_DTL
AFTER INSERT OR UPDATE
ON X_PO_DTL
FOR EACH ROW

DECLARE
CURSOR C1 IS
SELECT ORDR_QTY * ORDR_PRC X_AMT_PO_DTL
FROM X_PO_DTL
WHERE PO_ID = :NEW.PO_ID;

X_AMT_PO                    PO.X_AMT%TYPE := 0;

BEGIN
FOR C1_REC IN C1 LOOP
X_AMT_PO := X_AMT_PO + C1_REC.X_AMT_PO_DTL;
END LOOP;
UPDATE PO SET X_AMT = X_AMT_PO WHERE PO_ID = :NEW.PO_ID;
END;
/
```

Code Example 18-1

The drawback here is that we must create a third table, X_PO_DTL, that is essentially useless short of the denormalization it assists in performing. The trade-off is the additional storage of a table the same size as the PO_DTL table. While it is true that disk space is relatively cheap, it does add to the complexity of systems administration. Any modification to the PO_DTL structure must now also be propagated to the X_PO_DTL table. We can avoid the mutating table issue if we calculate and update the PO of every record in the application, instead of on the server side.

Using UPPER for Indexing

Text string matching is truly a performance nightmare. When matching addresses, it is quite common to see several variations of a given word. For example, 'AVE.', 'Ave.', 'Avenue',' AVENUE', and other variations all mean the same thing, although they will not match unless you manipulate the text strings for consistency.

An algorithm such as the one described earlier in the chapter makes a great deal of sense. Parsing each text string for common entries and then substituting a consistent format allows for accurate searching. Unfortunately, text strings have a way of being more complex than originally assumed. For example, the address '120 Park Ave Seagrave, CT, 65867' has two places where 'AVE' can be found. You must be able to identify some consistent format within your source data prior to attempting a match in order to have a chance for success. In other words, you must know that the street reference will only occur between characters 10–12, or something similar. Otherwise, you will not be guaranteed accurate matching.

You could implement this logic in a trigger on the table in which the text string is stored. You will only be interacting with data from the current record, so you will not encounter the mutating table issue. The basic assignment of

```
:new.x_addr_txt := upper(text_string)
```

is the simple part of the task. The complicated part is the matching logic. Not many organizations are willing to undertake such a task.

Extra Foreign Key Columns Where They Don't Belong

Extra foreign keys can certainly speed up aggregated reporting. The trade-off is the added complexity of the data model. The data model shown in Figure 18-1 indicates an implicit relationship from Claim Detail to Group through Claim, Policy, Cost, and Plan. Unfortunately, multiple table joins tend to be performance bottlenecks. This technique is demonstrated in Code Example 18-2.

```
CREATE TABLE GRP (
GRP_ID     NUMBER (10) NOT NULL PRIMARY KEY,
DESCR_TX    VARCHAR2 (40) NOT NULL)
/

CREATE TABLE PLAN (
PLAN_ID     NUMBER (10) NOT NULL PRIMARY KEY,
DESCR_TX    VARCHAR2 (40) NOT NULL,
GRP_ID NUMBER (10)  NOT NULL
   REFERENCES GRP (GRP_ID))
/

CREATE TABLE COST (
COST_ID     NUMBER (10) NOT NULL PRIMARY KEY,
AMT         NUMBER (10,2) NOT NULL,
PLAN_ID     NUMBER (10) NOT NULL
   REFERENCES PLAN (PLAN_ID))
/
```

```
CREATE TABLE POLICY (
POLICY_ID   NUMBER (10) NOT NULL PRIMARY KEY,
DESCR_TX    VARCHAR2 (40) NOT NULL,
COST_ID     NUMBER (10) NOT NULL
  REFERENCES COST (COST_ID))
/

CREATE TABLE CLAIM (
CLAIM_ID    NUMBER (10) NOT NULL PRIMARY KEY,
PATIENT_LNAME    VARCHAR2 (40) NOT NULL,
PATIENT_FNAME    VARCHAR2 (40) NOT NULL,
POLICY_ID        NUMBER (10) NOT NULL
  REFERENCES POLICY (POLICY_ID),
CREATE_DATE      DATE)
/

CREATE TABLE CLAIM_DTL (
CLAIM_ID   NUMBER (10) NOT NULL
  REFERENCES CLAIM (CLAIM_ID),
CLAIM_DTL_ID NUMBER(3) NOT NULL,
DESCR_TX       VARCHAR2 (40),
DIAGNOSIS_CD VARCHAR2 (10),
GRP_ID       NUMBER (10) NOT NULL
REFERENCES GRP (GRP_ID))
/
```

Code Example 18-2

We can avoid the six-table join by defining a foreign key from CLAIM_DTL to GROUP, as the highlighted bold portion of Code Example 18-2 demonstrates.

Another option is to make the unique identifier of each of these tables a concatenated key. This way, you could report Claim Details by Claim, Policy, Cost, Plan, or Group, and your query would only have to access Claim Detail and one or more of the other tables optionally, if additional information is sought in the requested query that can only be obtained from one of them. The code for this option is shown in Code Example 18-3.

```
CREATE TABLE GRP (
GRP_ID     NUMBER (10) NOT NULL PRIMARY KEY,
DESCR_TX   VARCHAR2 (40) NOT NULL)
/
```

```
CREATE TABLE PLAN (
PLAN_ID      NUMBER (10) NOT NULL,
DESCR_TX     VARCHAR2 (40) NOT NULL,
GRP_ID   NUMBER (10)  NOT NULL
  REFERENCES GRP (GRP_ID),
PRIMARY KEY (PLAN_ID, GRP_ID))
/

CREATE TABLE COST (
COST_ID      NUMBER (10) NOT NULL,
AMT          NUMBER (10,2) NOT NULL,
PLAN_ID      NUMBER (10) NOT NULL,
GRP_ID       NUMBER (10) NOT NULL,
PRIMARY KEY (COST_ID, PLAN_ID, GRP_ID),
FOREIGN KEY (PLAN_ID, GRP_ID)
  REFERENCES PLAN (PLAN_ID, GRP_ID))
/

CREATE TABLE POLICY (
POLICY_ID  NUMBER (10) NOT NULL,
DESCR_TX   VARCHAR2 (40) NOT NULL,
COST_ID    NUMBER (10) NOT NULL,
PLAN_ID    NUMBER (10) NOT NULL,
GRP_ID     NUMBER (10) NOT NULL,
PRIMARY KEY (POLICY_ID, COST_ID, PLAN_ID, GRP_ID),
FOREIGN KEY (COST_ID, PLAN_ID, GRP_ID)
  REFERENCES COST (COST_ID, PLAN_ID, GRP_ID))
/

CREATE TABLE CLAIM (
CLAIM_ID    NUMBER (10) NOT NULL,
PATIENT_LNAME    VARCHAR2 (40) NOT NULL,
PATIENT_FNAME    VARCHAR2 (40) NOT NULL,
CREATE_DATE      DATE,
POLICY_ID  NUMBER (10) NOT NULL,
COST_ID    NUMBER (10) NOT NULL,
PLAN_ID    NUMBER (10) NOT NULL,
GRP_ID     NUMBER (10) NOT NULL,
PRIMARY KEY (CLAIM_ID,
             POLICY_ID,
             COST_ID,
             PLAN_ID,
             GRP_ID),
```

```
FOREIGN KEY (POLICY_ID,
             COST_ID,
             PLAN_ID,
             GRP_ID)
  REFERENCES
     POLICY (POLICY_ID,
             COST_ID,
             PLAN_ID,
             GRP_ID))
/


CREATE TABLE CLAIM_DTL (
CLAIM_ID   NUMBER (10) NOT NULL,
CLAIM_DTL_ID NUMBER(3) NOT NULL,
DESCR_TX       VARCHAR2 (40),

DIAGNOSIS_CD VARCHAR2 (10),
 POLICY_ID   NUMBER (10) NOT NULL,
COST_ID     NUMBER (10) NOT NULL,
PLAN_ID     NUMBER (10) NOT NULL,
GRP_ID      NUMBER (10) NOT NULL,
PRIMARY KEY (CLAIM_ID,
             CLAIM_DTL_ID,
             POLICY_ID,
             COST_ID,
             PLAN_ID,
             GRP_ID),
FOREIGN KEY (CLAIM_ID,
             POLICY_ID,
             COST_ID,
             PLAN_ID,
             GRP_ID)
  REFERENCES
     CLAIM (CLAIM_ID,
             POLICY_ID,
             COST_ID,
             PLAN_ID,
             GRP_ID))
/
```

Code Example 18-3

As you can see, the policy of concatenated primary keys can make your data storage requirements go through the roof. Through careful analysis, you can determine the optimal path for your project.

Redundant Columns for History

Redundant columns for history are implemented in the same way as the denormalization technique for extra foreign key columns, and therefore require no additional information.

Typing Detail Tables

This approach is similar to the extra foreign key and redundant columns for history techniques, although a redundant foreign key here is a foreign key of the master table—as opposed to being the primary key of the master table. Again, this serves to enhance reporting, though it does clutter the model.

Violations of First Normal Form

Violating First Normal Form means that you are hard-coding a business rule that your organization currently lives by into the structure of your database. A decision such as this should not be taken lightly. Code Example 18-4 indicates that the current budgeting strategy of this organization is formulated by quarter. But what if this changes to a different time interval in the future? A change of this magnitude would require substantial changes to the database, all applications (i.e., forms and reports), and any interfaces that exchange information with this database. These trade-offs are quite costly and should not be dismissed lightly.

```
CREATE TABLE BUDGET (
BUDGET_ID               NUMBER    (10)    NOT NULL,
DESCR_TXT               VARCHAR2 (100)    NOT NULL,
ACCT_CD                 VARCHAR2 (20)     NOT NULL)
/
CREATE TABLE BUDGET_DTL (
BUDGET_ID               NUMBER    (10)    NOT NULL,
QTR1_AMT                NUMBER    (10,2)  NOT NULL,
QTR2_AMT                NUMBER    (10,2)  NOT NULL,
QTR3_AMT                NUMBER    (10,2)  NOT NULL,
QTR4_AMT                NUMBER    (10,2)  NOT NULL)
```

Code Example 18-4

Instead, we can implement a more flexible model that can accommodate changes to the budget structure over time. This approach would require additional data structures that we would use to define the budgetary structure.

Overloaded Columns

To implement the geographic subdivision example, we need to define two tables, CTRY and ST_PROV, as shown in Code Example 18-5.

```
CREATE TABLE CTRY (
CTRY_ID              NUMBER   (10) NOT NULL PRIMARY KEY,
DESCR_TXT            VARCHAR2 (50) NOT NULL)
/
CREATE TABLE ST_PROV (
CTRY_ID              NUMBER   (10) NOT NULL
   REFERENCES CTRY (CTRY_ID),
ST_PROV_ID           NUMBER   (10) NOT NULL,
DESCR_TXT            VARCHAR2 (50) NOT NULL,
STATE_YN             VARCHAR2 (1)  NOT NULL)/
```

Code Example 18-5

The DESCR_TXT column in the ST_PROV table stores the names of both states and provinces. It is not clear whether a given value in the DESCR_TXT column of the ST_PROV table is a state or a province without consulting the STATE_YN column, which indicates whether a given record defines a STATE or a PROVINCE.

Multiattribute Columns

A very common place this type of denormalization occurs is in inventory identifiers. Sometimes the unique identifier of an item is stored in a single column, but actually can be broken down into multiple components such as warehouse number, item type, and item number. Rather than placing these different data values into a single column, we recommend breaking them out individually. This certainly makes the model easier to read, and the values can still be displayed together in order to satisfy this user preference, as shown in Code Example 18-6.

```
CREATE TABLE ITEM (
   ITEM_ID       NUMBER (10) NOT NULL, PRIMARY KEY,
   DESCR_TX      VARCHAR2 (50) NOT NULL)
/

INSERT INTO ITEM (ITEM_ID,
                  DESCR_TX)
          VALUES ('0113561111',
                  'WIDGET')
/
```

Code Example 18-6

Code Example 18-6 uses the ITEM_ID column to store a combined string that contains the type of the item (i.e., '011' – characters 1–3), the item identifier (i.e., '356' – characters 4–6), and the warehouse identifier that stores that item (i.e., '1111' – characters 7–10).

There are a couple of problems with this approach. First, users of this system must know what item type '011' means, because the system does not store a description for it. Second, querying sales of items by item type cannot be indexed, because you would need to parse the item type out of the item identifier as a filter. This action would require a SUBSTR function, which inherently ignores indexes. Third, what if your item will be reclassified as some other type of item or stored in some other warehouse in the future? This would require updating the primary key—a very bad thing!

The most sensible approach is to normalize when you see these types of scenarios, and are convinced that their structure can and most likely will change in the future. The structures shown in Code Example 18-7 would be safe.

```
CREATE TABLE WHSE (
   WHSE_CD       VARCHAR2 (4) NOT NULL PRIMARY KEY,
   DESCR_TX      VARCHAR2 (50) NOT NULL)
/

CREATE TABLE ITEM_TYPE (
   ITEM_TYPE_CD    VARCHAR2 (3) NOT NULL PRIMARY KEY,
   DESCR_TX        VARCHAR2 (50))
/
```

```
CREATE TABLE ITEM (
ITEM_CD        VARCHAR2 (3) NOT NULL,
DESCR_TX       VARCHAR2 (50) NOT NULL,
WHSE_CD        VARCHAR2 (4) NOT NULL
  REFERENCES WHSE (WHSE_CD),
ITEM_TYPE_CD     VARCHAR2 (3) NOT NULL
  REFERENCES ITEM_TYPE (ITEM_TYPE_CD))
/
```

Code Example 18-7

This example will uniquely identify items by their item code, not the combination of item code, warehouse code, and item type code. This allows the items type or warehouse to change over time. If you are convinced that these values won't change over time, you could still use this design, and simply change the primary key of the ITEM table to include the warehouse and item type codes. This way, you get the descriptive text of warehouses and item types, and the guarantee that the combination of those three fields represents a unique item.

Of course, there are data sources that you will never be concerned with breaking apart. A classic example would be postal codes. Many of us might not even realize that the postal code is actually comprised of multiple, smaller codes for many countries. Actually, most of us don't have a reason to care. It is the entire postal code that is of interest to most systems, and therefore does not require normalization as the Item example from above did.

Conclusion

Each of the denormalizations discussed here with the exception of First Normal Form (which we do not advocate) involved starting with a fully normalized Third Normal Form database and adding an occasional redundant column. This is a key concept to good modeling since it maintains a conceptually clean underlying model. All we have done is add to the model without sacrificing any flexibility or conceptual clarity. By adding pieces that are clearly identified through naming conventions as denormalized, carefully documenting where those fields come from, and implementing these entirely through database triggers, we get the best of both worlds: a clean, theoretically correct model and adequate performance.

Does this approach always work? No. For very high-volume retail banking, large retail merchandise systems, airline reservation systems, or any other systems with thousands of transactions per second, some theoretical correctness may need to be sacrificed to support performance requirements. This should only be used as a last-ditch alternative. The benefits of a clean data model are its ease of maintenance and the ability of new sets of developers who will work on it to understand it.

CHAPTER
19

Introduction to Object Database Designer (ODD)

The primary focus of this book has been to enhance the productivity of systems development by designing more comprehensive data models. The introduction of UML as a data modeling language significantly improved our ability to capture complex business rules in a data model. Several examples of UML's ability to surpass the capabilities of Entity Relationship (ER) modeling have been supplied throughout this book.

Oracle Designer is the tool suite that Oracle provides for use in data modeling and for overall project administration. It provides functionality for both upper CASE and lower CASE information interaction.

Oracle has now released a new modeling tool, the Object Database Designer (ODD). ODD has been integrated into Oracle Designer so that both modeling techniques are based on the same set of tables and views.

This chapter will focus on the features of ODD with respect to logical and physical database design. It will not address any detailed aspects of C++ and Java-generated objects intended for the seamless access of data stored in Oracle by C++ and/or Java-based applications. A discussion of those topics is beyond the scope of this book.

Modeling Categories

As noted several times throughout this book, our approach is to develop a single data model that can be used from the beginning to the end of each project. Any modifications that must occur during the progress of the project are made to the logical data model and then retrofitted to the physical.

Of course, logical models cannot satisfy everyone, nor are they intended to serve this purpose. Oracle Designer has provided both a logical and physical modeling tool for some time now. This is necessary because there is information about tables and columns that is important for DBAs to see when they peruse a data model that is not reflected by logical data models. For example, a DBA would want to see the name of the tablespace in which the table resides. He or she would also want to review the sizing parameters that have been specified for storage.

The problem that inevitably arises is that enhancements are made using both logical and physical modeling tools independent of each other. This often results in substantial disconnects between the logical and physical data models. We suggest having the ability to specify parameters of logical data structures that would instruct the database design generator precisely how to physically implement the structures. Such an undertaking would be quite time-consuming, and not likely to be deliverable in any reasonable time frame. The problem is less of a technical issue than it is a management issue. If an organization applies stringent rules for managing the information stored in its repository, it will effectively shut the door on discrepancies between the logical and physical models.

ODD Modeling Types

ODD provides two types of models, Object Type and Server Type. The Object Type Model is the successor of Entity Relationship, or ER, models. The Server Model takes the place of the Database Design Modeler. Both the Object Type Model and the Server Model include a Navigator on the left side of the screen for more efficient exploration of object definitions. Toolbars have been added to provide access to the most frequently used features with a single button click. The Navigator and the toolbars are shown in Figure 19-1.

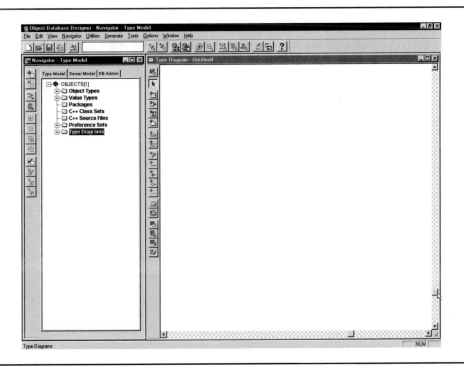

FIGURE 19-1. *ODD Navigator and toolbars*

Object Type Model

The Object Type Model allows users to specify all pertinent information regarding object types, including associations these types may have between them. Object Types can be created in any of three ways:

- Single-click on Object Types in Navigator, then press the first button on the toolbar to the left of the Navigator (i.e., the button with the green plus sign).

- Double-click on Object Types in the Navigator.

- Single-click on the Create Object Type button on the toolbar to the right of the Navigator.

Performing any of these options will display the Edit Object Type canvas shown in Figure 19-2.

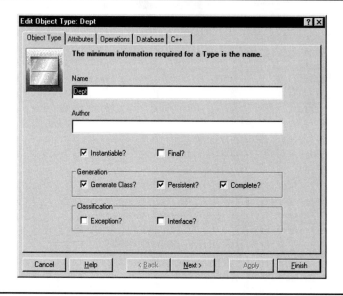

FIGURE 19-2. *Edit Object Type canvas*

The Edit Object Type Canvas contains five tabs: Object Type, Attributes, Operations, Database, and C++.

The Object Type tab is used to specify parameters pertaining explicitly to the object type itself. For example, you can name the object type, define whether a physical object type should be generated from it, whether the definition of the object type is Final or Complete, and whether or not to generate as an Object Class (i.e., Object Table based upon an Object Type).

The Attributes tab is where we define the attributes, or members, of the Object Type. In the Dept. Object Type shown in Figure 19-3, we have defined three attributes, DeptNo, Dname, and Loc.

The Attributes tab shown in Figure 19-4 permits the following types of information to be tracked for members of Object Types.

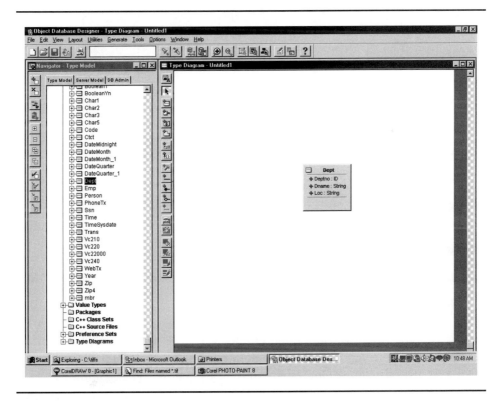

FIGURE 19-3. *Dept. Object Type*

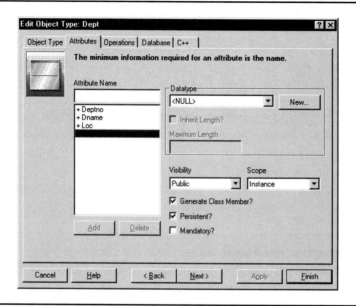

FIGURE 19-4. *Object Type Modeler – Attributes tab*

- The name of the attribute (member)
- The datatype of the member
- Whether or not the member should inherit the maximum length and decimal place allocation of the selected Value Type
- Whether the member has public or restricted access
- Whether or not the member should be generated in the Object Table
- Whether or not the member can be NULL

Value types refer to user defined data types. In Chapter 6, "Domains of Datatypes," we created several user-defined data types. Whereas Oracle Designer uses the term "Domains," ODD uses "Value Types," and the

Oracle8 Server simply calls them "Types." Keep in mind that the physical implementation of an object type can serve multiple functions. Value types refer to types on which an object member's data formatting may be based. Currently, object types defined via ODD allow you to specify value types for their members. When defining value types, you can specify the domain to which they pertain.

For example, the object type, Dept, shown above, reflects the use of value types in the definition of Dept's members:

- DeptNo (i.e., Value Type = Integer)

- Dname (i.e., Value Type = String)

- Loc (i.e., Value Type = String)

However, when defining an object type's member from within Oracle Designer, you cannot specify a value type. Instead, you can specify a domain. Most likely, domains and value types will be mapped directly to each other some time in the future.

If you intend to generate user-defined datatypes for value types, then create them as both value and object types. Value types cannot currently be generated. Unfortunately, when an object table is generated from an object type that contains members based upon value types, the columns will be defined based upon the datatype specifications in the value type. We would expect an object type to be created by the name of the value type, itself, but this is not currently available.

If you define a value type called 'ID', and specify that the value type was of type NUMBER with a maximum length of 10, and assigned the DeptNo member this new value type, the DDL shown in Code Example 19-1 would be generated:

```
-- Generated for Oracle 8 on Tue Aug 25  13:28:39 1998 by Server
Generator 2.1.19.5.0
PROMPT Creating Type 'DEPT_T'
CREATE OR REPLACE TYPE DEPT_T AS OBJECT
 (DEPTNO NUMBER(10)
```

```
,DNAME VARCHAR2(14)
,LOC  VARCHAR2(13)
)
/
```

Code Example 19-1

At this point, if you want to add a member to an object type via ODD's Object Type Model whose data type is user-defined as in the previous example, this procedure will have to be accomplished through an association. Future versions of ODD should tie value types in with domains, resulting in the generation of user-defined data types.

ASSOCIATIONS   *Associations* are relationships between object types. However, associations provide much greater flexibility in the definition of business rules than the relationships of ER modeling.

ODD supports four types of associations:

■ Generalization

■ Association

■ Strong Aggregation

■ Aggregation

Figure 19-5 is an example of an association between the Emp and Dept tables. Each Emp. object must be associated with a single Dept object in order to satisfy this association.

Each association can be identified by a single name; in this case, the name of the association is 'works for'. The association can also contain two role names, one for each of the object types involved in the association (i.e., 'Employee', 'Employer'). The appropriate way to read this association is 'Employee works for Employer'.

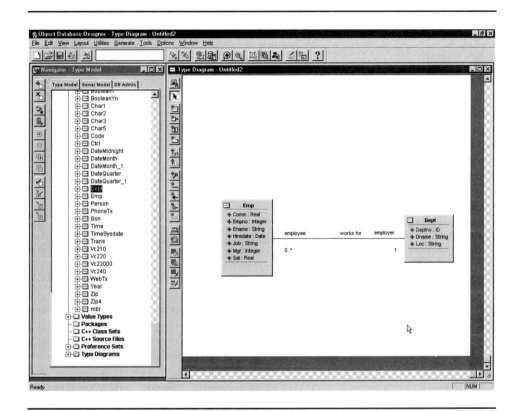

FIGURE 19-5.   *EMP/DEPT Association*

Generalization associations are used to categorize like object types—for example, if a system required multiple tables that all kept track of different sets of people for a variety of uses. Figure 19-6 exemplifies the use of generalization by creating an object type called Person and associating two object types to it using the generalization association.

If you set the 'Instantiable' flag and the 'Generate Class' = TRUE for CTCT and MBR, and FALSE for PERSON, then the following three object

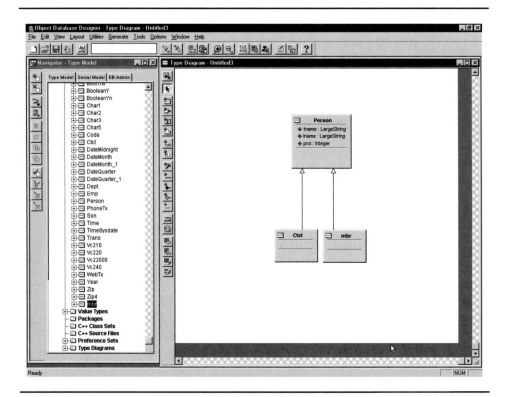

FIGURE 19-6. *Generalization association*

types and two object tables will be generated, as shown in Code Example 19-2.

```
-- Generated for Oracle 8 on Tue Aug 25  13:59:02 1998 by Server
Generator 2.1.19.5.0

PROMPT Creating Type 'PERSON_T'
CREATE OR REPLACE TYPE PERSON_T AS OBJECT
 (PNO NUMBER
 ,LNAME VARCHAR2 (40)
 ,FNAME VARCHAR2 (40)
 )
/
```

```
PROMPT Creating Type 'CTCT_T'
CREATE OR REPLACE TYPE CTCT_T AS OBJECT
 (PNO NUMBER
 ,LNAME VARCHAR2 (40)
 ,FNAME VARCHAR2 (40)
 )
/

PROMPT Creating Type 'MBR_T'
CREATE OR REPLACE TYPE MBR_T AS OBJECT
 (PNO NUMBER
 ,LNAME VARCHAR2 (40)
 ,FNAME VARCHAR2 (40)
 )
/

-- Generated for Oracle 8 on Tue Aug 25  13:59:02 1998 by Server
Generator 2.1.19.5.0
PROMPT Creating Table 'CTCT'
CREATE TABLE CTCT OF CTCT_T
/

COMMENT ON TABLE CTCT IS 'Created from Type Model'
/

PROMPT Creating Table 'MBR'
CREATE TABLE MBR OF MBR_T
/

COMMENT ON TABLE MBR IS 'Created from Type Model'
/
```

Code Example 19-2

Currently, ODD does not reference object types as datatypes within the object type DDL that it generates. In other words, if we were to create the above example manually, the code would most likely look like that in Code Example 19-3.

```
CREATE OR REPLACE TYPE PERSON_T AS OBJECT
 (PNO NUMBER
 ,LNAME VARCHAR2 (40)
```

```
,FNAME VARCHAR2 (40)
 )
/
CREATE TABLE CTCT OF PERSON_T
/

CREATE TABLE MBR OF PERSON_T
/
```

Code Example 19-3

This set of DDL is far more robust than what was generated, because we essentially have inheritance from PERSON_T to CTCT and MBR. In future releases of Oracle8, we will be able to modify the object types that tables are based upon. Those changes will be automatically propagated to the dependent tables and/or types. Currently, the generated code merely reproduced columns from the members of the PERSON_T object type for each of the Object Tables, resulting in no value added at all.

RECURSIVE ASSOCIATIONS   Recursive associations can be generated as of ODD V 2.0.19.5.0. However, these associations do not guarantee the integrity of the data being associated, as does a recursive foreign key. Figure 19-7 creates a table called 'Person', with a recursive association.

While the intent of this association is to relate two people as manager and employee, there is no guarantee that this relationship will not be violated. Oracle8i provides a new type of constraint that we can apply to REFS to eliminate this problem.

Server Model

The Server Model graphically represents the physical implementation of data structures. In the past, Oracle Designer provided a Database Design Modeler that enabled us to display tables, constraints, database links, and connect strings.

Today, a profile of your database can look substantially more complex. In the past, it was basically limited to tables, constraints, and views that we

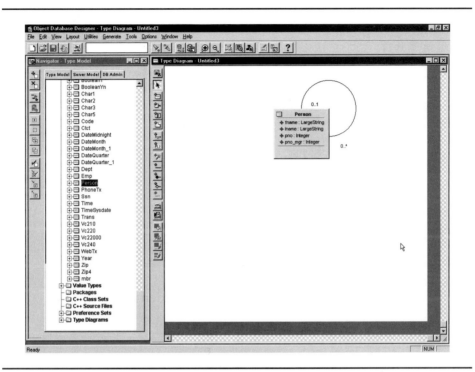

FIGURE 19-7.   *Recursive association*

wanted to see as diagrams. In the future, our diagrams will include these structures along with Object Types, Object Tables, Collections, partitioned tables, and other categories of objects, all in one integrated server model.

The ODD Server Model Navigator, as shown in Figure 19-8, displays tables (both relational and object-relational), views, snapshots, clusters, sequences, a variety of PL/SQL components, domains, object types, and collections. Currently, relational and object relational tables are separated in the ODD Navigator, although they are displayed under one common term called 'Table Definitions' from within the Oracle Designer Navigator. It is likely that these discrepancies between navigators will be smoothed out in upcoming releases.

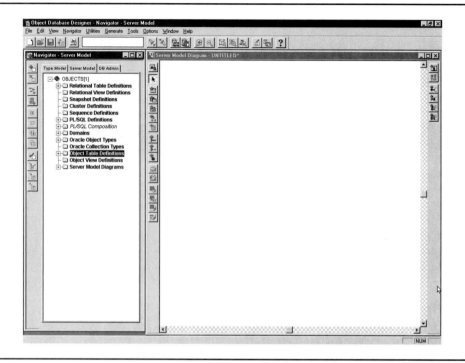

FIGURE 19-8. *Server Modeler Navigator*

The Server Model Toolbar provides single-click buttons for quick access to create the following physical structures:

- Relational tables
- Relational views
- Snapshots
- Clusters
- Columns
- Mandatory/Optional foreign keys
- Primary keys

Currently, the Table and View icons do not provide the capability of defining object tables or views. To define object tables or views within the Server Modeler, you must do so via the Object Table Definitions and/or Object View Definitions options on the Server Model Navigator.

TABLES   Though the interface has been somewhat modified, the relational aspects in ODD are similar to those in Oracle Designer. However, Oracle has provided a few little goodies for us in the meantime. For example, the Create Table canvas shown in Figure 19-9 now has a few new options:

■ The first, Create Audit Columns?, is a check box that will automatically generate CREATED_DATE, CREATED_BY, MODIFIED_DATE, and MODIFIED BY columns for the table when checked. Audit columns tend to be used quite heavily throughout most systems, whether or not they are appropriate. This feature saves a great deal of time and effort by automatically generating these columns.

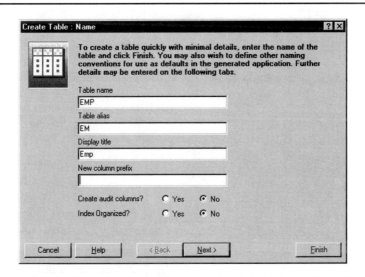

FIGURE 19-9.   *Create Table canvas*

- The second option is Index Organized?. Index Organized tables (IOTs), are tables that are essentially stored as indexes. Therefore, data retrieval is based upon user-defined values, eliminating the ROWID hit, because the entire contents of the table is loaded in memory. This check box will generate a given table as an IOT, when selected.

DOMAINS   Domains will be generated for you from value types when you generate to the Server Model. Figure 19-10 represents the Generator screen. The three options available for generating DDL are

- Generate DDL files Only

- Create on Database

- Repository held Server Model

Running the Database Generator from the Type Model today would not generate object types for user-defined value types. However, generating a

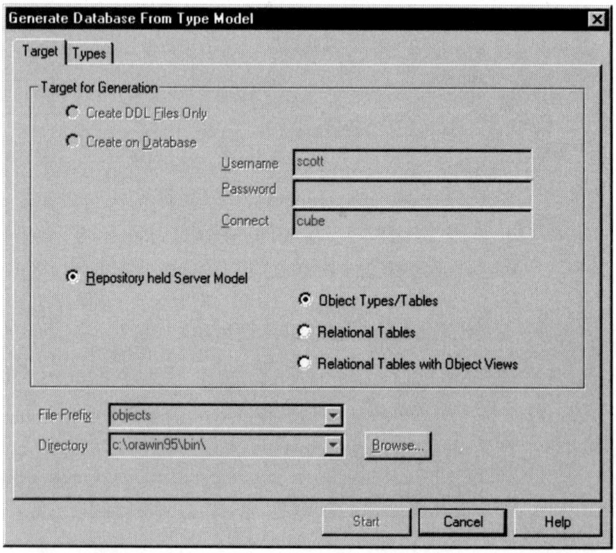

FIGURE 19-10.   *Generator screen*

Repository Held Server Model (i.e., option 3) will generate domains that match your user-defined value types. This third option will generate object types and their corresponding tables, either all relational tables or relational tables with object views. Remember that this third option (i.e., Relational Tables with Object Views) will eventually provide your organization with a seamless bridge from relational database designs to object-relational designs.

Unfortunately, there is no real differentiation among logical types intended to be user defined data types, types intended to be abstract data types, or types intended to be object types in ODD. Therefore, it is necessary to check off the Create Object Class indicator for all non-object type types.

ODD's current implementation of integrity constraints can be defined for relational tables, but not for object-relational tables. Check constraints, synonyms, and triggers can be defined for both relational and object-relational tables. ODD does not yet support referential integrity constraints because the server won't support them until Oracle 8.1 does.

Columns can only be defined for relational tables. Remember that object tables are strictly bound to an object type, meaning that their structure must not deviate from the structure of its object type. A future release of Oracle8 will support reclassifying an object table as a different object type. Columns can be based upon domains, which can be generated from value types.

Conclusion

While ODD is quite new, it is certainly a step in the right direction. Along with many people in our industry, the Oracle Designer group has struggled for years with the idea that data modeling should have a top-down approach. ODD is definitely the closest they have ever come to implementing this idea.

The ability to specify for a logical type—whether or not it should generate an object type, or both an object type and an object table—could be the foundation that we have been looking for. If Oracle expands upon this strategy and provides additional user-specified parameters for object types and associations in the Type Modeler that communicate to the generator precisely how to physically implement logical structures, we will be able to make changes solely in our Type models, and regenerate our Server Models on the fly.

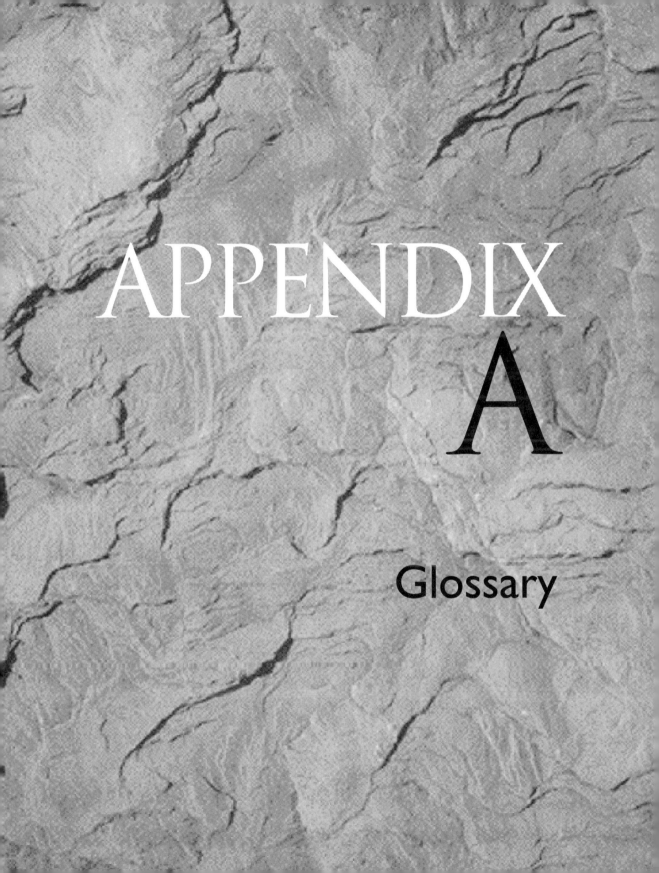

APPENDIX
A

Glossary

he following glossary includes definitions and descriptions of important terms used throughout the book.

Relationship	In ER modeling, a relationship between two entities (called an association in UML)
Abstract class	An abstract class has no objects of its own, but is only used to provide a template for refinement object classes based upon a generalization.
Aggregation	A type of close association. Class A is said to be an aggregation of class B if an object in class A is defined as a collection of objects from class B.
Association	In UML, a relationship between two classes
Association class	In UML, a class that arises from a many-to-many relationship between two other classes. An association class is a formal intersection whose unique identifier is exactly one object from each of the subordinate classes—similar to an intersection entity in ER modeling.
Boyce-Codd Normal Form	A table is in Boyce-Codd Normal Form if every non-key attribute is dependent on the entire primary key.
Candidate key	A collection of attributes in a class which could be used as the primary key
CADM	CASE Application Development Method—a method of systems development pioneered by Dr. Paul Dorsey and Peter Koletzke

CASE*Method	The process of designing and building automated information systems using Computer-Aided Software Engineering (CASE) programs to capture information about business requirements, create a design for the data structures to fulfill these requirements, and generate front-end and server program code. The CASE*Method was pioneered by Richard Barker.
Check constraint	A check constraint is used to restrict the values of a particular attribute to those in a given list. For example, gender attributes can be restricted to Male/Female, or Boolean attributes to Yes/No.
Class	A class is something of interest, a generalization of something of interest to the organization, or a means of classifying something of interest. A class always represents something in the real world. Similar to an entity in ER modeling.
Class diagrams	Graphic representation of the structure of a system in terms of classes and the relationships among those classes—one of the basic types of UML diagrams
Cluster	A storage method in Oracle databases where tables are stored in close proximity to improve performance.
Cluster key	The cluster key contains the column(s) that is used to join clustered tables. See Cluster.
Collections	In Oracle, collections are a means of storing a series of data entries that are jointly associated to a corresponding row in the database. Collections model a 1-to-many relationship between a row and a collection without necessitating integrity constraints. See VARRAYs and Nested tables.

Complex Generalization	A situation where there is more than one generalization structure from a given object class.
Composition	Strong form of aggregation. Class A is said to be a composition of class B if each object of class B is a part of an object of class A. Objects of class B may not exist unless they are part of a specific object from class A. Class B objects may not exist independently. An object from class B may not be a composition child of more than one object at a time, whether it is from class A or another class.
Constraint	In UML, a constraint is a method of restricting the definition of the UML object denoted with { }. Constraints may be attached to any UML object. In Oracle databases, constraint refers to a way of restricting allowable data values. Examples include check constraints or referential integrity constraints.
Constructor method	In Oracle8i, constructor methods are automatically created for object classes based upon their object type. This type of method is used to create new objects for the given object class. The constructor method assumes the name of the object type that it is based upon.
Contingent constraint	A contingent constraint is a database constraint enforced under certain conditions (for example, when an attribute has a certain value), but not at all times. Contingent constraints are frequently found wherever there are workflow-related rules.

Cyclical structure	A cyclical structure is present if you can return to the same class after passing through a series of associations.
Data Definition Language (DDL)	Language used to create, modify, or delete the structure of data to a Database Management System (DBMS)
Database triggers	In Oracle, database triggers are program units that are attached to specific tables, and executed based upon the specified action criteria. Database triggers fire based upon Insert, Update, and/or Delete requests to the table in which the trigger exists.
Denormalization	The process of breaking the rules of normalization in a database, usually for the purpose of improving performance
Dependency	In ER modeling, a dependent relationship exists when the child object is dependent on the parent object. "Dependent" means that the child object has no meaning outside of the context of the parent object. For example PO detail is dependent upon PO. Similar to composition in UML. In relational theory, an attribute is dependent on one or more source attributes if the value of the attribute is unique, given a set of values for the source attributes.
Domain	A set of properties used to help define the characteristics of an attribute. Domain definition includes data type and may include valid values.
«Dynamic»	In UML, an association is dynamic if it can be moved from one object to another after instantiation. By default, generalizations are not dynamic. If they need to be, the dynamic constraint can be added. This is the same as "transferable" in ER modeling.

Encapsulation	A class is encapsulated if we define all of the interface methods to the class and restrict access to the class to only those methods. This would mean that no applications would have direct access to a table based on that class.
ERD	Entity relationship diagram used in relational modeling
First Normal Form	In relational theory, an entity is in First Normal Form if it does not have any multi-value attributes.
Foreign keys	In relational theory, a foreign key is a set of attributes that act as pointers to a row in a different table. They are used to implement referential integrity between tables.
Generalization	In UML, a type of relationship between 2 classes. If class A is a generalization of class B, then class B inherits all attributes and methods from class A. This is similar to subtyping in ER modeling.
Index Organized Tables (IOTs)	In Oracle8i IOT tables, rows are physically clustered (and ordered) on the primary key.
Inheritance	In object theory where one object or class takes on the properties of another object or class
INSTEAD_OF trigger	In Oracle8i, the INSTEAD-OF trigger fires instead of the actual DML statement. For example, you can write an INSTEAD_OF trigger to replace Oracle's Insert functionality. This is new with Oracle8 and is only available for views.
Intersection entity	In ERDs, the entity arising from the many-to-many relationship is called an intersection entity. In UML, we call it an *association class*.

Linked list (recursive structure)	A linked list is chain of objects where each element has, at most, one parent and, at most, one child. In each chain, there exists an element with no parent (top) and an element with no child (bottom).
LOB	Large Objects (LOBs) are new data types available with the release of Oracle 8.0. LOBs provide substantially greater storage ability as compared to their predecessor, LONG. LOBs can store up to 4GB of data.
Logical data model	Data model designed to capture and represent data-related business rules with little or no attention paid to the ultimate physical implementation of the structure.
Mandatory relationship	Relationship where every object from Class A must be involved in the association.
Member method	In Oracle8i, member methods are user-defined access paths that declare the valid reporting and data manipulation guidelines for a specific object class. Member methods are physically implemented as PL/SQL procedures and/or functions, defined as part of the object type specification. Member methods are intended for data retrieval activity.
Method	In UML, a physical implementation of an operation
Moore's Law	Approximately every 18 months, the speed and storage capabilities of available computers will double.
Multi-linked list (recursive structure)	A group of linked lists. See Linked list.

Multi-network (recursive structure)	This type of structure is used when keeping track of the general interactions among objects. The reason it is called a multi-network is because this structure can contain any number of independent networks. Any particular object can have any number of parents and any number of children.
Multiple classification	A particular class may exist that refines to two or more other classes. For example, a person can be both a customer and an employee. In ERDs, this phenomenon is referred to as a *nonexclusive subtype*.
Multi-ring (recursive structure)	Multi-ring structures are linked lists with no bottom or top. Every element has both a parent and a child. The entire structure is made of closed loops. Any object may have any number of children and, at most, one parent. In addition, there is a stipulation that there is exactly one object in each tree (called the root object) that has no parent. The term "multi-tree" is used to allow for multiple independent tree structures.
N-ary association	Association where classes are linked to more than one other class
Nested tables	In Oracle8, nested tables are a type of collection that is based on object types that do not store their data in the same location as the master table. Nested tables are the logical equivalent of clustered tables, although they are not implemented in the same way.
Network (recursive structure)	Given any two objects in the structure, a series of relationships exists to get from one object to another. A single network would support the business rule that you can get from any one location in the network to any other location.

Normalization	The basic rules governing the design of relational databases
Notes (in a class diagram)	In the UML class diagram, Notes are graphically represented text objects that can be attached to any UML object. Notes are depicted in a text box that resembles the old flow chart symbol for punch card. Notes are useful for declaring data-related business rules that could not be represented otherwise.
Object Database Designer (ODD)	Oracle Designer's UML-based modeling tool, which has been integrated into Oracle Designer
Object ID (OID)	In object theory, the unique identifier of an object
Object Model	One of two model types available in the ODD component of Oracle Designer 2.1.
Object reference	In Oracle8, a pointer that can simultaneously support referential integrity and external programming languages
Object view	In Oracle8, an object view is very similar to a relational view. Object views are based upon a single SELECT statement that could reference one or more Relational and/or object-relational tables. The most common use of views is still primarily for providing a secure level of access to the actual data structures.
Object-oriented database	Object-oriented databases allow for objects to exist as non-volatile structures. Rather than connecting objects through referential integrity, they use reference pointers. Inheritance is fully supported and access to objects is typically restricted through the use of associated methods and operations.

Operation	Process in UML that accesses and/or changes the states of objects
Order/Map Method	In Oracle8, order and map methods are used to compare and/or sort data of the same object type. You must, in fact, define either a Map or Order method within your object type specification in order to perform non-equality comparisons.
Pairs (recursive structure)	Pairs of objects are equivalent to a two-element multi-linked list.
Primary class	In UML, a class that stores objects of interest to the organization as opposed to value list or abstract classes
Primary key	In relational theory, the unique identifier of a table
Procedure	A program that performs one or more actions
Recursive relationship	An association between an object class or entity and itself
Redundant attribute	A redundant attribute is a function of other objects existing in the database. For example, an UPPER (Name) where the uppercase values of a name are stored redundantly
Redundant class	A redundant class is any class that could be reconstructed from other data in the database if deleted. Aggregation classes in a data warehouse are redundant.
Referential integrity	In ER theory, relationships are implemented using foreign keys as pointers to parent rows in other tables. Enforcing that the values in the foreign keys reference valid rows is called *referential integrity*.

Relational database	A relational database implies that you have designed your database tables in such a way that they conform to basic relational theory and practices. These theoretical guidelines are expressed through the rules of normalization.
Ring (recursive structure)	This is a structure containing a single cycle.
Schema	A collection of tables that can be implemented either as a database or as a separate user account. Schemas allow us to reference tables throughout the system. There should be one schema for each subject area within the data model.
Second Normal Form	In ER modeling, an entity is in Second Normal Form if it is in First Normal Form AND no non-key attributes are dependent on a portion of the primary key.
Server Model	One of two model types available in the ODD component of Oracle Designer 2.1.
Specialization class	In UML generalization, if A is a generalization class of B, then B is a specialization class of A.
Stereotype	Stereotypes allow us to redefine or extend UML structures. Stereotypes are keywords that can be attached to any UML element to alter meaning or functionality. Stereotypes (designated by «guillemets») extend or redefine an element. There are predefined stereotypes such as "Abstract" for classes.
Stored programming units	Programs that are stored within an Oracle database instance that perform one or more specific tasks. These stored units can be executed from user interfaces such as SQL*Plus, or referenced within applications such as those built using Oracle Developer.

Subtype	In ERDs, subtypes are used when we can divide one entity into a number of mutually exclusive and collectively exhaustive subsets. The most common example is employees who are either paid at an hourly rate or who are salaried.
Supertype	In ER modeling, the parent entity in a supertype/subtype relationship. Each instance of a supertype must be instantiated as exactly one instance of exactly one of the subtypes. See Subtype.
Table alias	An alternate name of a table
Third Normal Form	In ER modeling, an entity is in Third Normal Form if it is in Second Normal Form AND no attribute is dependent upon a non-key attribute.
Tree (recursive structure)	Tree structures are similar to multi-tree structures except that they are restricted to support only one tree. Exactly one object in the class would have no parent and all other objects would have exactly one parent.
Types	In Oracle8i, types are physical structures that serve as templates or building blocks for other types and/or tables.
UID bars	The small horizontal lines on the ER relationship are called *UID bars*, indicating that the foreign keys will be part of the primary keys.
UML	The Unified Modeling Language (UML) was developed by Grady Booch, Jim Rumbaugh, and Ivar Jacobson. In an attempt to create a single system for modeling and documenting information systems and business processes, UML was created with an underlying object-oriented analysis and design philosophy.

Value list class	A class that stores a list of values valid for one or more attributes in one or more other classes
VARCHAR2	In Oracle, a variable length character field type with maximum length of 4000 characters
VARRAYS	VARRAYS, or varying arrays, are typically stored inline with respect to their containing row. VARRAYS are assigned an outer limit of values. Data stored within a VARRAY is stored in the same location as the data of the master table.

Index

Get Your **FREE** Subscription to Oracle Magazine

Stay informed and increase your productivity with every issue of *Oracle Magazine*. Inside each FREE, bimonthly issue you'll get:

- Up-to-date information on Oracle Data Server, Oracle Applications, Network Computing Architecture, and tools
- Third-party news and announcements
- Technical articles on Oracle products and operating environments
- Software tuning tips
- Oracle customer application stories

Three easy ways to subscribe:

1 MAIL Cut out this page, complete the questionnaire on the back, and mail it to:
Oracle Magazine, P.O. Box 1263, Skokie, IL 60076-8263.

2 FAX Cut out this page, complete the questionnaire on the back, and fax it to
+ 847.647.9735.

3 WEB Visit our Web site at **www.oramag.com.** You'll find a subscription form there, plus much more!

If there are other Oracle users at your location who would like to receive their own subscription to *Oracle Magazine,* please photocopy the form and pass it along.

☐ YES! Please send me a FREE subscription to Oracle Magazine. ☐ NO, I am not interested at this time.

If you wish to receive your free bimonthly subscription to *Oracle Magazine,* you must fill out the entire form, sign it, and date it (incomplete forms cannot be processed or acknowledged). You can also subscribe at our Web site at
www.oramag.com/html/subform.html or fax your application to *Oracle Magazine* at **+847.647.9735.**

SIGNATURE (REQUIRED) ✓ **DATE**

NAME _____ TITLE _____

COMPANY _____ E-MAIL ADDRESS _____

STREET/P.O. BOX _____

CITY/STATE/ZIP _____

COUNTRY _____ TELEPHONE _____

You must answer all eight questions below.

1 What is the primary business activity of your firm at this location?
(circle only one)
- 01 Agriculture, Mining, Natural Resources
- 02 Architecture, Construction
- 03 Communications
- 04 Consulting, Training
- 05 Consumer Packaged Goods
- 06 Data Processing
- 07 Education
- 08 Engineering
- 09 Financial Services
- 10 Government—Federal, Local, State, Other
- 11 Government—Military
- 12 Health Care
- 13 Manufacturing—Aerospace, Defense
- 14 Manufacturing—Computer Hardware
- 15 Manufacturing—Noncomputer Products
- 16 Real Estate, Insurance
- 17 Research & Development
- 18 Human Resources
- 19 Retailing, Wholesaling, Distribution
- 20 Software Development
- 21 Systems Integration, VAR, VAD, OEM
- 22 Transportation
- 23 Utilities (Electric, Gas, Sanitation)
- 24 Other Business and Services
  _____

2 Which of the following best describes your job function? *(circle only one)*
CORPORATE MANAGEMENT/STAFF
- 01 Executive Management (President, Chair, CEO, CFO, Owner, Partner, Principal)
- 02 Finance/Administrative Management (VP/Director/Manager/Controller, Purchasing, Administration)
- 03 Sales/Marketing Management (VP/Director/Manager)
- 04 Computer Systems/Operations Management (CIO/VP/Director/Manager MIS, Operations)
- 05 Other Finance/Administration Staff
- 06 Other Sales/Marketing Staff

IS/IT Staff
- 07 Systems Development/Programming Management
- 08 Systems Development/Programming Staff
- 09 Consulting
- 10 DBA/Systems Administrator
- 11 Education/Training
- 12 Engineering/R&D/Science Management
- 13 Engineering/R&D/Science Staff
- 14 Technical Support Director/Manager
- 15 Webmaster/Internet Specialist
- 16 Other Technical Management/Staff

3 What is your current primary operating platform? *(circle all that apply)*
- 01 DEC UNIX
- 02 DEC VAX VMS
- 03 Java
- 04 HP UNIX
- 05 IBM AIX
- 06 IBM UNIX
- 07 Macintosh
- 08 MPE-ix
- 09 MS-DOS
- 10 MVS
- 11 NetWare
- 12 Network Computing
- 13 OpenVMS
- 14 SCO UNIX
- 15 Sun Solaris/SunOS
- 16 SVR4
- 17 Ultrix
- 18 UnixWare
- 19 VM
- 20 Windows
- 21 Windows NT
- 22 Other _____
- 23 Other UNIX _____

4 Do you evaluate, specify, recommend, or authorize the purchase of any of the following? *(circle all that apply)*
- 01 Hardware
- 02 Software
- 03 Application Development Tools
- 04 Database Products
- 05 Internet or Intranet Products

5 In your job, do you use or plan to purchase any of the following products or services?
(check all that apply)

SOFTWARE

	Use	Plan to buy
01 Business Graphics	☐	☐
02 CAD/CAE/CAM	☐	☐
03 CASE	☐	☐
04 CIM	☐	☐
05 Communications	☐	☐
06 Database Management	☐	☐
07 File Management	☐	☐
08 Finance	☐	☐
09 Java	☐	☐
10 Materials Resource Planning	☐	☐
11 Multimedia Authoring	☐	☐
12 Networking	☐	☐
13 Office Automation	☐	☐
14 Order Entry/Inventory Control	☐	☐
15 Programming	☐	☐
16 Project Management	☐	☐
17 Scientific and Engineering	☐	☐
18 Spreadsheets	☐	☐
19 Systems Management	☐	☐
20 Workflow	☐	☐

HARDWARE

	Use	Plan to buy
21 Macintosh	☐	☐
22 Mainframe	☐	☐
23 Massively Parallel Processing	☐	☐
24 Minicomputer	☐	☐
25 PC	☐	☐
26 Network Computer	☐	☐
27 Supercomputer	☐	☐
28 Symmetric Multiprocessing	☐	☐
29 Workstation	☐	☐

PERIPHERALS

	Use	Plan to buy
30 Bridges/Routers/Hubs/Gateways	☐	☐
31 CD-ROM Drives	☐	☐
32 Disk Drives/Subsystems	☐	☐
33 Modems	☐	☐
34 Tape Drives/Subsystems	☐	☐
35 Video Boards/Multimedia	☐	☐

SERVICES

	Use	Plan to buy
36 Computer-Based Training	☐	☐
37 Consulting	☐	☐
38 Education/Training	☐	☐
39 Maintenance	☐	☐
40 Online Database Services	☐	☐
41 Support	☐	☐
42 None of the above	☐	☐

6 What Oracle products are in use at your site? *(circle all that apply)*
SERVER/SOFTWARE
- 01 Oracle8
- 02 Oracle7
- 03 Oracle Application Server
- 04 Oracle Data Mart Suites
- 05 Oracle Internet Commerce Server
- 06 Oracle InterOffice
- 07 Oracle Lite
- 08 Oracle Payment Server
- 09 Oracle Rdb
- 10 Oracle Security Server
- 11 Oracle Video Server
- 12 Oracle Workgroup Server

TOOLS
- 13 Designer/2000
- 14 Developer/2000 (Forms, Reports, Graphics)
- 15 Oracle OLAP Tools
- 16 Oracle Power Object

ORACLE APPLICATIONS
- 17 Oracle Automotive
- 18 Oracle Energy
- 19 Oracle Consumer Packaged Goods
- 20 Oracle Financials
- 21 Oracle Human Resources
- 22 Oracle Manufacturing
- 23 Oracle Projects
- 24 Oracle Sales Force Automation
- 25 Oracle Supply Chain Management
- 26 Other _____
- 27 **None of the above**

7 What other database products are in use at your site? *(circle all that apply)*
- 01 Access
- 02 BAAN
- 03 dbase
- 04 Gupta
- 05 IBM DB2
- 06 Informix
- 07 Ingres
- 08 Microsoft Access
- 09 Microsoft SQL Server
- 10 Peoplesoft
- 11 Progress
- 12 SAP
- 13 Sybase
- 14 VSAM
- 15 **None of the above**

8 During the next 12 months, how much do you anticipate your organization will spend on computer hardware, software, peripherals, and services for your location? *(circle only one)*
- 01 Less than $10,000
- 02 $10,000 to $49,999
- 03 $50,000 to $99,999
- 04 $100,000 to $499,999
- 05 $500,000 to $999,999
- 06 $1,000,000 and over

OMG